FITTskills
Global Business Environment

FIFTH EDITION

FITT
*The Professional Path
to Global Markets*

FITTskills: Global Business Environment, Fifth Edition

ISBN 978-1-894566-09-4

Revised edition, printed 2008

Reprinted 2009

For information contact FITT:
Tel.: 613.230.3553 or 800.561.3488
Fax: 613.230.6808
E-mail: info@fitt.ca
Web site: www.fitt.ca

Disclaimer
Every reasonable attempt has been made to contact the copyright owners of information and sample documents included in this textbook. If a copyright owner observes that permission was not obtained, he or she should advise FITT of this in writing, so that permission can be properly acknowledged in future publications.
While FITT has made every reasonable attempt to provide accurate information, this information may contain errors or omissions for which FITT disclaims any liability.

The opinions and interpretations in this publication are those of the author and do not necessarily reflect those of the Government of Canada.

Available in French under the title << FITThabiletés : Le milieu mondial des affaires >>

Cover designed by Mediaplus Advertising

This project is funded in part by the Government of Canada's Sector Council Program.

Table of Contents

Acknowledgments viii

Course Objectives 1

Course Introduction 2

1. The Global Business Environment 3
Chapter Objectives 3
Overview 4
The Dynamic Context of International Business 4
Global Power and Influence: New Players, New Paradigms 9
Global Flows: Capital, People and Trade 13
Multilateral Institutions 18
Pitfalls of Protectionism, Benefits of Engagement 21
Trade and Competitiveness 22
International Business, Security and Intellectual Property 24
The Old "Fringe" Goes Mainstream: Green, Fair and More 25
Leading Edge: Integrative Trade, Global Supply Chains and Virtual...Everything 27
International Trade: Through the Crystal Ball 29
Chapter Summary 30
Exercises 30
References/Resources 31

2. Canada's Place in the World 33
Chapter Objectives 33
Overview 34
International Trade: Its Role in Canada 34
Canada's Trading Partners 42
The Importance of Trade Agreements to Canada 44
The Supporting Environment for Trade 52
Chapter Summary 54
Exercises 54
References/Resources 55

3. Global Trader, Global Business 57
Chapter Objectives 57
Overview 58
The Business: Vision, Innovation and Commitment 58
Navigating the Pitfalls 61
The Attitude: Heart of an Entrepreneur, Spirit of a Leader 63
Positioning the Organization for the Global Marketplace 68
Before the Leap: Evaluating Global Trade Readiness 72
Chapter Summary 75
Exercises 75
References/Resources 76

4. The Global Supply Chain   77

Chapter Objectives 77
Overview 78
Value Chains and Supply Chains: Linking Nations Through Business and Trade 78
Trade: Physical, Financial and Information Global Supply Chains 79
Integrative Trade 82
Trade Transactions: Doing Business Across the Chains 83
Buyers, Sellers and a Cast of Many More: Parties to a Trade Transaction 83
Lights, Camera, Action: The Mechanics of a Trade Transaction 84
Import Considerations: Supplier Development and International Purchasing 85
Export Considerations: Client Development and Channel Management 87
View from Across the Table: Seeing the Deal As Your Trading Partner Does 92
Chapter Summary 93
Exercises 94
References/Resources 96

5. Trade and Technology   97

Chapter Objectives 97
Overview 98
Technology: The Transformation of Trade 98
Enhanced Global Supply Chain: From Manufacturing to Business Process Outsourcing. 102
Online Purchasing and E-Trade Platforms 108
E-Marketplaces: The "Middle Man" Returns 110
Security in the Virtual Marketplace 119
Defining the E-Business Plan 122
Chapter Summary 126
Exercises 126
References/Resources 128

6. Trade in Services   129

Chapter Objectives 129
Overview 130
The Growing Importance of the Global Service Sector 130
Modes of Delivery: Four Ways Services Are Traded 133
The Role of Services in Manufacturing 135
Goods vs. Services Trade: Different Circumstances, Different Approaches 137
Intangibles: Skills, Knowledge and Expertise 139
Value Proposition: Differentiating Your Service 140
Market Research: Implications for Services 141
Business-Process Outsourcing 143
Trade Policies and Issues Affecting Services Trade 145
Trade in Services Checklist 146
Chapter Summary 146
Exercises 147
References/Resources 148

7. Cultural Considerations   149

Chapter Objectives 149
Overview 150
Global Business: Multicultural Environment 150
Intercultural Effectiveness: Knowing the Rules of the Game 151

Cultural Concepts in Context 152
Effective Communication 154
Impacts of Culture...162
Intercultural Relationships: Built to Last...164
Chapter Summary...169
Exercises 169
References/Resources 172

8. International Business Practices   173

Chapter Objectives 173
Overview...174
Bribery and Corruption: Corrosive, Costly and Cancerous.....................176
Exploitative Child Labour: Critical, Complex and Compelling.................180
Human Rights: Trade, Invest or Sanction 184
Intellectual Property Rights...192
Codes and Integrity Programs: Theory to Practice 195
CITP Standards of Ethical Conduct...206
Business Ethics Checklist...208
Chapter Summary...209
Exercises 210
References/Resources 211

9. Market Research and Marketing   213

Chapter Objectives 213
Overview...214
Market Research: Trade Without Research = Tightrope Without a Net!...........214
Market Research: What and Where 215
Recognizing Market Types...218
Understanding the Marketing Plan 220
Market Planning and the International Business Plan 222
Finding the Right Mix: Elements of the Marketing Strategy....................223
Resources and Costs of the Marketing Activity 226
Market Research and Marketing Checklist 228
Chapter Summary...229
Exercises 229
References/Resources 230

10. Entering and Maintaining the Market   231

Chapter Objectives 231
Overview...232
Market Entry: Time to Sell...232
Market-Entry Options: Direct, Indirect, Investment and Strategic Alliances.....................235
Identifying and Implementing the Right Distribution Mix: Maximizing Coverage,
    Minimizing Conflict 252
Selling to Customers: Helping Them Make Informed Decisions..............254
Distribution Channel Management: Maintaining the Market 255
Out of Sight, Out of Mind: The Importance of Communication 256
Market-Entry Checklist...258
Chapter Summary...259
Exercises 259
References/Resources 261

11. Trade Finance   263

Chapter Objectives 263
Overview...264
International Trade Finance 264
Managing Currencies, Managing Cash 265
Elements of Trade Finance...266
Trade Finance: Getting Paid 268
Credit Insurance and Risk Mitigation 272
Trade Finance Across the Supply Chain 273
Trade Finance: Helping to Close the Deal 274
Banks, ECAs and IFIs: Trade Finance the Traditional Way 275
Other Sources of Trade Finance..276
Technology: Trade Finance Evolves 276
Project Finance, Countertrade and Other Flavours 277
Trade Finance Checklist 279
Chapter Summary...279
Exercises 279
References/Sources 280

12. Logistics and Distribution   281

Chapter Objectives 281
Overview...282
Logistics: Your Competitive Advantage..282
Materials Management: Reliability and Cost-Effectiveness 283
Physical Distribution: Options and Strategies.....................................284
Transportation: Issues and Challenges 285
Modes of Transportation: Making the Right Choice 286
Advanced Logistics: New Delivery Considerations.............................288
Incoterms: Must-Know Trade Terminology...288
Documentation: Requirements and Examples 291
Health and Safety: Dangerous Goods Certificate...............................291
Security: Mitigating Risks..293
Logistics and Distribution Checklist 294
Chapter Summary...294
Exercises 294
References/Resources 295

13. Law, Policy and Regulation   297

Chapter Objectives 297
Overview...298
The International Regulatory Framework 298
Trade Policy: National Interest, Global Citizenship.............................300
Law and International Trade 301
Extraterritoriality..307
International Security 309
Rules Against Dumping and Unfair Trade Practices 310
Technical Standards 312
Health and Environmental Regulations 312
Dispute Resolution: Negotiation, Mediation, Arbitration, Legal Action 313
Law, Policy and Regulation Checklist 316
Chapter Summary...316

Exercises 317
References/Resources 317

14. The International Business Plan — 319

Chapter Objectives 319
Overview.. 320
The Importance of the International Business Plan 320
The Planning Process: Gathering the Information................................... 322
Assembling the Components of the International Business Plan 324
Market Evaluation 327
Export Market Penetration: Step by Step or Full Speed Ahead?............ 331
Developing Contingency Plans and Exit Strategies................................ 333
The International Business Plan Key Points 334
Chapter Summary.. 334
Exercises 335
References/Resources 335

Index — 337

Acknowledgments

FITT would like to express its appreciation to the many industry professionals and supporters who contributed directly or indirectly to the development and publishing of this textbook.

In particular, FITT wishes to recognize the contributions of the co-authors, Global Links Network, a team of five international business experts:

- David Archer, ATM Export Management Inc.

- Mark Drake, CITP, Corsley Inc.

- Diana Girard, Global Links Network

- Alexander Malaket, OPUS Advisory Services International

- Theo Ward, Globeview

Several industry specialists and experts have developed this textbook through a combination of subject-matter expertise provided by Global Links Network and through primary and secondary research as well as review and commentary. In particular, FITT and Global Links Network wish to acknowledge several major sources that were referenced extensively throughout the development of this material: Canadian Manufacturers and Exporters (CME), Conference Board of Canada, Foreign Affairs and International Trade Canada, Industry Canada, International Trade Centre Geneva, Organisation for Economic Co-operation and Development (OECD), Statistics Canada, World Trade Organization (WTO) and Professor Errol Mendes, Human Rights Research and Education Centre, University of Ottawa.

In addition, FITT and Global Links Network would like to thank the Industry Review Panel for their valued input and validation of content:

- Larraine Adrain, CITP, Agricom International Inc.

- Toby Heaps, Corporate Knights

- Leroy Lowe, CITP, Nova Scotia Community College

FITT recognizes the major contribution of Human Resources and Social Development Canada's Sector Council Program and their support of our efforts to assist Canadians in becoming effective players in the international economy.

FITTskills | Global Business Environment

Course Objectives

- Understand the current and future global business environment, from global and national perspectives
- Recognize the new competencies required in the 21st century business environment and understand what it will take to master them
- Initiate a framework for a strategic plan to incorporate key elements of the international business process, including market research, market entry, financing, legal aspects, logistics, documentation and transportation

Course Introduction

FITTskills: Global Business Environment provides a comprehensive overview of key aspects of global business in the 21st century. Whether the participant is looking for general information, is seriously considering getting involved or is already participating in global trade, this course provides important information on the key elements of the global business environment.

The course emphasizes forward thinking and a positive perspective and highlights the considerable effort that any business, in any region of the world, must commit to in order to succeed, since we believe that this effort—properly executed—represents a fundamental "best practice" approach that goes beyond borders. In creating contemporary material that not only describes the current state of the environment, but also helps identify ongoing transformation of global business, it is of paramount importance that any "advice" be relative to the knowledge that any business in the world should assimilate in order to be a successful global trader.

The course is grouped into three key areas:

- **The Global Business Environment** and your country's place in the world provides the course participant with a big-picture overview.

- **New 21st Century Competencies** introduces the learner to key characteristics of new global traders and new core competencies that are relatively unique to the future of global trade, such as culture, ethics, technology, supply chains and trade in services.

- **Planning Your Global Business Strategy** is designed to provide a high-level overview of the fundamental elements of global business and encourages the participant to think strategically at an introductory level, while setting the stage for more advanced courses in the FITTskills offering, such as market research, marketing, supply chain management, finance, law and trade management.

Whatever the objective in reading this textbook—for general information, as a prospective Certified International Trade Professional (CITP), to build a career or expand a business—the investment of time and effort will be worthwhile, as it will undoubtedly help to further define the role and decisions needed to be successful in the new global business environment.

1

The Global Business Environment

A New Era

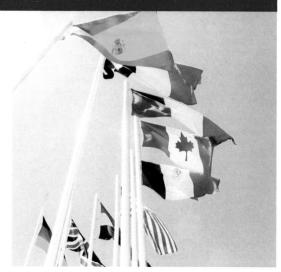

Chapter Objectives

- Gain an understanding of the changing global business environment
- Recognize the major forces shaping the global business environment
- Relate key characteristics of the global business environment directly to principles, practices and development in international trade

Overview

Global. Business. Environment. These three words, joined together, describe the introductory course of the FITTskills program. These words also reflect a reality of the nature of international trade: it is evolving in a fundamental way as a result of numerous forces shaping the nature and dynamics of global commerce.

It is indeed a "new era" in international trade; so much so that the subject can no longer effectively be treated in isolation or as a specialization, but rather, must be viewed more broadly as "global business" in the context of a shared, increasingly integrated environment.

Technology has enabled the development of international relationships and the conduct of international business and trade in ways—and at a rate— unimagined a decade ago, and the pace of change is increasing. Competitive dynamics across the globe are reshaping sourcing models and supply chains, the development of powerful economies is redefining the risk related to cross-border business, and a range of new product and service offerings are available to assist companies pursuing global commerce.

Intercultural effectiveness remains a critical element of success in global business, and although diversity remains fundamental, a certain level of convergence is evident in other areas, such as principles of ethical practices in international business, concerns about sustainability, human rights and other related elements.

The Dynamic Context of International Business

Business at home, commerce abroad: a classical view

The formerly common view that separated domestic business from international operations is no longer effective in the current global business environment.

Leading a commercial enterprise, whether a one-person SME (small and medium-sized enterprise) or a global multinational, involves some common challenges and requires a set of skills and experiences that are, at some level, related. These skills, experiences and capabilities, which include business vision, people and financial management, marketing and sales skills, commercial acumen and competitive mettle, are the subject of much writing, a great deal of teaching and vigorous discussion and debate.

Doing business in a familiar domestic environment involves enough of a challenge that the vast majority of start-up enterprises (up to 80 percent by some measures) fail within the first two years. From identifying and effectively communicating a value proposition or "unique selling proposition," to managing customer and supplier relationships, ensuring adequate cash flow, mitigating business and financial risk and developing a healthy "pipeline" of new and recurring business, there is no shortage of variety and complexity for the business executive.

When operating in a domestic context, business leaders are in a familiar environment. They know the requirements of setting up and managing a business, they're able to access whatever resources might be available in a given market and they're "connected" to valuable academic, personal and professional networks. There is, even for the novice, a certain support system that comes with operating in one's own domestic environment.

The contrast is sharp when considering the prospect of pursuing international trade or business on a global basis. The conduct of international business—even when it only involves crossing the border to a neighbouring country—adds a level of complexity, challenge and risk that is significantly beyond that encountered by domestically focused enterprises.

Basic procedures, such as the ability to conduct due diligence, or even an element as straightforward as a commercial credit check, can be difficult in international markets, and more so for companies with global aspirations. The broader the scope of operations, the larger the number of factors that will vary between markets and the more complex the overall management becomes. This reality is one reason why certain international business-development or trade-promotion agencies recommend a gradual expansion into international markets.

The overall infrastructure supporting the conduct of business, from government agencies to regulatory bodies, financial institutions and technology (such as the existence of reliable credit reporting) is at different levels of development in different parts of the world, a reality that has very direct implications for the successful conduct of business.

The all-important relationship between buyer and seller becomes more difficult to establish and more complicated to assess and monitor, and therefore, materially riskier. Communication is not straightforward, as much because of the logistics of engaging in communication from around the globe, as because of the cultural differences that can both enrich and complicate the process.

Fundamental concerns, such as dispute settlement (across multiple legal jurisdictions), assurances of timely payment and security from civil unrest, expropriation or nationalization are very real and ought to be very much on the minds of executives pursuing international business, depending on the markets being developed. This last set of factors illustrates the stark reality that a business operating internationally may be "doing everything right" when assessed against domestic standards of good management, yet be facing the prospect of failure and the risk of losing everything.

Pursuing trade and/or business on an international basis is, then, much riskier and more complex than conducting commerce domestically. This increased risk links directly to the potential for lucrative returns, and explains the attraction for many businesses in conducting trade (and other business activities) on an international basis.

How has this view evolved?

The accelerating pace of change
The reality of international trade and global business today is increasingly such that the classical distinctions between domestic business and international commerce are disappearing, and doing so at an accelerating rate.

The argument can be made that a purely domestic business is an endangered species; sourcing practices and patterns are increasingly international—even global—in nature. In almost every industry or line of business, the sourcing of inputs, components and even services on an international basis is not only a matter of sound business management, but a competitive imperative, and for many, no less than a matter of survival. Evolving business associations and partnerships, such as those between India and China, or China and various

The impact of technology and its promise as an effective enabler of global commerce is pervasive in the global business environment. Technology touches every aspect of international business, from communication to due diligence, logistics and financial settlement.

parts of Africa, will ensure that the reality of global sourcing will accelerate and will hasten the demise of the purely "domestic" commercial entity.

The evolution of technology and its increasing ability to deliver on a long-envisioned promise of new capabilities (such as full-scale e-commerce) has contributed to—perhaps even driven—the transformational changes reshaping the global business environment. The mind-numbing range of activities, transactions and interactions that can be conducted in the "virtual world" through the Internet touch every aspect of international trade and global commerce. Where the Internet was once a convenient vehicle for the exchange of small, low-value and low-complexity items such as Pez candy dispensers, it has evolved to enable full-scale electronic commerce across the globe that encompasses a broad range of products and services, from valuable antiques to high-end research consulting and other professional offerings.

From the previously noted credit-verification and due-diligence challenge, to full-scale online trading platforms, highly integrated supply chains and web-based "social networks" that facilitate the mobilization of networks around every conceivable undertaking, the impact of doing business internationally is broad and will only expand. The pace of change in emerging markets, for example, is assisted by the absence of antiquated, legacy technologies, so these economies can move directly to leading-edge capabilities, unhampered by the limitations of existing systems. As the importance of these markets continues to grow in the context of global sourcing, the pace of change of global commerce will be further accelerated.

Technology has evolved to impact every element of trade and global business, from near-instant communications across the globe through highly mobile devices to instantaneous inventory controls, detailed tracking of shipments and advances in logistics and security, including the increased use of Radio Frequency Identification Technology (RFID). From global positioning to in-transit tracking of shipments, the level of visibility through the global supply chain has increased dramatically, and the potential for enhancing trade and global commerce is in its early stages.

The changes are such that the evolution of virtual "states" based on people sharing common views, interests and objectives, rather than a common border, is being seriously contemplated as an emerging complement to traditional forms of social organization. Early versions of such virtual communities are already in evidence in the area of international trade and global commerce, and they demonstrate further that the classical distinctions between domestic and international business will eventually be historical, academic observations.

The recognition that there is a convergence between domestic and international business—even global business—will be a competitive advantage to a business if they can translate it from concept to action.

Shifting trade flows and trade priorities

The flow of international trade and international business has changed significantly and will continue to change in the coming years, as powerful new business and trade partnerships are concluded, and focus continues to shift from primary inputs and manufactured goods higher into the value chain to professional services. This shift may eventually transfer back to increasingly scarce natural resources, such as fresh water.

From the regional trade flows in the early Middle East to trade flows that enriched European colonial powers to the emergence of post-war U.S. economic power and hegemony, trade patterns and practices related to global business have shifted, and their characteristics and focus have evolved to re-shape the realities of global business today. Historical context is important in understanding the evolution of the global business environment; the critical contribution of trade routes and trade flows—across Europe, Asia, Africa and the globe—to the development of the international community and its institutions is self-evident. An illustration of the impact of trade flows is available through a multi-year (1999–2007) study of Old World trade routes (OWTRAD) at the Australian National University (www.ciolek.com/owtrad.html).

The largest single engine of trade and economic growth today is arguably the mammoth flow of goods and services between the United States and China. This bilateral relationship has reshaped the flow of global trade and redefined fundamentals related to international business, from the mechanics of global supply chains to the transactional characteristics of international payments. Despite the political differences between China and the United States, the commercial impact of these two nations trading and conducting business is that their combined influence shapes the global business environment as no two other partners today.

The European Union continues to expand its membership, and now includes economies that cover the full spectrum, from ailing to growing steadily to stable and robust. The EU is notable as a trading and commercial power, as well as for the fact that the trade and business conducted among members will become increasingly "domestic" in nature, and will change the approach that non-EU companies take to access the overall market. The requirement to obtain CE Markings (Conformité européenne) prior to exporting to EU member states is one example of the increasing integration of the EU market. Similarly, the union's ongoing initiative to create a unified payments process and infrastructure under SEPA (Single European Payments Area) has already impacted financial services firms locally and internationally.

A third major trend relates to the increasing value and importance of South-South trade: economies in the southern part of the globe are among the most dynamic and growth-oriented economies in the world, and are generally also those in development and evolution. The relevance of North-South trade, historically discussed primarily in the context of international development, has given way to some degree to the increasing dynamism and growing potential of South-South trade.

In addition to changing priorities and patterns of trade on a geographic level, major changes are reshaping the global business environment at the industry and sector levels. Service-sector trade has demonstrated significant and sustained growth, and similarly, international business in the areas of technology and other knowledge-based industries is reshaping entire industries. Perhaps the most visible example is the market for outsourcing many higher-value functions and professions, from the proliferation of global call centres to the veritable explosion of programming and technology development offerings in India and elsewhere.

A major automaker in India let it be known several years ago that strategic interests and partnership-development efforts would concentrate on China rather than the United States or Japan. Recently, General Motors lost its ranking as the largest auto maker in the world to Toyota. Expect top rankings in this industry to be more fluid and dynamic over the coming years than they've been in the last eighty years. Part of this dynamism will be the result of net new entrants in the market.

As with other areas in global business and international trade, the priority and impact of environmental considerations is increasingly central—and critical—to success. The emphasis on sustainability and environmentally friendly products, services and solutions is yet another illustration of the radical change in focus, interest and priorities in this new era of the global business environment.

Merger and acquisition trends

In the past couple of decades, we have also witnessed a dramatic period of corporate consolidation; the rate of global merger activity has risen exponentially. According to the New Economics Foundation (www.neweconomics.org), between 1980 and 2000, the value of global mergers rose 100-fold, reaching U.S.$15 trillion by the millennium. Mergers have been most prevalent in the telecommunications, pharmaceutical, media, automotive, energy, utilities, defence, food retail and financial services sectors. The most recent sector to experience this surge of business concentration is the resource sector. Years of under-investment combined with steadily increasing demands from China have led to supply shortfalls of many raw materials and have created demand-driven price increases in a broad spectrum of resource commodities. Accordingly, share prices in the resource sector have been rising and companies are actively combining while conditions for deal financing are optimal. In general, this acceleration in mergers and acquisitions has been enabled by the "integration of financial markets, trade liberalisation, deregulation and privatization of national industries."[1] And while the vast majority of these deals have involved European and North American firms, companies in developing countries have become popular takeover targets for larger multinationals. Thus, this is clearly a trend that should be carefully watched because it is also a self-perpetuating phenomenon (i.e., as smaller companies find it increasingly difficult to keep pace with larger competitors, it inspires more mergers).

Trade, investment and international business: the boundaries blur

There was a time when it was interesting to discuss whether the conduct of trade was a precursor to investment in an international market, or whether an investment ought to be made locally as a first step to developing a lasting trading relationship. Similarly, international trade was generally seen as a specialized subset of international business.

The current reality sees a much more holistic and integrated dynamic between these three elements, both in the business community and among public-policy specialists in many governments. The promotion of trade and exports is increasingly linked to the support and promotion of inward foreign investment, as well as to the facilitation of international investment by local firms and organizations. Trade promotion organizations, often primarily focused on export development, are now increasingly active on the investment side.

Commercially, the distinction between trade and investment is also less clear now than it has been historically. Global sourcing is increasingly a reality of business and often serves as a convincing argument in favour of establishing an in-market presence. Similarly, the role of inter-company trade continues to be critical in certain markets—North America being a notable example—and

---

[1] Oram, Julia. "Standing Up to the Competition? The Future of European Mergers," *The New Economics Foundation Corporate Breakdown*, Edition 5, Jan. 2003.

that reality will expand as emerging economic powers continue to extend their activities, ambitions and influence across the globe.

The global trends related to increased privatization of a whole range of activities will only magnify this reality as larger and larger enterprises and undertakings that might have operated under public-policy drivers seek to become more competitive and responsive to market forces and economic disciplines.

From large public-sector utilities to export finance and credit agencies across the globe, realities of privatization—including the frequent re-structuring of such organizations and the economic imperatives that drive those entities to seek engagement in the global business environment—contribute to the blurring of the trade/investment boundaries.

One striking illustration of the convergence between trade and investment in its purest form is the emergence of specialized investment vehicles (hedge funds), which are based upon trade finance transactions and the related returns and financial flows. The leading funds in this space are currently in London and New York; however, their investment focus is primarily in the area of emerging markets. As trade and as financial markets evolve globally, it is likely that similar trade-based investment vehicles will be increasingly common. Increasingly integrated financial markets, including stock market mergers across national boundaries, are a characteristic of the current environment, as is the emergence of new sources of capital pools—from rich pension funds with limited, but growing, appetite for international investment, to capital pools in emerging economies that can rival liquidity in leading economies. The implications for the continued evolution of the global business environment are significant and largely supportive of current trends.

The global business environment is proving to be "global" in more than just geographic terms: the environment within which businesses operate is "global" also in its increasingly integrated, boundary-crossing character. The relationship between trade, investment and the pursuit of global commerce is a compelling illustration of the changes to date, and a precursor of changes yet to come.

Global Power and Influence: New Players, New Paradigms

Global integration
The global economic and political integration that began, on some level, along political and ideological lines in the post–Second World War period, continues today, though along far different lines of commonality. The vision of the European Union, under development since the 1950s, being actualized despite seemingly insurmountable political and historical differences, is a striking testament to the imperatives of integration. The EU represents a level of integration among member states that crosses political, economic and social boundaries, and links EU members, some would argue, more closely than states or provinces that share a common national history and border.

Integration is also taking place at regional levels through bilateral and multilateral agreements of various types, from economic co-operation and customs unions to full-scale free-trade zones and agreements, across the globe. Major examples

According to the OECD, China averaged a meteoric 9.6 percent rate of growth between 1979 and 2005. By increasing its share of world trade (in goods) from less than 1 percent to 6.4 percent in the same period, it became the third-largest trading nation after the United States and Germany in 2005.
Source: China's Growth and Trade Impact...OECD Working Paper No. 44

include the European Union, the North American Free Trade Agreement (NAFTA), MERCOSUR in South America, ASEAN in Asia and CARICOM in the Caribbean community, as well as COMESA in Africa. Details on the nature and scope of each form of partnership are available from numerous sources, including the websites of the secretariats of each partnership.

Table 1.1—Stages of economic integration	
Free Trade Agreement (FTA)	Zero tariffs between member countries and reduced non-tariff barriers
Customs Union (CU)	FTA + common external tariff
Common Market (CM)	CU + free movement of capital and labour, some policy harmonization
Economic Union (EU)	CM + common economic policies and institutions

Source: Government of Canada (www.dsp-psd.communication.gc.ca/Pilot/LoPBdP/inbrief/prb0249-e.htm)

The emergence of new players and new powers
China

China is almost universally regarded as an example of stunning success in growth, trade development and expansion as well as effective, accelerated integration into the world economy and the global business environment. China's trade and economic power cannot be denied or overlooked, despite widely shared concerns related to political dynamics and issues of human rights and intellectual property, among others.

Where Hong Kong was historically a facilitator and "transit point" for trade, including exports originating from the mainland, China has taken the role of "final processing and assembly" for goods originating in various parts of Asia destined for ultimate export to Europe and North America. Additionally, China is shifting its emphasis to technology-intensive, complex goods, including capital-intensive exports. As of 2004, China became the world's leading exporter of information and communication technology (ICT) products—a reality well illustrated by the acquisition of IBM's retail computer business by China-based Lenovo, announced in late 2004.

China's demand for raw materials and resources to fuel its meteoric growth is impacting commodity prices on a global basis and has driven increasing interest in foreign investment and acquisitions by Chinese organizations and entities. Services trade remains a limited component (less than 10 percent) of China's overall trade activity, but is sure to increase in volume and impact.

China's increasing interest in trade and investment in Africa is a striking illustration of shifting priorities and trade flows—despite long-established trade and colonial ties with Europe, the level of trade and investment engaged in between China and various parts of Africa is growing at meteoric rates–surpassing U.S. $32 billion in 2006.[2] An overview of Sino-African relations can be obtained through the China-Africa Cooperation Forum.

---

[2] BBC website article, China-Africa trade jumps by 39%, January 6, 2006. (www.news.bbc.co.uk/2/hi/business/4587374.stm)

India

India is another emerging global power, which some say is in a close race with China to determine which country will become the example of success in transitioning from an emerging economy to a full-fledged power. India faces numerous political, social and economic challenges, yet is recognized as a generally stable democracy, and has effectively staked a position as a provider of high-quality services in technology, call centres and a range of other areas, including manufacturing. India's pre-eminent position as the world's provider of BPO (Business Process Outsourcing) services is well recognized, as is the entrepreneurial character of its people and its businesses.

India has achieved high levels of economic growth as well as very high rates of foreign direct investment, which soared from U.S.$103 million in 1990-91 to U.S.$5.9 billion in 2001-02—excluding significantly larger flows from institutional investors.[3] The influx of foreign investment has been one enabler in India's rapid rise upward on the global value chain, but Indian companies are equally active in foreign acquisitions, which in the first quarter of 2007 alone totalled 34 companies valued at more than U.S.$10.7 billion, according to *The Economist*.

The global growth in foreign direct investment in 2006 rose by one third over the previous year, to U.S.$1.23 trillion, propelled by both increased levels of mergers and acquisitions and higher overall share prices, according to the United Nations Conference on Trade Development (UNCTAD) as quoted by the World Trade Organization WTO, and India is well poised to take advantage of this trend.

Despite the challenges of leading a coalition government with a wide range of political views and economic visions, India has achieved growth rates in the 8 percent range, and is well positioned from a commercial perspective to continue this level of performance, provided political stability—both internally and with its neighbour, Pakistan—is maintained.

Other countries and regions

The CIS (Commonwealth of Independent States), a group of 12 former Soviet republics co-founded by the Ukraine and others, including some of the newer members of the European Union, such as Poland, are exhibiting potential and achieving levels of growth and development that contribute to the shifting focus of energies, investment and attention in the global business environment.

Global snapshot

The following table illustrates annual percentage growth in GDP and trade by region and for selected economies, according to the World Trade Organization.

---

[3] R. Kumar, and A.K. Sethi, *Doing Business in India*, 2005.

Figure 1.2—Annual percentage growth in GDP									
	GDP			Exports			Imports		
	2004	2005	2006	2004	2005	2006	2004	2005	2006
North America	3.9	3.2	3.4	8.0	6.0	8.5	10.5	6.5	6.5
United States	3.9	3.2	3.4	8.5	8.0	10.5	11.0	6.0	5.5
South & Central America	6.9	5.2	5.2	13.0	8.0	2.0	18.5	14.0	10.5
Europe	2.4	1.8	2.8	7.0	4.0	7.5	7.0	4.0	7.0
European Union (25)	2.3	1.6	2.8	7.0	4.0	7.5	6.5	3.5	6.5
Commonwealth of Independent States (CIS)	8.0	6.7	7.5	12.0	3.5	3.0	16.0	18.0	20.0
Africa & Middle East	6.0	5.5	5.4	8.0	5.0	1.0	14.0	13.0	8.5
Asia	4.8	4.1	4.4	15.5	11.5	13.5	14.5	8.0	8.5
China	10.1	9.9	10.7	24.0	24.0	22.0	21.5	11.5	16.5
Japan	2.7	1.9	2.2	13.5	5.0	10.0	6.5	2.0	2.0
India	8.0	8.5	8.3	15.5	20.5	11.5	16.0	20.5	12.0
World	3.9	3.2	3.7	10.0	6.5	8.0	—	—	—

a. Includes the Caribbean

b. Trade volume data are derived from customs values deflated by standard unit values and an adjusted price index for electronic goods

Source: World Trade Organization (WTO)

This table provides a stark contrast in growth rates between emerging regions and nations and established economies. U.S. exports growth of 10.5 percent in 2006 stands against 22 percent growth in China in the same year, and double-digit GDP growth in China over three years also stands in marked contrast to growth achieved in most parts of the world, with India also exceeding 8 percent each year. Several other comparisons, such as the high rate of growth of imports to the CIS, help to highlight the shift in economic growth and momentum.

While there is clearly an argument that high growth from a lower starting point is easier to achieve, the current reality is that the differences in growth rates are large. China's merchandise exports outpaced those of the United States for the first time in the latter part of 2006—a precursor of realities to come in the new global business environment.

New power, new partnerships
The emergence of new trade and new economic and global business powers has implications that extend far beyond purely commercial factors. Historical relationships, evolving political views and shared desires to exercise power on the global stage will all contribute to assuring active and motivated efforts to reshape the global environment—business and otherwise.

Chinese and Indian companies have quickly recognized the value and advantages of exploring partnership opportunities in preparation for the "century of Asia," and the continuing willingness, or need, of traditional economic powers to ignore or downplay political, commercial and other disagreements with the emerging players is perhaps the clearest indication of the shifting dynamics of global power. Serious concerns about nuclear capabilities in India, or the disregard for intellectual property in China, are consciously given lower priority and profile than the potential gains from commercial partnership, and that reality will extend over time to areas beyond the realm of business.

The automotive- and technology-industry sectors offer synergies and partnership opportunities based on complementary approaches in China and India, while both economies will continue their competitive drive upward on the value chain, focusing on service-sector activities and other high-value business. Colonial ties, historically important in the maintenance of trade and commercial relationships, are being replaced by new "partnerships of equals" and by active searches among middle- and low-income economies for win-win alternatives.

China's increased interest and activity in Africa, driven perhaps by a combination of objectives, including access to abundant and much-needed resources, is another striking development and a further illustration of the fundamental re-shaping of the global business environment.

Global Flows: Capital, People and Trade

South-South trade

Trade between low- and middle-income countries, referred to as "South-South" trade, is an area of increasing focus for a variety of business, political and development-related reasons, and was at the centre of the recent Doha Development Agenda promoted by the World Trade Organization.

South-South trade accounts for a small but growing percentage of world trade but has grown, according to the Organisation for Economic Co-operation and Development (OECD), at a rate that outpaces the growth of North-North and North-South trade. Additionally, South-South trade accounts for an increasing portion of the overall trade involving the South.

South-South trade offers potential for development of trade and of technological and industrial capabilities and capacity in lower- and middle-income countries, under commercial conditions that might be somewhat less competitive. Ultimately, the argument goes; enhanced capabilities will permit countries in the South to effectively and competitively penetrate markets of the North, and to do so at a higher level on the value chain than might otherwise be possible.

The OECD notes several empirical observations that are characterized as stylized facts or as "phenomena that have been observed in several contexts and are widely understood to be empirical facts." (As listed in the adjoining box)

The changing nature of the global business environment is, and will continue to be, impacted in a material way by the growth, evolution and broadening of South-South trade. The potential for a worldwide increase in benefits ("welfare") under a fully liberalized trade model is illustrated below.

The share of South-South trade in world trade has increased.

Economies of the South have grown much faster than those of the North.

Tariff barriers have gone down in major developing countries.

The bulk of observed expansion in South-South trade has been intra-regional, though not necessarily as part of a regional trade agreement (RTA).

Manufacturing trade has played a leading role in South-South trade and now accounts for two-thirds of such trade.

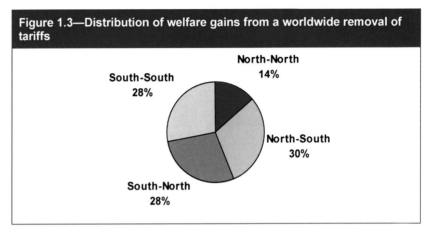

Figure 1.3—Distribution of welfare gains from a worldwide removal of tariffs

Source: OECD Working Paper No. 40, *South-South Trade in Goods*, October, 2006

Note: South-North indicates the gains that originate in liberalization by the South and accrue to the North.

The graphic suggests, at least notionally, that each combination of trading relationships shown would result in a net benefit; while North-North trade under a fully liberalized model is projected to generate a 14 percent increase in welfare between trading partners, each other combination (involving a "South" partner) generates a 28–30 percent increase in benefits.

While working papers can be academically rigorous, there are practical commercial realities that suggest that the worldwide elimination of tariffs is not attainable in the medium term, if at all; nevertheless, the potential of South-South trade and its increasing impact on the global business environment is illustrated even if we consider the benefit figures above as upper limits.

Services trade is also material and growing in importance. In a parallel study, the OECD notes, "While developing countries' exports to developed markets seem to be more important for the majority of non-OECD regions, the opposite is true for Asian developing countries: their services exports to developing regions represent more than half of their total services exports."

South-South trade is an important element of the character of the global business environment, and will increase in potential, profile and power over the medium term.

Capital markets
The capital markets are growing on a global basis, becoming more closely integrated—as well as automated, through the introduction of technology—and are increasingly becoming directly accessible by companies and organizations of all sizes.

Leading financial institutions have been concerned for some time, and across various lines of business, about the threat or prospect of "disintermediation"— simply put, being cut out of the process as product and service providers. The most striking illustration of this reality is the ability of world-class corporate clients (with credit ratings to rival that of top banks and financial entities) to access financing directly from the market, at rates that are far more attractive than those offered by the banks. Even the finance of international trade, long a banker's domain, is being reshaped by changing flows of capital, new sources of financing and the willingness of major parties in the global business environment to seek solutions beyond the traditional ones.

The capital markets themselves are becoming increasingly global, integrated and interdependent. Foreign investment and ownership restrictions are gradually being relaxed, large pools of investment capital from pension funds and other sources are combing the globe for attractive investments and perhaps most telling of all, stock exchanges are operating as businesses, seeking international partnerships, acquisitions and other alliances. Leading exchanges in Europe and the United States have merged, and the largest exchanges are looking for additional merger and acquisition opportunities in Asia and elsewhere as capital markets evolve and mature globally.

Outsourcing and offshoring

Outsourcing business processes and operations to low-cost markets has been a significant trend in the global business environment for more than a decade, and continues to expand as technology solutions evolve to meet the needs of business process outsourcing clients and providers. The scope of business activities that can be outsourced is ever broadening, to the delight of certain markets such as India, and to the chagrin—and political dilemma—of others, such as the United States.

The worldwide market for business-processing outsourcing (BPO) was to exceed U.S.$130 billion in 2005, according to Gartner Research, with major BPO deals in the U.S.$300 million range. The impact on the global business environment has been nothing short of transformational in terms of pure business, commercial ventures and trade-related activities, and in the context of distribution of wealth and resources to emerging markets. Areas traditionally viewed as professional, and "immune" to outsourcing, are in fact increasingly under pressure or, from the provider's perspective, increasingly a viable opportunity: Gartner projected that the outsourcing market for finance and accounting services in Europe would exceed U.S.$4 billion by 2008, and the scope of BPO, outsourcing and offshoring continues to expand.

The global trend in outsourcing trade finance banking operations is perhaps a useful illustration. In the early days of trade operations outsourcing, a few global financial institutions explored the feasibility and viability of providing outsourced or offshore processing capabilities to other banks. While there was some interest in such models in the 1990s, the advent of effective technologies and proven business models, together with market imperatives driving banks out of the trade-finance business, have combined to make BPO one of the major trends and forces in trade banking today.

Cross-border mobility and skills flow

The global business environment is evolving and operating at a pace that, in many regions, demands or motivates a flow of resources and skills across borders. The European Union is perhaps the most striking example of the future of skills flow and mobility of resources; yet this challenge is central to many parts of the global business environment, both from a private sector, commercial perspective and public-policy view. The global business environment is in the early stages of evolution in the area of efficient flow of people, resources and skills across the world.

In addition to broader issues related to immigration and the flow of people across the globe, a specific concern in terms of the global business environment relates to the recognition of educational and professional equivalencies between countries and jurisdictions. The availability of universally (or at least, very widely) recognized professional designations may mitigate this challenge to some degree; however, the vast majority of skill sets, educational credentials and technical/professional accreditations are poorly understood and thus inadequately matched across jurisdictions.

Leading economies appreciate that a resolution to this issue—recognizing legitimate and demonstrable skills, training and credentials—represents a significant competitive advantage and an excellent opportunity to better leverage resources and expertise to the benefit of all concerned.

Social and demographic issues

Despite the acknowledged evolution in the global business environment, significant challenges remain in terms of population growth and continuing poverty, and even in the established economies, the trend toward the "greying" of populations—with implications of future productivity declines, higher health-care costs and the need, as some have already recognized, to ensure ongoing growth through active encouragement of immigration. Additionally, pension reform is a critical issue in many parts of the world, including Europe and North America, where provisions for aging populations are increasingly inadequate, especially as life expectancies rise.

Social inequity has been a constant in the human experience; the existence of powerful modes of communication such as the Internet—even in censored form, as it operates in some parts of the world—allows a greater awareness of the gulf that separates the poorest from the wealthiest. At its extreme, this inequity is identified as a motivator for terrorist activity, either directly or indirectly.

The CIA, as quoted by the National Research Council of Canada,[4] cites the following four types of large-scale demographic shifts that will contribute to social stress:

- Age cohort differences, such as the widening youth bulge in the developing world

- Population growth, exacerbating environmental degradation in some areas

- Movements from rural to urban areas

- The destabilizing effect of migratory population flows in the developing world

---

[4] CIA, as quoted by the National Research Council. (www.nrc-cnrc.gc.ca/aboutUs/ren/nrc-foresight_10_e.html)

Given 9/11, protectionism, security and defence of trade interests could be added to this list.

The effects of some of the major social issues that shape the global business environment extend far beyond the economic consequences that are often an area of focus.

International businesses, particularly multinational corporations, are often identified as significant contributors to the ongoing polarization of wealth and standards of living across the globe. Many argue that the ongoing search for lower-cost labour and factors of production perpetuates very large differences in economic progress and development. Others will argue, of course, that properly led multinationals are good global citizens, bringing opportunity and (some) economic benefit to areas that would otherwise remain completely impoverished.

Reaching higher into the value chain

The global business environment is still heavily impacted by commodity trade and commodity- and resource-based business. The effect of oil prices on the world economy and the increasing concern about limitations and depletion of natural resources—even water—are clear illustrations of this reality.

Concurrently, however, there is an emerging trend in many parts of the world, from leading economies to emerging markets and developing nations, to reach higher into the global value chain, seeking to identify, provide or even create—through effective marketing and brand management—significant and profitable value-added. Some markets have taken a nearly completely commodified textile business and developed a high-value niche industry through the creation, promotion and support of an effective fashion-based brand. Similarly, it is argued by some that even traditional and powerful manufacturing industries, such as the automotive sector, will inevitably become commodified and that the value of an automotive business and franchise will eventually be based on brand recognition and brand value.

It may be sufficient as a starting point to have a "unique selling proposition;" however, sustainable venture and businesses will increasingly be based on a clear and differentiated value proposition, which will often mean being solution-oriented and holistic rather than product-focused and transactional in the conduct of trade and global business.

The global business environment continues to require a focus on commodities, primary industries and traditional business activities, yet the most complex and (some would suggest) high-value activities, from engineering, technology, and professional services, to health-care, medical and even surgical "services," are increasingly a part of the global business environment.

The increasing importance and impact of service-sector trade on a global basis is fully acknowledged, with several emerging economies shifting from barely nascent industrial capabilities—partly through enabling technology—directly into service-oriented business and trade. India has enjoyed success in creating value through service-based business services, such as computer programming, accounting, engineering and management consulting. The WTO General Agreement on Trade in Services (GATS) is a high-profile and high-impact element of the global business environment, and the overall subject of trade in services receives significant attention at the WTO.[5]

Multilateral Institutions

Overview
Following the Second World War, several multilateral institutions were created to foster global trade and provide a framework for the effective management and evolution of a rules-based and inclusive international trade and global business environment. As international economic relations grew in volume and complexity, the number of these institutions increased.

The numerous multilateral institutions funded by the contributions and membership dues of member states focus on areas such as international development, infrastructure, trade support and business facilitation. Some such institutions, notably the World Trade Organization, also assist in resolving trade disputes. Additionally, they prepare emerging and developing nations to join the international trade and business community, which agrees to conduct business on the basis of a shared set of agreements, principles and rules, such as the General Agreement on Trade in Services. An overview of the history of the WTO and its precursor institutions is available on the WTO website, and provides useful context for the evolution to the current global business environment (www. wto.org).

The multilaterals, or international financial institutions (IFIs), may fund or guarantee trade transactions or larger capital projects, and together represent a multi-billion dollar procurement market for businesses active in international markets.

While the pursuit of IFI and development business may be administratively complicated and challenging, it can be quite lucrative, and recent efforts by the IFIs to standardize procurement documentation, processes and practices are easing the burden on interested organizations.

The multilaterals are excellent sources of statistics, market insight, analysis and rigorous studies on a wide range of subjects related to the global business environment, with some emphasis on international development.

World Bank Group
The World Bank Group includes the following organizations:

- The International Bank for Reconstruction and Development (IBRD), commonly called the World Bank

- The International Development Association (IDA)

- The International Finance Corporation (IFC)

- The Multilateral Investment Guarantee Agency (MIGA)

---

[5] World Trade Organization. (www.wto.org/English/tratop_e/serv_e/serv_e.htm)

These institutions, like other regional development banks (IFIs), mainly lend money to developing nations or encourage investment in various regions. IFIs generally seek to contribute to economic growth in developing countries, though anti-globalization movements often target these institutions as enablers of perpetual injustice and inequity through burdensome and intrusive aid programs.

Like the United Nations, multilateral agencies operating in the global business environment face numerous complex challenges and have been required to adapt to the changing landscape of business. The World Bank Group's Environmental Health and Safety Guidelines (EHS), described in detail on the IFC website (www.ifc.org), provide some evidence of the group's efforts to respond to changing priorities and realities.

A detailed history of the World Bank, including an online archive, is available on their website at www.worldbank.org.

United Nations (UN)
The UN is a major element of the global business environment. Some argue that it is the best hope for a meaningful global basis for dialogue and collaboration, while others perceive an inherently imperfect and largely failed, impotent organization with limited success, but with catastrophic failures, such as the genocide in Rwanda and the scandal-plagued Oil-for-Food program in Iraq.

Whether the UN is a shadow of the hopes and aspirations that flowed after its establishment in the post-war period, or an idea whose time in history has not yet arrived, it remains, however imperfectly, the only global forum for dialogue on a broad range of issues. Among its major current areas of focus, the Millennium Development Goals (MDGs) have been given some attention and profile in the global business environment. As the UN describes it, "The eight Millennium Development Goals (MDGs)—which range from halving extreme poverty to halting the spread of HIV/AIDS and providing universal primary education, all by the target date of 2015—form a blueprint agreed to by all the world's countries and the entire world's leading development institutions. They have galvanized unprecedented efforts to meet the needs of the world's poorest."[6]

United Nations Development Programme (UNDP)
The UNDP is the world's largest source of multilateral technical and pre-investment co-operation, as well as the co-ordinating organization for UN development activities worldwide. It has its headquarters in New York and has regional offices in 128 developing countries. The UNDP provides financial and technical support to more than 6,000 projects in developing countries. Some 130 countries support it, making voluntary contributions in addition to their regular UN contributions. Through a network of specialized international agencies and development banks, the UNDP offers technical assistance in almost every area of economic activity.

International Monetary Fund (IMF)
The IMF is a specialized agency of the UN with headquarters in Washington. It promotes international monetary co-operation, fosters the expansion and

---

[6] United Nations. (www.un.org/millenniumgoals)

balanced growth of international trade and promotes stability in foreign exchange. Most developed countries and many developing ones are among the 185 members of the IMF.

One of the IMFs major roles is to help members meet short-term balance-of-payment problems by allowing them to draw temporarily on the fund's reserves. The IMF also supervises the operation of the international exchange-rate system to maintain stability among world currencies and prevent competitive devaluations.

United Nations Conference on Trade and Development (UNCTAD)
In 1964, the first conference on trade and development was held in Geneva, Switzerland. It led to the establishment of the UNCTAD as a permanent UN body. This meeting brought together representatives from industrialized and developing countries to discuss trade issues. It is also called the North-South dialogue.

During the sixth UNCTAD meeting in 1983, the industrialized countries agreed to open access to their markets if the developing countries would do the same for their poorer neighbours. The South contended that its "infant" industries needed the protection of tariff and non-tariff barriers to allow them to develop.

UNCTAD has also implemented the Trade Point Program to establish, operate and connect trade points in all regions of the world. Almost 90 trade points in 55 countries had been established by 1995. Trade Point Development Centres (UNTPDCs) have been established to help trade points become electronically connected, especially through the Internet.

International Labour Organization (ILO)
The ILO became a UN specialized agency in 1946. Its purpose is to promote international action aimed at achieving full employment, raising workplace standards and improving labour conditions. The ILO is unique among international organizations in that it is based on a tripartite system of representation that includes not only governments, but employer and employee groups as well.

The ILO adopts conventions and recommendations for ratification by member governments. While members are not bound to adopt ILO conventions, they must bring them to the attention of national legislators and report periodically to the ILO on relevant aspects of their own labour laws and practices. Under a widely used special procedure, the governing body of the ILO investigates alleged violations by governments of trade unionists' right to "freedom of association."

Organisation for Economic Co-operation and Development (OECD)
The OECD is a multilateral organization that provides a forum for representatives of industrialized countries to develop and co-ordinate economic and social policies. The OECD is a well-respected source of economic research, statistical information and publications.

The OECD was formed in 1961 and is based in Paris. Its membership comprises the most economically advanced countries in the world, and it engages in research and policy analysis related to major issues of importance to the global business environment. The OECD is also a key forum relative to the development of global standards around the conduct of business by export credit agencies around the world.

It must be noted that the very existence of various international financial institutions and development agencies is a matter of some controversy. Are these agencies benefactors to the poor and dispossessed of the world, or are they ruthless instruments of political power and policy? Some allege that these institutions fundamentally sustain and perpetuate a system that keeps developing nations crushed under insurmountable debt, the service payments of which generate huge, net inflows of capital and economic benefit to the lending countries.

A detailed review of the negative perceptions related to the various agencies, including the IMF and its frequently observed ironclad application of market principles, even in the face of economic devastation for the recipient country, can be effected through various sources, including NGO groups such as ECA Watch and the Halifax Initiative, among others.

Pitfalls of Protectionism, Benefits of Engagement

Pitfalls of protectionism

Protectionism had its place and its time in the evolution of leading global economies, and despite the prevailing anti-protectionist "economic wisdom" of today, many developing and emerging markets argue their entitlement to a certain level of "protection" to ensure adequate development of companies, industry sectors and national economies.

International development experts at leading institutions such as the OECD suggest that one advantage of healthy and sustained "South-South" trade is that it lets developing and emerging economies nurture industries and commercial capabilities, allowing them to develop under less competitive conditions than in the broader global business environment.

More generally, however, there is a tendency to favour free trade, a rules-based regime with broad international membership and adherence, and the shaping of the global business environment by market forces. One reality of the new era in trade and global business is that even formerly "pure" command economies are displaying—and encouraging—characteristics that look suspiciously like entrepreneurship and market-based activity. The emergence of China's entrepreneurial class, millionaires and all, is perhaps the most striking example, though similar developments in Russia also demonstrate the new reality. China's careful handling of Hong Kong after 1997, as well as its welcoming of foreign-educated expatriates—bringing with them expertise and ventures ranging from real estate mega-projects to Internet-based ventures—provides another illustration of emerging realities and converging practice.

At the highest level, protectionism imposes additional costs on economies engaging in such activity and, taken in aggregate, on the global economy and on every aspect of global business. The Great Depression is arguably a stark historical example of this phenomenon; a more current challenge with global implications relates to the global battle over agricultural subsidies with positions taken by the United States, Canada, the EU and Japan having effectively frozen progress in several rounds of WTO talks. These countries have persistently sought to encourage other countries to agree to a "level playing field" in agriculture trade, but they continue to heavily subsidize their own agricultural sectors and have refused to eliminate these distorting practices. These subsidies have led to the dumping of staple commodities into less developed countries, which has had severe and negative ramifications for smaller, "unsubsidized" farmers in those markets. So, this situation has created a deadlock in trade negotiations as many countries have seen the level-playing-field argument as a highly hypocritical posture.

Engagement through trade

The impact of international trade and global commerce is believed by many to have transformational potential at all levels, from political and economic considerations to elements of social structure and every macro-aspect in between.

"A country does not have to be best at anything to gain from trade. The gains follow from specializing in those activities which, at world prices, the country is relatively better at, even though it may not have an absolute advantage in them. Because it is relative advantage that matters, it is meaningless to say a country has a comparative advantage in nothing. The term is one of the most misunderstood ideas in economics, and is often wrongly assumed to mean an absolute advantage compared with other countries."
Source: www.wto.org

The argument in favour of engaging in international business and trade with oppressive regimes or dictatorship, for example, is that sanctions rarely work, and a more effective approach is to engage in what might be termed "co-operative influence": trade and commercial engagement is a win/win and involves contact and some level of partnership. The business relationship becomes a basis for positive influence and increases the likelihood of engagement in the international community in future.

Trade is extremely important on a range of levels, from basic survival to less fundamental but perhaps still compelling considerations of standard of living, luxury and prestige. Trade obligations, especially short-term ones, are settled promptly and consistently. This generally healthy flow, even when less progressive economies and regimes are involved, is an indication of the potential in "engagement through trade."

There are arguments that suggest that even matters of international security can be addressed, at least partially, through poverty reduction and enhanced quality of life and progress beyond bare survival for a larger portion of the world population. Dissatisfaction with the current state of the world, it is said, can be mitigated through equitable trade as one strategy for encouraging and fostering engagement in the global community.

A historical and academically rigorous treatment of the effectiveness of "engagement through trade" can be reviewed in a paper published by Princeton University,[7] which argues that engagement is most effective when it targets multilateral integration as opposed to bilateral relations, with the U.S.-China relationship figuring prominently in the analysis.

Trade and Competitiveness

The classical "advantage" model

Textbooks on international economics refer to "absolute" and "comparative" advantage in international trade. Absolute advantage refers to the scenario

---

[7] Soo Yeon Kim, *Structure and Change in International Trade and Militarized Conflict: When Is Engagement Constructive?* Princeton University. (www.people.fas.harvard.edu/~johnston/GOV90ia/Kim.pdf)

between two trading partners where one partner has a net, clear advantage in the production (or acquisition) of a product—an abundant resource, a cost or production efficiency—that allows the partners to trade in a way that enhances value for both.

Comparative advantage relates to the idea that gains from trade can arise when a country applies resources to specialize in areas where it is relatively more efficient (taking into account world pricing) and uses the higher returns to import items from trading partners, even if it could produce those items domestically.

Partners and competitors: the networked environment

The global business environment is being shaped by an interesting new dynamic. Competitors and partners are still very much a reality of business and trade; however, the global reach that is now attainable by the smallest business in the tiniest economy creates the double-edged sword facing businesses today.

The opportunity to identify, assess and consummate business partnerships across the globe with organizations of all sizes and value propositions is unparalleled in history. This is due in large measure to the advent of Internet-based technologies and communications, and has resulted in access to global markets for the smallest of private businesses in remote locations across the globe.

Similarly, business competition is no longer restricted to businesses that are proximate to one another. It is a reality that competition can come—directly or indirectly—from any part of the world for a broad range of industries, from manufacturing to programming. Sourcing options have been greatly expanded, and much is being invested in optimizing global supply chains on every level, including the selection of competitive suppliers that will assist in driving costs down and enhancing the competitiveness and profitability of the buyer.

Global trade: zero-sum or win-win?

International trade, like business in general, is often approached with implicit reference to an agreement with the principle of scarcity. Trade partnerships between buyer and seller and agreements between nations and regions are shaped by the view that trade is a competitive dynamic, often involving maximization of value for one partner at the expense of another.

This approach is inconsistent with the win-win and partnership-based approach to business that characterizes commercial relationships in certain parts of the world. The competitive view of international trade may well be at the root of many of the greatest challenges facing the global community. Is the global business environment prepared to accept a new paradigm around trade, based upon principles of equity and maximized joint value between partners?

The next generation of trade professionals will face fundamental questions about the nature of trade and will be challenged to allow and enable the evolution of a new model for global commerce and international trade.

International Business, Security and Intellectual Property

Challenges of jurisdiction

A major complexity faced by leaders engaged in international trade and global commerce relates to the different legal and political jurisdictions that can claim authority over a transaction or a business venture.

The largest multinational mergers and acquisitions provide clear examples of this reality and its potentially deal-breaking impact. A corporate merger in the United States may be subject to review by European Union authorities if either or both entities have operations in the EU; competition policy often applies across borders, and the question of transfer pricing between affiliated companies is a direct result of jurisdictional issues affecting inter-company trade.

Issues of jurisdiction can, and do, arise at the transactional level as well. Payment for an import-export transaction between Brazil and the United Kingdom may occur under a U.S.-dollar denominated banking instrument—a New York bank, for example. Even if the goods traded never enter the United States, the financial flow through New York adds a further layer of jurisdiction and makes the transaction subject to certain U.S. regulations.

Jurisdictional questions and their impact—typically felt only when a deal or transaction becomes adversarial—are of critical importance to business partners and ought not to be treated lightly.

Security

Issues of security are pervasive in the current environment—at every level and extending across jurisdictions and borders. Security considerations affect every aspect of business, from the cross-border flow of funds to heightened security risks in certain markets and the logistical challenges now associated with international travel. Mundane aspects of these special considerations, such as longer transit times due to increased security screenings, involve an economic cost. So do numerous other security enhancements, such as the use of biometric technology and the requirement for enhanced technology in customs inspection and in securing shipments in transit—the scope of the security issue is huge, and is a reality of the global business environment that is likely to get more complex, pervasive and expensive over the medium term.

Security is being re-defined in the current environment, to the extent that the security of individual citizens is now being recognized, increasingly, as paramount and superseding national sovereignty. This notion, promoted by Canada, allows international intervention in cases where a government is clearly violating its citizens' basic rights. Security reaches from the highest macro-level aspects of the global business environment down to the level of human and individual security. A unique illustration of the issue is available through the Human Security Network (www.humansecuritynetwork.org).

In some sense, the issue of human security encompasses the increasing risk posed by various pandemics, including HIV/AIDS, West Nile virus, avian flu, influenza and malaria, that threaten the most vulnerable and poorest of global citizens. Numerous groups and resources are available to assist businesses in preparing for a possible or eventual pandemic, such as avian flu (www. pandemicflu.gov). Numerous specialist firms are providing business-continuity planning advice and services, and some industry groups are proposing options to prepare for and respond to possible pandemics, with HIV/AIDS addressed in numerous contexts, including a report by Booz Allen Hamilton[8]. The Canadian Manufacturers and Exporters (CME) have also prepared a guide, "Influenza Pandemic: Continuity Planning Guide for Canadian Business."[9]

Intellectual property and the risk/reward trade-off

The protection of intellectual property (IP), whether related to design, technical specifications, process patents or professional methodologies, is a critical consideration in the decision whether to pursue commercial opportunities on an international or global basis.

The discipline, professional practice and legal standing of IP is strictly respected and firmly enforced in certain markets and almost completely disregarded—some even say, actively contravened as a strategy for advancement of capabilities—in other markets.

Organizations pursuing opportunities in the markets that most flagrantly violate IP regulations do so at significant risk, though also with a view to the prospect of accessing large new markets. Enforcement mechanisms related to violations of IP are evolving but are far from effective as deterrents; stories about pirated designs and technologies reaching market before the original, legal versions, are easily found in writings related to international business. The question of intellectual property, including mitigation strategies, enforcement options and legal remedy is a critical one and will be increasingly central as an issue in the global business environment.

The Old "Fringe" Goes Mainstream: Green, Fair and More

Non-governmental organizations (NGOs)

NGOs, once considered voices of the fringe, hardly worth a glimpse in the landscape of international trade and global business, are now very much at the centre of fundamental issues shaping the current reality of global business, and are increasingly influencing the evolution of that environment in substantive ways.

Historically in an adversarial relationship with other major players in the global business environment, the NGOs, which form part of what is collectively referred to as "civil society," have garnered significant political currency as the issues they champion take increasing profile and priority across the globe. NGOs have gone from "fringe" to very much mainstream in the international trade and global business environment.

---

[8] Allen Hamilton, Booz. "The State of Business and HIV/Aids 2006, A Baseline Report." (www.boozallen. com/media/file/State_of_Business_and_HIVAIDS_2006_v2.pdf)

[9] Canadian Manufacturers and Exporters (CME). "Influenza Pandemic: Continuity Planning Guide for Canadian Business." (www.cme-mec.ca/pdf/CME_Pandemic_Guide.pdf)

Corporate social responsibility, anti-corruption measures, environmental issues, questions of sustainability and transparency (in trade, export and project finance, for example) are all very central to the activities of NGOs. The fair-trade movement, which seeks to direct a larger proportion of export revenues to the producers of goods in developing markets—as opposed to wholesalers and other intermediaries—is also gaining increasing support and becoming a characteristic of the global business environment.

Some argue that the efforts of NGOs—active in influencing the funding of large infrastructure projects based on the monitoring of local and environmental impacts, as well as advocating and promoting standards in the extractive industries—have the net effect of reducing competitiveness. Others contend that nothing less than the long-term health of the planet is at stake and that at any rate, those who lead in these areas become market makers in new lines of business, such as "green" products.

Environmental issues, from the all-encompassing climate change issues, to specific considerations about the environmental impact of long-range road transport, are at the core of political dialogue and, increasingly, at the centre of economic calculations related to business and economics. Sustainability is a factor or requirement in every major endeavour, and the development of markets for trading carbon emissions represents a creative mix of NGO green-friendly efforts, driven through mechanics and disciplines that closely mirror those present in leading stock exchanges and securities markets across the world.

Carbon markets allow countries that generate high emissions to "purchase" carbon credits from nations that are low emitters, effectively imposing an economic cost on polluters and creating a windfall benefit for those whose emissions are below agreed levels. Sophisticated trading and financing models have been developed (and continue to evolve) around carbon credits, and these mechanisms are shifting from macro, country-to-country models, down to the level of individual farms, businesses and consumers. Several international institutions, including the European Bank for Reconstruction and Development (EBRD) are active supporters of carbon credit programs and investment vehicles, as indicated on the EBRD site (www.ebrd.com).

Exercising stewardship in terms of sourcing practices to ensure the "greening" of supply chains (i.e., the design and management of eco-friendly supply chains) is now a matter of good business practice and is increasingly an effective brand differentiator in the market, as consumer concern over issues of sustainability and environment continues to evolve. The global sourcing of wood covering products, for example, with increasing activity from China, Russia and other sources, is increasingly influenced by concerns related to the source of the woods used, including clear-cutting practices, the use of endangered woods and increased interest in the use of reclaimed timber.

Automotive developments in hybrid technologies, the gradual shift to ethanol-based fuels and other crop-based inputs to chemical processes provide another illustration of the increasing demand for sustainable solutions and product offerings.

NGOs were given significant profile as stakeholders in the global business environment during a crucial period in the history of the World Bank and international development,[10] when the debate over contributions to international development—as opposed to looking after national interests—was distilled to the slogan "Grandma versus Ghana." The underlying suggestion of this slogan is that limited financial resources ought to be focused on resolving pressing domestic problems, such as health care and adequate pensions for seniors, rather than being squandered (so goes the extreme version of this argument) in developing nations through ineffective aid programs managed by bureaucratic development banks. It is alleged that most of the aid funds end up enriching corrupt government officials and others at the expense of the intended recipients, so why not apply those resources locally?

NGOs have joined the debate and have succeeded in raising the profile of a set of issues to the highest levels of government and to the senior levels within multilateral institutions. Corporations and multinationals have codes of ethical conduct and statements about CSR and banks are acknowledging and adopting guidelines, such as the Equator Principles (www.equator-principles.com), meant to ensure that social and environmental issues are considered in assessing project finance.

Issues that were once considered "fringe" now drive global agendas and shape policy: the international attempts to address global warming through the Kyoto Protocol are an example of the growing profile of NGO-promoted issues. Specifics around corporate social responsibility, such as proactive attempts to address corrupt practices and promote ethical business standards, illustrate the scope and impact of NGOs and demonstrate the increasing political effectiveness and leverage of these organizations and their global networks.

"The Equator Principles Financial Institutions (EPFIs) have consequently adopted these principles in order to ensure that the projects we finance are developed in a manner that is socially responsible and reflects sound environmental management practices.... We believe that adoption of and adherence to these principles offers significant benefits to ourselves, our borrowers and local stakeholders through our borrowers' engagement with locally affected communities."
Source: www.equator-principles.com

Leading Edge: Integrative Trade, Global Supply Chains and Virtual...Everything

Integrative trade
"Global commerce has entered a new phase of 'integrative trade.' This term captures all elements firms use to achieve the lowest possible cost and maximize the return for their products: exports, imports used to create exports, inward and outward foreign direct investment (FDI), offshore outsourcing and insourcing, and sales (mostly services) from foreign affiliates created through FDI."[11]

The global business environment is fundamentally recast, with trade and other commercial activities becoming interconnected and part of a larger whole. Global sourcing activities and supply chain models are such that exports are increasingly produced with imported components, and investment activities are closely linked to international trade and global commerce.

Trade finance
Payment, financing and risk-mitigation options, as well as approaches related to international trade finance, are being fundamentally redesigned to respond to the changing requirements of importers and exporters, driven by the evolution of global supply chains and the technology that supports and enables these

---

[10] See Mallaby, Sebastian. *The World's Banker.* Penguin Press, 2004.
[11] Conference Board of Canada, "Canada Project" 2005–2006 Performance and Potential, Chapter 2.

complex networks. Shifts in transaction types are driving global financial institutions to re-think their value proposition in support of international trade, just as risk insurers, export credit agencies (ECAs) of national governments and others are doing the same.

ECAs have long been indispensable to the conduct of trade and global business, while at the same time attracting unfavourable attention from NGOs and others for financing controversial, sometimes disastrous projects and activities. In more recent years, ECAs have been motivated by numerous factors to adopt principles linked to corporate social responsibility, sustainability and related areas. The activities of export credit agencies, for better or worse, have significant impact on the global business environment and merit balanced consideration.

GE Capital and UPS Capital have now been offering trade finance services for years, though with the closer link between trade finance and logistics-supply chains in recent years, the entrance of new providers will increase.

A major factor in the finance of trade and global business relates to the nature and dynamics of the international currency markets and the historical and current central role of the U.S. dollar. The greenback has clearly been the currency of the globe since the emergence of the United States as a superpower, and particularly since the end of the gold standard as the basis for determining the value of a currency internationally. While this reality remains and is likely to remain for some years, the fundamentals have shifted significantly—both in terms of the nature and power of the U.S. economy and in terms of the global landscape in foreign exchange and currency-market dynamics.

The level of debt (and continued borrowing) of the U.S. government raises questions about the long-term stability of the U.S. currency, including the ability of the Federal Reserve to effectively control the currency through open-market operations when so much debt is held by foreign investors, including emerging powers such as China. Additionally, the Euro is now an established currency, and a popular option in the conduct of international trade and global business. Over the long term, the Chinese yuan could rival both as a viable currency of global commerce.

The reality of the "contest" between the U.S. dollar and the Euro for leadership as a global currency of business—with all of the economic advantage and political leverage implied—is illustrated by the increasing interest in this topic. From senior political levels through to central bankers, economists and other specialists, the debate draws increasing attention and, as with other aspects of financial markets, the expectation is accounted for in market dynamics before it becomes a reality. If, or when, the EU reaches a critical mass as a global currency, the implications of that reality will have been "built in" as part of the new economic reality. A Federal Reserve Bank of New York economist has provided a treatment of the subject in relation to international trade and trade balances.[12]

Virtual…everything?

The transformational power of the Internet cannot be overstated. Taken together with complementary technologies and advances in security, the current set of

[12] Goldberg, Linda and Tiele, Cédric. *The International Role of the Dollar and Trade Balance Adjustment.* Occasional Paper No. 71, Group of Thirty, Washington, DC, 2006. (www.newyorkfed.org/research/economists/goldberg/GRP30_op71_all_FNL.pdf)

technological capabilities has enabled the evolution of global virtual trading communities, which include the trading platform, a proxy "quality measure" that arguably acts like a credit report, as well as payment mechanisms and dispute-settlement processes between buyer and seller. There is even an export financing solution attached to the model we reference: eBay, together with PayPal (the online payment service) and Skype (Voice over IP, or Internet Telephony) bring together the capacity to trade, communicate globally and effect near-immediate payment.

More complex virtual trade models have been developed now and facilitate hundreds of millions of dollars worth of international trade. The market has now adopted the idea that there are at least two concurrent supply chains at work in any deal: the physical supply chain and the financial supply chain. Some also refer to an "information" supply chain related to the deal, transaction or shipment.

Trade and international commerce in the virtual environment is a reality.

International Trade: Through the Crystal Ball

Global business tomorrow

The pursuit of international trade and global commerce has been a constant element of the human experience, regardless of how the idea of borders has been defined over time. That reality will continue, and the importance of how we conduct global commerce will only increase.

The basis upon which we conduct international business will continue to shape whatever prosperity exists in the world and will either sustain poverty and a skewed distribution of wealth, or it will become more inclusive and share its benefits more broadly across the globe. The effectiveness of multilateral institutions, together with the committed engagement of governments, civil society and others, has the potential to transform trade and commerce from a purely competitive process to one that looks to the overall welfare of the international community.

An international system based on maximizing overall gain and value as opposed to being driven by zero-sum competition, where one partner gains at the expense of another, is perhaps an ideal; however, there are clear indications that the current approach serves few at the expense of many. In the long term, such drastic inequity is unjust, dangerous and unsustainable.

The promise of technology as an enabler and an equalizer is beginning to be evident, and the application of that promise to enhancing international trade and global commerce is inevitable.

Change is a given, and its pace will only increase. International commerce will see significant transformation over the next decade, and the implications of that transformation will shape the fabric of global society, from economics to politics to security.

Global. Business. Environment. Each of the words in the title of this course will be redefined within the next ten years in ways that we cannot yet conceive of.

Global business environment checklist

☑ Appreciate the historical context, but keep a forward-looking view.

☑ Identify major global issues and related trends, such as the importance of environmental issues, the development of carbon credit markets and the pervasive nature of security issues.

☑ Identify emerging global leaders and understand their drivers and needs, as well as challenges in engaging with them.

☑ Appreciate the complexities of the many contradictions that shape and drive the global business environment.

☑ Think holistically and in terms of integration, interdependence and win-win-based partnerships.

☑ Embrace and leverage information technology (IT): it is everywhere.

Chapter Summary

The environment in which we conduct international trade and global commerce today has been, and continues to be, transformed by a series of factors that include emerging global powers, technological progress and shifts in priority related to former "fringe" issues.

The trade and international business professional of today cannot take a narrow, silo-based view of this specialized expertise, but must look at context and be mindful of evolution and the speed of transformational change.

While there is certainly still a conscious decision to be made about "going global," the reality of today's market is that the pure domestic enterprise is an endangered entity. Even a company that chooses not to go global is actually competing on a global basis, simply because competitors are sourcing from international markets, pursuing partnerships globally and thereby eliminating the now artificial insulation provided by a national border.

Go west, young executive? No longer. Go global: the globe is coming to you.

Exercises

Exercise 1 (small group activity)

Work in a small group of two or three and select a business or enterprise that is ideally suited to operate locally. Describe how you would manage that business solely within the domestic market. Ensure that the company or business remains active only within domestic borders and then identify any difficulties that you might face (e.g., finding certain types of suppliers) and argue the benefits of remaining a local company. Now, take that same enterprise and identify ways in which it could reach beyond domestic borders to the global business environment. Identify the advantages of operating across national borders and argue the benefits for acting as an international business. Then, summarize your choice, your assumptions and your conclusions for both scenarios and nominate a presenter to present your conclusions to the class.

(Estimated time 15 minutes)

Exercise 2 (class discussion)
Discuss three major forces shaping the global business environment from your and your country's perspective. Select another country at random, and consider the major trends and developments influencing its role, activities and opportunities in the global business environment. Now select a product or service and consider the issues that would impact a business transaction between these two countries.

(Estimated time 10 minutes)

Exercise 3 (small group activity)
Globalization is an encompassing term that is used to capture all of the recent ongoing trends in international business and international relations. These trends have both ardent supporters and strident detractors. Indeed, most people have seen the massive anti-globalization protests that have accompanied recent high-profile meetings of governments and ministers. Work in small groups of three or four to answer the following questions:

1. What are some of the most controversial business practices that you are aware of that have been drawing fire from activists, NGOs and other concerned citizens?

2. What issues have you heard something about but don't really understand the details of?

Work with your group to develop a list of all the controversial business practices that you know about and those that you have heard about (but don't know the details of) and then present your findings to the class. Your instructor will capture on a whiteboard or flipchart all the issues that either warrant further explanation or aren't understood. Once all of the groups have reported, your instructor will review the issues that need further discussion and those that remain unexplained. Alternatively, they can be the basis of a brief research assignment to be reported on at the beginning of the next class—instructor to decide.

(Estimated time 20 minutes)

References/Resources

Kumar, Rajesh, and Kumar Sethi, Anand. *Doing Business in India*. Palgrave MacMillan, 2005

Mallaby, Sebastian, James Wolfenson and the World Bank. *The World's Banker*. Penguin Press, 2004

ASEAN (www.aseansec.org)

Australian National University (www.ciolek.com/owtrad.html)

CARICOM (www.caricom.org)

Catholic Agency for Overseas Development (www.cafod.org.uk)

China-Africa Cooperation Forum (www.china.org.cn/English/features/China-Africa/81869.thm)

COMESA (www.comesa.int/about)

Conference Board of Canada (www.conferenceboard.ca)

Corporate Watch (www.corporatewatch.org)

Human Security Network (www.humansecuritynetwork.org)

MERCOSUR (www.mercosur.int/msweb/)

Multinational Monitor (www.multinationalmonitor.org)

NAFTA (www.nafta-sec-alena.org/DefaultSite/index.html)

National Research Council of Canada (www.nrc-cnrc.gc.ca)

New Economics Foundation (www.neweconomics.org)

Radio Frequency Identification Technology (RFID) (www.privcom.gc.ca/fs-fi/02_05_d_28_e.asp)

World Bank (www.worldbank.org)

World Trade Organization (www.wto.org)

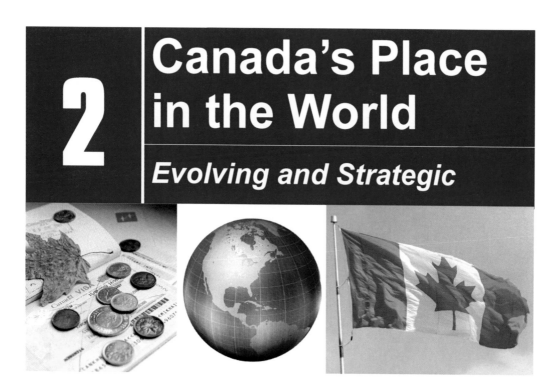

Canada's Place in the World

Evolving and Strategic

2

Chapter Objectives

- Understand and describe the relative position of Canada in the global business environment
- Recognize major elements of Canada's trade activities and objectives
- Gain insights into Canada's key characteristics, strengths and global opportunities

Overview

In an age of ever-increasing trade and travel, global security concerns and environmental problems, Canada and its citizens are advancing a wider sense of community around the world.[13]

Canadians are citizens of the world. They study, they read, they watch, they travel and they learn. They are aware of global issues, and they care. They care about wars, poverty, security, the environment and issues involving women and children. They care, but does the average Canadian ever wonder why they are in the enviable position to be able to enjoy such a high quality of life? Do they know that one in four Canadian jobs rely on international trade? Do they know that each day, we export and import several billion dollars worth of goods and services with the rest of the world? Do they realize that trade enhances our quality of life, and that of others around the world?

Canada's participation in international trade is driven by a fundamental reality: the country must look outward for prosperity, given it has an abundance of production in natural resources, manufactured goods and services, but a relatively small domestic market. This means that it is critical for Canada to continue to evolve in this new age of globalization and to think strategically about Canada's place in the world. The more Canadians understand this, the better their chances will be of continuing to enjoy one of the highest standards of living in the world.

International Trade: Its Role in Canada

A resilient trading nation

Currency fluctuations affect Canada's trade performance, especially with the growing strength of the Canadian dollar against U.S. currency—importers thrive while exporters struggle.

Canada is a trading country, and international trade is integral to its continued prosperity. Canada is the world's ninth-largest exporter and tenth-largest importer—trade is equivalent to 70 percent of GDP,[14] up from 51 percent in 1990, and exports account for 36 percent of the Canadian economy. Throughout much of the last decade, the expansion of trade has promoted employment and growth.

Externally, Canada has faced escalating global competition and a strong appreciation of the Canadian dollar. China has made major inroads in the important U.S. market while the Canadian dollar has appreciated some 38.4 percent since January 2002, when the currency dipped below U.S. 62¢, to almost U.S. 86¢ at the end of 2005. The share of exports in GDP fell to about 38 percent in 2005 from over 45 percent just five years earlier, while imports declined from 40 percent to 34 percent. The Canadian dollar appreciated against the major currencies in 2005 and, moreover, was the only G7 currency to appreciate against the resurgent U.S. dollar in that year.

An estimated one in four Canadian jobs is linked in part to exports, with Canada's total exports of goods and services representing about 38 percent of our gross domestic product.

Notwithstanding the currency appreciation and competitive challenges in the U.S. market, that country still remains Canada's principal trading partner, representing 76 percent of total exports and 65 percent of all imports in 2005 (though these figures may be overstated due to transhipments). Two-way trade in goods and services with the United States amounts to over C$2 billion on a daily basis, more than double the value registered for 1993.

---

[13] Pico, Iyer, *Canadian Geographic*, "Canada: Global Citizen," Nov.–Dec. 2004.
[14] Statistics Canada. (www.statcan.ca)

Canada's economic performance has benefited from a flexible labour market that has permitted it to reallocate productive resources in response to shifts in terms of trade and exchange-rate appreciation. On average, 250,000 new jobs are created every year, almost all of them full-time positions, and an estimated one in four jobs is linked in part to Canada's export success in global markets. While Canada's trade balance has its ups and downs, it remains nonetheless largely favourable.

Canadian exports of goods and services

Exports of goods and services were equivalent to 36 percent of Canadian gross domestic product in 2005. This was down somewhat from 2004 as a result of strong growth in the domestic economy but was sufficient to place Canada second in the G8 countries. As shown in Figure 2.1, Germany was the most trade-dependent economy in the G8, followed by Canada, Italy, France and the U.K.

Solid growth in the global economy and in Canada, robust growth in the main emerging economies of China and India and increased demand for natural resources, including energy products, all contribute to Canada's trade performance.

Table 2.1—Exports of goods and services as a proportion of GDP (2000–2005) (percentage (%) of GDP)						
	2000	2001	2002	2003	2004	2005
Canada	45.4	43.4	41.3	37.8	38.1	37.7
France	28.6	28.1	27.1	25.7	26.0	26.1
Germany	33.4	34.8	35.7	35.7	38.0	40.2
Italy	27.1	28.4	27.0	25.8	26.6	27.2
Japan	9.9	9.4	10.1	10.6	11.8	12.5
U.K.	28.0	27.4	26.2	25.5	25.2	26.1
U.S.	10.9	9.9	9.3	9.3	9.8	10.2
G7 Total	17.4	16.9	16.8	17.1	18.2	n.a.

Source: Statistics Canada (www.statcan.ca)

Despite the continued appreciation in the Canadian dollar against the U.S. dollar, exports of Canadian goods and services increased 5.2 percent to C$516.4 billion in 2005, surpassing the previous record of C$489.0 billion reached in 2000). Like exports, imports also rose, increasing 5.8 percent to C$463.1 billion. These developments resulted in the trade surplus widening to C$53.3 billion, with a goods surplus at C$66.7 billion and a service trade deficit at C$13.4 billion.

Growth of Canadian exporters

The number of exporting companies continues to grow. In 2004, Statistics Canada recorded 43,800 exporters, up 59 percent from 27,600 in 1993. The United States is the main destination for these products and services, with 70 percent exporting to the U.S.; however, there is a growing trend towards market diversification as can be seen in the chart below.

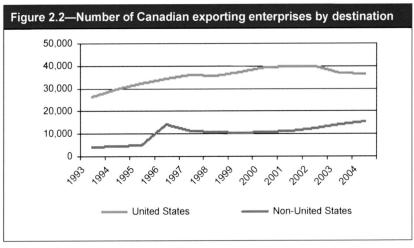

Figure 2.2—Number of Canadian exporting enterprises by destination

Source: Statistics Canada Exporter Registry (www.statcan.ca)

The largest number of exporters is in the manufacturing sector, making up 47 percent of all exporters and contributing over 66 percent of export value. The value per exporter is dominated by mining, oil and gas extraction and utilities.

Table 2.3—Canadian exporters by industry group (C$)			
Industry group	Exporter population (%)	Export value (%)	Value per exporter (millions $)
Agriculture, forestry, fishing and hunting	4.8	1.1	2.0
Mining and oil and gas extraction	1.3	5.9	38.2
Utilities	0.1	0.7	38.6
Construction	2.6	0.3	1.0
Manufacturing	47.3	66.3	11.8
Wholesale trade	22.4	11.7	4.4
Retail trade	4.6	0.4	0.7
Transportation and warehousing	3.2	4.2	11.1
Information and cultural industries	1.2	0.1	1.0
Finance and insurance	2.0	6.4	27.1
Business services	7.5	2.4	2.7
Other	2.9	0.4	1.1

Source: Statistics Canada Exporter Registry (www.statcan.ca)

Trade in goods

The goods sector is an important part of the Canadian economy—it employs approximately one in five Canadians. Of the seven major categories of goods, three have consistently posted a trade surplus since 1971. These are rooted in Canada's traditional resources: agricultural and fish products, forestry and energy products.

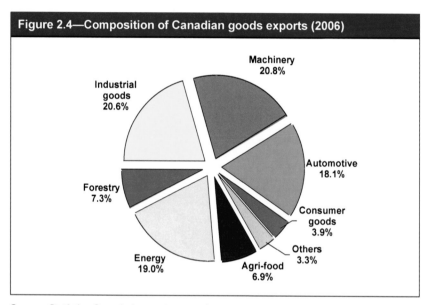

Figure 2.4—Composition of Canadian goods exports (2006)

Machinery 20.8%
Industrial goods 20.6%
Automotive 18.1%
Forestry 7.3%
Consumer goods 3.9%
Others 3.3%
Energy 19.0%
Agri-food 6.9%

Source: Statistics Canada (www.statcan.ca)

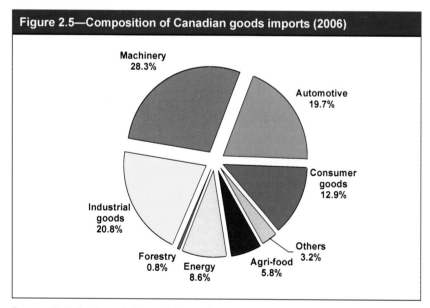

Figure 2.5—Composition of Canadian goods imports (2006)

Machinery 28.3%
Automotive 19.7%
Consumer goods 12.9%
Industrial goods 20.8%
Others 3.2%
Forestry 0.8%
Energy 8.6%
Agri-food 5.8%

Source: Statistics Canada (www.statcan.ca)

Automotive products and industrial goods and materials are also important sectors from both the import and export perspectives. Globalization is having a major impact on the Canadian economy, and increasingly, Canadian businesses need to continue to search for ways in which they can add value to their products and services.

Impact of global business on manufacturing

A majority of Canadian manufacturers now see markets outside Canada as their prime focus for sales and business development. A recent survey conducted by the Canadian Manufacturers and Exporters (CME) indicated that while 23 percent report that they are focused primarily on regional or local markets and 21 percent sell primarily across Canada, 38 percent say that they focus on the entire North American market and 18 percent report that their primary market is global.

Figure 2.6—Primary market for Canadian manufacturers

Global 18%

Local/ Regional 23%

Canada 21%

North America 38%

Source: Canadian Manufacturers and Exporters, "Manufacturing 20/20 International Business Report"

Canadian manufacturers sell into markets around the world. They also source raw materials, products, services, skills, knowledge, and technologies on a global basis. Many companies have investments and production facilities in other countries as well as in Canada, and more and more international business partnerships are being formed among manufacturers and service, sales and distribution companies to deliver high-value, competitively priced products to customers in Canada and international markets.

- Canada exported about C$400 billion worth of manufactured goods in 2003.

- Manufacturing accounts for 77 percent of Canada's merchandise exports and for 66 percent of our total exports of goods and services.

- Manufactured exports have grown by 96 percent since 1990.

Access to international markets, and particularly to markets in the United States, has provided Canadian manufacturers with the customer base they require to expand production and to specialize in higher-value goods and services.

Exports have become an increasingly important part of most manufacturers' business strategies. When the Canada-U.S. Free Trade Agreement came into

Figure 2.7—Canada's export performance in manufacturing

Source: Canadian Manufacturers and Exporters, "Manufacturing 20/20 International Business Report." (www.cme-mec.ca/mfg2020/index.asp)

effect in 1989, about 37 percent of Canada's total manufactured output was exported. Today, over 55 percent of the goods manufactured in Canada are sold outside the country. Over 50 percent of what is made in Canada is exported into or through the United States.

Manufacturing powers export growth across Canada. Ontario and Quebec are both heavily dependent on international exports of manufactured products; for example, Ontario manufacturers exported C$178 billion worth of goods to other countries in 2003, and manufactured exports from Quebec exceeded C$63 billion. In 2003 almost C$50 billion worth of goods were manufactured for international export in western Canada, while manufactured exports from Atlantic Canada totalled C$14.6 billion.

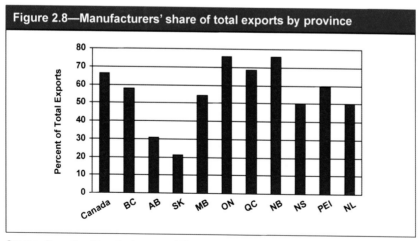

Figure 2.8—Manufacturers' share of total exports by province

Source: Canadian Manufacturers and Exporters, "Manufacturing 20/20 International Business Report." (www.cme-mec.ca/mfg2020/index.asp)

Canada and trade in services

The past decades have seen a broad structural shift towards services in the Canadian economy. Since 1961, services have increased from just over half to two-thirds of Canada's gross domestic product. The percentage of workers employed in services is also on the rise—about three Canadians in four, compared to just over half in 1961. Furthermore, services created more than 90 percent of new jobs between 1990 and 2006, and in 2006, 331,000 new jobs were created in the services sectors alone, while about 16,500 jobs were lost in the goods sector.

Services are, on balance, more knowledge-intensive than other sectors and therefore employ many more well-educated workers than other industries. For example, almost 20 percent of workers in the services sector have post-secondary education. Interestingly, some of the best-paid jobs in Canada are in the services sector—in financial, legal, advertising, computer software and engineering services.

Investment

Enhancing Canada's investment opportunities abroad is essential to Canada's ongoing international competitiveness. Foreign investment links Canadian companies, consumers and workers to the new knowledge-based global economy. It enhances Canada's competitiveness by revitalizing domestic industry and increasing the flow of goods and services between Canada and its trading partners. Foreign investment not only produces jobs, but also introduces new technology, new management techniques and new market access. Canada has a clear interest in providing stability, transparency, predictability, non-discrimination and protection for Canadian companies and individuals that invest abroad, as well as for foreign investors wishing to invest in Canada. Good investment rules make for a positive economic climate, which favours growth and jobs. Thus, Canada has consistently supported a strong, rules-based system, multilaterally, regionally and bilaterally.

The openness of the Canadian economy and the importance of international trade are reflected in the significant growth in total stocks of both inward and outward foreign direct investment (FDI) that Canada has experienced over the past 25 years.

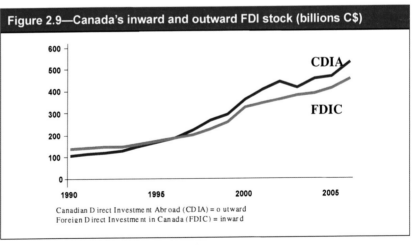

Figure 2.9—Canada's inward and outward FDI stock (billions C$)

Canadian Direct Investment Abroad (CDIA) = outward
Foreign Direct Investment in Canada (FDIC) = inward

Source: Statistics Canada (www.statcan.ca)

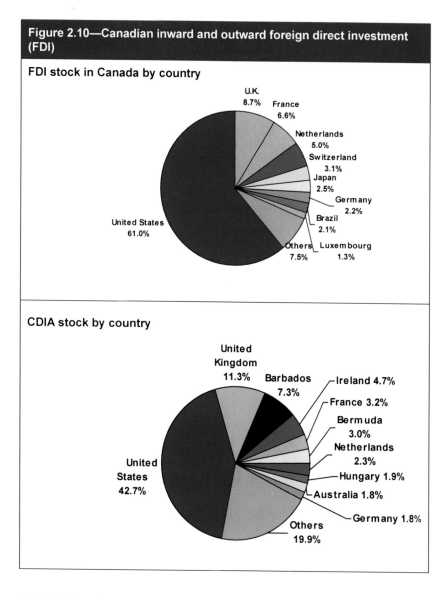

Figure 2.10—Canadian inward and outward foreign direct investment (FDI)

FDI stock in Canada by country

U.K. 8.7%
France 6.6%
Netherlands 5.0%
Switzerland 3.1%
Japan 2.5%
Germany 2.2%
Brazil 2.1%
United States 61.0%
Others 7.5%
Luxembourg 1.3%

CDIA stock by country

United Kingdom 11.3%
Barbados 7.3%
Ireland 4.7%
France 3.2%
Bermuda 3.0%
Netherlands 2.3%
Hungary 1.9%
Australia 1.8%
United States 42.7%
Germany 1.8%
Others 19.9%

Global integration

Canadian businesses will restructure their operations, production systems and supply chains to serve global customers. They will continue to move where the money is—to the rapidly expanding markets of emerging economies. Production and services will become more integrated worldwide, to take advantage of the best in terms of skills, technologies and cost structures, allowing companies to boost their profit margins while offering customers higher value at a lower price. E-business technologies will allow manufacturers to connect anywhere at any time with customers around the world. And the world of manufacturing itself will be characterized by global operations, global competition, global business networks and competing global supply chains. Canada is already on its way.

Canada's Trading Partners

Canada's economy continues to be closely linked to that of the U.S. As illustrated in the chart below, exports to the U.S. represent a significant portion of Canadian merchandise trade, although we see diversification to other markets from 2002 to 2006.

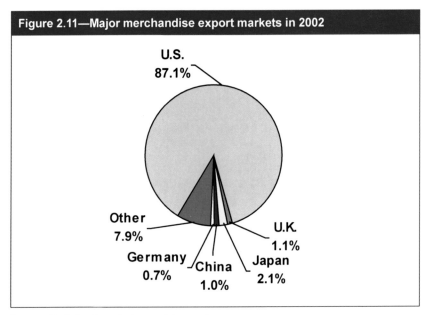

Figure 2.11—Major merchandise export markets in 2002

U.S. 87.1%

Other 7.9%

Germany 0.7%

China 1.0%

Japan 2.1%

U.K. 1.1%

Source: Statistics Canada (www.statcan.ca)

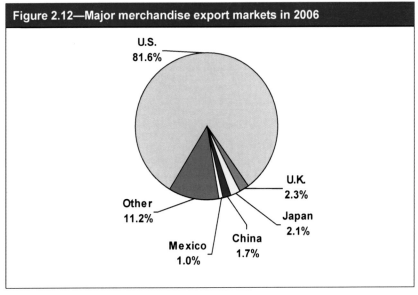

Figure 2.12—Major merchandise export markets in 2006

U.S. 81.6%

Other 11.2%

Mexico 1.0%

China 1.7%

Japan 2.1%

U.K. 2.3%

Source: Statistics Canada (www.statcan.ca)

The world's largest trading relationship: Canada–United States

The links between Canada and the United States are deep, diverse and complex. We share a long tradition of co-operation in defending our continent and fighting for freedom. We share a common language, common interests and common traditions. We share the world's largest trading relationship and a common border that stretches across 8,893 kilometres, or 5,526 miles, of land and three oceans. We share stewardship of a rich and diverse environment, including 20 percent of the world's supply of fresh water in the Great Lakes.

Canada and the United States share the largest bilateral flow of goods, services, people and capital between any two countries in the world, moving over C$2 billion worth of goods and services across the border each day. Canada and the United States are each other's largest customers and biggest suppliers. In 2005, Canada exported C$368.6 billion in goods to the United States and imported C$259.8 billion in return. That same year, services exports totalled C$35.9 billion, with corresponding imports of C$45.3 billion.

The Canadian and U.S. economies are becoming increasingly intertwined. Canada sends close to 80 percent of its exports to the United States and is the leading export market for 39 of the 50 U.S. states. The history of the close economic integration of the two countries has been punctuated by the signing of three important trade agreements—the Auto Pact signed in 1965, the Canada-U.S. Free Trade Agreement signed in 1989, and the North American Free Trade Agreement signed in 1994, which brought Mexico into the fold.

Canada's most important trade and investment partner will continue to be the United States. Close to $2 billion worth of goods and services cross the border each day.

The last two free-trade agreements were controversial in much of Canada. There was a widely held perception that the Canadian economy simply would not be able to compete against the sheer size and power of the United States, or against the lower labour and business costs in Mexico. While there certainly was a period of adjustment, it became clear that free trade was bringing major benefits to Canada. It opened new markets, and the resulting competitive pressure on Canadian entrepreneurs spurred innovation and productivity efforts that are showing a real payback today in the growth of Canadian exports.

Emerging markets

As part of its present and future strategy, Canada will need to strike the right balance in the geographic orientation of its trade and investment policy. It must continue to pursue the growth opportunities offered by the emerging markets, including Brazil, Russia, India and China (commonly referred to as the BRIC countries), among others, while fostering its core trade relationship with the United States.

For decades, many Canadians have searched for a trade alternative to the United States in the hopes of diversifying ties to the world economy and making the country less dependent on one dominant partner. The global economy is undergoing huge shifts. The large emerging BRIC markets, especially China, will drive growth and shape future investment, trade and commerce. The economic clout of western Europe and Japan will fade, weakened by aging populations, falling birth rates and structural economic problems. Canada's status is also slipping.

It follows that the BRIC emerging markets will be important for Canada's future trade growth and diversification. They are fundamentally altering the structure of the global economy, including the competitive space within North America, and Canadian firms cannot afford to ignore them. However, despite the attractive growth potential of these markets, it would be a mistake to view the BRICs primarily as an alternative to Canada's existing heavy concentration on the U.S. market. Even with the potential gains from enhanced trade with the BRICs, our trade and investment relationship with the United States will remain Canada's top international economic priority over the next two decades, simply because of the reality of North American integration. Canadian policy makers and business leaders must act accordingly.[15]

Focus on Africa

Trade agreements build a strong foundation between countries and open doors between buyers and sellers.

Canadian trade with sub-Saharan Africa has increased substantially over the years. Linkages have strengthened between Canada and Africa due to projects financed by the Canadian International Development Agency, the World Bank and the African Development Bank in areas including the provision of engineering and construction, forestry, geomantic, air, educational and other services. Investment has increased significantly. Mining is often the face of Canada in many African countries, with Canadian investors making up the largest foreign and most important non-African investors in the continent's mining sector. Much of the exploration and production technology, as well as the consulting engineering expertise that these operations employ, originates in Canada.

The Importance of Trade Agreements to Canada

History of Canadian trade agreements

In recognition of its dependence on trade, Canada has a history of pursuing international trade agreements.

- The first modern trade agreement with the United States concluded in 1935

- The first major multilateral trade agreement, the General Agreement on Tariffs and Trade (GATT), entered into force in 1948

- Eight subsequent rounds of negotiations under the GATT to further liberalize trade, including the Uruguay Round, established the World Trade Organization (WTO) in 1995

- The Canada-U.S. Free Trade Agreement (FTA) concluded in 1987

- The North American Free Trade Agreement (NAFTA) entered into effect with the United States and Mexico in 1994

- Bilateral free trade agreements were forged with Israel (1997), Chile (1997) and Costa Rica (2002)

---

[15] Adapted from Conference Board of Canada's "Performance and Potential 2005–2006."

Table 2.13—Canada's trade agreements	
Current free trade agreements	**At negotiation or exploratory stage**
Canada currently has free trade agreements in place with the following partners: • Chile • Costa Rica • Israel • United States • United States and Mexico (NAFTA)	Canada is negotiating or exploring free trade with the following partners: • The Americas (FTAA) • Central America Four • European Free Trade Association (EFTA) • Republic of Korea • Singapore • Andean Community Countries • CARICOM • Dominican Republic • Regional and bilateral agreements

Note: Although not at the agreement stage, there are also initiatives underway with the EU and Japan.

Benefits of trade agreements

Canada participates in these agreements and ongoing negotiations for a simple reason: it is in the Canadian interest to do so. The benefits include a clear and stable framework to conduct business, secure access to markets for Canadian exporters, protection for Canadian investors abroad, access to greater choices and better prices for Canadian consumers and increased productivity and efficiency for the Canadian economy. This all contributes to a higher standard of living for Canadians as well as Canada's trade and investment partners.

There is ample evidence of this. For example, since the GATT came into effect in 1948, global trade has increased more than a hundredfold. For Canada, total two-way trade in goods and services reached more than C$929 billion in 2004— that equals C$2.5 billion every day. From 1993 to 2004, merchandise trade with the U.S. and Mexico more than doubled to reach an annual level of over C$573 billion. Total foreign direct investment in Canada rose to nearly C$368 billion in 2004, surpassed by Canadian direct investment abroad of C$438 billion.

While obtaining these very substantial benefits, Canada has not given up any core values or policies. Canada retains the right to regulate in the public interest, which includes areas such as public health and safety, education, social services and the environment. Canada will also safeguard the right of all countries to promote and preserve their cultural diversity.

Of course, there continue to be protectionist pressures around the world and Canada is sometimes affected by actions against its exports. Canada's trade agreements cannot always prevent such actions, but they do provide binding dispute-settlement procedures to help defend the country's interests. This is particularly important for countries that might otherwise not have the political clout to challenge unfair trade measures.

The vast majority of Canadian exporters are small- and medium-sized enterprises. Trade gives these Canadian businesses access to larger markets for their products and services and more varied sources for cost-effective inputs, technology and investment. This, in turn, delivers increased efficiency, productivity and competitiveness, all of which translate into jobs and higher incomes for Canadian citizens.

Multilateral agreements: from GATT to WTO's Doha Round

The initial focus of Canadian trade agreements, particularly with the GATT, was on removing barriers to trade in goods, such as tariffs and quantitative import restrictions. In more recent years, the focus, at both the multilateral and bilateral levels, has shifted towards trade liberalization and the establishment of a rules-based system for services, intellectual property, investment and non-tariff barriers.

Canada is one of the original 23 founding members of the Uruguay Round of the General Agreement on Tariffs and Trade (GATT), which eventually led to the creation of the WTO.

Work to expand the benefits of the international trading system continues on a number of fronts. In November 2001, a new round of multilateral trade negotiations was launched at the Fourth World Trade Organization (WTO) Ministerial Conference in Doha, Qatar. Ministers agreed to continue negotiations on trade in agriculture and services; to begin negotiations to further liberalize trade in non-agricultural goods; to strengthen rules on subsidies, trade remedies and dispute settlement; and to negotiate on certain aspects of trade, the environment and intellectual property rights.

The Doha Development Agenda (DDA) holds the promise of benefits for all countries, developed and developing. Canada believes that active participation in the multilateral negotiations is essential, given that an ambitious and broad-ranging outcome to these negotiations could significantly reduce poverty, enhance security and improve the quality of life for people around the world. The negotiators of the Doha Development Agenda continue to struggle in their attempts to bring this to a close. For ongoing updates on the current WTO negotiations, go to www.wto.org.

Regional and bilateral trade initiatives

As a trade-oriented and globally integrated economy, Canada benefits from a healthy, open, transparent and rules-based international trading system. While Canada maintains its focus on the WTO, it also recognizes the importance of bilateral and regional trade initiatives in further liberalizing trade in goods and services. Bilateral and regional initiatives can complement and reinforce multilateral liberalization by generating political momentum, developing and refining elements of the trade regime and preparing domestic industries for the further multilateral opening of markets. Bilateral and regional initiatives can also serve as capacity-building tools for developing countries.

Canada's multilateral and bilateral initiatives are designed to be mutually supportive. Rather than detract from multilateral efforts, bilateral agreements allow us to explore new commitments and disciplines in areas such as investment, services and trade facilitation, making them broader than existing multilateral rules. In this sense, Canada believes that regional and bilateral agreements can help place new issues on the global agenda and provide innovative solutions to the challenges posed by trade integration.

Regional and bilateral free-trade agreements (FTAs) also serve to secure markets for Canadian businesses and to provide them with access to lower-cost goods and services. Furthermore, FTAs can help strengthen markets by creating opportunities for increased specialization and productivity and providing competitive stimulus. Closer economic relations, as well as the closer governmental relations forged by the negotiating process, also contribute to progress on the broader social, political and environmental fronts.

North American Free Trade Agreement (NAFTA)

In January 1994, Canada, the United States and Mexico launched the North American Free Trade Agreement (NAFTA) and formed the world's largest free trade area. The agreement has brought economic growth and rising standards of living for people in all three countries. In addition, NAFTA has established a strong foundation for future growth and has set a valuable example of the benefits of trade liberalization.

Well into the second decade since the North American Free Trade Agreement (NAFTA) came into effect, it is clear that the agreement has contributed to making the conduct of business in North America more predictable and transparent, thus significantly increasing the trade and investment flows between the three countries. Canada's annual merchandise trade with its NAFTA partners has nearly doubled since 1994, reaching C$598.9 billion in 2005. Canadian merchandise exports to the United States grew at a compounded annual rate of 8.2 percent between 1990 and 2005, and Mexico is now Canada's fifth-largest export destination and ranks fourth as a source of imports worldwide. Under NAFTA, Canada's trade in services with the U.S. and Mexico has also increased (from C$46.4 billion in 1994 to C$82.7 billion in 2004), and there has also been a positive impact on investment. The stock of foreign direct investment in Canada reached C$415.6 billion in 2005, of which more than 64 percent came from our NAFTA partners.

Maximizing the free flow of goods, services and capital with the United States is a key priority for Canada. Areas of ongoing interest in the Canada-U.S. relationship include streamlining border-control measures and enhancing regulatory collaboration.

Free Trade Agreement of the Americas

The FTAA is a collaboration among 34 democratic governments in the Americas, including Canada, to ensure prosperity, democracy and free markets for goods and services by 2005. The Free Trade Area of the Americas (FTAA) process has been suspended since 2004. At the 2005 Summit of the Americas in Argentina, Canada, along with the majority of FTAA participants, supported the resumption of formal negotiations.

Mercosur

Canada and Mercosur (Argentina, Brazil, Paraguay and Uruguay) continue to further enhance their trade and investment ties by exploring which policy tools and instruments are best suited to promoting this objective. Bilateral trade

The Canada–United States Softwood Lumber Agreement, a mutually agreed resolution of the softwood lumber dispute, took effect on October 12, 2006. As part of this seven- to nine-year agreement, the United States revoked all anti-dumping and countervailing duty orders against Canadian softwood lumber exports and refunded over 80 percent of the duty deposits collected since 2002.

between Canada and the Mercosur bloc totalled C$5.6 billion in 2006 with Canada exporting C$1.6 billion and importing C$4 billion.

Association of Southeast Asian Nations (ASEAN)
As a group, the ASEAN member countries (Brunei, Darussalam, Burma, Cambodia, Indonesia, Laos, Malaysia, the Philippines, Singapore, Thailand and Vietnam) represent a major trade and investment partner for Canada—in 2006, two-way trade totalled over C$12 billion. The year 2007 marked the 30th anniversary of Canada-ASEAN relations, and Canada continues to undertake initiatives to engage with AEAN countries, particularly as these countries play an important role in global value chains.

Bilateral trade initiatives
Canada-European Union Trade and Investment Enhancement Agreement (TIEA)
Negotiations between Canada and the European Union (EU) were launched on May 17, 2005. The Trade and Investment Enhancement Agreement (TIEA) seeks to address "new generation," non-tariff trade issues, such as investment, trade facilitation, regulatory cooperation and services, as well as government procurement and intellectual property. Canada and the EU expected that the TIEA, once completed, would complement improved market access achieved via the WTO negotiations. In May 2006, Canada and the EU agreed to pause the TIEA negotiations until the results of the WTO Doha Round talks are known. Despite the pause in the TIEA negotiations, Canada and the EU continue to discuss regulatory co-operation.

Canada-Japan Economic Framework
In November 2005, Canada and Japan agreed to a flexible and innovative economic framework. The framework addresses new and emerging economic challenges and opportunities and promotes economic co-operation through policy- and business-development initiatives. It is structured to focus on forward-looking, strategic priority areas of co-operation. Since its creation, discussions under the Economic Framework have resulted in a co-operation agreement on anti-competitive activities, a co-operation arrangement on enhanced customs, a memorandum of understanding on bilateral investment-promotion co-operation, an agreement on social security and an informal framework document on food-safety co-operation. The framework also launched a joint study on the benefits and costs of further promotion and liberalization of trade and investment.

Canada-Chile Free Trade Agreement (CCFTA)
This agreement was signed in 1997, and bilateral trade was virtually tariff-free as of January 1, 2003. The agreement undergoes regular review, and new chapters are added, for example, the chapter on government procurement, which requires each country to treat each other's suppliers in the same manner as their domestic suppliers.

Canada-Israel Free Trade Agreement (CIFTA)
This agreement came into force January 1, 1997, eliminating tariffs on almost all industrial products manufactured in Canada and Israel. In November 2003, the CIFTA was expanded to provide preferences to a wide range of agricultural and agri-food products that Canada exports to Israel. Of note is Canada's elimination of tariffs on various products including fresh-cut roses, various vegetables and

juices. Israel largely eliminated tariffs on various Canadian exports, including animals for breeding, various vegetables, grains and oilseeds. The CIFTA contains disciplines on government procurement but does not cover cross-border trade in services or investment.

Canada-Costa Rica Free Trade Agreement (CCRFTA)
This agreement was signed in 2002. The CCRFTA offers a market-access package that provides comprehensive tariff reductions on both industrial and agricultural goods. Canada will eliminate all tariffs on imports from Costa Rica by January 2011, except for beef and certain supply-managed dairy and poultry tariff lines, which are not subject to tariff reduction commitments under the agreement. Canada has implemented five stages of tariff reductions pursuant to the agreement since the CCRFTA came into effect. The agreement does not contain disciplines on services, investment or government procurement.

EFTA States—Iceland, Norway, Switzerland and Liechtenstein
On June 7, 2007, Canada and the EFTA countries announced the conclusion of free trade agreement negotiations. As Canada's first trans-Atlantic free trade agreement, it will provide a strategic platform for expanding commercial ties with these countries in particular and the European Union in general. It will offer advantages in key European markets ahead of competitors, such as the United States, and will put Canada on an equal footing with other competitors, such as Mexico, Chile, Korea and the European Union, which already have FTAs with EFTA.

Canada and Singapore
Negotiations towards a free trade agreement were launched in October 2001. To date, there have been six rounds of negotiations, the last of which was in October 2003. In November 2006, Canada and Singapore agreed to resume negotiations with a view to concluding by early 2007. Canada is seeking a comprehensive agreement that covers a wide range of topics including trade in goods, cross-border trade-in services, temporary entry, financial services, investment, government procurement, dispute settlement and competition policy.

Central America Four (CA4)
Canada launched FTA negotiations with the Central America Four (CA4) countries of El Salvador, Guatemala, Honduras and Nicaragua in 2001. The negotiations are well advanced. Canada and the CA4 countries continue to explore ways to overcome the remaining obstacles with a view to concluding an agreement in the near future. Canada remains committed to concluding a comprehensive agreement covering market access for goods, services, investment and more.

Canada and the Republic of Korea
Negotiations towards a free trade agreement are currently in progress. The negotiations, which were launched in July 2005, include tariff elimination, trade facilitation, non-tariff measures, cross-border trade-in services, temporary entry, investment, competition policy, government procurement and intellectual property rights. An eighth round of negotiations was held in Seoul in November 2006, with a ninth round scheduled for early 2007 in Canada.

Andean community, Dominican Republic, Caribbean community and Caricom
Canada supports the goal of free trade with the countries of the Andean

community, the Dominican Republic, the Caribbean community and Common Market (Caricom). Exploratory discussions towards potential free trade agreements have been productive, and Canada hopes to be in a position to launch formal negotiations in the near future.

Initiatives to promote efficient borders
The Government of Canada has also launched initiatives with the following partners:

Canada-United States Smart Border Declaration
The catastrophic events of September 2001 have had a profound impact not only on the lives of those directly affected by the terrorist attacks, but also in an unprecedented tightening up of all entry points to the U.S. To protect two-way trade of close to C$2 billion a day, Canada and the United States signed the Smart Border Declaration. The declaration provided an effective framework for addressing border issues and was supported by a 32-point action plan that has been the mechanism for progress on cross-border transportation initiatives.

Since the signing of the declaration, the Canadian government has announced more than C$1.3 billion in border infrastructure improvements in co-operation with provinces and other partners. The improvements have been funded through the Border Infrastructure Fund (BIF) and the border component of the Strategic Highway Infrastructure Program (SHIP). These projects address border congestion and facilitate cross-border trader flows by providing additional infrastructure capacity and dedicated lanes to support enhanced low-risk traveller facilitation programs, such as Free and Secure Trade (FAST).

Security and Prosperity Partnership
In a March 2005 joint statement, the leaders of Canada, the United States and Mexico unveiled a new Security and Prosperity Partnership for North America (SPP) that speaks of increasing continental integration and the need to work trilaterally to make our societies more secure and our economies more resilient. Border initiatives figure prominently on the SPP agenda. The Government of Canada recognizes that infrastructure investments are crucial to maintaining Canada's economic competitiveness, productivity and quality of life.

Canada in other multilateral forums
Asia-Pacific Economic Cooperation (APEC)
Since Canada's last trade policy review, it has used its participation in APEC to advance key Canadian trade policy interests, including support for the WTO Doha Development Agenda; to support its regional trade and investment promotion and policy objectives; and to make the Asia-Pacific region more accessible to Canadian businesses, including women-owned enterprises. These goals are addressed through APEC's work on trade facilitation, transparency and anti-corruption, and intellectual property rights.

Organisation for Economic Co-operation and Development (OECD)
Canada has worked to ensure effective OECD support for the Doha Development Agenda. In many important ways, the OECD trade-policy work program parallels the efforts of the DDA.

The promotion of trade liberalization has been central to the OECD mandate. Canada participates in the Trade Committee (TC) and Working Party on Trade, whose focus is on interdisciplinary consideration of trade issues. It provides a unique forum in which to set out the analytical basis required to understand the issues, and it complements the work of the WTO, promoting the multilateral trading system. The government continues to support the work of the OECD in examining the benefits and challenges of trade and investment liberalization in a globalizing world.

In support of developing countries
The needs of developing countries deserve special mention, as advancing the cause of development through WTO negotiations is a key objective of the Doha Development Round and, more generally, of the WTO. To that end, the Government of Canada is actively seeking to address some of the administrative, commercial and economic challenges that many developing countries face in implementing trade agreements. It is also seeking to address developing countries' concerns about taking on new commitments.

Trade-related technical assistance and capacity building (TRTA/CB)
An integral part of Canada's approach to trade and development is the delivery of co-ordinated, needs-based and trade-related technical assistance and capacity-building (TRTA/CB) programs. Specifically, such assistance aims to help developing countries negotiate effectively, to mainstream trade into plans for national development and to build both institutional and supply-side capacity to take advantage of emerging trade opportunities that will achieve poverty reduction.

Least developed countries (LDCs): accessions
The Doha Ministerial Declaration also reflected a commitment to work to facilitate and accelerate negotiations with acceding LDCs. Recognizing that WTO accession will help least developed countries in their development and transition efforts, Canada is active in the negotiations of all applicants. Canada's approach to least developed countries has been to reduce requests to a minimum and show considerable flexibility on, for example, the number of tariff lines, request rates and transition periods. Canada was also very active in the WTO Sub-committee on Least-Developed Countries in promoting an agreement to facilitate least developed countries' accession to the WTO.

LDC Market Access Initiative
Since January 1, 2003, Canada has provided duty-free and quota-free access to all imports (excluding the over-quota tariffs on dairy, poultry and egg products) from 49 LDCs, 34 of which are in Africa. In 2004, Canada renewed its LCDT program for a ten-year period. The current scheme covers approximately 99 percent of tariff lines. Canada's initiative is among the most far-reaching in the world in terms of eligible countries, product coverage, rules of origin and overall ease of administration. As well, it encourages trade between these countries (South-South trade) in the inputs used to make these products. As a result of this initiative, Canadian imports of apparel from LDCs have increased significantly, and since 2003, merchandise imports into Canada from LDCs have more than tripled, from C$632 million in 2002 to C$1.9 billion in 2005.

Aid for Trade
In Hong Kong, ministers directed the creation of an Aid for Trade (AfT) Task Force to provide recommendations on how AfT might contribute most effectively to the development dimension of the Doha Development Round. Canada was

a member of this task force and supported the recommendations, which aim to help developing countries, especially LDCs, build the supply-side capacity and trade-related infrastructure they need to assist them in implementing and benefiting from WTO Agreements and to expand their trade more broadly. Canada's view is that in order to reach these goals, AfT should strictly adhere to the principles of aid effectiveness.

Canada believes that AfT is important in its own right and that it should and must move forward, despite the current challenges that are being faced more broadly in this round. Canada has been, and will continue to be, actively engaged in advancing the AfT agenda set forth in the Hong Kong Ministerial Declaration.

Official development assistance (ODA)

In 2002, Canada committed to increasing official development assistance funding by 8 percent per year, with the aim of doubling ODA volumes by the end of the decade and raising ODA as a percentage of gross national income to roughly 0.35 percent. In this regard, Africa would be a major recipient of government programming, but Canada will also continue to apply these resources to address important needs elsewhere—be they in the Caribbean, Latin America or Asia.

Complementing efforts to liberalize trade with developing countries, Canada has been increasing its aid effectiveness and opening markets to stakeholders in developing countries through aid untying and increased flexibility in procurement. While the aid-untying ratio to all developing countries was 32 percent in 2001, it reached 59 percent in 2005. In September 2005, the Government of Canada announced it was changing its food aid policy, so that up to 50 percent of Canada's food aid could be purchased in developing countries. This shift in policy will mean that Canada will buy more food from farmers in developing countries, supporting local agricultural sectors and making the delivery of food more efficient.

The Supporting Environment for Trade

Many departments of the federal government and of provincial or territorial governments manage programs that encourage international business expansion. Federal departments and agencies work together and co-operate with provinces and territories to provide business intelligence and international market-access information and advice to Canadian businesses. Training programs focused on trade practices and the rules that govern international business activities assist in providing services to new and smaller exporters with a view to enhancing their capacity and preparedness in international market development.

The Government of Canada manages approximately 140 trade offices in Canadian embassies and consulates around the world. A principal responsibility of trade staff is familiarity with the regulations, policy issues and barriers that Canadian businesses may face in exporting goods and services or making a direct investment in a foreign market. Trade offices provide a direct point of contact for Canadian firms in foreign markets, teach companies how to build partnerships in an international environment and help resolve trade-policy issues that negatively impact commercial relationships.

This international business-development network is a main source of information for Canadian trade-policy initiatives, together with domestic consultations.

The agencies within Canada are well placed to inform domestic enterprises of their rights under international-trade and investment-protection rules. They also identify aspects of business policy that limit the expansion possibilities of Canadian firms, while offering the government practical advice on handling problems and assessing priorities. The international network examines how other governments implement the disciplines that they have accepted and advises the Government of Canada on new issues.

The following are some of the main government organizations supporting trade in Canada. They can all be accessed via ExportSource—Canada's most comprehensive source of information and practical tools for new or existing exporters. (www.exportsource.ca)

Foreign Affairs and International Trade Canada

This organization helps Canadian companies expand and succeed internationally by promoting Canada as a dynamic place in which to invest and do business and by negotiating and administering trade agreements. (www.international.gc.ca)

Trade Commissioner Service

Their website offers

- hundreds of reports on foreign markets organized by industry sector;

- help from officers located in 12 cities across the country to find new markets abroad and implement business strategy; and

- help from officers located in more than 140 cities worldwide to assess export potential, identify key foreign contacts and obtain relevant advice and intelligence. Six core services are available. (www.infoexport.gc.ca)

Export Development Canada (EDC)

EDC (Canada's official export credit agency) provides innovative financing, insurance and bonding solutions to Canadian companies that export goods and services or invest in other countries. EDC operates in 200 markets worldwide, including 130 emerging markets. It also helps Canadian enterprises—mainly small- and medium-sized ones—manage risk and capitalize on trade opportunities around the globe. (www.edc.ca)

Industry Canada

The department's mission is to foster a growing competitive, knowledge-based Canadian economy. The department works with Canadians throughout the economy and in all parts of the country to improve conditions for investment and Canada's innovation performance, to increase Canada's share of global trade and to build a fair, efficient and competitive marketplace. Program areas include developing industry and technology capability, fostering scientific research, setting telecommunications policy, promoting investment and trade, promoting tourism and small business development and setting rules and services that support the effective operation of the marketplace.

Trade Data Online provides the ability to generate customized reports on Canadian and U.S. trade in goods with over 200 countries. (www.strategis. gc.ca)

Statistics Canada

Statistics Canada publishes data and analysis in the form of survey results, research reports, technical papers, periodical magazines, census products and research compendia. Online publications date from 1996 to the present, and historical material can be located using the library catalogue. (www.statcan.ca)

Figure 2.14—Canada's place in the world checklist

- Become familiar with the economic importance of trade to Canada.

- Keep a list of quick facts and figures on Canada's trade performance—one never knows when they might become useful.

- Study trade statistics between Canada and the organization's target markets.

- Review and understand trade agreements that are relevant to the markets under consideration.

- Keep abreast of developments relating to border access.

- Determine what role the organization might plan in the support of trade in developing countries.

Chapter Summary

Increased exposure to international competition has energized Canada's economy, spurred innovation, attracted foreign investment and created jobs for Canadians. Canada's current and future prosperity depends on its ability to continue to develop an international framework that provides access to growing world markets and keeps pace with changes in technology, business practices, social systems and public interests.

Canadian businesses need to take advantage of this opportunity to better understand Canada's place in the world and to explore ways in which they too can become important contributors and participants in the future global business environment.

Exercises

Exercise 1 (class discussion)

Foreign Affairs and International Trade maintains a staff of trade commissioners at "posts" (i.e., embassies, consulates, high commissions, etc.) around the world. The trade commissioners assess export potential for companies, identify key foreign contacts and obtain relevant advice and intelligence, but they are often swamped with requests for assistance from exporters (because their services are free). As trade commissioners, they are also posted to a new country every few years and the selection of postings available often depends on their past performance (i.e., how successful they have been at helping companies). As a result, trade commissioners are often more eager to help companies that are well positioned to act when they contact the embassy looking for help.

While trade commissioners will ultimately help all companies, getting a trade commissioner to go the extra mile for your firm often depends on whether or not he/she believes that you are prepared, capable and serious. In an instructor-led discussion, use inputs from the class to develop a list of qualifying criteria that you think would demonstrate to a trade commissioner that your company is well positioned to act and very worthy of assistance. Once the list of criteria has been developed, discuss how this information could be conveyed to the trade commissioner effectively.

(Estimated time 15 minutes)

Exercise 2 (research assignment)

Your organization is planning to expand throughout the Americas. Review this chapter to identify the key trade agreements that might be relevant. Then go online and research some of the anticipated benefits to be yielded from those trade agreements. Finally, select one trade agreement and do some additional research to find out whether or not there are any activists or detractors raising concerns about that particular trade agreement. What are the controversial issues? Who potentially benefits and who/what is potentially harmed? How might these issues impact your decisions as a Canadian business seeking to operate in that region? Summarize your findings on a single page as follows:

- Relevant trade agreements

- Summary of the benefits to be yielded from each agreement

- Main controversies associated with selected trade agreement

- Potential impact of most controversial issues on Canadian businesses

(Estimated time 30–45 minutes)

Exercise 3 (research activity)

You are currently preparing to travel to another country to explore the potential for exports for your firm. Select one country and then spend 20 minutes online familiarizing yourself with the ExportSource website (www.exportsource.ca). What are some of the key sources of information accessible from that site that might be useful for pre-trip planning?

(Estimated time 20 minutes)

References/Resources

Canada's State of Trade—Update 2007 (www.international.gc.ca/eet)

Canadian Manufacturers and Exporters (www.cme-mec.ca)

Conference Board of Canada (www.conferenceboard.ca)

ExportSource website (www.exportsource.ca)

Foreign Affairs and International Trade Canada (www.international.gc.ca)

Free Trade Agreements of the Americas (FTAA) (www.ftaa.gc.ca)

NAFTA—Text of the Agreement (www.international.gc.ca/nafta-alena/agree-en.asp)

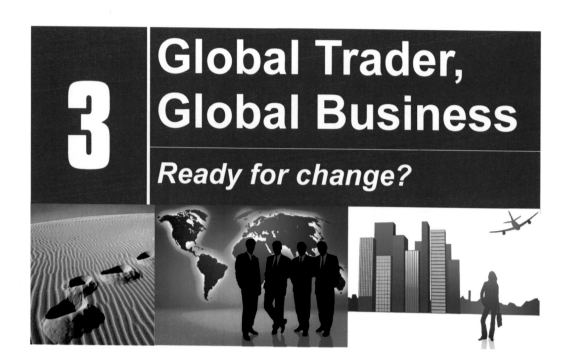

3 Global Trader, Global Business
Ready for change?

Chapter Objectives

- Understand the key factors impacting the enterprise in today's global marketplace
- Identify key strategies and characteristics that ensure the competitiveness of an organization and the global trade professional
- Perform a brief analysis of an organization's readiness to participate in global markets

Overview

The word "globalization" is over-used in the media, is often amorphously defined, is regularly abused by both sides of political and social commentary and is typically dismissed as yet another cliché of modern times. This can happen when words become so absorbed into the global lexicon and so much a part of daily routine that they come to be taken for granted. This is exactly the case with the concept of globalization. In the business context, the necessity of looking beyond the domestic market is now completely absorbed in the pursuit of sustainable competitiveness.

For the company, the concept of "going global" must be considered on a lateral plane along with other business strategies, rather than being conceived as some vague progression that occurs once the domestic market has been exhausted. If a company's domestic market has become exhausted, it is very likely due to either the presence of foreign competitors or the importation of more competitive products or services.

It is clear from the previous chapters that the global business environment has radically changed in recent years and continues to evolve with increasing speed. Engaging in business and growing profits requires business people and organizations to consistently define themselves as global traders in a "globalized" world.

The Business: Vision, Innovation and Commitment

The level of attention that global business now receives, due to an increasing number of viable markets and enhanced access to those markets, presents unprecedented levels of opportunity along with many new challenges to doing business. A reason that companies often try but fail in global markets is a lack of awareness of what makes a successful global trader and global organization. Entrepreneurship is a very important quality for navigating the complexities of global business and will be discussed later in this chapter.

However, entrepreneurs can make the mistake of placing too much importance in their own passion and strength of conviction and not enough importance on self-examination and strategic preparation. Taking a "leap-before-you-look" approach to pursuing foreign opportunities is likely to be costly and has a high potential for failure.

Whether the CEO of a medium-sized firm, a small-business owner or a lone consultant, a business person should be aware of some of the strengths of today's successful global companies as well as the weaknesses that most new traders must overcome.

Many companies succeed in the current global marketplace by concentrating on niche positioning and innovation. These companies also realize that success and profits in global trade are directly tied to the amount of energy, commitment, planning and follow-up they put into it.

Focusing on niche value

Today's higher concentration of global competition has made refining the value proposition and focusing on developing niche markets an attractive and often necessary strategy. Until recently, a niche approach was viewed as the domain of small companies competing with larger firms, but now companies of all sizes are developing products and services for increasingly segmented global markets.

One of the drivers of this trend is the complete penetration of the Internet and e-commerce into the global business environment. The Internet is the ultimate niche marketplace. The level of choice, combined with the ever-increasing demand for end-user customization, means that successful online companies are usually those that define their value with an intensely refined focus. This trend is mirrored in the offline global marketplace, where heightened competition has required many companies to reposition their product or service, or their market strategy and market orientation.

Niche marketers specialize in products and services that, at the time, might not appeal to other companies because of non-existent or limited demand. Once recognized, the niche can be developed "under the radar" of potential competition until enough demand for the product or service has been created to attract their attention. By that time, niche strategists may well have protected their position with patents, brand loyalty or a reputation for excellence.

The original market entry of Google Inc. is a popular example of using a niche focus to capture a global audience. The renowned Internet search engine company, officially launched in 1999, when it was barely more than a home-based business, concentrated on providing a single service—a search tool for locating relevant web-based content with superior quality and accuracy of results. At the same time, other more established Internet companies, such as Yahoo!, were attempting to add value to their search functions by providing news services and other types of content. By 2002, while Google's competitors continued to dilute their original strategy, Google had managed to gain enough market share through user loyalty that their website became and continues to be the world's most-used search engine.

Innovate, innovate, innovate!

Companies that innovate can create their own demand by generating new products and processes. But an inventive product or service, even if it finds success in the domestic market, will not necessarily translate into success in foreign markets. Global business leaders are turning their focus towards innovation in the organization itself. For many companies, innovation in the corporate approach may simply mean a commitment to proper awareness of and preparation for the differences between conducting domestic business and doing business globally.

Innovation is a process through which economic or social value is extracted from knowledge—through the creation, diffusion and transformation of ideas—to produce new or significantly improved products, services or processes.
Source: Conference Board of Canada

Table 3.1—Survey of innovation as a global success factor

Technology executives in some regions and industries are more bullish on innovation than their counterparts elsewhere. In North America, 87 percent of Chief Information Officers (CIOs) and Chief Technical Officers (CTOs) see it as a significant driver of profitability. A smaller proportion of Asian (77 percent) and European (74 percent) executives see a strong link between innovation and profits, perhaps because technological innovation tends to reduce the labour content of work, and labour regulations are tighter in western Europe and Japan. There is less pressure in the rest of Asia to optimize labour, since it is relatively cheap in that region.

Fifty-three percent of CIOs and CTOs—compared with 45 percent of business executives—cite the ability to innovate as the most important capability for growth.

It is interesting that 33 percent of technology executives see improving their companies' current products as the key driver of growth—a significantly higher proportion than the 19 percent who favour developing new products.

Source: As reported by CNET News, based on data contained in the 2005 McKinsey Global Survey of Business Executives

Commitment to sustainability

"So it is said that if you know your enemies and know yourself, you will win a hundred times in a hundred battles. If you only know yourself, but not your opponent, you win one and lose the next. If you do not know yourself or your enemy, you will always lose."
Source: Sun Tzu's The Art of War, Chapter 3

The quality of leadership and a flexible attitude towards change are inherent aspects of innovators. For a number of decades now, Sun Tzu's The Art of War has been required reading for corporate executives the world over, particularly in the context of global business competitiveness. The application of the strategies of war has inspired many business managers on how to approach "the enemy." However, global managers have since begun to take a more innovative view of what it means to be competitive. Valuing collaboration, awareness, accountability and understanding of the marketplace, partners and customers are key elements in how competitiveness is defined in an environment that is more connected and interdependent than ever.

Consequently, in addition to vision and innovation, a commitment to sustainability is seen as a vitally important management commitment in any business. Corporate sustainability borrows elements from four well-established concepts: sustainable development, corporate social responsibility, stakeholder theory and corporate accountability theory (see Figure 3.2).

In other words, companies that are going global recognize the necessity of balancing the need for economic growth with environmental protection and social equity (i.e., sustainable development). They also acknowledge that ethical managers should consider the needs of society, not just the interests of the shareholders or themselves (i.e., corporate social responsibility). Finally, firms recognize that there are many groups and individuals who can affect or who are affected by the achieving of the organization's objectives (i.e., stakeholder theory)[16] and that the firm has both a legal and an ethical responsibility to provide an account for the actions of the firm (i.e., corporate accountability).

---

[16] See R. Edward Freeman, Strategic Management A Stakeholder Approach, Pitman Books, Boston. Mass., 1984.

While this commitment to sustainability may appear too far-reaching in principle, it is the very soundest foundation for business, in that it is a commitment that will help firms avoid short-sighted business decisions that can be catastrophic to the firm in the long run.

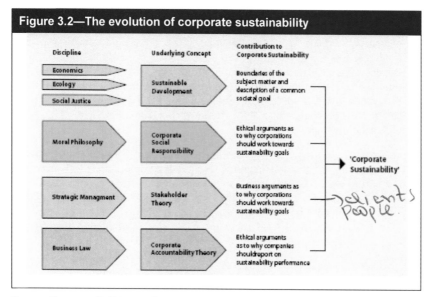

Figure 3.2—The evolution of corporate sustainability

Source: Freeman, R. Edward. *Strategic Management: A Stakeholder Approach,* Pitman Books, Boston, Mass., 1984

Navigating the Pitfalls

When companies or individuals that are new to trade seek to be global players, the biggest challenges they face usually are

- insufficient financing;

- lack of knowledge;

- lack of competent individuals; and

- insufficient planning.

Small companies critically need funds for start-up, growth and survival in downturns. Global business adds to this need, as the costs of developing export markets are high. Foreign-market research yields valuable results, but it can be expensive—visiting foreign markets entails travel and accommodation expenses. Maintaining a sales presence adds to the costs, and market adaptation (of products or promotional materials, for example) also needs to be considered.

The cost of capital may also be a challenge. In Japan, companies sometimes pay only a fraction of one percent for their capital; in comparison, interest rates for certain kinds of venture capital can reach 20 percent or higher in Canada. Many small companies find that financial services are geared to larger firms, and under-capitalization and a lack of financial guidance work against many small businesses. Skilled global traders face these challenges as well but may perhaps be more aware of what it takes to overcome the problems of financing international transactions.

Successful conduct of global trade requires certain skills. For a small firm, going global usually means adding international responsibilities to the existing domestic responsibilities of a particular executive—often the CEO or the marketing manager, but these executives may not already possess the required skills to handle these extra responsibilities. Furthermore, a small company may have trouble finding staff with the basic skills for international trade activities. Moving from the domestic market to global markets, even if the necessary skills are in place, usually contributes to another danger for smaller companies: costly failure due to lack of planning.

Companies new to the global marketplace must recognize that international business, marketing and financial planning are essential in pursuing foreign market opportunities. Supported by critical analysis of the company and of the opportunities, these plans provide direction, establish the means of implementation, delineate responsibilities and resource requirements and lay the groundwork for future corrective action. In short, plans provide a strategic direction that can constantly be revisited, revised and used to measure performance.

Other common pitfalls to avoid are:

- **Over-extension:** Attempting to enter too many diverse markets at the same time can be a drain on company resources. Patience is key! Following leads too quickly prevents proper formation of a market strategy.

- **If it works at home, it will work anywhere:** Sales and marketing efforts need to be tailored for the target market. Cultural differences must be observed in all market preparation processes—from businesses communications to product modification. Pricing, shipping, payment terms and packaging are also aspects of the export process that are likely to require alteration.

- **Assuming business will be done in English:** Familiarity with the language of the target market is critical. It can be considered the height of arrogance to expect buyers to learn the language of the seller.

Table 3.3—Potential reasons for failure in the target market
• Misunderstanding the target market and committing errors in pricing
• Advertising and distribution that lose potential customers
• Failing to plan
• Starting without enough money to maintain operations until sales start to be made
• Mismanaging the finances of the business, leaving it low on cash and high on inventory or capital equipment

Table 3.3—Potential reasons for failure in the target market *(continued)*

- Failing to allow for "backup money" to cover unforeseen circumstances

- Failing to negotiate appropriate payment terms with suppliers

- Growing too quickly

- Failing to develop a commitment to the venture, and not spending enough time and energy on it

- Assuming that good performance today automatically means continued success in the future, and thus failing to adjust to changing circumstances

- Failing to compensate for inexperience through appropriate skills development

- Failing to deal appropriately with family pressures that place demands on the entrepreneur at a time when the business requires attention

- Recruiting the wrong employees

- Behaving dishonestly

- Communicating poorly with employees

- Assuming that the same skills that launched the successful venture will be the ones needed on a day-to-day operational basis

The Attitude: Heart of an Entrepreneur, Spirit of a Leader

To succeed in today's competitive environment, the global trade professional requires a number of characteristics. Fundamental ones include the following:

- the vision and initiative to seek out opportunities

- a commitment to achieving long-term goals using sustainable business practices, improving and developing new skills, understanding customer needs and delivering total quality at the best possible price

- inexhaustible energy, which is necessary to follow through with a plan

- the patience to bring the venture to successful completion

Characteristics also include technical knowledge, cultural sensitivity and a commitment to ethical conduct. Most importantly, the global trader must have the self-confidence of an entrepreneur and cultivate strong leadership skills in order to manage the sometimes unstable nature of foreign market development.

Who is the entrepreneur?

The entrepreneur is the person with vision, the team leader who is driven to achieve set goals. This person has the ability to find, involve and motivate people with similar energy, drive and dedication.

The ongoing general interest in entrepreneurship and its importance to global trade demonstrates an appreciation of the way it energizes a society and—more politically appealing—the way it contributes to job creation. Typical contributions include the following:

- providing innovative and improved products and services
- finding new ways to make products and services available to more people
- improving quality and keeping prices down by competing to be the "best"
- creating jobs in the community
- increasing the quantity of products and services produced in the economy (that is, stimulating economic growth)
- creating new opportunities for others through initiatives and innovations
- providing a spirit of energy, initiative and potential for progress in a community
- creating role models for young people, which encourages entrepreneurial study

Table 3.4—Common characteristics of successful global traders
Technical Knowledge
Knowledge of economic geography and foreign markets
• International marketing and research skills
• Familiarity with technology tools such as the Internet
• Familiarity with documentation
• Knowledge of laws regulating trade
• Knowledge of the role of forwarders, brokers, agents and similar professionals
• Familiarity with the terminology of international trade
• Knowledge of transportation and insurance services
• Knowledge of letters of credit and other trade-financing instruments
Cultural sensitivity
• An awareness of cultural differences and an understanding of how to accommodate them
• Cross-cultural negotiating skills
Entrepreneurial characteristics
• Drive, energy, commitment, creativity and flexibility

One study of the entrepreneurial spirit defines entrepreneurs as champions. Champions are individuals who "emerge to take creative ideas and bring the ideas to life." This study concluded that champions are the driving force behind successful ventures and that they share the attributes outlined in the following table.

Table 3.5—Characteristics of champions	
• High self-confidence	• High level of energy
• Risk-taking potential	• Gravitation towards leadership
• Persistence	
• Attraction to challenges	• Seemingly inexhaustible drive

Source: Howell and Higgins. *Champions of Change: Identifying, Understanding and Supporting Champions of Technological Innovations* (University of Western Ontario)

In addition to these personality traits, the entrepreneur also tends to[17]

- have a spirit of adventure;

- have a strong need to seek and achieve personal accomplishment;

- demonstrate self-reliance;

- be goal-oriented;

- be creative and versatile;

- have a positive attitude;

- be willing to take the initiative; and

- have a strong sense of commitment.

Five myths of entrepreneurship
Myth #1: Entrepreneurs are unique and relatively rare.
Fact: Entrepreneurs are everywhere, but only a small number get a lot of the attention as "superstars" of success. However, the efforts and achievements of thousands of entrepreneurs across the country often go unrecognized because these people may not fit accepted "media images."

Myth #2: Entrepreneurs are money-driven.
Fact: Research shows that most entrepreneurs are primarily motivated by a desire for personal accomplishment. Entrepreneurs compete with themselves, seeking to better past achievements and reach new goals. Money, while important, is often used as an indicator of success rather than as a goal in itself.

Myth #3: Entrepreneurs are born, not made.
Fact: Traditionally, schooling has done little to encourage entrepreneurial initiative. This has lead successful people to believe that their behaviour originates from within. Research suggests, however, that they are a product of

---

[17] Canadian Foundation for Economic Education (CFEE). (www.cfee.org)

various influences, including their own innate qualities and their experiences, environment and schooling. Exposure to entrepreneurial activity leads to understanding and encourages imitation. Entrepreneurship can be taught, but it requires a new educational approach that fosters the appropriate attitudes.

All too often, people lack confidence in their creativity and their ability to acquire the right skills. This doubt, more than anything else, is the key impediment to entrepreneurship, but ultimately, we all have the ability to be entrepreneurial. Emerging entrepreneurs need to focus on the challenges of the venture. Successful exporters will tell you that success in new markets is highly correlated to vision, effort and determination. Nowhere is the concept of multiple solutions more apt than in international trade, where there is never a single "best" way to proceed.

Myth #4: Entrepreneurs take high risks.
Fact: Entrepreneurs are not gamblers. Gamblers take chances on things over which they have no control. Entrepreneurs want to know that whatever the outcome, it was due primarily to their own efforts. Otherwise, the personal satisfaction they seek cannot be realized. They will do everything possible to minimize risk and then examine the risk that remains, comparing it to the potential benefits, before deciding whether to proceed. Successful entrepreneurs take careful, calculated risks, not high risks. In international trade, they are very cautious and conservative operators who know that taking unnecessary risks may cause their entire venture to fail.

It is absolutely vital to gain as much knowledge and experience as possible in preparation for a venture. Going into new and uncharted waters is risky. It is challenging enough to operate in areas that are already familiar in a domestic context, without also coping with what is new and unfamiliar in distant foreign markets.

Myth #5: Entrepreneurs are highly independent individuals.
Fact: Most successful entrepreneurs know they cannot do it all alone. They tend to be very honest about their own needs and shortcomings, and will seek assistance from others who can complement their own skills. Those who try to do everything themselves usually fail. Successful entrepreneurs are good "team builders," and they know how to use teams effectively. Finding the talent necessary to ensure the success of a venture is a key skill.

An entrepreneur may often be frustrated by an inability to "share the dream." Most are involved in initiatives they have nurtured and care a great deal about; however, the other people needed to make the idea work may not share this excitement. After all, it is the entrepreneur's idea, not theirs. They may view the undertaking as simply a job, not a dream. This can frustrate the entrepreneur— at times to the point where he or she refuses to delegate responsibility for fear that the outcome will not meet expectations. This can lead to serious trouble. It is crucial to use other people's talents effectively, while accepting the fact that these people may not be as driven as the entrepreneur.

Far from being independent, entrepreneurs crave trust, and they are motivated when people express confidence in them. The trust of others builds their self-image. Entrepreneurs thrive in an environment that not only challenges them but also expects them to live up to the challenge.

The global mindset and the global leader

Simply put, to work globally one must develop a global mindset. A survey of over 220 global executives around the world revealed that they share similar traits, several of which are included below.[18]

- Cognitive complexity

- Cultural intelligence

- Open-mindedness

- Cosmopolitanism

- Willingness to experiment

- Sensitivity and empathy

- Ability to connect to and work with people from other parts of the world

- A global perspective

- Respect for others

Table 3.6—Four traits of global leaders
A successful global leader is inquisitive and welcomes learning opportunities, is energized when surrounded with diversity—different people, languages, cultures, foods and customs. To develop this, [one must] be open-minded. Cultivate your sense of adventure. Push yourself to be curious about that which you do not know. Don't ever stop learning.
A successful global leader must be able to connect, on an emotional level, with people from various backgrounds. This connection is built when you show an interest and concern, when you listen well and when you can understand and respect differing points of view. Making the emotional connection as a leader earns you respect and commitment from those whom you want to follow you. It is a powerful skill.
A successful global leader is grounded in personal and professional values. It is your actions that demonstrate your integrity. Don't compromise yourself; integrity is one of your most valuable assets. A consistent demonstration of high ethical standards, in personal and company matters, in any part of the world, increases trust. People who trust you are more apt to follow you. Having followers defines a leader.
A successful global leader is capable of managing uncertainty and changing conditions and of tolerating ambiguity in situations. With a tolerance for ambiguity, you will find yourself more comfortable in a foreign culture. You will be more effective in working with people from different backgrounds different from you and creating followers from this group of people.

Source: Elizabeth A. Fessenden. *Executive Staffing and Leadership Development*. Alcoa Inc.

---

[18] *e-Thunder newsletter*, Thunderbird School of Global Management, November 2006.

Positioning the Organization for the Global Marketplace

Know the process and the players

In addition to entrepreneurial and leadership skills, success in global trade also requires expertise in areas such as languages, law, culture, politics, economics and foreign business practices.

Certain areas of knowledge need particular treatment to heighten their usefulness from a global business perspective. Assumptions made in the context of domestic markets are unlikely to hold true when doing business in foreign markets. Preparation and planning are critically important in international trade. Consequently, special attention must be paid to conducting market research, understanding customer needs and accommodating cultural differences. Preparation also means understanding the language of international trade, documentation requirements, regulations affecting trade, and the workings of trade finance, insurance and transportation systems. The ability to create and implement a foreign market-entry strategy is no less important.

Some aspects of company operations that were once viewed as removed from the marketing function are now recognized as central to competitiveness.

- Effective logistics management ensures that products are delivered to customers in the best condition, in the shortest time and at the lowest cost to the firm.

- Communications systems affect the responsiveness of the firm to customer and supplier needs, as well as the costs and reliability of the firm's service.

- Effective quality management holds the potential for companies to maintain or expand market share while ensuring maximum profitability.

- Strong investment in human resources is a high priority.

- A strong commitment to sustainable business practices is very important.

- Export functions are not restricted to trading, export management or production; other professions are extensively involved in trade. They include people who provide logistical services, such as carriers, freight forwarders, customs brokers, warehouse operators, distributors, couriers, purchasing agents and inventory and materials managers.

Table 3.7—Other professions involved in trade development		
• Bankers • Consultants • Accountants • Lawyers • Transportation and shipping firms	• Translation houses • Packaging and design firms • Travel agents • Trainers and instructors	• Research organizations • Federal and regional government departments

Clearly, not all of these functions exist within the organization, and others may be outsourced. However, strong relationships with providers of these services are vital to the global organization's support structure.

Qualities of global managers

Since exporters commit considerable resources to meeting the global business challenge, it is vital that they have the right attributes, technical knowledge and cultural skills training for the job at hand. Several characteristics are of particular importance: creative thinking, problem solving, adaptability to new business and cultural environments and flexibility in a world of relentless change. Those who display these characteristics have the best chance of succeeding in global business.

Figure 3.8—Testing export quotient (EQ)	YES	NO
1. Are you entrepreneurial?	☐	☐
2. Do you have a reliable, service-oriented character?	☐	☐
3. Are you a natural networker, building and maintaining relationships?	☐	☐
4. Do you see yourself as highly organized and research-oriented?	☐	☐
5. Do you possess good communication skills?	☐	☐
6. Are sales, marketing or distribution backgrounds featured in your resumé?	☐	☐
7. Do you excel in finance and business-related subjects?	☐	☐
8. Do you pride yourself on your strong negotiating skills?	☐	☐
9. Are you experienced in handling complex documentation?	☐	☐
10. Are you an avid follower of global politics?	☐	☐
11. Do you have the ability to speak and write in more than one language?	☐	☐
12. Are you sensitive to different cultures?	☐	☐
13. Do you consider yourself able to adopt ideas easily, even under pressure?	☐	☐
14. Are you well travelled or curious about other cultures?	☐	☐
15. Do you understand the basic principles of sustainable business?	☐	☐
Total (award one point for every answer marked "Yes") _____		

Figure 3.8—Testing export quotient (EQ) *(continued)*

Score:

1–6   Although you have acquired some skills related to exporting, you need further assessment to find out whether you are suited to this field.

7– 10   You show a keen interest in the subject. However, you should consider increasing your knowledge, language and technical trading skills.

11–15 You have a high rating in the critical factors that make companies and individuals successful in global trade

Working towards transnational status

Economic integration and interdependence has eroded many of the barriers that used to separate national and regional markets, while the Internet has had the effect of fading political borders. Today it is possible—even mandatory—to adopt a commercial perspective that embraces the entire globe. As a result, a growing number of companies are doing precisely that. They are thinking about their mission and goals in terms of the world market, not just a narrow part of it.

The transnational company

A truly global organization plans and organizes without geographic bias. However, it also recognizes the need to adapt products and marketing to local conditions. The companies that are able to organize their activities across national boundaries in this way are termed transnationals.

For instance, a transnational company that produces running shoes and athletic wear might locate running shoe and garment production in southeast Asia, where labour costs are lowest and raw materials are abundant. At the same time, it might establish its design and R&D in the United States, where top technical talent can be easily attracted and retained. It might set up separate marketing, sales and distribution companies in each country where consumers are located. Finally, it might locate the legal and financial functions of the company in an offshore jurisdiction to take advantage of specialized accounting, legal and insurance expertise, or to consolidate and capture profits in a low-tax jurisdiction. Each of these business units might be internal to the company or aspects of its global supply chain.

The end of true multinationals?

In contrast, many international firms still exhibit some kind of country or regional bias. Companies that are organized along country lines but operate many subsidiaries and branch plants in other countries are termed multinationals. A multinational corporation traditionally would set up separate companies in each jurisdiction where it plans to do business. These subsidiaries would carry out almost all corporate functions locally. Essentially, a multinational corporation functions as a group of related but largely independent companies whose operations are based entirely in the jurisdictions where they are located.

A classic example of this type of structure would be an automobile parts manufacturer with country-based operations in each country where major customers are located. So, for instance, the company might have a subsidiary that designs, builds, markets and sells brake components in the United Kingdom. It might have similar subsidiaries in the United States, Brazil and Japan.

The key thing to note here is that each part of a true multinational corporation tends to be self-serving. This structure creates entities that are very focused on the needs of local markets, but it also creates redundancies. In the example above, one would have to question why a car-parts company would need to have separate design teams independently creating the same types of components.

This approach also ignores the efficiencies that are possible when a company looks at the world as a single location. Again, using the example above, if a multinational company has six plants producing car brake parts, isn't it possible that a single plant located in the lowest-cost, most appropriately skilled jurisdiction could serve all six countries more efficiently and with better economies of scale? This is how a transnational corporation would view the world, and this is exactly what has evolved over recent years. The advancement of the global supply chain concept, business segmentation, near-shore and offshore outsourcing and global digital networks have all but done away with the redundancies and inefficiencies of the traditional multinational company.

Virtual corporations and business networks

As the global market has presented new opportunities, companies have formed teams with the sole purpose of working together on a specific project or approaching a specific business opportunity. These teams differ from traditional joint ventures, which are actually independent business entities, because they are temporary and virtual—brought together by digital networks and special objectives. Each party, big or small, contributes its core competence. Acceptance of such entities as a legitimate part of the global business environment has made opportunities even more abundant for traders.

The weaving of the Internet into the fabric of global trade has given rise to virtual business networks of global service providers. It is common for whole project teams never to meet face-to-face, with the abundance of online communication and file-sharing tools available. While virtual business will never replace face-to-face contact, the obvious cost savings of minimizing global travel are undeniable.

Networks of suppliers

Specialization allows an organization to become more skilled and efficient at a particular activity. By dealing with specialists rather than doing all the work themselves, global companies can reap the benefits of better-quality services at lower costs, while retaining multi-skilled workforces that can respond quickly to new opportunities. As a result, their organizational structures have become increasingly less centralized. For instance, design, engineering, production and marketing are all aspects of production that companies are buying as services from outside suppliers. This global supply chain has given rise to new opportunities and new industries. From India's booming software and business process outsourcing industries, to supply-chain management and e-procurement, the support network for global trade continues to grow.

Some supplier relationships are purely local. When these relationships work well, however, purchasers and suppliers both have a natural interest in extending them when requirements for similar services originate elsewhere. For global companies seeking to establish consistent processes throughout their operations, maintaining key supplier links around the world is strategically important.

The challenge, of course, for ethical managers seeking to maintain a sustainable business model is to ensure that these partners share the same values and have the same commitment to sustainability. Otherwise, an ethically sound business can quickly find itself immersed in controversy (i.e., if their supply-chain partners are engaged in unethical business practices).

Before the Leap: Evaluating Global Trade Readiness

Before moving on to a greater appreciation of the organizational structure and processes of today's successful global trader, it is important to have an understanding of the company's current state of readiness to pursue foreign-market opportunities. Having the desire and even a number of sales leads is not enough. Preparing the organization by ensuring that the right staff, skills and systems are in place comes with its own costs. The following checklist may be used to determine to what extent the company is ready to proceed with global business preparation.

Table 3.9—Global trade readiness checklist
Commitment to developing international markets
A lack of commitment and co-ordination, undefined management roles and responsibilities and inexperienced staff are all weaknesses to be identified. Any company members with exporting experience and management should be involved in developing the global business plan.
☑ Does exporting fit into your company's overall marketing objectives?
☑ Does top management strongly support pursuing exporting?
☑ Will your company develop an international marketing plan with defined goals and objectives?
☑ Has your company committed an appropriate budget for initial export development? This budget should include items such as international travel, market research, business training and/or outsourcing and consulting costs.
☑ Has your company conducted market research using secondary sources of information (government statistics and market briefs, industry data, privately-produced reports and the Internet)?

Table 3.9—Global trade readiness checklist (continued)

Commitment to a sustainable business model

☑ Does the firm recognize the need to balance economic growth with environmental protection and social equity?

☑ Does the firm acknowledge that managers should consider the needs of society, not just the interests of the shareholders (i.e., corporate social responsibility)?

☑ Does the firm recognize that there are many stakeholders who can affect or who are affected by the achievement of the organization's objectives and that the firm has both a legal and an ethical responsibility to provide and account for the impact that the actions of the firm has on those stakeholders.

International trade operations

☑ Will your company ensure that export sales orders will be processed with the same expediency of domestic sales orders?

☑ Will your company give its foreign representatives and customers the same attention and level of service given to domestic representatives and customers?

☑ Will your company appoint someone internally to develop export sales? Ideally, this person would be familiar with the language and practices of your target markets.

☑ Does your company have sufficient production capacity that can be committed to the export market over the long-term?

☑ Is your company willing to modify product packaging and ingredients to meet foreign import regulations, food safety standards and cultural preferences?

☑ Does your company have a staff member who can handle export documentation?

☑ Is your firm prepared to look carefully at the impact that business operations will have on those who are located in the foreign jurisdiction of interest and take proactive measures to ensure that the needs of all stakeholders are carefully balanced?

Financial commitment

Exporting is an advisable strategy to pursue only at the appropriate point in each company's unique development process. A company not yet ready to export is much better off devoting its resources to further strengthening domestic business than prematurely attempting to export.

Table 3.9—Global trade readiness checklist *(continued)*

☑ Is your company well established in the domestic market and financially stable?

☑ Will management accept a payback of three years or more on exporting?

☑ Will your company's management set yearly export sales goals with long-term objectives of making export sales a substantial percentage of total corporate sales?

☑ Is your company aware of how currency exchange rate fluctuations can affect company sales and profits?

☑ Does your company have the financial resources to actively support the promotion of your products in the targeted markets over the long term?

☑ Does your company have liability insurance and/or a plan to deal with worst-case situations where the firm causes injury or loss to stakeholders in the foreign jurisdiction where the company is engaged in business?

Supplier, customer and contact network

☑ Does your company already have contacts in the markets being considered?

☑ Has your company established relationships with trade services providers at home to help facilitate export transactions?

☑ Has your company ever imported products?

☑ Have any of your company's suppliers or customers exported to your target markets?

☑ Are you aware of public- or private-sector trade representatives in your target markets?

Technology

The Internet and other digital networks are now everyday tools in preparing for and managing global trade.

☑ Does your company have an office network and the staff (in-house or outsourced) to maintain it?

☑ Does your company have a well-designed corporate website that is kept up-to-date?

☑ Does your staff regularly use e-mail and other online tools for communication?

Table 3.9—Global trade readiness checklist (continued)
☑ Do you use the web to stay up-to-date on trends in your industry, customer buying trends and competitive intelligence?
☑ Do you maintain a company intranet for internal management and communications, and/or an extranet for interaction with suppliers and customers?
☑ Has your company ever engaged in other networked activities with suppliers or customers, such as an Electronic Data Interchange system for managing supply chains?
Answering "no" to any of the above questions does not necessarily mean that the company is unfit for global business, but it does present issues for later consideration.

Source: Portions of the checklist adapted from Pennsylvania Economic Planning and Development Council (www.pasourcenet.com)

Chapter Summary

Understanding what it means to be a global trader is no longer a choice; that is the reality of the current interconnected business world. If a company is not self-diagnosing its capacity for global business and ensuring that the right skills, systems and processes are in place, it runs the risk of declining market share—even in its domestic market.

However, there are choices for how an organization may structure itself in preparing for trade, and what strategy is to be used for any given market. What is common for every successful global business is the fact that the entrepreneurial spirit is thriving within the company and there is strong leadership at its helm.

Exercises

Exercise 1 (class discussion)

An entrepreneurial person is often an enthusiastic person who is very passionate about what they do. In considering global trade, what potential risks might this type of person present as they take the company forward?

(Estimated time 5 minutes)

Exercise 2 (discussion in pairs)

Ease of communications and competitive forces have caused many businesses to look for low-cost suppliers in other countries. Yet, in many instances, the best prices for goods and/or services are coming from companies located in developing countries where labour is very inexpensive and business regulations (e.g., labour laws, environmental regulations, etc.) and enforcement are weak. So, for companies that are committed to sustainable business, supplier conduct is often a significant issue. With this in mind, work in pairs and walk through the meaning of each of the following four concepts that form the foundation of sustainable business (Refer to Figure 3.2.).

1. Sustainable development

2. Corporate social responsibility

3. Stakeholder theory

4. Corporate accountability theory

Be sure that you fully understand each concept. Once you have discussed each of these areas, answer these questions:

1. How can a company that is committed to sustainable business compete with a firm that is willing to chase the lowest-cost offers (i.e., irrespective of the conduct of the suppliers)?

2. Why is it important for companies to articulate a commitment to sustainable business in some form of company mission statement or widely circulated policy document (i.e., something that has been vetted at the highest level by the president or CEO)?

(Estimated time 15 minutes)

Exercise 3 (class discussion)
How does the concept of the transnational change in the context of the Internet and e-commerce?

(Estimated time 5 minutes)

References/Resources

Freeman, R. E. *Strategic Management: A Stakeholder Approach*. Boston: Pitman, 1984

Interactive Export Readiness Diagnostic (www.exportdiagnostic.ca)

The Interactive Business Planner (www.cbsc.org/ibp)

What is Competitiveness? The Competitiveness Institute (www. competitiveness.org/article/articleview/774/1/32/)

Do you have a global mindset? Thunderbird School of Global Management (www.thunderbird.edu)

The Global Supply Chain

4

Optimizing pathways to trade

Chapter Objectives

- Understand the increasing impact of global supply chains, integrative trade and multi-sourcing in all aspects of international trade
- Differentiate between the different parties in a trade transaction and explore their objectives, roles and responsibilities
- Understand the mechanics of a transaction from both import and export perspectives

Overview

"A production supply chain refers to the flow of physical goods and associated information from the source to the consumer. Key supply chain activities include production planning, purchasing, materials management, distribution, customer service, and sales forecasting. These processes are critical to the success of any operation whether they're manufacturers, wholesalers, or service providers."[19]

Technology, particularly the Internet, is enabling significant advances in the evolution of supply chains across industries and all over the globe. The ability to conduct business throughout the world as a result of the increased transparency of international markets and potential business partners, as well as advanced logistics and the shortening of transaction cycles, has resulted in increasingly global sourcing practices, even for small business ventures.

Exporters find it cost-effective, and in some cases even necessary, to import components that will be used to produce goods for export, so that the historical distinctions between importer and exporter are less meaningful today. The concept of "integrative trade," widely promoted by Canada's export credit agency EDC, proposes that import, export and investment activities across borders are elements of a holistic, integrated set of complementary activities that make up international business and global commerce.

Value Chains and Supply Chains: Linking Nations Through Business and Trade

Value chains versus supply chains

"The value chain describes the full range of activities that are required to bring a product from its conception, through its design, its sourced raw materials and intermediate inputs, its marketing, its distribution and its support to the final consumer. In other words, the chain can be seen as incorporating production, exchange, distribution and consumption—from the cradle to the grave of a given product or service."[20]

Given that supply chains focus primarily on enabling the flow of goods or services from producer to consumer, and value chains look at the "process" independent of specific firms, on a "vertical" basis, it is perhaps appropriate to view supply chains as a specific subset of global value chains.

Supply chains have historically operated in what is now referred to as "push" mode, where manufacturers, distributors and retailers all have agendas and objectives and a role in shaping the final product. More recently, supply chains, enabled through the Internet and e-commerce, have been characterized as "pull"-oriented, with consumers exercising increased power and authority in shaping the products and services that ultimately fill their needs. The balance of market power has been shifted in favour of consumers through "pull"-based supply chains.

---

[19] Supply Chain Basics—Western Economic Diversification Canada. (www.e-future.ca/alberta/pdf/efc_ supply_chain_basics.pdf)

[20] The Institute of Development Studies, U.K. (www.ids.ac.uk/ids/global/valchnconcept1.html)

The advent of Internet technology has significantly enhanced the functions and capabilities of global supply chains, providing greater (and accelerated) visibility to every aspect of a trade transaction. The Internet facilitates efficiency and improved function in several areas:

- Cost control and efficiency/streamlining of processes

- Enhanced service through improved communication, status reporting and related capabilities

- Real-time status checking of shipments, from container to individual product

- Accelerated receiving of shipments

- Improved freight audit processes and procedures

- Standardization of documentation, reduction of error rates

All of these enhancements combine to greatly improve the speed, accuracy and cost of supply chains, and have enabled supply chains to truly extend across the globe, even for small businesses sourcing production inputs to be included in exports.

By extension, the more efficient supply chains can be, the more attractive global value chains become as business models and means of entering international markets.

> Individual firms participate in value chains differently; their approach determines their role in the value chain:
> - Increased income
> - Firm's role in the value chain
> - Access to niche markets
> - Upgrade of processes and products
> - Capacity to change their role in the chain (for example, taking greater responsibility for design)
> - Ability to move into new and more profitable chains
>
> Source: IDS UK (www.ids.ac.uk)

Trade: Physical, Financial and Information Global Supply Chains

Physical supply chain

The movement of goods, even services, through the chain from manufacturer to consumer, perhaps using the services of a freight forwarder or logistics/transport specialist, as well as a customs broker to facilitate clearance of the goods, is the traditional and well-known type of supply chain.

More accurately, it is the most commonly seen layer of the supply chain, which in reality functions on several levels simultaneously. Advances in technology and evolutions in business practices are such that the layers of the supply chain have been peeled and closely examined, resulting in new services and value propositions being proposed, touching each layer of the supply chain and doing so on a global basis.

Financial supply chain

Just as goods move across the world from manufacturer to consumer, so does a corresponding financial flow. It moves, ultimately, from consumer to manufacturer through the various intermediaries.

Just like the physical flow of goods or services, the flow of monies between parties has been the subject of significant improvement over the last decade, largely due to the Internet and the increasing effectiveness of e-commerce.

There has been increased focus and attention on understanding the value "trapped" in longer global value chains, through inventory, orders, receivables and extended payment terms, as well as general inefficiencies in process. Global supply chains are the equivalent of business "ecosystems". It has been estimated that large corporations can face financial expenses in the range of 3-4 percent of revenues, which for a billion-dollar company translates to a significant expenditure per year.

Extensive research has been carried out in recent years on efficiencies in the finance function of trade and international business, including considerations of financial supply-chain management and optimization.[21]

The concept of a financial supply chain is now a mainstream idea in the business of international trade, and the financial layer of the global supply chain has been given its due attention.

Information supply chain

The global supply chain, including the physical, financial and information flows, is very similar to an organic, evolving ecosystem of entities, mutually dependent in survival as well as in success. Like any significant ecosystem, the global supply chains of today have an impact far beyond their immediate members or participants.

Global business and international trade activities are being assessed, undertaken and concluded at rates of speed that, a few years ago, would have been impossible to attain, or at the very least, would have been imprudent due to lack of timely information and very limited transparency.

Advances in technology, improvements in business processes and communication and a competitive drive have combined to demand quicker responses from business executives, often with limited visibility. Service providers and financial executives have focused on the importance of timely, holistic and accurate information about individual transactions, as well as about the "portfolio" of transactions that comprise a company's international activities.

At the transactional level, near real-time insight into the status of shipments, the expected settlement of invoices or the maturity of future-date payments is of central importance to financial managers. Optimization of cash flow is a financial discipline that has earned increased attention, and similarly, expeditious delivery of shipments and the ability to track the status of containers or individual products is critical to retail organizations.

Large global retailers have logistics systems and capabilities that rival those of world-class military. Inventory control is a well-developed art and science, and understanding financial dealings and the status of trade receivables, or foreign currency accounts on a net basis, across multiple financial institutions (a so-called "multi-bank" view) is an increasingly common expectation.

Information is king: the physical and financial supply chains may be perfectly tuned and functioning optimally; however, if that is not visible to a business through near real-time reporting or query capabilities (information), those accomplishments do not translate into business value.

The effectiveness of a company's information supply chain is inextricably linked to the technology infrastructure supporting the enterprise. Questions of data

---

[21] See Aberdeen Group. *CFO's Agenda for Global Trade Benchmark Report.* September 2005. (www. aberdeen.com)

quality or access, which appear at first glance to be "an IT problem," can quickly lead to serious business issues when critical information fails to reach decision makers in a timely manner.

The increasingly critical importance of the information supply chain is highlighted through the broadening use of e-commerce in the conduct of global trade and international commerce. E-commerce is enabled through "virtual proximity"— the sense of being "closer" to a trading partner as a result of the availability of information, and the much higher levels of transparency enabled through technology and near real-time information flow.

E-commerce is nothing less than a specific flavour of the conduct of international trade and business, with its own variations of global supply chain and associated technologies. The perfect illustration of mainstream e-commerce and a truly global "supply chain" would perhaps be eBay. It is enabled through a series of features and processes which give traders and auction participants a certain level of assurance about the trading partner (through "information" provided via user feedback), the security of a verified online payment system, and the availability of rudimentary dispute settlement mechanisms. The system effectively allows users to "segment" potential trading partners through various search features, as well as through quality- and volume-based membership tiers. E-commerce, originally restricted to lower-value goods, now extends into higher-value merchandise. It also extends into areas such as professional services, through specialized sites providing, for example, the services of expert consultants in a wide range of domains.

One representation of the financial supply chain, illustrated by George Marinos, Partner, National Data Quality, PricewaterhouseCoopers, looks as follows:

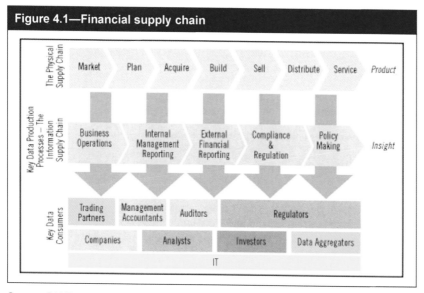

Figure 4.1—Financial supply chain

Source: *DM Review*, April 2005 (www.dmreview.com/article_sub.cfm?articleId=1023896)

While the financial supply chain is not explicitly represented in this view, the inclusion of management accountants, auditors and other financial professionals provides the implicit sense that a financial view is a key derivative of the information supply chain.

Integrative Trade

The new paradigm

Integrative trade is a model used to describe the increasing interrelationship between imports, exports, foreign investment and the global supply chain—ultimately, the conduct of international business.

Integrative trade recognizes that export trade is no longer as independent or "stand-alone" as once might have been the case. Competitive dynamics, closely integrated economies and the ability to source inputs and skilled resources on a global basis are creating a dynamic where importing, outsourcing and foreign investment combine to allow for the manufacture (or other creation) of competitively priced but profitable exports. This new model of global business envisions its participants reaching further up into the value chain related to the product or service being exported, and sharing in a net overall gain from the specialization and trade that drives the model.

Integrative trade requires certain components to be traded twice—once as an import on the supply side, and subsequently as a component of the final export. Similarly, investments in markets where inputs are sourced show a marked increase and high-profile business models built around outsourcing and offshoring are now very much a reality of the global business environment.

According to Stephen Poloz, SVP Corporate Affairs, and Chief Economist for Export Development Canada, "One consequence of the growth in trade and cross-border investment is that economies today are even more intimately interconnected than they were in the past. Indeed, taking the fall of the Berlin Wall back in 1989–90 as a point of departure, the importance of international trade to income generation in the world has increased by approximately 50 percent in just 15 years. Back in 1990, less than 40 percent of global GDP depended on trade, while today that number is approaching 60 percent."[22]

Integrative trade also links to the ideas of business and economic integration across the globe and "functional" integration between national economies and businesses. Linking integrative trade to global value chains, Timothy J. Sturgeon, Senior Research Affiliate at MIT writes: "An earlier era of 'internationalization,' characterized by the simple geographic spread of economic activities across national boundaries, is giving way to an era of 'globalization,' which involves the functional integration of these internationally dispersed activities. It is this functional integration that drives our growing interest in 'integrative trade.'"[23]

Five trends driving global integration:
1. Doubling of the global workforce
2. Enhanced and economical global communications
3. Standardization and digitization of work
4. The global supply base
5. Rise of the global startup
Source: Timothy Sturgeon

---

[22] *Financial Intermediation under the New Trade Paradigm: EDC and Integrative Trade*, February 2007.
[23] *Conceptualizing Integrative Trade: The Global Value Chains Framework*, 2006. (www.international.gc.ca/eet/research/TPR_2006/Chapter_3_Sturgeon-en.pdf)

The concept of integrative trade captures a transformational reality in international trade and global business, with implications ranging from practical business tactics to the highest-level policy considerations for national governments. The reality of closer integration and the linkage to both global supply chains and value chains will require active and informed leadership from executives engaged in international trade, outsourcing and global business.

Trade Transactions: Doing Business Across the Chains

Practical implications?
International trade and global commerce have never been simple or straightforward.

The realities of increasing interdependence and integration, continuously evolving enabling technologies and competitive pressures combine to generate implications in nearly all aspects of international trade and global commerce.

Exporters can no longer be content to produce a final good for export, based solely on domestic inputs—the final product will often prove too expensive. The advent of effective and fully enabled outsourcing arrangements across a wide range of industries and professions further creates direct and practical implications related to resourcing and/or foreign investment decisions in markets where outsourcing arrangements may be concluded.

China and India are emerging powers and major suppliers to the global economy both in terms of inputs to manufactured goods for export and in terms of outsourced expertise, from assembly-line work to computer programming and professional services. Exporters in North America and Europe, for example, must re-assess their business models in light of these realities, and competitive pressures may well force them to engage in global sourcing, whether they wish to do so or not.

> Due diligence and good faith are critical to the success of trade transactions. There are processes, instruments and remedies available to provide security or to mitigate losses, but the value of upfront analysis and good judgment in the selection of business partners cannot be overstated.
>
> Taking good care of the relationships will magnify successes and reduce challenges to manageable proportions.

Certain markets, such as Hong Kong and Dubai, are very familiar with the import and re-export business model, having engaged in this form of business activity for much of their commercial history. Other markets may try to hold on to familiar business models but do so at some peril, given the pace of change in the global business environment.

The reality of increased global integration, truly global sourcing, supply-chain models, the growing focus on vertical value chains and the explosion of outsourcing solutions across industries strongly suggests that integrative trade is a reality for the long term and will affect the conduct of global business on every major level.

Buyers, Sellers and a Cast of Many More: Parties to a Trade Transaction

Trade is a people business
The business of international trade and global commerce is very much a business of people and partnerships. Few are masters of every aspect of trade or global

business, even among experts or experienced veterans of the international business scene.

If we consider an international trade deal by way of illustration, there are many variations of these transactions, and even in the most straightforward structure, several "cast members" are required to make the production a success.

Lights, Camera, Action: The Mechanics of a Trade Transaction

The actors
Exporter
Is a driven and internationally oriented business person, with entrepreneurial qualities, the heart of a deal maker and the soul of an explorer. The exporter's interest in international trade may be purely profit- or opportunity-driven, yet many have a certain attraction to extending business activities (increasingly at the start-up stage of business) into the global marketplace. The exporter's primary concern, with apologies to Jerry Maguire, may be summarized as "SHOW ME THE MONEY!"

Importer
The importer is very comfortable operating in the familiar domestic environment. They may identify an opportunity to bring an innovative new product to the home market and could imagine a contribution being made to raising the standard of living at home by importing the latest new technologies or luxury items. The importer is an acquirer and is focused on successfully sourcing and safely receiving that shipment, to be turned around at a profit on the home market or perhaps as a re-export.

Both characters may have a dual role, particularly under a screenplay influenced by integrative trade.

Financier
This character finances the transaction, through a range of product and service offerings. The financier may require the participation of other financiers—bankers, export credit agencies, non-bank providers of trade finance—to be able to support the transaction adequately. This character will earn revenue by granting access to monies (generally on a short-term basis, but possibly well into the five-to-seven-year medium term) required by either or both the importer and exporter.

Transporter
This actor is an expert at moving goods across the globe: he knows the most secure and optimal routes and is fully versed in the various components of freight costing and the regulations related to transport. The transporter and the exporter work very closely together to produce documentation that correctly describes the goods, ensures that they meet the standards of the importing market and clearly identifies and allows transfer of ownership and risk.

Broker
The customs broker is often the first point of contact for the goods on arrival at destination. The broker may provide temporary accommodations to store the

goods pending customs clearance and is an expert on the requirements related to the final import of goods into the receiving country after the transporter has completed his task. The broker may collect any taxes and duties due.

Agent
This actor is skilled in the mechanics of commerce, is well-connected in the home market and most commonly represents the exporter in the country of destination. The actor assists in the sales process and, depending on the script, remains active as the local representative of the exporter in the destination market.

Government
This actor is always on stage, collecting taxes, regulating the interaction of the rest of the cast, negotiating with other governments and the various actors' guilds, and providing financing or guarantees in support of the financier's transactions. This role is broad and varies on each stage and with every deal.

Supporting Cast
There is a group of additional actors, such as the inspector, who verifies shipments and issues certificates attesting to their nature/condition, and the lawyer, whose presence is generally underemphasized, and numerous others, depending on the exact nature of the production.

A major supporting actor is technology: this member of the cast is reshaping nearly every aspect of international trade and global business in ways that revise practices that are hundreds of years old—shifting business processes, documentation and even transaction decisions from the "real world" to the virtual world.

Import Considerations: Supplier Development and International Purchasing

Importing: second-string no more?
Importing has generally been given secondary focus and attention in the international trade equation, due to the old perspective that exports brought wealth and prosperity and imports drove the trade deficit up and generally represented an outflow of value from the economy.

Imports are a matter of quality of life—sometimes even of survival—but have generally benefited less from government support, promotion and the availability of resources than exports.

Under the integrative trade model, imports and global sourcing are critical to the success in exports and export development, and therefore are afforded greater focus and resources. Successful importing is now a matter of competitive advantage.

Supplier relationships
Partnering or improving supplier relationships is a way to improve supply-chain management. By partnering with suppliers—instead of just doing business with them—a company can extend the reach of its logistics system for the benefit of the total supply chain. Partnering implies developing more personal relationships and trust, sharing information and making decisions that will improve the

efficiency or cost base of the supply chain. There may be times when some decisions could put one of the chain's partners at a disadvantage; however, any total supply-chain savings will eventually benefit all partners in the supply chain. And, if the supply chain system improves customer service, then all partners should benefit from increased business volume.

Partnerships will develop most readily between companies that have a vertical relationship (operate within different but complementary industry sectors) in the supply chain. Partners may be suppliers of products or services. In international trade, it is particularly important to have good working relations with third parties, such as freight forwarders and foreign distributors.

One of the first steps in selecting a supplier is to establish that the supplier has the potential to improve profitability for the total supply chain, through efficiency and/or cost reductions. Management commitment and involvement in establishing and maintaining solid business relationships with all supply-chain suppliers is necessary. While it may at times be tempting to expedite the whole process and to devote less time to some of the minor participants in the chain, this would not be wise. Each participant or supplier in an integrated supply chain is vitally important, and one non-committed supplier can have a negative impact on the entire logistics strategy.

Import considerations

Foreign trade is an essential ingredient in the economic development and prosperity of most nations. Many countries have entered into trade pacts or agreements and, through negotiation, have established rules and regulations to govern orderly trade. These trade agreements, along with the relative reduction in trade barriers that ensue, make it simpler to import goods into Canada.

Importers of materials, finished goods or products for resale either identify unfilled niches in the domestic market and seek to fill them from foreign sources or identify promising foreign products for which they try to develop domestic demand. In either case, importers run the risk of importing products for which there is no viable resale market. Effective market research is the key to minimizing that risk. Similarly, once a promising market opportunity has been identified, a rigorous approach to product sourcing and supplier evaluation can reduce the risk of entering into arrangements with unreliable suppliers. Supplier evaluation may involve a considerable investment of time and effort, but it is well worth it if the result is a smoothly functioning and mutually beneficial long-term business relationship.

It is usually best to evaluate different foreign suppliers before settling on one. Even after a deal has been initiated, it may be wise to keep track of several alternative suppliers. This helps to avoid dependence on one source and to minimize risk if the foreign supplier selected turns out to be unsatisfactory.

Once a potential foreign supplier has been identified, the buyer initiates the process with a purchase order or with a request for a quotation to supply the goods required. The initial request may open up a process of offer and counter-offer as the importer and the foreign supplier clarify, negotiate and agree upon trade terms. Once an offer has been accepted, it constitutes a legal contract.

Negotiating price is a critical element of the process, and several key questions ought to be kept in mind:

- What volume is being purchased?

- Are discounts available as volumes increase?

- What logistics costs related to importing the products are covered in the price?

- Does the price include packing, transportation, cargo insurance and customs duties? Each of these items will be borne by either the exporter or the importer and will be included or excluded from the quoted price of the goods.

- When do the seller's responsibilities end and those of the buyer begin?

The importing firm should clearly set out its requirements in writing. The importer should also respond in writing to the exporter's requests for clarification in a clear, direct style and in as much detail as required. The aim is to avoid misunderstanding and to secure a deal that will benefit both parties.

Additional considerations include agreement on payment methods and terms and clear agreement on the documents (including content and format, specified to the appropriate level of detail to ensure payment as well as transport and clearance of the goods).

The sales contract will typically be complemented with a purchase order, which may serve as the basis for issuance of a documentary letter of credit—a payment and financing mechanism provided by banks in support of trade transactions.

Another important consideration includes the classification of an imported item, which determines any associated tariff due as well as import-valuation procedures.

It should be noted that, in the same way the importer verifies the reliability of the potential foreign supplier, that supplier also investigates the reliability and creditworthiness of the importer. Recognizing this fact, the partners can go a long way toward instilling mutual confidence while accelerating the validation process by providing each other with appropriate information and references.

Export Considerations: Client Development and Channel Management

Exporting: high-level view

Exporting, to some, is primarily about business development and sales. From identifying a product or value proposition to selecting a target market, planning and executing an entry strategy and ensuring growth and a healthy pipeline, it seems everything is primarily about sales.

Successful exporting is also, however, about due diligence and risk management: the market and its characteristics must be very well understood, as must various strategies and options for managing the market and ensuring successful entry and ongoing business growth.

Exporting requires a strong client orientation and an ability to operate in-market, with intercultural effectiveness and finesse. This requirement applies equally to business and social interactions with prospects and clients, as it does to adapting the product or service to be exported to meet the needs and expectations of end-clients. Exporting involves a combination of diplomacy and commercial orientation and savvy, together with the competitive or "exploratory" drive to venture into international markets.

Export: supply chains and logistics

Successful exporting depends on a tightly integrated process that includes product planning, design, production adaptation, order processing, packaging, documentation, transportation and delivery. In order to be cost-effective, this should be a seamless process—all participants must take direct responsibility for the success of the process. Logistics management ties all of these steps together and ensures they occur the way they are supposed to.

Logistics embraces a spectrum of activities designed to move goods and, increasingly, services from the producer to the customer, as quickly and cost-effectively as possible. This process involves issues such as cargo assembly, packaging, handling, inspection and transportation. Logistics is increasingly viewed as a key strategic capability that binds together virtually all functions within a company. It has an impact on—and a direct relationship with—product development, manufacturing, marketing, sales and even financial management.

All of this is significant enough in domestic transactions, but logistics is even more critical in international trade, where the distance between producer and customer is greater, more steps are involved, the process is more complex and the options are less well known. International traders that learn how to execute the logistics function properly can enjoy a decisive competitive advantage in the global marketplace.

The export process

Today's highly competitive international environment does not allow for a simplistic approach to exporting. What is required instead is an overall vision supported by a concrete plan for streamlining the process, reducing costs and shrinking total transaction time.

Table 4.2—The export process
1. **Product development**: market research, R&D, testing, refinement and modification
2. **Manufacturing**: materials handling, directing human resources (labour), process management, product adaptation and packaging
3. **Warehousing**: product handling, labelling and marking, and inventory control
4. **Marketing**: foreign travel, participating in trade missions, trade fairs and exhibitions and personal contacts

Table 4.2—The export process *(continued)*

5. **Order processing**: responding to inquiries, issuing quotations, dealing with offers and counter-offers and contract negotiations

6. **Shipment preparation**: removal from storage, cargo assembly, packing, marking, document preparation, securing insurance and arranging for transportation

7. **Transportation**: loading onto domestic transportation, physical movement from the manufacturer's facilities to a port of embarkation, unloading and loading onto international carrier and physical movement to the destination

8. **Reporting to customs**: submission of documentation, valuation, customs processing and payment of duties

9. **Delivery to customer**: unloading at destination, movement to storage site, engagement of local transportation, loading, physical movement to the customer's address, unloading and providing an acceptable level of post-sales service

10. **Payment process**: submission of transaction documentation to exporter's bank with request for payment, verification by exporter's bank of documents, resubmission to importer's bank with request for payment, verification by importer's bank of documentation, issuing of credit to the exporter's bank and request from importer for payment

The individual steps must not be thought of as expense items that add to the costs of the whole, but as investment opportunities to enhance efficiency, reduce expenses, provide better service and improve the company's bottom line. Supply chains, once established, tested and proven, can be used for expanded volumes of existing products or for new product lines as they evolve.

Producing or adapting for export

In selecting what products to market and determining what modifications need to be made and what design options to offer, the exporting firm must consider issues such as:

- Can the company simply sell its existing product line without modification? If so, what will additional sales do to existing capacity, supply requirements, production schedules, storage capacity and transportation facilities? If not, exactly what changes must be implemented to make the product fully acceptable to the foreign customer?

- Are proposed modifications compatible with existing equipment and processes used for both production and transportation?

- Is the proposed product easily manufactured and transported?

- Will the features and options proposed require a different approach to materials planning, production, warehousing, transportation, assembly and delivery?

- What are the costs associated with sourcing, production, storage, transportation, assembly and delivery to customers?

Adapting products or services to suit the unique needs, expectations and preferences of export-market customers has always been advocated as good practice by those experienced (and successful) in international markets.

This competitive advantage of the past is almost the "price of entry" today, given the shift to "pull" supply-chain models and the increasing power of the consumer, as well as the powerful communication infrastructure, which allows buyers to identify options on a global basis and sets an expectation that exporters should be informed and educated about the characteristics of a market, and therefore be able to tailor offerings to its preferences.

Optimizing the export process

Exporting is a complicated, multi-phased process with unique characteristics for each product, customer and market. Nonetheless, certain industry practices can be identified that tend to drive an export program to success. The following table illustrates actions that can be taken to enhance or optimize the export process:

Table 4.3—Optimizing the export process	
Function	**How to reduce cost/complexity/time**
1. Product development	Purchase or licence external technology and engage external specialists in market research—if they are familiar with the target market, co-development of a product with a foreign partner in the target market might be possible.
2. Manufacturing	Move from serial to parallel manufacturing processes, design modular products for parallel manufacturing and rapid assembly, transfer labour-intensive functions to countries with lower labour costs, subcontract parts of the process to external suppliers, produce components simultaneously in different locations for final assembly close to the customer.
3. Warehousing	Use JIT inventory processes to reduce time in storage and use electronic and automated systems for coding, handling, storing and identifying products. Plan warehousing function to determine optimal geographic locations (what can or should be stored in the country of origin, what can or should be stored close to the customer).
4. Marketing	Engage agents or distributors located in the foreign market to handle marketing functions. Use advanced logistics to improve delivery times, offer product customization or enhance product-related services.

Table 4.3—Optimizing the export process	
Function	**How to reduce cost/complexity/time**
5. Order processing	Use advanced telecommunications technology and e-commerce or EDI technologies to deal with order processing.
6. Shipment preparation	Engage the services of a freight forwarder to handle some or all of the functions involved in this step. Automate warehousing to enhance efficiency, treat the warehouse as a staging area for grouping and assembling shipments and employ advanced packaging and bar-coding techniques to protect the product while identifying it for easy picking and preparation.
7. Transportation	Engage a freight forwarder to deal with carriers and optimize shipping arrangements through discounts on long-term contracts or consolidation of small shipments into larger ones. Use containers, pallets and state-of-the-art handling equipment.
8. Reporting to customs	Engage the services of a customs broker or consultant to process the goods through foreign customs.
9. Delivery to customers	Engage a foreign distributor to handle the goods after they leave customs. Ensure that facilities at the receiving end can handle the shipment appropriately. Engage a foreign distributor or joint-venture partner to assume responsibility for delivering goods to the customer. Consider using facilities in the target country for storage, final assembly and customization.
10. Payment processing	Engage the services of an export house to handle invoicing and payments processing. Use EDI for the documentation needed to process payments.

View from Across the Table: Seeing the Deal As Your Trading Partner Does

Is trade about besting your partner, or win-win?
International trade and global commerce are increasingly conducted in an environment shaped by the principles and practices illustrated in the concepts of value chain and integrative trade. The global business environment today is underpinned by partnerships and interdependence. Trade is less about net competition and "who won," and increasingly (both commercially and between governments) about maximizing overall value and benefit.

Global sourcing models supported by local investments and resource access through outsourcing arrangements are expensive and time-consuming to arrange and maintain. These systems are not built for the short-term or with one-off transactions in mind: they are for the long term and are intended to support lasting commercial partnerships and relationships.

Just as the best philosophers and statesmen of old could argue the positions of their opponents—often more eloquently than their own positions—importers and exporters today must be acutely aware of the objectives, concerns and expectations of their partners.

The global business environment today is a complex and highly integrated ecosystem, and traders who take a purely competitive and combative approach to global commerce will erode value and will eventually run out of business "partners" due to the range of partnership options offered by enlightened enterprises active in international trade and global commerce.

A small Canadian consultancy in international trade uses the tag line "Winning Partnerships in World Trade," with the word "winning" serving as both a verb and an adjective. Collaboration within competition is the way of the present. The global business environment demands a value-based approach to international business, and effective partnerships create value.

Figure 4.4—Global supply-chain checklist

☑ Understand the evolution of supply chains, including the shift of leverage from producers to consumers.

☑ Appreciate the relationship between the physical and financial supply chains and the emerging focus on the information supply chain.

☑ Understand the roles and responsibilities of the major "actors" in the supply chain.

☑ Understand the partnership-based supply chain and the importance of technology as an enabler.

☑ Assess the implications of integrative trade.

☑ Understand the main processes related to import and export transactions.

☑ Apply the understanding acquired to be able to see a transaction or deal from the perspective of your trading partner.

Chapter Summary

Transformational forces are reshaping the conduct of international trade and global commerce: tighter integration and interdependence, global sourcing in every industry sector imaginable and the increasing interconnection of import, export and investment activity on a global basis.

Integrative trade is a reality that will shape and drive the conduct of international business. Global supply chains continue to evolve to meet the new realities, and the character of imports and exports, including the "differences," continue to merge and to blur their points of distinction.

Exercises

Exercise 1 (class discussion)
Discuss the concept of integrative trade. Illustrate its practical implications by selecting a manufacturing industry and considering its sourcing practices and their impact on the industry's export development efforts and successes.

(Estimated time 5 minutes)

Exercise 2 (class discussion)
Consider the impact and contribution of outsourcing (including offshoring) on the global business environment. Consider its role in the interdependent global business environment, specifically in terms of the value chain, in a service industry sector.

(Estimated time 5 minutes)

Exercise 3 (class discussion)
Wal-Mart is arguably one of the leading global supply-chain innovators in the world. Read the *Financial Times* article below on Wal-Mart's recent entry into India and the work in small groups (three or four people) to discuss this case and answer the following questions:

1. Who are the stakeholders (i.e., groups and/or individuals who can affect or who are affected by the achievement of the Wal-Mart's objectives) in this situation?

2. What impact will this undertaking have on each of those stakeholders (positive and negative)?

3. Does Wal-Mart appear to be committed to sustainable business (why or why not)?

4. What sort of additional actions might the company take to balance the need for business growth with the needs of the various stakeholders?

(Estimated time 15 minutes)

Wal-Mart in joint venture for India

Wal-Mart has succeeded in getting its toe in the door of the Indian market, via a long-planned joint venture with local partner Bharti Enterprises.

The world's largest retailer stressed it would "work with and develop local supplies and create local beneficiaries along the supply chain," in an apparent effort to play down controversy over the potential disruptive effects of corporate retail in India.

Wal-Mart in joint venture for India *(continued)*

The 50-50 joint venture, called Bharti Wal-Mart, is a "wholesale cash-and-carry" business that will use Wal-Mart's back-end logistics technology, inventory systems, cold chain infrastructure, truck tracking and fuel management.

Bharti, one of India's largest companies and owner of Airtel, the country's leading mobile phone operator, recently announced investments of up to $2.5 billion in Bharti Retail, its own 100 percent-owned supermarket chain that will be supported by Wal-Mart's logistics and supply chain technology through a agreement.

The plans come amid controversy over Wal-Mart's entry into India. Activists and small trade associations insist corporate retailers will disrupt millions of Indians whose livelihoods depend on farming and retail dominated by small "mom-and-pop" shops.

Manmohan Singh, Indian prime minister, this spring called for an independent study on corporate retail advances into the country. The report is yet to be finalised.

Dharmendra Kumar, head of India FDI Watch, which opposes big retail, said: "The government is still to know the likely impact of corporate retail. In the meantime, they are allowing corporations to expand their retail plans at an alarming pace."

India FDI Watch and other activist groups plan demonstrations across India this week. Hakim Singh Rawat, president of the Hawkers Association, said street traders would be hit hard by Bharti Wal-Mart and warned the Indian government about favouring "only a few huge corporations."

Opponents insist the joint venture is a "back door" into India's $300 billion retail industry. Under current law, "multi-brand retailers" that sell more than one brand of products are barred from India. Single-brand retailers such as Benetton and Nike are allowed 51 percent foreign direct investment.

In the next seven years, Bharti Wal-Mart plans to open 10 to 15 wholesale centres in smaller cities, starting late next year. A typical facility will sell groceries, stationery, clothing and consumer durables. The companies did not disclose details of their investment in the joint venture.

Formal shops, or "organized retail," comprise just 2–3 percent of India's $300 billion retail industry. The majority of shopping takes place in small "mom-and-pop" shops, roadside vendors and open air market. About 35–45 percent of farm products never make it to market because of lack of cold storage and poor transport and roads.

Copyright The Financial Times Ltd. All rights reserved.

Source: Yee, Amy. "Wal-Mart in joint venture for India." *The Financial Times*, August 6, 2007. New Delhi. Reprinted with permission

References/Resources

Aberdeen Group: CFO's Agenda for Global Trade Benchmark Report, September 2005 (www.aberdeen.com)

DM Review, 04/2005 (www.dmreview.com/article_sub. cfm?articleId=1023896) (PricewaterhouseCoopers)

Sturgeon, Timothy J. *Conceptualizing Integrative Trade: The Global Value Chains Framework.* As prepared for the CTPL conference, December 2006

IDS UK (www.ids.ac.uk)

Institute of Development Studies, U.K. (www.ids.ac.uk/ids/global/ valchnconcep1.html)

Supply Chain Basics—Western Economic Diversification Canada (www.e-future.ca/alberta/pdf/efc_supply_chain_basics.pdf)

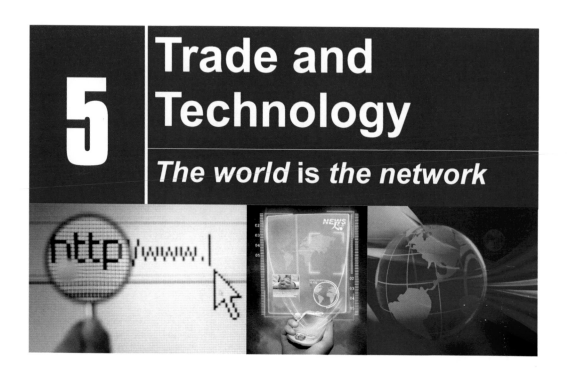

Chapter Objectives

- Describe how network technologies and tools have changed the fundamental processes of trade development activities
- Understand the transformation of the global supply chain as a result of technology
- Realize the heightened levels of market access and competition as a result of technology
- Identify the various technology tools that enable global trade

Overview

Advancements in technology have historically led to advancements in the way nations conduct trade with one another. Over four thousand years ago, the use of camel trains on the Silk Road facilitated early regional trade between China and its economic partners for millennia. The introduction of sailing ships had a profound impact, not only on the transport of goods, but also on international trade law. The rise of independent shipping carriers resulted in new legal and documentary processes, most notably, the bill of lading. Early "technological" advancements such as these shaped many of the transport, legal and financial activities of global trade that have remained essentially the same for centuries. More recent advances, such as the widespread use of the telephone and later the fax machine also made an enormous impact on how global business was done over a number of decades.

Illustrating one way that the Internet has created ultra-niche markets and trade opportunities, the first item ever sold on eBay in 1994 was a broken laser pointer, for U.S.$14.83. When the founders of eBay contacted the buyer and asked whether he understood that the product was broken, the reply was, "I'm a collector of broken laser pointers."
Source: ebay.about.com

In contrast, it took only six years for the Internet to penetrate almost all aspects of global business within the world's wealthier economies. Once it did, any business or individual potentially became a global trader. New companies with new user-friendly online tools emerged, turning home offices into home-based trading companies. The arrival of virtual companies like eBay revolutionized online trading and resulted in the birth of hundreds of thousands of small businesses, many of them representing an explosion in the number of new exporters and importers. Out of necessity, people who had never thought about global logistics or foreign payments began to familiarize themselves with the options, the risks and the opportunities. If there was a product to sell, no matter how obscure, there was a means to find someone to buy it. And for established businesses, it began to dawn on them that a market segment could be as small as a single individual, located anywhere on the globe, with infinitely customized needs and the expectation that they could find the perfect product to fulfill those needs.

In developed economies throughout the world, the application of network technologies has changed the nature of trade processes and trade opportunities with near-ubiquitous use. While networked business technologies such as Electronic Data Interchange (EDI) were once used only by larger businesses and multinational corporations, the democratizing effect of today's network technologies on the global supply chain has given even the smallest companies access to powerful business-development tools. This same effect has also been a major contributor to the rapid shift of many developing countries towards becoming viable markets on the global stage.

Technology: The Transformation of Trade

Electronic Data Interchange (EDI) The computer-to-computer transmission of (business) data in a standard [machine readable] format.
Source: UN/EDIFACT

The advent of the digital age has brought about a tremendous amount of business- and industry-level restructuring. National economies are more closely linked than ever before. The concept of the supply chain has become far more decentralized and globalized as companies have greater access to new markets and more cost-effective sources of supply to boost competitiveness. The value of data and the activities involved in analyzing, manipulating and managing it have allowed many developing nations to move beyond the bonds of their traditional export sectors. The world economy has become transnational, shaped more by the flow of money, credit, investment and information than strictly by the trade of goods and services.

A new mindset: If it's not on the Internet, it doesn't exist

Digital networks are certainly not the only drivers of technology innovation, but the "global network mindset" is a by-product of their evolution over the last ten years. It is already taken for granted—although not entirely accurately—that any product or service is available somewhere, and that most information can be found on the Internet. Conversely, there is an already widespread assumption that if particular information or a specific product cannot be found online, then it will be difficult or impossible to find at all. Despite the potential inaccuracies of these assumptions, this new mindset is the reason that daily activity increasingly involves "plugging into" one digital network or another. More importantly, it is also the reason for the transformation of how buyers—whether industry or consumer based—research, analyze, value and purchase goods and services worldwide.

How big is the Internet audience?

To gain an understanding of the size of the potential online market and the opportunities for connecting with customers and suppliers around the world, one must begin with an appreciation for the approximate size of the Internet population.

A January 2007 estimate indicated that the number of individual worldwide users of the Internet over the age of 15 totalled almost 747 million (see the following table for a breakdown by country). This estimate does not include users who accessed the global network via public terminals, such as Internet cafés, or by using mobile technologies such as cell phones and Personal Digital Assistant (PDA) devices.

Table 5.1—Top ten countries by Internet penetration: unique visitors age 15+			
	Jan. 06 (000s)	**Jan. 07 (000s)**	**Percentage change**
Worldwide	*676,878*	*746,934*	*10%*
United States	150,897	153,447	2%
China	72,408	86,757	20%
Japan	51,450	53,670	4%
Germany	31,209	32,192	3%
United Kingdom	29,773	30,072	1%
South Korea	24,297	26,350	8%
France	23,712	24,560	4%
India	15,867	21,107	33%
Canada	18,332	20,392	11%
Italy	15,987	18,106	13%

Note: Excludes traffic from public computers such as Internet cafés or access from mobile phones or PDAs.

Source: comScore, Inc. World Metrix, March 2007. (www.comscore.com)

Acceptance of digital commerce

Certainly the most well-known example of the transformative effect of technology on trade is the activity of global electronic commerce, also known as e-commerce or e-comm. E-commerce is not strictly a phenomenon of the Internet and the World Wide Web, though the concept has evolved over the last 30 years. Pre-Internet technologies, such as EDI standards, have been used since the early 1970s to conduct commercial and non-commercial transactions by some electronic means, such as the exchange of purchase orders and invoices between two parties or the transfer of medical information. The 1980s and early 1990s saw rapid mass-market acceptance of electronic banking tools, such as Automated Banking Machines (ABMs) and telephone banking.

While the ongoing issue of business transaction security over mainly open networks has caused a slower adoption rate than these earlier, consumer-focused types of e-commerce, the value of trade that is facilitated through the Internet continues to grow. The global market for e-commerce spending alone is predicted to grow beyond U.S.$10 trillion by 2010.[24] Increasing levels of trust in digital networks has helped set the stage for the adaptation of the Internet to form a new platform for commercial activity and new tools for conducting almost every aspect of global trade.

e-this and i-that: Has the Internet really contributed to increased global trade?

Between 1994 and 2001, while the use of the Internet for business was rapidly growing, there was a large increase in the value of exports as a percentage of gross world product (GWP). In 1994, international trade in goods, services and investment was 20 percent of GWP, or U.S.$5.9 trillion (in 1995 U.S. dollars). By 2001, this had increased to 29 percent, or U.S.$9.6 trillion. What is significant is that during the 15 years prior to this period, exports accounted for between 18 and 20 percent of GWP. While there is no definitive data to prove a link between these two events, analysis conducted by the same study reporting these figures supports the fact that countries that export more tend to have a higher level of Internet penetration than countries that export less.[25]

Altering the way the world works

What is more difficult to quantify is the immense impact that information technology has had over the last ten years on the way the world works to transact trade.

- **Communications.** Internet-based communication tools have enabled any company to become truly global in scope. While e-mail continues to be the most common online form of communication, instant text messaging, online audio and video conferencing, and Internet telephony are fast becoming mainstays of the global business toolkit. Not only do these tools provide more immediate connections with clients and collaborators around the world, but they are usually far more cost-effective than offline forms of communication. Instant connectivity has also affected the etiquette of global business. Companies are often expected to be responsive 24 hours a day, seven days a week, and the acceptable waiting time for responses to inquires has been considerably shortened.

---

[24] *Worldwide Internet Usage and Commerce 2007–2010.* IDC/International Data Group Inc., April 2007.
[25] Clarke, George R. G. and Wallsten, Scott J. "Has the Internet Increased Trade?" World Bank Policy Research Working Paper. February 2004.

- **Collaboration.** In manufacturing and service industries, aggressive global competition has forced companies of all sizes to be more productive, making effective collaboration essential. The Internet has allowed for greater and more frequent collaboration among customers and suppliers spread throughout the world. This high level of business interaction has not only transformed marketing, customer relationship management, trade financing and logistics, but has also allowed for greater remote distribution of internal business processes, such as production and sales for strategic or cost advantage. It is in this last area that the application of technology to the management of global supply chains is becoming commonplace.

- **Business development.** Communication and collaboration are the building blocks of networking, and networking is an effective means of opportunity development. No matter how advanced technology becomes, business always begins with connections between people. Numerous examples of online "social networks" targeted towards business users have emerged over the last couple of years. These social or contact networking platforms allow business users around the world to stay in touch with one another and to connect with one another through referral systems within communities of shared interest.

Clearly, the Internet provides an immense resource for market research and planning. From free government market briefs to in-depth analysis conducted by major marketing firms, any business can conduct a great deal of their marketing tasks from the desktop. An increasing number of high-quality sources of trade leads and procurement notices are also available for any geographic market.

- **Business transparency and competitive intelligence.** One of the fundamental steps to making use of the Internet for global business is the maintenance of a website. For years, companies have set out to achieve a balance between promoting a high-quality image and making sure not to give away competitive insights into the direction or strategy of the business. While this is largely still true today, there is a wealth of intelligence to be gained about potential customers, suppliers and competitors from company websites.

However, through a recent trend that is truly unique to the commercial Internet, many companies have begun to alter their Internet promotion strategy. The concept that has been dubbed "radical transparency" is demonstrated by companies that allow their employees to openly participate in as many targeted online forums as possible, such as in Internet discussion groups or through blogging, with the ultimate goal of enhancing a perception of expertise. Quite often, this practice has the double-edged effect of allowing for extraordinary levels of insight into a company's culture and attitude towards their marketplace.

Websites to visit:
Contact networking—
www.LinkedIn.com or
www.ecademy.com
Trade leads and
e-procurement—
www.Importers.com or
www.dgmarket.com or
www.sourcecan.com

Blogging, or web logging, is the activity of maintaining a public, online journal usually based on a specific topic. Blogging has become a major marketing tool of businesses that want to use their internal knowledge to build on perceptions of leadership.

Enhanced Global Supply Chain: From Manufacturing to Business-Process Outsourcing

This evolution of how global companies operate due to Internet and digital technologies is evidenced by the maturing of global supply-chain management processes and tools, and also by the accessibility of these tools to companies of all sizes and levels of sophistication. The digitization of the supply chain increasingly dictates how companies trade globally and how these activities are co-ordinated, measured and communicated. Real-time tracking of shipments, on-demand manufacturing and fully automated management functions between supply-chain partners are only a few examples of the tools available to literally any company today. Linking the real world to the virtual world, bar code scanning and Radio Frequency Identification Technology (RFID) microchips are being used to globally pinpoint everything from shipments of parts to crates of pineapples, and even people!

Global sourcing and supply includes the integration of sourcing, operations and design or development processes located in different countries. The information requirements may include goods and service specifications, required volumes, quality and standards data, delivery timelines and methods, packaging and labelling requirements, shipping documentation and so on.

Table 5.2—Typical reasons for global sourcing
• Achieving the best price or cost
• Profitability requirements
• Supply availability
• Supply quality
• Labour cost and availability
• Availability of technology
• Supplier responsiveness
• Level of market penetration
• Tax and other financial considerations
• Countertrade and other co-operative agreements

Source: Adapted from *Effective Global Sourcing and Supply for Superior Results,* Institute for Supply Management, 2006

Electronic Data Interchange (EDI)
Electronic automation of supply and value chains began with Electronic Data Interchange (EDI). EDI is defined as the company-to-company electronic exchange of business transactions in a machine-readable, standardized format.

Some sources claim that EDI originated from the use of Morse code by the railways and Western Union to transmit business information in the mid-1800s. In a very basic sense, the dots and dashes of Morse code are an early representation of digital binary data.

A number of international standards define how computers send, receive and process business documents without the need for human intervention.

In the late 1960s and early 1970s, a number of large corporations began to realize that the use of electronic systems to transmit business documents in a standardized format could improve the domestic and international supply chain through quicker communications, improved customer service, reduced paperwork and faster processing of supplier quotes and sales. Examples of the types of documents exchanged between buyers, suppliers and other stakeholders include, among others:

- purchase orders;

- design specifications;

- production line status notifications;

- invoices;

- shipping notifications;

- export and import documentation;

- carrier waybills;

- funds transfers; and

- health insurance claims.

These first adopters represented a handful of industries that typically managed remote operations as part of their overall business model, such as transportation, banking and the automotive industry. General Motors and K-mart were among the pioneers of the integration of EDI technology into all aspects of the supply chain.

Early instances of EDI were largely proprietary, and the systems and data sets that were developed were unique to each industry or even to individual supply chains. By the early 1980s, it became clear that more structured EDI standards were required to allow for greater interaction across industry sectors and national boundaries. While a number of international organizations and business associations have worked to establish appropriate standards, there is no single, unifying structure for EDI interactions.

Two of the most common standards used for EDI today are UN/EDIFACT (the United Nations Directories for Electronic Data Interchange for Administration, Commerce and Transport) and the ANSI X12 standard first drafted by the U.S. Transportation Data Coordinating Committee.

Challenges for smaller firms

For smaller domestic and global suppliers, engaging EDI solutions was—and still can be—a very costly venture. For example, smaller automotive parts manufacturers had to invest in expensive computer systems and software and in expert staff that understood the EDI standards in use by General Motors if they wanted to continue to respond to requests for quotation (RFQs). Often, these companies would act as suppliers to a number of other large buyers, requiring them to interact with numerous other proprietary systems and standards for electronic transfer of documentation.

The Value-Added Network (VAN)

A major evolution of EDI to ease the costs of hardware and software acquisitions, data security and multiple proprietary formats was the emergence of the Value-

Added Network (VAN) within the EDI model. For smaller businesses where the supply volumes are relatively low, an investment in EDI may not be justified by the efficiencies that could be achieved. VANs help to reduce the complexities of participating in EDI networks.

A typical EDI network may be linked by a number of VANs. These networks reduce the technology and skills burden on the company by translating the transactions moving between systems that employ different hardware, software and electronic transport standards. VANs also provide an extra layer of security by acting as a buffer between the senders and receivers at either end of the communication path.

The open RosettaNet standard is named for the Rosetta stone. Created in 196 B.C. and rediscovered in 1799, the Rosetta stone is an early translation "technology." The message carved on the stone was written in three different Egyptian scripts, which later allowed modern researchers to better understand each of the ancient writing forms.

Figure 5.3—An EDI model incorporating a value-added network interaction

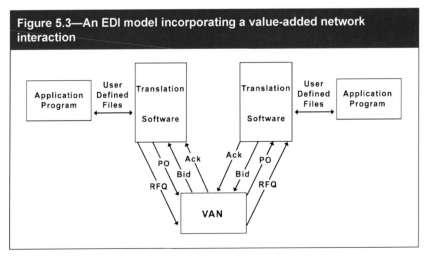

Source: *Electronic Data Interchange: Concepts and Effects*. The Internet Society (ISOC). www.isoc.org

Extensible Mark-up Language (XML) is a mark-up language for electronic documents containing structured information. Unlike HTML, the original mark-up language of the World Wide Web, XML provides for customized tagging of various types of information that may be contained within a document, allowing it to be used for virtually any kind of information exchange between otherwise incompatible systems.

Value-Added Services (VAS)

Value Added Services, or VAS, complement VAN systems by easing the skills challenges for the business. EDI software can be expensive, and the common formatting standards are complex. If a company is using the X12 standard, for instance, it must still have employees that understand the X12 data set and can properly format documents for transfer. A VAS can offer this and other EDI-related services as an outsourced function of the business, which may allow smaller companies to integrate with EDI networks at a far lower cost and with greater efficiency.[26]

The Rosetta stone goes digital

Another key development in EDI, again facilitated by the progression of Internet technologies, was the foundation of the RosettaNet consortium in the late 1990s. The core objective of the consortium is to guide the definition of a standard set of supply-chain business processes so that a platform-independent method of binding e-commerce global trading partners can be formed.

---

[26] Adapted from *Electronic Data Interchange: Concepts and Effects*. The Internet Society (ISOC). (www.isoc.org)

RosettaNet standards are developed by users for users, allowing for greater speed, efficiency and reliability. They enable greater collaboration and improved communication between trading partners. Non-proprietary and freely available to the public on the RosettaNet website (www.rosettanet.org), the standards encompass data dictionaries, implementation frameworks, and XML-based business-message definition sets and process specifications.[27]

As with the benefits of VANs, the introduction of RosettaNet standards to the EDI world have resulted in greater accessibility and cost savings for small- to medium-sized enterprises that need to maintain EDI links with suppliers and customers. The RosettaNet consortium comprises over 1,000 member companies representing almost every industry and every type of trade service, from global-payment to logistics services, and is global in scope. More and more large corporations support the standard, and therefore smaller suppliers are no longer at the mercy of costly proprietary systems imposed upon them by their supply-chain partners.

The Internet and the services boom

Near-worldwide penetration of the Internet and the ongoing development of devices that access it is arguably the most important factor in the expansion of the global services economy.

The intangible nature of the services sector naturally lends itself to its own transformation to digital bits and bytes. By extension, the Internet allows for not only the global marketing and delivery of services, but also for the creation of global services supply chains, business networks and other forms of collaboration.

Table 5.4—Examples of Internet-enabled services trade	
Architectural services	Competitive architectural firms have been producing and transferring drawings electronically for some time, allowing for faster modification of specifications, duplication of sketches and rescaling of plans. More recent uses include the development of intranets for ongoing consultations, not only with domestic and international clients, but also with all members of a project team throughout the life of the project. Virtual reality modelling software is also being used to allow for virtual tours and engineering analysis and testing prior to finalizing plans.
Commercial, education and training	While accurate measurement of services trade, not to mention services traded on the Internet, is difficult at best, estimates by the Gartner Group Inc. indicated that at least half of all training was conducted via the web in 2005. Delivery has shifted from in-person presentations to self-paced, learner-centred multi-media training packages. Popular modalities for export include CD-ROMs (as portable multimedia tools) and web-based training supported by video-conferencing, file-sharing and voice-over-Internet (VoIP) technologies. One of the challenges in international delivery is the issue of managing multiple languages, which has in turn spurred the growth of Internet-based translation-service networks.

---

[27] From the RosettaNet. (www.rosettanet.org)

Table 5.4—Examples of Internet-enabled services trade *(continued)*	
Computer, software and other IT services:	By their very nature, computer service firms are extensive users of enabling technologies, some of which they create themselves. Competitiveness is presently linked to using non-proprietary platforms for applications to ensure interoperability. Innovative technologies used in support of export earnings focus particularly on enhanced uses of the Internet, including developing and managing extranets in rapid-growth sectors like call centres. Firms are equipping Internet service providers with value-added features such as audio and video conferencing, the scheduling of virtual meeting rooms and enhanced security features for their customers. In 2005, the estimated global export of computer, software and IT services from all reporting countries was valued at just over U.S. $78 billion.[1]
Consulting engineering	Consulting engineers have tended to follow their clients' adoption of enabling technologies. Computer-aided design (CAD) has made international design partnerships possible as well as the electronic transmission of blueprints and designs. Through CAD, engineering firms are able to reduce drafting time, increase accuracy, and achieve greater design-phase flexibility, ultimately resulting in faster project turnaround, higher quality and greater profitability. Newer technology uses include creating secure extranets for virtual client consultations and effective project management. Advances in and greater accessibility to high-bandwidth global networks has also facilitated real-time design collaboration between remote locations through the transfer of very large amounts of data.
Geomantic/ GIS	Many of the enabling technologies for remote sensing and satellite technology industries, such as intranets, extranets and CD-ROMs are a part of daily business. Access to online spatial data, as well as the digital delivery of mapping and reports, is assumed. Competitive firms are able to manage distributed geographic information in response to remote on-line queries. Newer technologies include electronic journals and the use of graphic tools, space-imaging technologies, Advanced Network Technologies (ANT) and the Internet to demonstrate capabilities using virtual reality and consumer-targeted services such as Google Maps.

Table 5.4—Examples of Internet-enabled services trade *(continued)*	
Management consulting	Management consulting firms tend to be on the cutting edge in the use of enabling technologies, as they advise clients on the technology and need to model its use themselves. Even consulting firms without a technology-related practice are finding electronic accessibility to clients a must and corporate websites an important tool for enhancing credibility. Management consulting firms are also likely to use a wide range of software tools, including presentation, database, document- and project-management software. Leading edge technology uses focus in two areas: research and overhead reduction. To remain competitive, management-consulting firms rely on data mining to identify trends and on websites that incorporate client interaction. Smaller management consulting firms in particular are using a range of online technologies to create a virtual presence, thereby lowering overhead.

[1] 2007 International Trade Centre UNCTAD/WTO estimate, based on International Monetary Fund (IMF) data collected for 64 reporting countries in 2005.

Source: Adapted from *Enabling Technology and Trade in business and professional services*. Industry Canada, www.strategis.gc.ca

Offshore Business Process Outsourcing (BPO)

The outsourcing of services is not a new phenomenon, but the enhancement of the Internet is responsible for not only the expansion of the industry and the overall services boom, but also for the creation of new economies within the developing world. For years, companies have been outsourcing business functions such as payroll processing, check processing, insurance claims processing and more. BPO covers a wide range of IT-enabled services that are related to some form of business process. It encompasses mature industry segments such as payroll transaction processing, and less mature segments such as client relationship management and call-centre operations.

BPO is not itself a technology market, although services that target the Information and Communications Technology (ICT) sector are certainly among the biggest growth contributors. BPO is a combination of "people," "processes" and "technology," which in turn also describes the general nature of service industries as a whole. Regardless of the mode of service delivery, the topic of BPO exports is now synonymous with global online services delivery.

The Internet and other digital technologies have also accelerated the maturity of the BPO marketplace. The packaging of BPO offerings has experienced a shift in the last few years, from being primarily vendor-driven to a more demand-driven market. New sub-segments, niche services and multi-process packages are appearing at a rapid rate because of customer demand for added value in back-office operation management. For instance, processes such as payroll, employee benefits and recruiting, which were once offered as single outsourced services, are now becoming more commonly included within higher value, multi-process human-resource BPO offerings.

Just-in-time (JIT), is "an inventory control system [or strategy] that controls material flow into assembly and manufacturing plants by co-ordinating demand and supply to the point where desired materials arrive just in time for use. Developed by the auto industry, it refers to shipping goods in smaller, more frequent lots."
Source: Forbes (www. forbes.com)

Online Purchasing and E-Trade Platforms

The Internet has not only made seamless supply chains in the form of EDI-type solutions more accessible and more affordable, but it has also resulted in the creation of new and highly competitive business models that have altered the course of most industries by bringing the supplier and the customer closer together. The Internet-based tools that allow for this tighter global integration of producer and end-user have made it possible for even the smallest companies to plan and apply their own unique strategies for online collaboration. An illustrative example of one small company—now a very large company—that has used the Internet to create a new and often-mimicked global business model is Dell Computer Corporation.

"Gotta get a Dell": Selling direct and just-in-time

The enormous global success of Dell is only partly due to creative and memorable advertising campaigns. The company that Michael Dell founded in 1984 is partly responsible for pulling the computer retail industry from the grasp of IBM, which enjoyed a near-monopoly in earlier years. Dell's accomplishment is a well-known example of how direct sales and just-in-time manufacturing strategy transformed one of the world's highest grossing industries.

In 1996, just three years after being cited as one of the top-five computer systems makers in the world, Dell put this strategy on the desktops of its customers by introducing web-based purchasing and order fulfillment. By the next year, Dell shipped its 10-millionth system, and by 2000, Dell's Internet sales reached U.S.$50 million per day, while at the same time being named the number one global shipper of computer workstations. With Dell's application of e-commerce and online order tracking technologies, the industry—and many others, such as amazon.com in the online retail book industry—was transformed once again.[28]

The Internet cuts out the "middle man"

By shifting primary sales to the Internet, Dell put its alteration of the manufacturing supply chain to the test through disintermediation, which is essentially the removal of the "middle man." In this model, gone were the retail distributors and resellers. While not an entirely unique approach, Dell was one of the first companies of the "new economy" to realize that the Internet vastly improves the viability of the direct sales strategy. Through Dell's successful example, traditional value-added services in the global supply chain all but lost their value and were forced to adapt to this new e-reality of worldwide supply and demand.

Exactly the right place at exactly the right time

Rapidly decreasing component costs and competitive price cuts for fully built computer systems were a major threat for smaller companies seeking to increase their market share against the dominance of companies like IBM. A leaner, more efficient production line was needed, from parts warehousing to product shipping, to increase profit margins if Dell was going to survive. With a just-in-time approach to parts procurement at its core, Dell developed a "build to order" approach for every computer system it sold. Not only did this represent yet another alteration of its supply-chain strategy, but it also required full modularization of its product design and build process. Again, Dell's online

---

[28] Dates obtained from the website of Dell Inc. (www.dell.com)

ordering system facilitated the strategy. Consumers and businesses use Dell's website to customize almost every aspect of the transaction, including

- the components to be used;

- the number of systems required;

- the desired amount of after-sales service;

- the preferred shipping method for the final product; and

- the method of payment and financing.

Rather than pre-purchasing and stocking a massive supply of component parts at enormous cost, the introduction of the online ordering system allowed Dell to quantify what parts were needed when, and from which supplier, based on in-depth and real-time analysis of trends in customer choices. Only the most common components require regular stocking, while Dell's electronic vertical supply network automates the remainder of the order and fulfillment activities. During the build process, Dell uses wireless RFID tags to electronically track every step of the production of every system using every component received from suppliers. As added value for the end-user, this same data are pushed to Dell's website so that the customer can monitor the assembly and shipping of the purchase.

A model of technology application for global competitiveness

Dell's integration of supply, production and purchasing technologies—many of them Internet-based—created the most competitive company in the computer industry, as outlined below.

- A direct-sales-via-Internet strategy was refined to remove retailers and distributors from the mix, thus maintaining a higher per-unit profit margin.

- Their online e-commerce systems were linked to an EDI network of part suppliers to drive just-in-time delivery of components. This greatly reduces the pre-purchase, warehousing and inventory tracking costs.

- An Internet-based "build to order" approach was used. Combined with its EDI-powered supply network, this level of buyer customization allows Dell to stay ahead of the curve in an industry where products quickly become obsolete, resulting in less waste inventory.

- A highly functional e-commerce website was developed that takes almost every customer need into account, from questions about the product to financing the purchase. Because the website accomplishes the work of a number of departments within an offline sales strategy, the product almost sells itself.

- A personal brand was built with its customers. The marketing affects of Dell's online direct sales, combined with almost total buyer customization, has resulted in strong brand loyalty because:

    - customers perceive a high degree of company transparency—they know exactly what is going into the product and they can "watch" every step of the production and delivery process online;

Radio frequency identification, or RFID, refers to technologies that use radio waves to automatically identify people or objects. The most common method is to store a serial number that identifies a person or object on a microchip that is attached to an antenna (the chip and the antenna together are called an RFID transponder or an RFID tag). The antenna enables the chip to transmit the identification information to a reader. The reader converts the radio waves reflected back from the RFID tag into digital information that can then be passed on to computers that can make use of it. *Source: Adapted from The RFID Journal (www.rfidjournal.com)*

- there is only one company to deal with for both manufacturing and for after-sales service and support;

- Dell's website allows customers to view, research, build and purchase the product, and also to communicate directly with the company without leaving their desks; and

- the e-commerce website also helps to educate the customer about the product, thus removing a potential barrier to making the sale.

While Dell's production model remains relatively the same today, the company has realized that Internet-based direct sales are perhaps not a long-term sustainable model on their own. The company has an agreement with Wal-Mart to sell its computers through the ubiquitous retail chain, thus augmenting its mass consumer penetration, especially in light of Hewlett-Packard's gain on the market. While this does not affect the efficiency of Dell's supply-chain solution (a similar approach is used for Wal-Mart's supply needs, though in bulk orders), it shows that Internet sales alone are not necessarily enough to sustain the market share of even the largest of companies.

E-Marketplaces: The "Middle Man" Returns

Dell, like many companies large and small, increasingly utilizes outsourced solutions to access global supply and purchasing networks. Online vertical and horizontal trading portals and e-trade platforms exist for nearly every industry, and extend global sales channels to nearly every geographic market.

Figure 5.5—Creative use of an online marketplace

Dawson's Antiques is a 23-year-old small antique business. With the emergence of online auction sites, the owner foresaw the need not only to accommodate the Internet in their business strategy but also to take advantage of it in order to survive as a business. This came with the recognition that many of her clients were exposed to a wide range of antiques from competitors at online auction sites at prices lower than she was charging.

Meanwhile, Sotheby's, then a growing (and now one of the largest) online auction site, realized the merit of increasing its auction inventory to attract a bigger audience on the Internet. It revised its Internet strategy by opening its website, sothebys.com, to smaller dealers and auction sites, instead of competing directly with its competitors in the online auction business. With this approach, Sotheby experienced exponential growth in its inventory, which attracted a bigger market. Dawson's enlistment in Sotheby's was instrumental in expanding its client base. To make things easier, Sotheby's not only provided the website for its members (Dawson's included) but also arranged to handle all billing and collection. Under the new strategy, Sotheby's enlisted 4,660 members, which translated to an expansion of its auction inventory by five times the previous average stock or about 5,000 lots per week. For Dawson, e-business sales accounted for 25 percent of total sales in the first year and 50 percent less than a year later.

Source: Adapted from *e-commerce and e-business*. e-ASEAN Task Force, UNDP-APDIP, May 2003

The most well-known example of a self-service, horizontal online marketplace is eBay (www.ebay.com). Originating strictly as an online auction—before online payment and other digital value-added services had been created—eBay has now become a full-service, end-to-end e-trade portal. By offering automatic purchase notification, advanced online payment solutions, a variety of buying and selling options and delivery quotation and tracking tools, eBay has moved from being a website used by "garage sale hunters" to being a central hub for ad hoc supply chains and purchasing networks. Hundreds of thousands of small businesses around the world have become exporters by taking their business online through eBay's easy-to-use and cost-effective tools and services.

Online goods, services and commodities exchanges
While eBay caters mainly to a consumer and small-business marketplace, there are many other examples of online trading systems that have grown out of the needs of specific industries to more efficiently buy, sell and trade across all time zones. These e-marketplaces typically provide supplier search capabilities, virtual auction services, fulfillment services and electronic payment tools. Examples of well-established e-marketplaces include the following:

- Ariba (www.ariba.com): Sourcing, procurement, financial services and online horizontal marketplace

- Commerce One Inc. (www.commerceone.com): Turnkey software solutions for setting up customized online supplier networks and trading platforms

- eHub (www.ehubsoft.com): Online, managed supply and procurement

- ChemConnect (www.chemconnect.com): Third-party online commodity exchange for the chemical industry

- Elemica (www.elemica.com): Another online marketplace for chemical buying, selling and supply-chain management

- IBX Intergrated Business Exchange (www.ibxeurope.com): A leading European provider of e-sourcing solutions and online supplier network

- Onvia (www.onvia.com): Online marketplace for public sector procurement

- Axiom (www.americanexpress.com/axiom): Online marketplace for the travel services industry

- Ework (www.ework.com): Horizontal platform for global services acquisition

- Reardon Commerce (www.reardoncommerce.com): Online marketplace for suppliers of business and consumer services

Figure 5.6—Factors in selecting an appropriate e-marketplace

General requirements

1. Is there a statement of privacy on the website?

2. Does the e-marketplace describe its business on the website? For example, who are the shareholders, managers and clients/customers and what are the technologies used, etc.

3. Are the terms and conditions for doing business in the e-marketplace stated on the site?

4. Has the e-marketplace documented a process for resolving disputes that may arise?

5. Does the e-marketplace state the full contact details of the main office, including phone number, street address, and e-mail address?

6. Does the e-marketplace regularly review its services and update them to meet members' needs?

Ethical requirements

1. Does the e-marketplace have an ethical policy? An ethical policy should cover aspects like the e-marketplace's vision, mission and values/principles. It may also cover what stakeholders can expect if any illegal activities occur on the e-marketplace that breach the User Agreement.

2. Does the e-marketplace have an ethical code of conduct for employees in line with the ethical policy? This may include employees' being required to sign a declaration of secrecy.

3. Are the ethical policy and code of conduct communicated internally, and are they on the website?

4. Are processes for managing unethical and illegal behaviour defined?

5. Within the scope of the privacy policy, does the e-marketplace show respect for privacy by

   • using information collected from interested parties only for the purpose explicitly stated when collected;

   • keeping the information confidential through the use of the best available security measures;

   • enabling customers to manage their own personal information; and

   • avoiding the use of "spam" promotions by conducting e-mail marketing campaigns only to parties that have explicitly indicated that they wish to receive information about specific products or services?

Figure 5.6—Factors in selecting an appropriate e-marketplace *(cont'd)*

Infrastructure requirements

1. Has the e-marketplace documented the various methods used for collection of data and the intended purpose of such collected data?

2. Is the e-marketplace content comprehensive, correct and up-to-date?

3. Are the ICT systems under surveillance, and are there processes to ensure system availability and business continuity?

4. Are mechanisms implemented to protect the e-marketplace from malicious attacks?

Security requirements

1. Has the e-marketplace established and documented a policy regarding e-business security?

2. Are potential security risks identified and their significance periodically assessed? For example: viruses, unauthorised staff accessing data, control of user passwords, etc.

3. Does the risk assessment cover organizational, physical and logistical security?

4. Are responsibilities related to computer security in the organization and its service providers clearly defined?

5. Are physical assets and data protected from accidents and natural disasters? (With back-up systems and data-recovery processes, for example.)

6. Are relevant employees trained in their roles and responsibilities in business contingency plans?

7. Does the organization have suitable data-access controls and authentication methods?

8. Are there systems in place to back up software and data in case of any kind of threat?

9. Are secure data-disposal procedures in place (covering hardcopy, disks, diskettes, magnetic tapes and obsolete equipment)?

10. Does the organization monitor, analyze and review its performance with respect to security periodically? This might include:

   - security breaches;
   - network intrusions;
   - incident handling;
   - audit trails;
   - alarms;
   - intrusion response; and
   - virus protection.

Figure 5.6—Factors in selecting an appropriate e-marketplace *(cont'd)*

Process and organizational requirements

1. Does the e-marketplace reveal all relevant information that describes the characteristics of the products and services it offers and applicable terms for engaging in an electronic transaction?

2. Is support provided to help users make a request/order? This could be in the form of online training, telephone support or clear guidelines.

3. Is request/order acceptance confirmed to the seller and/or buyer? This may vary depending on the e-marketplaces' business processes.

4. Are terms and conditions of sale in accordance with local and/or international laws?

5. Does the e-marketplace keep track of customer requests/orders?

6. Is customer support provided? For example 24/7 help desk, scaled levels of support and support in the local region (relevant if the e-marketplace is global in scope).

7. Is customer feedback collected and analyzed? This feedback could be about various things, including business processes, functionality, site content and quality of support service provided by the e-marketplace.

8. Are customers informed at some stage in the business process:

   • about how collected information will be used?

   • that they can opt out from issuing information that is not necessary for transactions?

Web-marketing requirements

1. Has the e-marketplace identified potential markets and potential customers within those markets?

2. Have expectations of target customers relative to e-business policy been determined and analyzed?

3. Are competitors being monitored?

4. Does the organization have a marketing plan?

5. Does the organization have a communication strategy focusing on online brand value, website identity, reputation and web traffic?

Source: Adapted from *Self-assessment checklist for quality e-marketplaces*, version 2.0. eMarketServices, Innovation Norway, Sept. 2005

E-procurement

The process of searching for goods and services suppliers, inviting bids and placing orders using Internet technologies is referred to as e-procurement, and has become one of the most important aspects of the digital supply chain.

E-procurement is more than simply putting company purchasing decisions online; it is a means of connecting suppliers directly to the company's procurement needs and decision-making processes on an ongoing basis. For larger companies, e-procurement allows efficient centralization of procurement processes without removing the decision input of individual purchasing groups within the organization.

At the top level, e-procurement solutions give managers a way to track company buying patterns in real time and alter the approach as soon as might be necessary to achieve greater cost savings, quality or production efficiency. For example, since most of Dell's sales are to the purchasing departments of large companies, the company has essentially created an outsourced e-procurement service for its largest buyers.

Online tender systems

There are few governments, multilateral organizations and international financial institutions in the world that are not engaged in some form of e-procurement to disseminate tenders for public-sector goods and services. Frequently, government offices will dedicate a section of their own website to publishing tender notices and will sometimes provide suppliers with an online means of responding.

There are also a growing number of tender aggregators or feeding systems—both free and fee-based—that collect and disseminate global online tenders with added-value services such as e-mail notifications and response mechanisms. A few examples of these are the following:

- **Merx** (www.merx.com)
  Merx is a source for public and private tenders issued by Canadian federal, provincial and municipal governments and by U.S. federal, state and local governments. Most Canadian public tender information is provided free of charge. For U.S. government and North American private tenders, registration and payment are required.

- **dgMarket** (www.dgmarket.com)
  dgMarket is a major source of worldwide tender and consulting opportunities. While e-mail summary notifications are free of charge, dgMarket charges monthly or annual fees for up to 200 detailed tender notices per month. Users may

  - view tender notices for projects financed by the World Bank Group and other multilateral development banks;

  - view all larger government tenders of EU member states, the U.S. and many other countries; and

  - post procurement information for an international audience of suppliers.

The types of notices available include the following:[29]

- Prior Information Notice (PIN). Prior Information Notices, sometimes called General Procurement Notices (GPN) or Periodic Indicative Notices, are issued by some buyers to indicate that tenders (invitations to bid) are soon to follow.

- Invitation for Bids (IFB). An Invitation for Bids, Invitation to Tender or Contract Notice informs suppliers that bidding documents are available and provides them with information on availability of bidding documents, deadlines and other details of tendering procedures.

- Invitation for Prequalification (IPQ). An Invitation for Prequalification is issued when complex and detailed bids are required. IPQs inform suppliers that prequalification for a contract is open and invites them to apply. Only those suppliers who prequalify will be issued an invitation to bid on that contract at a future date. Prequalification is common for complex construction projects, turnkey plants and some specialized goods, such as complex information-technology systems.

- Request for Expressions of Interest (REI). Requests for Expressions of Interest provide consultants with general information about upcoming consulting assignments and invite firms to submit information on their capacity to perform the assignment. This information is used to help create a short list of qualified firms that will be issued the formal request for proposals.

- Contract Award (CA). Once a contract is awarded, the purchase authority publishes a contract award notice for this contract. Contract award notices provide information on the date the contract was awarded, the name of the successful supplier and the value of the contract.

- **SourceCAN** (www.sourcecan.com)
  SourceCAN is a tender-feeding and business-matching system and is free of charge to Canadian companies. It allows users to search for posted opportunities originating in Canada and abroad and from both government and private sector sources. Through user registration of business interests, a company can receive notifications of tenders within a pre-defined set of industries. In addition, SourceCAN provides

  - domestic and international partner search functions;

  - a virtual trade show where companies can upload text and multimedia promotional materials;

  - information on upcoming trade missions and events;

  - business news from around the world; and

  - links to e-business information and training.

---

[29] dgMarket (www.dgmarket.com/eproc/userGuide.do)

Ad hoc supply and e-procurement

Global accessibility, available bandwidth and programming protocols have reached a level that makes small- to large-scale procurement and supply in real time over the Internet a reality. Larger-volume exporters have the option to choose from a myriad of web-based supply-chain and e-procurement solutions, with turnkey technology and outsourced management services. However, for small- to medium-scale operators, it is possible to create ad hoc supply-chain networks and engage an e-procurement strategy at relatively low cost and on an "as-needed" basis.

This example represents a basic network of supply-chain communication and process of e-procurement using now-common Internet-based tools and services. The initial cost of setting up the system might range between U.S.$15,000 and U.S.$25,000, but the cost to maintain the system would be minimal. Where the cost of a larger-scale supply-chain management solution may outweigh the return on investment, smaller companies now have the ability to create a scenario such as this one to achieve efficiencies in production, communications and client management.

Table 5.7—An ad hoc supply/e-procurement scenario using web-enabled tools

1. **Online order received:** A small Canadian manufacturer and exporter of specialty running shoes receives an order from Germany, via its website, for a sample shipment of 100 units that incorporate new custom specifications. The manufacturer is given one week to respond with a price and delivery terms, given the custom requirements of the buyer.

2. **Supplier RFQ published online:** The Canadian company will need to engage its supply chain for the manufacture of the new moulded sole of the shoe. In a password-protected supplier section of its website, the manufacturer publishes a Request for Quotations (RFQ). The RFQ document is created in a secure, encrypted Portable Document Format (PDF), which contains the full specifications for the part, the materials to be used, the design/manufacture/delivery timelines and expectations and digitally signed form fields that the respondents can use to submit their individual quote details. The RFQ is accompanied by Joint Photographic Experts Group (JPEG) graphics of the draft designs. The company can either publish the RFQ as a blind bid or as an open auction to drive the bid prices down if cost is the most significant factor in developing the prototype.

3. **Suppliers notified:** As the RFQ is published to the website, an automatic notification is sent by e-mail to all relevant suppliers within the company's online database. The company may also seek out other potential suppliers through vertical online marketplaces, or by utilizing search engines such as Google, Yahoo! and AskJeeves.com.

4. **Suppliers bid:** Suppliers respond by accessing the manufacturer's website and downloading the RFQ documents to their own computer.

Table 5.7—An ad-hoc supply/e-procurement scenario using web-enabled tools *(continued)*

The suppliers then respond to the RFQ by filling out the standardized form fields within the PDF document on their screens. Once completed, the suppliers return to the manufacturer's website and submit their bids using a simple file-upload function. Each bidding supplier receives an automatic acknowledgement and confirmation via e-mail.

5. **Bids assessed:** Until the RFQ deadline, the manufacturer's online system reads and reviews the responses, in real time, and flags the quotes that score highest, based on a predefined set of criteria. The system that handles this process is based on XML, or Extensible Mark-up Language, which allows the standardized data in the PDF to be machine-read, imported into an online database and analyzed against the manufacturer's benchmarks for the quotation.

6. **Manufacturing process begins:** After a final human review, the supply contract is awarded. The running shoe manufacturer then responds to the German buyer with the price and delivery timelines for the sample shipment.

7. **Virtual meetings and project tracking:** The supplier that will make the new sole for the shoe is located in São Paulo, Brazil. The Canadian manufacturer and the supplier maintain contact through e-mail and by using free voice-over-Internet (VoIP) tools for teleconferences. During the design phase, the two parties use webcams and free video-conferencing software with on-screen whiteboard capabilities to review the CAD drawings and technical specifications of the new sole. The manufacturer is also able to stay up-to-date with the supplier's progress through a low-cost, web-based project management tool that reports on every phase of the process, based on input made by the supplier. This same tool is used by the manufacturer to give the German buyer insight into the production phase of its order, with timeline adjustments as necessary.

8. **Real-time shipment tracking:** For both the import of the soles into Canada from Brazil and the export of the final sample product to Germany, the manufacturer uses a worldwide logistics firm that offers a number of web-based tracking options with their services. Most of the customs, shipping and licensing documents are securely filled out and submitted online. During the guaranteed 10-day delivery timeline, the logistics firm provides real-time information on the ocean co-ordinates of the shipment, followed by its progress through customs clearance in Germany using barcode scans transmitted to a secure website so that both the manufacturer and the buyer can view the real-time status of the shipment.

9. **Delivery and payment:** The logistics firm updates the secure website to indicate successful delivery to the German buyer. With this notification, and based on the agreed-upon payment terms, the Canadian manufacturer transmits an electronic invoice to the buyer. Instant payment is made within the contracted terms to the manufacturer's bank account using an online payment system.

Security in the Virtual Marketplace

By initiating an aggressive global e-business strategy, customers, suppliers, contractors and business partners are routinely allowed access to critical business systems. The use of value-added networks within a networked supply chain and within vendor-based online trading communities minimizes the security risk through their own applications. However, small companies in particular tend to underestimate the risks of conducting trade over inherently open digital networks. By taking a risk-based approach rather than a purely operational one, security is considered, assessed and managed with the business and its goals in mind. The fundamentals of any security program are confidentiality, integrity and availability.

Building and maintaining trust and credibility at every point in the supply chain is a necessary element of successful business. One of the potential disadvantages of today's level of network connectivity is the increased opportunity for unauthorized access. The risks to business data have increased exponentially. By ensuring that the e-business strategy facilitates confidentiality, integrity and availability, these risks will be minimized and security efforts will not impede necessary online business interactions.

Typical security threats

The sources of online threats to any organization can be both internal and external. The main threats to information assets can be categorized as follows:

- **Internal and unintentional**

  - Uninformed workers can make mistakes, destroy information and expose confidential data and access to malicious websites.

  - Uninformed contract workers, if not fully briefed, can compromise security.

- **Internal and intentional**

  - Disgruntled employees might leave bugs and other malicious programming behind in the company network.

  - Technical contract workers may try to exaggerate work to increase their employment value.

  - Technical contract workers may request network access to do their job despite knowingly exposing the company network to security risks.

- **External and network-based**

  - Online criminals or hackers stealing credit card numbers and other financial data

  - Political activists or "hactivists"

  - Information brokers and competitive intelligence agents

  - Indiscriminate Internet viruses and "worms," commonly distributed via e-mail and false documents

"We are all security consumers, and the smarter consumers we are, the more we can make security into something that betters our lives instead of worsens it."
Source: Bruce Schneier, noted technologist and expert on digital and network security

The risks associated with e-mail

E-mail continues to be the dominant form of communication on the Internet, despite the growing use of "Voice over IP" (VoIP) or Internet telephony and video conferencing. While the convenience and cost advantages of e-mail remain, the risks caused by those seeking to do harm—whether indiscriminately or by targeting specific victims—are now well known.

A drawback of linking the business to the networked world is that such attacks, when successful, can have catastrophic effects, due to instantaneous and widespread infiltration of a company's information systems. A recent incident involving the electronic theft of an enormous amount of customer credit card data from a major North American department store chain was initiated by a virus-laden e-mail that eventually allowed the attackers "back-door" access to the company's credit-processing systems.

Since many such attacks occur through the receipt of unsolicited e-mails, computers protected by up-to-date Internet security software and spam filters are often the first line of defence. However, successful attacks are usually the result of uninformed employees inadvertently allowing malicious software to enter the network. Therefore, one of the most effective means of preventing e-mail-based attacks is to ensure that all employees are aware of a company-wide policy on the use of e-mail, such that

- e-mail communication using company computers and networks is limited to business use only;

- all unsolicited e-mail, regardless of whether it appears to have a business-related objective, is treated with a level of caution, especially if the e-mail includes one or more attached files;

- the person responsible for maintaining the company's network adheres to a predetermined update schedule of all security software;

- e-mails suspected of containing malicious software are never forwarded to another party on the network;

- mobile devices, such as notebook computers and personal digital assistants (PDAs), adhere to the network security policy;

- regular data backups are conducted in the case of an emergency; and

- all employees are aware of the response process should the network be breached by malicious software.

Determining the required level of network security

With the initial introduction of a network security plan, the following five-step process may be considered.

1. Analyze and assess the level of:

- Confidentiality—only authorized parties can read the details of transactions on the networked systems

- Integrity—unauthorized modifications of transactions are detected

- Availability—systems are reliable and recoverable

2. Determine the requirements:

- What needs to be protected?

- What business information requires a high level of confidentiality and integrity?

- What information and systems must be reliable and available?

3. Review the current state of the existing security program, if any:

- What is the company currently doing to ensure the confidentiality, integrity and availability of important business information and systems? Does management assume that the Internet service provider is taking care of security?

- What data are being protected? Employee data, customer data, business data?

- Are networked systems password protected?

- Are timely backups of critical data conducted?

- Who has restricted access to sensitive data?

4. Determine what the potential losses could be, including the impact on the company's reputation:

- What level of risk is the company willing to accept when weighed against the cost of network security measures?

5. Determine the cost threshold based on realistic assessment of the security threat to the business:

- What would the cost to the business be if other potential suppliers knew what was paid to the competition?

- What would happen if a competitor found out the next product line, procurement plan or market-entry strategy?

With a defined set of requirements and an understanding of the real threats to the business, the right mix of technical, procedural and organizational controls needed to meet security requirements can be determined. Does the security program address confidentiality, integrity and availability of business information and e-business systems? Unless there is in-house expertise, the company should consider consulting someone outside the company who can discuss the various technical options available and help evaluate offerings from different vendors. Not every piece of data that is potentially exposed can be completely secured. The appropriate controls should be devised based on the associated risk.

Table 5.8—Best practices for enterprise network-security management	
Authentication	Implement processes and procedures to authenticate, or verify, the users of the network. Potential techniques might include smart cards, secure tokens, biometrics or a combination of efforts.
Configuration management	Plan e-business architecture and deployment with security in mind. Manage configurations to know exactly what hardware, operating systems and software are in use; create robust access and software change controls; segment responsibilities; implement best practices; and do not use default security settings.
Training	Train all employees in the need for network security and ensure that security is factored into developing business operations. Foster an enterprise culture of safety and security.
Incident response	Develop an enterprise capability for responding to incidents, mitigating damage, recovering systems, investigating and capturing forensic evidence and working with law enforcement. Define the appropriate response for customers and suppliers to maintain trust and integrity.
Organization network	Organize security-management, IT-management and risk-management functions to promote efficient exchange of information and leverage corporate knowledge.
Network management	Create a regular process to assess, remediate and monitor the vulnerabilities of the network and consider developing automated processes for vulnerability reporting, patching and detecting insider threats. Internal and external IT security audits can also supplement these efforts.
Smart procurement	Ensure that security is embedded in the business operations and the systems that support them. Embedding security is easier than "bolting it on" after the fact.

Source: Adapted from the U.S. *National Strategy to Secure Cyberspace*. 2003

Defining the E-Business Plan

Trade in today's global environment necessitates consideration of the role that the Internet and other network technologies will play in all aspects of the international business plan. E-business planning should not be an afterthought and it should extend, support and amplify the overall global business objectives of the company. The following checkpoints should act as guidelines for building the company approach towards implementing an e-business strategy.[30]

---

[30] Adapted from *e-businessguide*, Australian Department of Communications, Information Technology and the Arts (DCITA), Information Economy Division.

E-business description

- How is the company currently using the Internet? How will it be using it two years from now? (e.g., e-commerce, marketing online, educating, providing access to services and products, etc.)

- Why does the company want to implement Internet technologies in the organization? (i.e., a brief statement on the e-business vision)

- How will the new e-business plan affect staff, customers, clients, suppliers and business partners?

Rationale

- Is there a detailed explanation of objectives? (e.g., to cut costs, save time, increase customer base, meet business requirements)

- How do the e-business objectives meet the overall objectives of the organization?

- How will the e-business meet stakeholders' needs or demands? (i.e., the results of market research into what the target audience wants and does not want in terms of online service and delivery)

Management

- Is there a statement as to who is ultimately responsible for the e-business, who will manage it and the people or organization maintaining it, and what committee, group or team will oversee it?

- Is there an outline of the management methodology/strategy to be adopted?(e.g., in meetings and communication)

- What are the risks, and how does the company intend to deal with them? (e.g., intellectual property and contracts with suppliers)

- Is there an outline of the schedule of the roll-out of the e-business plan?

Marketing strategy

- How will the use of e-mail and the website enhance the organization's existing marketing plan? What unique marketing tools will e-mail and the website provide that the organization has never had before?

- How will the e-business be promoted—with what strategies, to whom and when?

- What promotional features will be included in the website or e-mail to help drive traffic to the website? (e.g., e-mail subscriptions, virtual postcards)

- How do the website's look, feel and content complement and add value to the branding of the organization?

- What are the likely costs and required time allocations for implementing and monitoring the promotional strategies?

Resourcing
People
- Who will be involved in the development and maintenance of the e-business? What will their respective roles be? (e.g., updating, technical, promotion, etc.)

- What is the approximate time commitment required of each during the development and in the on-going maintenance of the e-business?

- What new skills and roles might be needed, how will they be met (re-training, outsourcing, engaging new staff) and what time and costs are involved?

Equipment
- What hardware or software may be required by the organization's staff in the development and maintenance of the e-business? (e.g., a computer and Internet connection for everyone in the office)

Funding
- What is the estimated dollar amount required to fund the establishment (or re-alignment) of the e-business and its on-going maintenance and promotion?

- Where will the funds come from?

Outsourcing
- What part (if any) of the redevelopment is to be outsourced, and how is the outsourcing to be conducted (e.g., open tender)?

Benefits of the e-business
- Who benefits?

- How will they benefit and over what time frame?

Revenue streams
- What, if any, are the likely revenue streams from the e-business over the next two to three years? (e.g., from sales, purchases of information, uptake of services)

- What features will be included to create these revenue streams (e.g., e-commerce, shopping carts)?

Efficiency gains
- What, if any, are the likely areas of efficiency gains resulting from the e-business, and what are the likely extent and nature of those gains? (e.g. 20 hours/month saved by providing online application forms, reduced number of inquiries, and automated processing)

Challenges and constraints
Technical
- What limitations should be placed on the range and sophistication of e-business features to accommodate the audience's level of computer power, browsers, plug-ins, Internet access speeds?

- What resourcing (time and money) is required to interface the organization's back-end databases, accounting systems etc. with the website?

- What degree of security of the website is required?

Legal
- Are there concerns about intellectual property and copyright? (e.g. ownership of the IP and copyright of the content and concepts to be placed in the website)

- What privacy laws and regulations does the site needs to comply with?

- What public legislation and regulations does website have to comply with and how will they impact the project?

Organizational changes
- What potential changes might result in the organization's market role, and how might these impact the e-business project over time?

- To what extent is the culture of the organisation conducive to change and to embracing the online world?

- What are the change-management plans?

Resources and timeframes
- Is there a plan for collating, editing and clearing all website content in time to meet milestones?

- What are the complexities and time involved in altering office workflow and processes to incorporate maintenance of the site?

- What special events or outside forces may challenge the milestones?

> "The Internet is at once a worldwide broadcasting capability, a mechanism for information dissemination and a medium for collaboration and interaction between individuals and their computers without regard for geographic location."
>
> Source: A Brief History of the Internet (www.isoc.org)

Competitors and collaborators
- To what extent do competitors and the status of their Internet strategies and websites affect the company's ability to meet the aims and vision for the online presence?

- Is there a possibility of collaborating? What are its mutual benefits?

Project evaluation
- What criteria will be used to judge the degree of success of the e-business? (e.g., 30 percent cost savings or reduction in staff time allocated to a particular area or task, level of site traffic equivalent to similar sites)

- Is there a measurement methodology in place? (e.g., who will conduct the evaluation and via what method—collection of statistics, surveys, focus groups, etc.)

- Who will report on the evaluation, when will they do it and in what format?

Chapter Summary

Within a very short time, the Internet and other global networks have become fully integrated into the global business environment. Regardless of the level of e-business integration that a company decides to achieve, it cannot be viewed as a discretionary option by any company that wishes to be competitive in global markets. To do so would be to ignore a fundamental component of the international business strategy.

Companies of any size can e-enable the business strategy—whether it is through the use of the Internet to conduct market research and identify buyers or to fully automate communications and interactions with suppliers and customers. Like any other aspect of the strategy, the approach should be weighed against the overall business objectives, management commitment, cost thresholds and capacity to manage risk.

Almost every country in the world is connected to a global network in one form or another. Whether it is through a desktop workstation, a PDA or a mobile phone, anyone using these devices to send and receive information is a potential customer—and a potential competitor.

Exercises

Exercise 1 (class discussion)
A common trend in the use of Internet tools for e-business is that many of these tools were originally created for personal, social or entertainment use. Taking this into account, an importer of handicrafts from a number of African nations has established a network of suppliers located in regions with consistent and reliable Internet connectivity. The imports are destined for re-export to niche Japanese markets. Given the level of sophistication of the supply network and the fact that the importer is a small business operation employing a staff of ten, describe some of the Internet tools they could use to maintain communications, track supply and delivery and facilitate payment in an ad hoc, low-cost supply network.

(Estimated time 5–10 minutes)

Exercise 2 (class discussion)
The Internet has brought markets closer together, linked suppliers directly to buyers and increased the speed at which business communication is done—at times to the point of being instantaneous, regardless of geographic location. What effect might this have in the context of doing business with different cultures that speak different languages and have different definitions of appropriate business etiquette?

(Estimated time 10 minutes)

Exercise 3 (class discussion)
Canada recently passed privacy legislation to protect consumers on the Internet. Read the brief description of the *Personal Information Protection and Electronic Documents Act* (below) and then discuss some of the reasons that this act might have been put in place.

(Estimated time 5–10 minutes)

Table 5.9—Office of the Privacy Commissioner of Canada

The *Personal Information Protection and Electronic Documents Act*, also known as PIPEDA, has been coming into effect in stages. In the first phase, the act applied to personal information about customers or employees in the federally regulated sector, such as banks and telecommunications companies. In the second phase, PIPEDA was extended to cover personal health information collected, used or disclosed by these organizations.

PIPEDA entered its third and final stage of full implementation in January 2004 and now covers all personal information of customers that is collected, used or disclosed in the course of commercial activities by private-sector organizations, except in provinces that have enacted legislation deemed to be substantially similar to the federal law. To date, this has happened only in Quebec, although it is expected that legislation in Alberta and British Columbia will soon be substantially similar.

The act applies to personal information collected, used or disclosed in the course of commercial activities, whether in the "real" world or on the Internet. It also applies to personal information disclosed to another province or country for profit or gain where the information is the subject of the transaction. The act specifies what information a website can collect from you and how. It also specifies how this information can be used. As well, it gives you control over how your personal information, including your e-mail address, is used.

The act in brief

Organizations covered by the act must obtain an individual's consent when they collect, use or disclose the individual's personal information. The individual has a right to access personal information held by an organization and to challenge its accuracy, if need be. Personal information can only be used for the purposes for which it was collected. If an organization is going to use it for another purpose, consent must be obtained again. Individuals should also be assured that their information will be protected by specific safeguards, including measures such as locked cabinets, computer passwords or encryption.

Complaints

An individual may complain to the organization in question or to the Office of the Privacy Commissioner of Canada about any alleged breaches of the law. The commissioner may also initiate a complaint if there are reasonable grounds.

Application to the Federal Court

After receiving the Office of the Privacy Commissioner of Canada's investigation report, a complainant may apply to the Federal Court for a hearing under certain conditions as set out in Section 14 of the act. The Privacy Commissioner of Canada may also apply to the Court on her own or on the complainant's behalf. The Court may order an organization to change its practices and/or award damages to a complainant, including damages for humiliation suffered.

Table 5.9—Office of the Privacy Commissioner of Canada *(continued)*

Audits

The commissioner may, with reasonable grounds, audit the personal information management practices of an organization.

Offences

It is an offence to

- destroy personal information that an individual has requested;

- retaliate against an employee who has complained to the commissioner or who refuses to contravene sections 5 to 10 of the act; or

- obstruct a complaint investigation or an audit by the commissioner or her delegate.

Source: Office of the Privacy Commissioner of Canada, www.privcom.gc.ca

References/Resources

A Brief History of the Internet (www.isoc.org/internet/history/brief.shtml)

Business 2.0 Magazine (www.business2.com)

Commerce One Inc. (www.commerceone.com)

ebiz.enable (www.strategis.gc.ca/ebizenable)

E-commerce Digest (www.ecommerce-digest.com)

The E-commerce Times (www.ecommercetimes.com)

IBX Intergrated Business Exchange (www.ibxeurope.com)

The Institute for Global Electronic Commerce (www.igec.umbc.edu)

ITbusiness.ca (www.itbusiness.ca)

The MIT Center for Digital Business (ebusiness.mit.edu)

Reardon Commerce (www.reardoncommerce.com)

Simon Fraser University e-Loyalty Project (www.eloyalty.ca)

Web Marketing Today (www.wilsonweb.com)

6 Trade in Services

The new economy

Chapter Objectives

- Understand the growing importance of the service sector and how it is changing the global economic and trade environments
- Identify the key differences between trade in goods and trade in services
- List services being traded in each of the four modes of delivery
- Outline the key considerations in contracting and delivering services

Overview

The economy of the world has experienced a major shift in the past century. In less than 100 years, countries whose economies were once dependent on resources and agriculture joined the industrial revolution. Now the focus is on the new knowledge-based economy, brought about by globalization and the information age.

The future will be one of global suppliers, global customers and global business relationships based on skills, knowledge and expertise. Services will be sourced from a different type of community—not necessarily one which is in the local neighbourhood, but a community of people and organizations that develop buyer-supplier-partner relationships, regardless of whether they live and work in the same community, country or even continent. It is not their geographic proximity that will bring them together, but common interests, complementary services and the mutual pursuit of business opportunities.

The Growing Importance of the Global Service Sector

Services account for approximately two-thirds of the world's economic activity today, and it is estimated that the service sector employs more than half of the world's workforce. Service industries are responsible for the creation of the overwhelming majority of new jobs, they employ more women than any other industry sector and they account for the majority of GDP in countries around the world. Estimates range from 40 percent to as high as 90 percent in some cases.

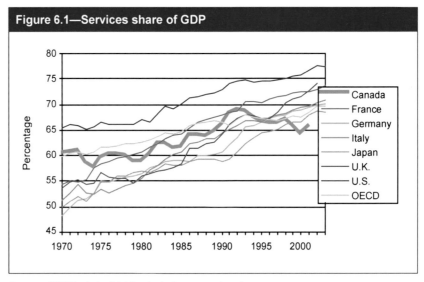

Figure 6.1—Services share of GDP

Source: OECD—Industrial Analysis (www.oecd.org)

Global trade in services

Services represent in excess of 20 percent of world trade. Forecasters predict that this figure will reach 50 percent by the year 2025, as information and communication technologies continue to increase the tradability of services. The shift to knowledge-based economic activity also results in the assimilation of economic activities, which creates an increasingly integrated global economy. The outsourcing of inputs, including services, further fuels the integration process.

The service sector in Canada

In Canada, the service sector is an important contributor to the economy. According to Industry Canada, services accounted for 68 percent of GDP in 2005 and employed 75 percent of Canada's workforce. Although hard to track (no cross-border supporting documentation) and therefore likely underestimated, services are reported to account for over 13 percent of Canada's total exports. Services exports have been growing at over 9 percent per year and are estimated to exceed C$60 billion annually.

"International trade is no longer about exchange; it is about integration." Source: Conference Board of Canada. April 2007

Worldwide, Canada is the 12th largest exporter of services, with a market share that fluctuates between 2 and 2.5 percent annually. Canada is particularly strong in the export of business services, especially computer services, which have recently been growing by 11 percent per year.

Types of services

Services include a wide range of activities. At one end of the spectrum are what might be termed personal services, such as training, live artistic performances and medical care. At the other end are impersonal services, such as telecommunications or the services embodied in manufactured products. In the case of telecommunications, for example, the service is delivered through automated equipment by a telephone company or a cable television operator. Figure 6.2 offers some examples of common service categories.

Figure 6.2—Examples of major service categories	
Services purchased primarily by business and industry	
Financial	• Banking (including investment banking and brokerage) • Insurance • Leasing
Shipping and distribution	• Freight forwarding • Transportation (ocean, rail, truck, air) • Warehousing

Figure 6.2—Examples of major service categories *(continued)*	
Professional and technical	• Architectural design • Engineering and construction (engineering design, architectural design, construction management and contracting) • Management, legal and accounting services • Technical licensing and sales
Other business services	• Information technology services (including software, telecommunications, data processing and information services) • Franchising, legal services, advertising and other services (commercial real estate, business travel, security, translation, postal and courier services)
Services purchased primarily by individuals	
Retail trade	• Retail services • Restaurant dining
Health care	• Private and public services • Medical care • Dental care
Travel, recreation and entertainment	• Travel services • Sports tickets • Cinema and theatre tickets • Hotel accommodations
Education	• Public-school and university tuition • Private-sector training and courses

Not all the services listed in here are exportable. Among those regularly traded internationally are financial services (banking, insurance and investment brokerage); construction and engineering (architectural design, construction supervision and project management); business services (management consulting and accounting); travel and tourism (the hospitality industry); and transportation (freight forwarding and shipping).

As mentioned above, international trade in services is difficult to measure. Any estimate of its value should be considered a minimum. A significant proportion of this trade does not appear in official statistics, because defining and tracking service exports is extremely complicated.

Modes of Delivery: Four Ways Services Are Traded

The World Trade Organization (WTO) lists four modes of delivery or ways in which services are exported.

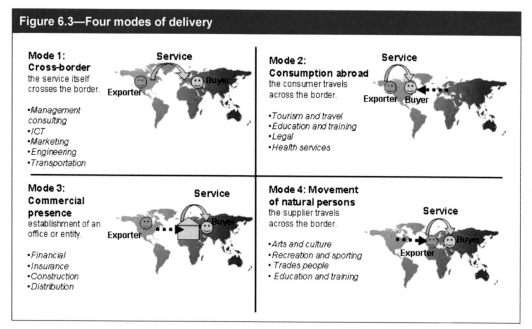

Figure 6.3—Four modes of delivery

Mode 1: Cross-border
the service itself crosses the border.

- Management consulting
- ICT
- Marketing
- Engineering
- Transportation

Mode 2: Consumption abroad
the consumer travels across the border.

- Tourism and travel
- Education and training
- Legal
- Health services

Mode 3: Commercial presence
establishment of an office or entity.

- Financial
- Insurance
- Construction
- Distribution

Mode 4: Movement of natural persons
the supplier travels across the border.

- Arts and culture
- Recreation and sporting
- Trades people
- Education and training

Source: World Trade Organization, Illustration by Global Links Network, Canada.

Mode 1: Cross-border

Cross-border trade takes place when the service itself crosses the border from one country to another without the movement of persons. The service is transported either via electronic means (e-mail or fax) or by infrastructure, such as transportation services (air, rail, land or sea) or telecommunications (telephone or radio).

Examples:

- Management consulting: studies, reports, business plans, financial advice

- Information and communication technology: Internet service provision, cellular telephony

- Marketing: market research, advertising, articles

- Consulting engineering: feasibility studies, drawings

- Health: tele-health

- Education and training: e-learning, distance learning

- Transportation: courier services, other transportation services

Mode 2: Consumption abroad

Consumption abroad relates to services used by nationals of one country in another country where the service is supplied. This requires the consumer to travel across the border to another country to actually use the service. The supplier of the service, who is being paid by a "non-resident" customer, is technically exporting a service (even without leaving the country).

> Companies become service exporters if they are paid for their services by a "non-resident" customer, regardless of where the service is provided.

Examples:

- Tourism and travel-related services: tour operators, hospitality industry, business tourism, agri-tourism, eco-tourism, edu-tourism

- Education and training: study tours, conferences, foreign students, seminars

- Legal: client seeks legal advice in local market and so travels to the market

- Health: patient travels to foreign country for diagnosis and treatment

Mode 3: Commercial presence

Commercial presence refers to instances where a company from one country sets up subsidiaries or branches to provide services in another country.

Examples:

- Financial services: banks, investment companies, insurance brokers

- Construction engineering: sets up project offices to manage local infrastructure projects

- Information technology: local offices set up to service local clients

- Distribution: shipping, warehousing, logistics

Mode 4: Movement of natural persons

Movement of natural persons refers to individuals travelling from their own country to supply services in another country.

Examples:

- Arts and culture: film industry—actors, directors, production crew, performers

- Construction: architects, tradespeople

- Education and training: trainers, professional speakers

- Environmental: consultants, specialists

- Geomatics: mapping, oceanography

- Recreational and sporting: coaches, trainers, promoters

Examples of how services are traded

For an export to take place, residents of one country pay residents of another for some kind of benefit. In the case of trade in goods, merchandise is physically shipped from one country to another, making tracking and measurement relatively straightforward. Trade in services is much more subtle.

Take, for example, the case of a multinational corporation with offices in two adjacent countries. If the subsidiary in one country ships components to the subsidiary in the other, the transaction is recorded both within the corporation and in the customs offices of both countries. But if a manager from one subsidiary travels to the subsidiary in the other country to participate in meetings and offer advice, the export of that manager's services is not recorded anywhere. Yet, value—in the form of several days of the manager's time—has been transferred from one country to the other.

Services may also be part of more complex international transactions. For example, a firm may be hired to build a subway system in another country. Part of the export will consist of subway cars, but an equally important component will be the design, planning, project management and training involved in constructing and operating the finished system. Some of these services will be delivered in person by individuals travelling to the site of the contract, falling under mode 4. Others, such as plans and schedules, can be transferred electronically, falling under mode 1.

As information technology has become more sophisticated, databases, advanced software applications and the Internet have made it possible for many businesspeople to export their services without travelling abroad. This makes counting, controlling and regulating service trade more difficult. For example, medical services are rigorously regulated in virtually every country of the world. A doctor qualified in one country cannot practise in another without first passing a series of examinations in the second country. Yet, medical technology already allows X-rays and other types of body scans to be transmitted over long distances for examination and diagnosis. In another example, a doctor in one country may be asked to offer an opinion on the case of a patient in another—in effect, practising medicine in the patient's country.

The Role of Services in Manufacturing

Transactions involving manufactured goods often have a significant service component built into them. For example, as much as one-half the cost of a car may be for services such as styling and design, advertising and marketing, data processing, translation, legal services, strategic planning and insurance. It is often difficult to draw a clear distinction between trade in goods and trade in services.

Today, manufacturing is a system encompassing all the activities that are required to deliver products that meet customer needs—it includes research and development, design and engineering, production, finance, sales and marketing and after-sales service. It is a system that extends beyond any single enterprise, across supply chains and business networks that are increasingly global in scope and that incorporate services as well as production activities.

The business of manufacturing is rapidly changing in the face of competitive challenges. New market opportunities and global trends are redefining the industry. Available statistics by and large reflect the performance of companies that are primarily engaged in production activities. Therefore they underestimate the total value of goods manufactured and exclude the value added by services companies that are an integral part of manufacturers' networks. Even so, the statistics tell the story of two dynamic sectors that have become an even more important part of the global economy over the past ten years.

Figure 6.4—Canadian facts on manufacturing and services	
The facts on manufacturing	**The facts on services**
• 2.3 million Canadians are employed in manufacturing. • Manufacturing is Canada's largest business sector, accounting for 18 percent of the Canadian economy. • Every dollar of manufacturing output generates C$3.05 in total economic activity. • Canadian manufacturers produced and shipped goods valued at C$546 billion in 2003. • Manufacturing has grown 16 percent faster than the Canadian economy as a whole since 1990. • Manufacturing accounts for two-thirds of Canada's total exports of goods and services. • Manufacturing accounts for two-thirds of all business investment in research and development in Canada.	• Services account for two thirds of Canada's GDP. • Services are estimated to exceed C$60 billion. • Services have been growing at over 9 percent per year. • Services account for over 13 percent of Canada's total exports. • Worldwide, Canada is the twelfth-largest exporter of services, with a 2-3 percent market share. • Worldwide, Canada is the fourth-largest in engineering services. • Canada is also particularly strong in business services, especially computer services, which have recently been growing by 11 percent per year.

Source: Canadian Manufacturers and Exporters and Industry Canada.

Many service areas are closely linked to manufacturing, and these offer significant opportunities for partnerships. The following chart demonstrates one approach to mapping the services component in the manufacturing process.

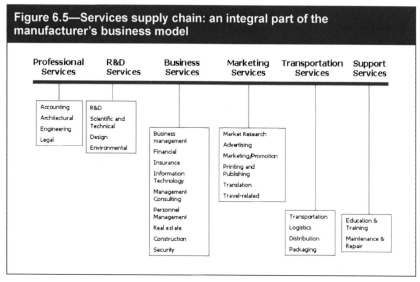

Figure 6.5—Services supply chain: an integral part of the manufacturer's business model

Source: Global Links Network, Canada.

Goods vs. Services Trade: Different Circumstances, Different Approaches

The most obvious difference between exporting a good and exporting a service is that a service export is invisible or intangible. When selling a product, samples can be sent, tried and replaced if they do not work. When selling services this is not the case.

Different circumstances—selling a promise

Selling a service is in fact selling a promise to perform. It is a promise by the service firm to meet the needs of clients at a pre-determined price and within a pre-determined timeframe. To sell a promise a company must "sell the individual" who will deliver the service. This will affect the marketing, price and delivery of the promise. The following comparisons illustrate some of the differences.

Table 6.6—Difference between exporting products and services		
Issue	Products	Services
Resource needs		
Cultural factors	Product design and packaging	Interpersonal dynamics
Government procurement	Goods acquisition	Services contracts
Local partners	Production/distribution firms	Other service firms

Table 6.6—Difference between exporting products and services *(cont'd)*		
Issue	**Products**	**Services**
Marketing your product or service		
Demonstrations	Sample product	Presentation of capabilities
Initial marketing	By sales representatives	Principals of the firm raise awareness, profile, credibility
Marketing skills	Demonstrate product features	Networking, relationship marketing
Stages of marketing	Marketing a product *and* a service	Marketing value and solutions
Local market presence	Sales/distribution facility	Office or virtual office in target market
Local events	Trade shows	Conferences (as speaker)
Media	Product advertising	Press coverage, magazine articles
Delivering your product or service		
Transportation	Products shipped by air/sea/land	Service, client or service provider travels
Technology	E-marketplace to show products and transactions online	Essential for communication and timely delivery of services
Distribution	Importer/distributor	Local partner
Delivery challenges	Replacement or exchange of malfunctioning parts	People are not interchangeable, close contact with client is required

Source: Adapted from Industry Canada, *Export Your Services Take a World View* (www. exportsource.ca/worldview)

Intangibles: Skills, Knowledge and Expertise

People with highly valued skills, specific knowledge and first-rate expertise are in demand around the world. Here are some examples.

- *Design.* An essential component of all quality manufacturing. Think Scandinavia for furniture, Italy for shoes, Japan for reliable retail electronics. Manufacturers need this skill to enhance product value whether they provide it in house or outsource to a service company.

- *Engineering.* Germany has been a traditional leader, now challenged by the Japanese. (Is China next?—they are qualifying huge numbers of engineers.) How can this service skill be harnessed for improved margins?

- *Training.* Companies that professionally train their staff, agents and customers need presentation, technical writing, cultural awareness and language skills. Is this value included in their prices? Can they charge customers separately? Can they look outside the parameters of existing products and customers to create unique added-value profit centres? Countries—particularly in the developing world—are hungry for skills and knowledge, as witnessed by the proliferation of training seminars and workshops on everything from running a trade show to corporate social responsibility. Manufacturers and service providers need to work together in this area.

- *After-sales service.* It is well known that many companies—especially in the auto sector and other capital equipment sectors—make a high profit on spare parts and after-sales service when they sell through dealers to the end customer. With industrial buyers, technical service is usually built into the price of the product, but increasingly it is being sold as a separate service, giving customers the option of buying different levels of support according to their needs. Again, an opportunity for enhanced profit.

The World Trade Organization lists 12 major service categories and over 150 subcategories. By being aware of these services, global traders can strategically consider their approach to integrating services within their offerings. Adding skills, knowledge and expertise adds value. Adding value increases profits.

Different approaches—marketing a service

How does one market an intangible? The following approaches and strategies are examples of how service firms are marketing their outputs.

Services marketing is actually relationship marketing. Service firms need to continually find innovative ways of linking their skills and knowledge to satisfy a customer need. Some of the steps in achieving this include

- building rapport;

- probing the client's services needs;

- presenting the service, shaped around client need; and

- seeking commitment.

The key goal of relationship marketing is to build a trusting relationship, out of which a sale will result.

Successful strategies

The following strategies for selling services have proven themselves successful in a number of markets:

- customization to meet client needs;
- fulfilling an immediate need vs. marketing an entire portfolio;
- selling solutions and demonstrating benefits;
- bundling with other service suppliers;
- delivery of superior value; and
- creativity vs. innovation.

Core competencies

As competition in the global economy intensifies, firms are focusing more and more on producing outputs that are centred on their core competencies. Consequently, they contract out other business activities.

For example, an architectural-services firm may contract out the following activities:

- market research
- promotion (website content, brochures, presentations)
- information technology support

Bundling services

Often, two or more service offerings are combined. For example, in southern Poland, health- and dental-care services and tourism are promoted together as a package. Advertisements on the Internet suggest to potential clients that they can have some dental work done and then recover and relax in a scenic location.

Value Proposition: Differentiating Your Service

A value proposition articulates the essential benefits and experiences the client can expect to get and at what cost, and how that combination is superior to other choices.

Building your value proposition

The outcome or the positive experience a client will receive as a result of doing business with you is the essence of your value proposition.

Things to do:

- Customize your value proposition to meet your client's need
- Clearly demonstrate how your solution is the best option
- Set priorities and timelines to reinforce your value proposition
- Deliver superior value without sacrificing your profitability

Things to avoid:

- "one-size-fits-all" value propositions

- generic statements: "we are the leader"

- overselling features of your service without properly demonstrating the benefits

- confusing, complex, difficult-to-remember value propositions

The desired outcome
Clients will recognize value if the services exporter is

- good at understanding their needs;

- conscious of the importance of the bottom line;

- creative and brings innovative solutions; and

- determined to deliver satisfaction.

Examples of value propositions
In order to be successful, service firms need to differentiate themselves from their competitors. Many service firms are realizing that the outcome or the positive experience a client will receive as a result of doing business with them is the essence of their value proposition, in other words, the value they will bring to their client.

> Good value propositions appeal to solving a problem or fulfilling a dream. A successful value proposition is synonymous with quality.

Important points to remember in building value propositions is to include customization to meet the client's need, to focus on the provision of solutions, clearly demonstrating the benefits, and to deliver superior value without sacrificing profitability. The best value propositions are clear and succinct, innovative and solution-oriented and will succeed in differentiating the service firm from its competitors.

Market Research: Implications for Services

Business-opportunity indicators and market-research methodologies are unique for service firms. Exporters must be clear on what represents an opportunity for them. They need to perform standard market research, as well as monitor potential markets, looking for special signs, solid information and competitive intelligence.

Opportunity indicators
Potential opportunity indicators may come from a variety of sources and result from a variety of activities.

Sources include

- news items;

- press releases;

- magazines and trade journals;

- policy statements;

- program announcements;

- contract awards to potential partner firms or the competition; and

- the Internet (procurement and partnering notices, general research).

Activities include

- becoming a member of an association (domestic and/or foreign);

- attending meetings, conferences, workshops and special events as a participant or presenter;

- raising awareness;

- increasing profile;

- building credibility; and

- networking.

Market-entry strategies
Market-entry strategies for service firms may vary from market to market. Choosing the right strategy can be the difference between success and failure, profitability and financial loss.

Table 6.7—Market-entry strategies for service firms			
	Direct exports	**Indirect exports**	**Partnerships and alliances**
Description	• You negotiate, contract and work with the foreign end user	• You negotiate, contract and work with an intermediary who negotiates and contracts with the end client	• You form an alliance, whether formal or informal, comprising two or more parties all from your country or from a combination of countries

Table 6.7—Market-entry strategies for service firms *(continued)*			
	Direct exports	**Indirect exports**	**Partnerships and alliances**
Advantages	• You have the resources • You have the cultural and language skills • You have the commitment to work directly, probably on site, with clients in a foreign market	• Your service is world-standard • You have identified target markets • You prefer to focus on your technical expertise • You have the ability to work within the target market in co-operation with a lead company that can provide the necessary strong market knowledge, cultural and language skills, significant resources and stamina	• You are relatively new to the target market's cultural and language differences • You require professional accreditation • You need to offer competitive pricing • You need breadth of technical expertise • You need to create links and synergy between providers of goods and services • You require mobility of personnel • Taxation is an issue • Legal status in the target market is mandatory • Eligibility to bid on target contracts is required

In addition to considering the above options, organizations worldwide are increasingly looking at outsourcing non-core functions.

Business-Process Outsourcing

What is business-process outsourcing?
Business-process outsourcing (BPO) is the practice of hiring outside service providers to handle selected non-core business processes of a firm. Offshore BPO is the practice of importing services from a lower-cost country or from a country where greater value or quality can be obtained.

The practice of outsourcing services has been growing steadily for some time, owing to continuous improvements in communication technology and

Typical reasons for pursuing a BPO arrangement include labour-cost savings, enhanced focus on core business, greater operational efficiency and higher quality of service.

infrastructure. Examples of business processes that have been outsourced frequently include payroll processing, workforce training, cheque processing, hiring and recruitment, insurance-claims processing, logistics and dispatch, answering services (call- or contact-centre functions) and engineering and architectural services.

Why outsource?
Firms engage in BPO for a variety of reasons. These include:[31]

- 36 percent to reduce operating costs

- 32 percent to focus on the core of the business

- 13 percent to create a variable cost structure

- 5 percent to increase speed to market

- 5 percent to improve quality

- 5 percent to conserve capital

- 2 percent to foster innovation

- 2 percent to grow revenue

Global market size
According to the Everest Group Research Institute, the total global services outsourcing market (including offshore and information technology [IT] outsourcing) in 2004 was valued at U.S.$362 billion in terms of total contracts or spending. IT outsourcing accounted for 64 percent of this market at U.S.$233 billion, while BPO's share of 36 percent amounted to U.S.$129 billion.

Success factors for BPO exporters
The success factors for BPO exporters are the same as for any other service provider in foreign markets:

- A clear focus on core value

- A client-oriented value proposition

- An ability to communicate credibility and competitive advantage to prospective clients in the target market.

Market-entry strategies
Potential market-entry strategies for BPO exporters include:

- Joint venture/consortia: To take advantage of the trend in multi-service BPO demand

- Language targeting: To gain market share in non-English markets (e.g., Morocco targeting France)

---

[31] Helios Innovations, White Paper: *Busines Process Outsourcing Overview.*

- Near-shore outsourcing: To take advantage of competitive labour costs and comparable skills (e.g., Bangladesh to India rather than Canada to India)

- Third-party representation: The use of brokerage firms or strategic partnerships to provide instant credibility, enhanced market access and greater supply chain knowledge

Trade Policies and Issues Affecting Services Trade

The World Trade Organization (WTO) strives to liberalize trade in services and global service standards. The General Agreement on Trade in Services (GATS) is the instrument governing the way services are traded around the world. The main purpose of GATS is to improve access to international markets for service providers. It aims to foster competition, lower prices, encourage innovation, increase employment, provide greater transparency and predictability and boost technology transfer. In particular, the focus is on trying to improve the opportunities for participation of small- and medium-sized service suppliers in the global marketplace.

Policies

Many countries have expressed the desirability of liberalizing trade in services; at the same time, countries want to preserve their ability to maintain or establish policies, regulations, subsidies, administrative practices or other measures in sectors such as health, public education and social services. As well, they want to continue developing rules for emergency safeguard mechanisms, subsidies, government procurement and domestic regulations.

Services are central to the development and strengthening of economies. In combination with strategic education policies, investment in various infrastructures and the continuing trend towards outsourcing, services trade is quickly modernizing developing countries while providing access to a global talent pool and boosting productivity in developed countries.

A particularly important element of GATS for service exporters is the effort to put a process for the mutual recognition of professional credentials into place. Without mutual recognition, architects cannot design, doctors cannot practise and engineers cannot innovate in many countries where their skills and expertise are in demand.

Issues

Negotiations of services trade agreements are inherently more complex than those dealing with goods, given that services account for the largest portion of most economies and they are highly diversified. In addition, services trade in a more complex manner than goods, involving cross-border trade as well as movement of providers, consumers and investors.

Countries that have liberal rules governing trade in services tend to benefit from innovation, due to easy access to capital and technology. The availability of world-class services assists both goods and services producers in becoming more competitive in the global market.

Some developing countries have expressed concern that the opening up of services markets could have an undesirable impact on their national policies, such as education and health care. GATS is exploring ways to address the interests and concerns of developing countries, and hopefully in the process will create a level playing field for all concerned.

Trade in Services Checklist

The following checklist can be helpful when considering trade in services.

Figure 6.8—Trade in services checklist

☑ Understand how important the service sector is in the world economy and what influence it has on the global trade environment.

☑ Be aware of the work of the World Trade Organization and the General Agreement on Trade in Services aimed at liberalizing global trade in services and related policies and other issues.

☑ Ensure that there is recognition of the difference between goods and services trade within your firm and an understanding of the different circumstances and different approaches required when trading in services.

☑ Know what is being traded (skills, knowledge and expertise) and the four different ways services cross borders.

☑ Create a value proposition and differentiate the service offering from the competition.

☑ Realize what represents opportunities for service exporters and how to use services-specific techniques to research the market.

☑ Know how to finance services.

☑ Be familiar with key considerations in the contracting and delivery of services.

☑ Understand business process outsourcing (BPO), the reasons for it, success factors and market-entry strategies.

Chapter Summary

The service sector has become a significant economic force in the 21st century. As a result, countries are re-thinking national strategies, entrepreneurial service firms are re-inventing themselves and economists are delighting in having new trends and numbers to assess, analyze and forecast.

It may be relatively easy to anticipate new trends, but being in a position to capitalize on them is a different matter. Services are invisibles. They cannot be demonstrated, shipped and returned as products can. Successful service firms have recognized that in selling these kinds of invisibles, the key to success is in the building of relationships, the adaptation of services to meet customer needs and the continuous innovation of unique high-value solutions.

Exercises

Exercise 1 (class discussion)
In how many ways do services trade? Provide three examples for each of the ways.

(Estimated time 5 minutes)

Exercise 2 (class discussion)
Your international business-development team is exploring ways to bundle two or more of your service offerings. Discuss how you would go about bundling and provide rationales for your choices.

(Estimated time 5 minutes)

Exercise 3 (small-group discussion)
In small groups of two or three people, discuss the following scenario: Your efficiency-management team is examining business process outsourcing possibilities. Discuss which of the processes within your firm may be candidates for outsourcing and why. Who are the stakeholders in this instance, and from a sustainable-business perspective, what unique actions might the firm take in an attempt to balance the needs of the various stakeholders?

(Estimated time 10-15 minutes)

Exercise 4 (assignment/research activity)
The General Agreement on Trade in Services has been a highly controversial element of WTO negotiations. Do some online research on this topic to identify the most controversial aspects of the agreement. What does the WTO website (www.wto.org) have to say about GATS? What does the Canadian Centre for Policy Alternatives (www.policyalternatives.ca) have to say on the topic? Summarize your findings in a two-page report that includes the following elements:

1. General overview of GATS

2. Proposed benefits of GATS

3. Major criticisms of GATS

4. Your opinion on GATS

(Estimated time 90 minutes)

References/Resources

A.T. Kearney (www.atkearney.com)

Conference Board of Canada (www.conferenceboard.ca)

E-Business Strategies Inc. (www.ebstrategy.com)

Everest Research Institute (www.outsourcing-bpo.com/2006-bpo.html)

ExportSource (www.exportsource.ca)

Industry Canada (www.strategis.gc.ca)

International Trade Centre, Geneva (www.intracen.org/servicexport)

WTO/GATS (www.wto.org/english/tratop_e/serv_e/gatsintr_e.htm)

7 Cultural Considerations

Know before you go

Chapter Objectives

- Describe the value of different cultures, business practices and social customs

- List the basic negotiating skills required to be successful in different parts of the world

- Understand how an organization needs to change to ensure that it is prepared to deal with cultural differences

Overview

"Culture is more often a source of conflict than of synergy. Cultural differences are a nuisance at best and often a disaster," said Prof. Geert Hofstede, Emeritus Professor of Maastricht University, one of the world's leading authorities on culture in international business. If this is true, careful study of culture prior to entry into foreign markets is more than advisable—it is crucial.

Some may argue that cultural differences are simply superficial, and that "deep down, people are people." However, it should be recognized that in many cases culture, and the values and beliefs that make up its foundation, hold an even deeper significance than the ultimate *raison d'être* for international commerce— money and profit. Developing cross-cultural relationships that lead to successful global business transactions requires careful preparation, strong commitment and a clear understanding of the cultural context within which one is to do business.

Global Business: Multicultural Environment

The impact of culture on marketing, negotiations and developing relationships with business partners in foreign markets was once generally restricted to larger companies with the resources to do business internationally. However, in the global economy of the 21st century, with worldwide business opportunities driven by recent advances in Internet and communications technology and increasingly multicultural societies, cultural awareness and sensitivity have become a key competency for almost everyone doing business today.

The importance of culture in business success has never been more important and will continue to increase. This chapter will provide knowledge and insights into how to bridge cultural differences and turn them into a competitive advantage.

Culture defined
First, what exactly is culture? It is the set of customs, values, beliefs, behaviours and traditions that have developed among groups of people over decades and centuries. It is influenced and defined by geography, language, religion, history, war, food, clothing, climate and other variables that not only make cultures unique, but also facilitate comparisons and allow us to learn and grow from cultural knowledge and awareness.

One of the most interesting and important features of international trade is the cultural aspect. The most successful international traders make a study of culture and learn to adapt their products and services, strategies, tactics, behaviour and activities to their advantage. They enjoy and appreciate all there is to learn from other cultures and embrace the opportunities that lie within international markets while internalizing the diversity, as strong corporations do when they ensure its existence within their own workforces.

Cultural understanding is critical to success when doing international business because of the huge number of small differences that exist between cultures, and how big an impact those small differences can have. A word may mean something innocuous (or simply be a name) in one language, but may create a negative connotation in another (the Chevrolet "Nova" did not sell well in Latin markets because its name means "doesn't go"). It is critical for a company to have the internal and external capability to carefully review all aspects of a product or service, as well as its associated support and advertising materials, from the perspective of the local culture in a target export market.

A culturally diverse workforce can help to fast-track entry into new markets by assisting in the development of language and slogans, packaging and design, colour and graphics, and adaptation of the product or service to the preferences of the target markets from which employees originate. As part of their job responsibilities, personnel from different cultures can provide highly informed and useful recommendations to their employers on how that culture is oriented to issues such as symbols, humour, gift giving, property and other important cultural considerations.

Organizations that do not have the advantage of a multicultural work force should consider using third parties, such as consultants and other outsourced options, to ensure that they are fully capable of effective cross-cultural communications and activity.

It is crucial to the success and survival of companies operating both locally and globally to take culture into account in their marketing initiatives, negotiation styles and relationship-building techniques. Moreover, companies that adopt the philosophy that "culture counts" will find it easier to make the transition from local to global player and, indeed, to grow their business around the world. As important as ever in global business, cultural awareness and sensitivity are not only for international traders any more!

Intercultural Effectiveness: Knowing the Rules of the Game

For companies that have not already made the transformation to a culturally effective organization, what is to be done? It is important to first understand the "rules of the game," that is, the attributes of a culturally effective company.

This competency is the base upon which all other competencies are built. If an individual does not fully understand the importance of culture on a people's activities and how it affects views of proper behaviour, communication practices, social structure and business negotiations, all other competencies that follow will be eroded—perhaps even meaningless. The more exposure individuals have to other cultures, the more likely they are to understand the importance culture plays in daily activities, and leverage that understanding to the mutual advantage of themselves, their organizations and their business partners.

What is cross-cultural marketing?
Cross-cultural marketing involves learning how to adapt a company's marketing strategies and communications to the cultural differences in various international markets. By applying cross-cultural marketing techniques, companies can increase the overall effectiveness of their international marketing. International marketing is far more effective, profitable and successful when it is clearly understood and appeals to each culture's particular values and behavioural traits.

Consider the advantages of changing a company's approach to a cross-cultural marketing orientation:

- Acceptance and understanding of the marketing message in each of a company's international target markets is significantly increased.

- The features, benefits and advantages of products and services that most appeal to potential customers in each different market are clearly communicated.

- The positioning of a company's image, products, and services against international competition in each market is strengthened.

- The chances of establishing positive long-term brand loyalty and customer/supplier relationships are greatly enhanced.

- Increased overall marketing effectiveness leads to optimization of international sales in each international target market.

Identifying and understanding the values of another society is a complex exercise that involves differentiating between the significant core values and the superficial features of a culture.

Gaining cross-cultural competency
When considering an international business venture, a good place to start is to prepare a profile of existing personal and corporate values.

People from different cultures do not necessarily see and do things in the same way. That does not make their customs and ways of thinking, interacting, and doing business superior or inferior—just different. It's important to be non-judgmental, open-minded and flexible.

Cultural Concepts in Context

To fully understand the different dimensions of cultural diversity, one should have a basic understanding of the following two cultural concepts:

High-context culture
In this culture, the context in which a conversation occurs is as important as the words that are actually spoken. Cultural cues are extremely important in understanding what is being communicated because unspoken communication and interpersonal relationships in business are more important than in low-context cultures.

Low-context culture
In this culture, the words used by the speaker explicitly convey the message to the listener. Low-context cultures rely less on relationship building and non-verbal cues than high-context cultures. Below is a figure demonstrating a few selected countries along a context continuum.

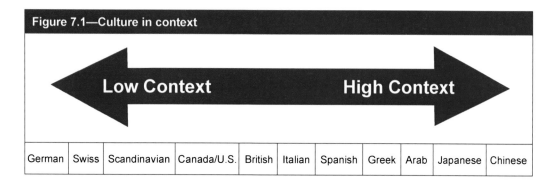

Figure 7.1—Culture in context

| German | Swiss | Scandinavian | Canada/U.S. | British | Italian | Spanish | Greek | Arab | Japanese | Chinese |

Relationships with foreign business partners: How much of a relationship is required?

The difference between traditional and non-traditional cultures is in many ways parallel to high-context and low-context cultures, as shown in the table below. The key difference between them is the relative importance of non-verbal communication and relationships to the success of a business relationship.

Generally speaking, the higher the context, the more important relationships and non-verbal communication are.

Table 7.2—Non-traditional vs. traditional cultures	
Traditional (Asia, Africa, Middle East, Latin America)	**Non-traditional (North America, western Europe)**
• Co-operation and harmony are valued	• Competition is valued
• Some information is physical and hidden	• Most information is clear from the words
• Religious beliefs are usually pervasive and entrenched	• Religious background is more limited and often irrelevant
• Time is a continuum. People do several things at once for as long as it takes	• Time is compartmentalized, as evidenced by appointments
• Orientation is toward the present	• Orientation is toward the future
• Work is motivated by need	• Work is motivated by ambition
• Harmony and nature are valued	• Materialism is valued over nature
• Patience is common	• Impatience for change or action is common
• People may say one thing and mean something else	• People are straightforward and say what they mean

Table 7.2—Non-traditional vs. traditional cultures *(continued)*	
Traditional (Asia, Africa, Middle East, Latin America)	**Non-traditional (North America, western Europe)**
• Saving face is crucial. Decisions are made to avoid embarrassment or to preserve honour	• Decisions are made on a practical basis. People worry less about saving face or being embarrassed
• Decision making is personal and is often done by consensus	• Decision making is impersonal and is often done independently

Effective Communication

Because communication is a cornerstone of business activity, every effort should be made to ensure that communication with people in a target market is clear and easily understood.

Cross-cultural communication presents challenges that are not always faced in home markets. This is because of cultural filters—perceptions formed over long periods of time—that affect how the world and our environment are understood. Particular cultural filters have been influenced by past experiences and societal influences, as well as by ethics and morals instilled by family, religion and peer groups. These filters determine what is viewed as appropriate or inappropriate, but are not necessarily transferable across cultures because formative influences differ from culture to culture. To be effective internationally, it's important to be aware that one's cultural filters might not be relevant or acceptable in a particular foreign market.

Table 7.3—Effective communicators
• Attempt to enhance communication by avoiding stereotypical presumptions
• Check to ensure that foreign counterparts have understood key communication aspects
• Try to learn the foreign language over time so as to reduce reliance on interpreters
• Experiment with, but do not necessarily adopt, local mannerisms and means of communication

Non-verbal communication

By definition, communication is the exchange of ideas and information between people. A large part of this process involves non-verbal communication that consists of body movements, gestures, facial expressions, touching, eye contact, tone of voice and others. Every culture receives and interprets non-verbal communication in a different manner. To avoid unintentionally insulting someone, it is important to understand the cultural aspects of non-verbal communication in foreign environments.

Gestures

The improper use of gestures has caused businesspeople considerable embarrassment in various cultures around the world. For example, if the host of a business luncheon asks how the meal is, and he receives the "OK" or "thumbs up" sign, there is a risk of insulting a great many people!

Touching

Touching is a primary form of non-verbal communication. In most cultures, a handshake between men is a common welcoming gesture and, if not accepted, a possible insult. However, if two men were to walk down the street in public holding hands, the meaning would be perceived as entirely different. Across different cultures, humans have appropriate touching customs ingrained at an early age. In some Asian cultures, men who are close friends holding hands is quite normal. This may be disturbing to many, even if they are fully aware of the Asian culture.

Dancing is another aspect where touching differs greatly among cultures. In North America, close dancing and the resulting contact between men and women are considered normal and non-sexual. However, other cultures would be horrified by this public display of touching between a man and a woman. The reverse is true in parts of Latin America, where couples openly display their affection in ways that would not be acceptable in other parts of the world.

Facial expressions

One common expression in Canada is the term "face-to-face communication." It implies that we will be communicating with others in person rather than by phone, e-mail, fax and so on. It could also serve as an explanation for how much communication is expressed through facial movements. Watching children interact with each other brings this aspect to light. Children are well versed in the meaning of facial communication from a very young age. They growl, smile, frown, stick out their tongue, squint and pout all the time, understanding each other without any formal education in this area. Within cultures, facial expressions may be interpreted in a similar manner—but across cultures, misunderstandings can easily occur.

Space

The space we maintain around ourselves reflects a desire to control who gets close to us, and under what circumstances. Ideas about appropriate distance vary from culture to culture and are symbolic of the society's style and tone.

For example, people from some African cultures stand quite far apart, while people from the Middle East who are of the same gender are likely to stand close to each other, yet frown on public displays of affection between men and women. On the other hand, Americans with European backgrounds are somewhere in between. The exact distance depends on the type of relationship they have with the other person—the more personal the association, the closer they stand to each other.

This is more than just an interesting sociological observation. Body language has practical business ramifications. Proper distance should be maintained in circumstances where workers, colleagues or clients are in danger of feeling emotionally or physically threatened by the invasion of their personal space. It should be noted that the sense of security or threat associated with personal space can be at the subconscious level, and may be difficult to assess or gauge effectively.

What should be done when people meet who have different interpretations of body language? Should an effort be made to "speak the same language"—that is, match their movements and ideas about space, touching, eye contact and gestures, or should one simply try to avoid doing anything that might offend? The answer depends on the relationship between the parties and how their body language differs.

For example, if one is speaking with someone who stands close and touches their arm during conversation, it would be unwise to try to match this behaviour. Instead, one should observe the behaviour, but not back away or rebuff the touch—unless, of course, it is inappropriate—and be reassured that this closeness most likely shows this person's desire to communicate. Conversely, when the other person stands at a distance, one should honour this difference by modifying one's behaviour accordingly. The reason for this distinction is that erring in the direction of too much intimacy can be far more damaging than appearing a bit reserved.

Verbal communication

The role of words and the way words are interpreted varies widely across cultures. North Americans mean what they say and say what they mean, and have a direct form of communication that is designed to be efficient and free of ambiguity. They do not generally go out of their way to avoid arguments, or consider too deeply the feelings or image of people they do business with. This is not to say they seek to insult or hurt, but their culture is more accepting of arguments, criticism, debate and controversy than some other cultural environments are. If a proposal is unacceptable to them, they say "no." When asked about the objection, they will give an opinion based on what are perceived to be the merits (or lack thereof) of the subject under discussion.

This is not always an acceptable method of communication around the world. In Japan, the word "no" is rarely used. Instead, a negative response is deflected with statements such as: "It may be difficult," "Perhaps," "We will see" and "We will think about it." The word "no" is not said, but the meaning is the same, only framed differently.

The objective here is to understand that the meaning of spoken words will differ from culture to culture. At times the absence of words also has meaning. Take for example a college professor who taught an international business class made up of Canadian and Mexican students. A large part of the class was debate-oriented, and students were given marks for participation. It was difficult to engage the Mexican students in this manner since they wanted to avoid conflict, which occurred frequently between the Canadian students when opinions differed. The lesson is that silence does not always mean consent, but is perhaps an effort to avoid conflict. Knowing the cultural aspects associated with the spoken word is important for each market.

The use of humour, colloquialisms, silence, expression, volume, speed and pitch are all characteristics of cultural norms in spoken language. It is important not to hastily judge what is being said by how it is being said.

Humour

Humour can be a very effective part of a deal and can help you through difficult situations. Travel can be stressful, as can new environments and change in general. This stress can limit both your flexibility and your ability to handle cross-cultural situations. Combat stress with humour. Be able to step away (at least mentally) from situations and find the humour in them.

Humour is a particularly challenging aspect of language as far as cross-cultural communications are concerned. Humour is often helpful in building interpersonal relationships, and it can diffuse stress in all sorts of uncomfortable situations; however, it doesn't always translate well across cultures and the response to humour can vary considerably. In particular, humour that involves making fun of someone else is not understood in many parts of the world and is considered disrespectful in many others. Therefore, the best strategy is to pick up on the humour being used most frequently by your business colleagues and/or potential customers and use a similar approach (sparingly, at first) until the nuances of the culture in question are better understood.

Spoken language
When we are talking to people who speak a different language, the challenges are obvious. However, even when we speak the same language, there can be significant hidden filters. Some examples of hidden language filters include speed, animation (reserved or excitable), volume, and the time lapse allowed for responses (if any). These filters are viewed differently in different cultures. Emphasis on a particular word in a sentence can dramatically change its meaning.

Culturally speaking, there are two distinct styles of communication: implicit and explicit. With implicit communication much of the meaning is carried by the context. Who says it, how it is said and in what setting it is said may be more important than the words spoken. The ability of the audience to "read" the context is expected; words only restate the obvious. Silence can communicate a variety of meanings, and cultural knowledge helps decode which one.

> Repeat the sentence "I didn't say he raised his price" and emphasize a different word each time. Note how it changes the meaning.

With explicit communication, the context is less important. Words carry the meaning and are used to ensure understanding and clarification. Silence is often seen as a lack of engagement or comprehension. Generally speaking, occidental cultures tend toward explicit communication, while oriental cultures gravitate toward the implicit. However, one must be aware that there are always exceptions to these generalizations and adapt to the communication style of a specific audience.

Learn the language
Speaking in the customer's language, or the language of the place one is physically located at the time, is the general rule for international business. There is no better window to understanding another culture than language. If this is not feasible, one is well advised to learn twenty or thirty words—and use them! Although it may not be possible to carry an entire conversation, it will demonstrate respect and interest in the business partner and his or her culture and earn goodwill for taking the time and effort to be accommodating. Presentations should begin with at least a few words in the local language.

Internationalizing language
If English is a business partner's second language, an effort should be made to ensure that they will understand presentations and conversations as clearly as possible. Words should be enunciated clearly and spoken at a relatively

slow pace to ensure clear understanding of the key messages that are being communicated.

Table 7.4—Tips for when verbal communication crosses languages
1. Acronyms, slang, colloquialisms, and sport- or culture-bound analogies (e.g., "rule of thumb," "ballpark estimate") will be meaningless to a foreign audience and should be avoided.
2. Standard and consistent terminology familiar to your audience should be used.
3. Key terms should be explained when first used.
4. Moderate pace and clear enunciation are critical, along with pauses after each main point.
5. Using words that have alternative meanings may cause misunderstanding, (i.e., "accurate" instead of "right").
6. Short words and sentences are best; taking a breath means a sentence is too long.
7. Superfluous words and sentences may cause confusion, such as "for all intents and purposes."
8. The word "not," if missed, will be taken opposite to that which was intended.
9. Visual aids should not be overloaded with text.

Written communication

Written communication in two or more languages presents a challenge to most global business representatives unless they are literate in both languages.

Key difficulties with written communication between languages are

- use of slang or idioms;

- ineffective translations that do not convey the initial meaning; and

- inaccurate interpretation of written contracts.

We use slang or idioms so often in our daily lives that they become a part of our spoken language. The problem occurs when we use them in written communication that is to be translated into a second language. If the translator has knowledge of the meanings, then the problem may be averted. If not, then the translation may not accurately reflect what one is trying to communicate.

Even without the use of slang or idioms, translations often do not convey the message originally intended. This may be because some parts of a language do not have similar meanings in the second language or because translators apply their own meanings, which may not be applicable. Back translating—using two translators, one to translate a message from the home language to a new language, then having it translated back by someone different—is one way to ensure that a translation is accurate when it is particularly important, such as a legal agreement.

Intercultural meetings

When attending meetings in foreign markets, the cultural aspects there should be considered carefully. A checklist is useful in preparing for a meeting.

Table 7.5—Meeting checklist
Room set-up
The set-up of the meeting table and chairs should be appropriate to meet the cultural and logistical needs of the meeting. Enough chairs and table space should be set for all the participants, with attention paid to specific seating arrangements. In cultures that are hierarchical in nature, participants should not be insulted by seating a subordinate in a higher position than his or her superior. Participants of equal rank should be treated equally. Space that is too tight will be uncomfortable for cultures that do not like close proximity. Gender issues can also come into play when arranging seating. The greeting of participants should be appropriate to their culture. Issues such as handshakes and eye contact should be taken into account. When making introductions, titles should be used if they are important in the culture.
Time
The scheduling of the meeting agenda should allow enough time for everyone to arrive, greet, get refreshments and be seated without being rushed. Time should be kept in mind—punctuality and staying on schedule have different levels of priority in different cultures. In some cultures (Latin America, for example), being late is generally an acceptable practice, while in Japan or Germany a late arrival to a meeting will almost certainly get it off to a poor start.
Refreshments
Refreshments must be appropriate to the culture and its special needs. Alcohol is acceptable in some cultures but offensive in others.
Business attire
Appropriate attire should be worn. When in doubt, dress conservatively.
Small talk
In some cultures it is polite to allow time for some initial small talk before a meeting takes place, and in others people want to get straight to business.
Interpreters
Interpreters who are competent, aware of technical terminology and fluent in the correct languages should be available if required.
Room decor
Room decor should be appropriate with respect to colours, flowers, furnishings, and ambience.

Table 7.5—Meeting checklist *(continued)*
Protocol
Protocol can be very important in meetings, especially in a formal, hierarchical society. Should the host chair the meeting? Who should speak first, and to whom? As always, preparation is crucial.

Face
The term "saving face" is used often in the context of global business. But what is "face"? How is it defined? Face is basically image. It is how one is perceived by the outside world and, more importantly, by co-workers and associates. To "save face," precautions should be taken to ensure that one's image, or that of a client, is not tarnished or injured.

In an international context this becomes more important in cultures that highly value image or "face." When negotiating, meeting or socializing with someone to whom image is important, care should be taken that nothing is done to cause them to lose face. Insulting, embarrassing or backing a business client into a corner, from which they cannot escape gracefully, makes the business process more difficult, if not impossible. Some people will take every measure to save face—even if it means terminating discussions and sacrificing an agreement. In business communications it is important to ensure that clients are always afforded the ability to change position. Statements should be framed as questions that encourage co-operation.

Eye contact
Inappropriate eye contact can make people feel uncomfortable, often without knowing why. Eye contact is unique from culture to culture, and awareness of culturally accepted norms is critical. For example, in some North American and European cultures, failure to "look one in the eye" might project an impression of untrustworthiness, as if the person had something to hide. In France, men and women look at each other to a degree that might make North Americans uncomfortable. In Canada, eye contact is considered an indication of attention that is being paid to a conversation, but one is expected to give strangers their space when it comes to eye contact in public settings. Typically, eye contact can be seen as a sign of honesty (or lack thereof) in some cultures, or as an invasion of privacy in others.

Silence
In all cultures there are moments of silence during communication. The importance of silence, however, is reflected in how these moments are perceived. In low-context cultures, where messages are explicit and words hold great meaning, the lack of words or silence can be disturbing and people may feel the need to fill their communication time with words. If a question is asked of a counterpart and they do not answer immediately but rather maintain a moment of silence, a common response might be "what's wrong?" The phrase "the silence was deafening" aptly describes this uncomfortable feeling.

In high-context cultures, where body language forms more of the transmitted message in conversations, silence is not treated as a breakdown in communication, but rather as a period to reflect, digest what was said and give one's full attention to the matter at hand. Generally, people from high-context cultures are more comfortable than their counterparts from low-context cultures with the concept of silence. They do not believe that every moment needs to be filled with conversation. People from high-context cultures (such as Japan) have often used silence (along with prolonged eye contact) against low-context cultures (such as the U.S.).

Interpreters

When using interpreters, one should be aware of how their role is perceived in the local culture. Canadians, along with Americans, Germans, Scandinavians and the British and Dutch, view an interpreter's role as providing an accurate, unbiased account of what is said. This is different in other cultures. For example, the role of a Japanese interpreter is not only to translate words but also to interpret the language, gestures, context and meanings. Rather than a neutral participant, Japanese interpreters are seen as part of the team. In Germany, one would probably be safe using an interpreter provided by the host, but in Asia one should consider engaging one's own to ensure they are truly part of the team.

If an interpreter is required, it is wise to also consider translating visuals and handouts. This may mean changing graphics as well as words. In the Middle East, for example, English-language graph axes and flow charts do not directly translate into Arabic, which moves from right to left. The interpreter's credentials should be checked thoroughly to engage someone who is fluent both culturally and linguistically.

Figure 7.6—Tips for working with interpreters

- Interpreters should receive the text of presentations and speaker's notes in advance.

- A vocabulary list of all acronyms and technical terms should be provided, as well as background information on the client company and participating personnel.

- When possible, time should be allowed to get to know the interpreter.

- Material should be broken up into clear sections so that one idea or thought can be translated at a time.

- Frequent pauses should be used to give the interpreter time to catch up.

- Words should be carefully planned to avoid ambiguities.

- The audience should be addressed, not the interpreter.

- If appropriate, the interpreter should be acknowledged.

Gift giving and Protocol

Protocol, formalities and etiquette differ according to country and circumstance. In cultures with a high degree of formality, formal speech and conduct are valued and titles and academic degrees are highlighted. Prescribed "parameters" exist around dress, hospitality and seating arrangements. In cultures that value informality, people conduct themselves in a friendly and familiar manner. Personality and achievement are more important than titles, and spontaneity is welcome.

The degree to which local protocol is understood and adhered to may have as much impact on credibility and success as what is said. A conservative approach should be taken when presenting in new or unfamiliar settings; it's easier to become progressively more informal as time goes on than the other way around.

Gift giving is another area of cultural concern that warrants careful consideration. Customs vary greatly from country to country, and what is considered appropriate for a gift in one country may be entirely inappropriate in another. But, as a general rule, gifts can be a very important aspect of protocol. Countries/regions fall into three broad categories based on the importance they place on gift giving.

Table 7.7—Gift-giving importance		
High priority	**Medium priority**	**Low priority**
Japan	Pacific Rim: South Korea, Taiwan, China, Thailand, Malaysia, Indonesia, The Philippines, Hong Kong and Singapore The Middle East Latin America	United States Canada Australia Europe

Mainly, it is important to first find out whether or not a gift will be expected and then to decide what type of gift would be most appropriate. For example, to the Japanese, gift giving shows respect, friendship and appreciation and it is centuries-old ritual that is associated with a whole host of associated protocol. For example, when meeting with a group of Japanese business people, higher-quality gifts should be given to those with the most seniority. Also, certain colours of wrapping paper are to be avoided (e.g., white symbolizes death and bright colours are considered to be flashy). There are many other gift-giving tips that are relevant to gift giving in Japan, but the message from this example is clear—it is important to carefully research the traditions in each country before travelling. New business relationships can quickly be derailed if someone is offended; therefore, research is essential to ensure that a "faux pas" is avoided.

Impacts of Culture

Religion
Religion can have a significant impact on business dealings. Adherence to religious concepts varies from culture to culture and among individuals. In some countries several religions are practised, which may make it harder to find out how much influence a certain religion holds in business dealings. It is also important to note that most religions have special requirements that may affect business operations. For example, many religious events are paid holidays for employees. Religion may also dictate dress and appearance, which can often

conflict with norms in another country. Strict followers of Islam in Saudi Arabia stop work five times a day to pray. In some religions, separation of men and women is prevalent, which may also affect business operations.

Values and attitudes

Understanding the values, beliefs, assumptions and superstitions of a target market can provide insight into local goals, priorities and motivations. Though difficult to access, this information is essential. A Canadian who knows that Japanese people value harmony would avoid contrarian behaviour. An architect working in China would understand the importance of accommodating feng shui—the belief that a building's layout affects the lives of those who live and work in it.

Age

In North America, not as much value is placed on older members of society as in some other cultures; instead, there is a tendency to value youth and seek young and energetic employees. In addition, older employees are often retired early with special incentives to help reduce costs. Other cultures, however, particularly in Asia, value age and the accumulated wisdom that older individuals may be able to contribute for the benefit of the group.

Hierarchy

Cultures that maintain a higher level of value for older individuals and group (rather than individual) orientation often feature a greater emphasis on hierarchy, with more decisions made by those in a position of power. Societies that value independence and personal accomplishment tend to have decision-making systems that are less centralized.

Education

Countries that restrict certain fields of education based on status or gender are often at a disadvantage in international markets since these restrictions greatly limit the potential talent pool. In some cases, this is because the concepts of marketing, competitive pricing, capital markets, customer service and so on were not widely taught in these countries.

Gender

Some societies have legislated and widely accepted gender equality. Others maintain a more traditional stance whereby a man's role is to earn income for the family, while the woman's is to remain at home to take care of domestic responsibilities. It is unfortunately still true that in some cases, women from gender-equal societies continue to be regarded as less than equal when dealing with a male-dominated culture.

Behaviour

Behaviour is how people act and what they do (or don't do). Are we outgoing and expressive or quiet and reserved? Casual or formal? Punctual or late? All behaviours have particular meaning and communicate something—whether intentional or not.

Property and materialism

Materialism is defined as "a set of centrally held beliefs about the importance of possessions in one's life."[32] In effect, people in different cultures attach varying

---

[32] Richins, M.L., and Dawson, S. "Consumer Values Orientation for Materialism and Its Measurement: Scale Development and Validation," *Journal of Consumer Research* (1992): 19, pp. 303–316.

degrees of importance to the ownership of personal property. It cannot be assumed that employees, business partners and/or customers will value property ownership the way same that we do. Therefore, assumptions about incentives and consumer needs/wants can be off track without adequate research.

Intercultural Relationships: Built to Last

The importance of personal relationships varies throughout the world, but relationship-building skills are important for any business professional. This is affected by other competencies since knowledge, understanding, communication and respect are the cornerstones of meaningful relationships.

Successful relationships are developed over time and need to be continually strengthened to endure the test of time. They are fashioned from intercultural understanding, investment in time and expense, and the combined vision of all parties about the business advantages that can be realized through a long-term business relationship.

Critical attributes of successful relationship builders include the following:

- In-depth knowledge of the similarities and differences in the norms of socializing in the home country and the foreign country

- An ability to initiate conversations in the foreign language

- An understanding of how personal and professional relationships are intertwined in the foreign culture

- An awareness of negative perceptions that may exist in the foreign culture and the ability to overcome stereotyping

- The capacity to instil confidence and trust in a cross-cultural environment through effective business practices, fair and equitable treatment of all counterparts and ethical practices

How relationships affect business costs

Today's highly competitive business environment makes reducing the costs of business a top priority. International business is generally more expensive than domestic business because of a variety of additional costs, including airfares, accommodation, per diems, ground transport, visas, translations and others. Doing business in a high-context culture that requires time for developing relationships is normally more costly than in a low-context culture where relationships are less important, at least in the short term.

But relationship-based business environments may be more cost effective—especially in the long term—than they first appear. Once a strong relationship has been established, it is less susceptible to attack by competitors who offer a slightly lower price. With a solid existing relationship, the new competitor may not be given a good opportunity to take away the existing business, or the existing supplier may receive a call to warn him of the impending threat and have time to take defensive action by offering a similar price concession or opportunity to add value for the existing customer.

The lesson to be learned is that both cultural business environments have advantages and disadvantages. The key is to understand which form best suits the situation and business structure and proceed accordingly. Where long-term relationships are preferable, the initial cost of developing business in a high-context culture can be well worth the investment.

Personal commitment

Finally, for businesspeople to be interculturally effective, they must be highly dedicated and committed to their business venture to overcome the difficulties and challenges of cross-cultural business operations. Without a high level of professional commitment, the business venture is prone to failure. Global business practitioners must develop and maintain clear and realistic expectations of what they wish to accomplish in a foreign market within a particular period of time. They must plan for success by prioritizing expectations, identifying problems and challenges in advance and preparing to resolve them.

Success in intercultural environments involves long-term commitment to gain all of the competencies discussed here, and to continue to improve by applying new skills and knowledge gained through experience.

Intercultural negotiation

Negotiation should not be a zero-sum game (win all you can at the expense of the other person or organization); win-win negotiations are preferable, since they promote long-term business relations and enhance trust between partners. Any relationship based on mutual benefit is easier to manage and grow—a one-sided agreement is a recipe for failure.

Negotiating in a multicultural environment is very challenging. Because culture affects everything that people do and think, it has a significant impact on the negotiation process. Different languages also add a challenge to the communication process, which is central to negotiating.

There are four common phases of negotiation in most cultures. What differs from culture to culture is the time spent on each phase.

Figure 7.8—Four phases of negotiation

1. Developing a relationship with the other negotiating parties

2. Exchanging information about the topic or issue under negotiation

3. Persuasion

4. Concession and agreement

Relationship development

Relationship development is the first phase and is a prerequisite of any negotiating process. The negotiating parties need to develop a respect and trust for each other before a successful relationship can be built. For high-context cultures, which value relationships, this process will involve more time and effort than for low-context cultures. Relationship-based cultures will spend some time early in the process getting to know the other negotiating team. This may be accomplished through social activities such as dinners and lunches and even sightseeing tours and welcoming activities. The purpose is to gain a perspective on the other team's lives, beliefs and values. This form of initial negotiating is common in many parts of the world, including most of Latin America and many parts of Asia.

One way to develop the business relationship is to identify common goals. Once both sides know these goals, future negotiations can refer to them as a benchmark of the negotiating process. Developing trust between the two sides is realized through open and honest communication. Questions need to be answered honestly and respectfully, always taking care to avoid causing insult or loss of face.

Exchange of information and positions

Generating trust in negotiations may require disclosing certain facts at the beginning of the negotiation process, including background information and the positive outcome one believes can result from the exercise. It is important to disclose opening positions and to receive information from the counterpart to facilitate meaningful negotiations. One way to obtain information from a counterpart is to ask open-ended questions rather than wait for disclosure.

Table 7.9—Asking open-ended questions	
Developing the Relationship	• To determine common ground
	• To show you are listening
	• To demonstrate your interest
Understanding Facts	• To clarify information
Managing the Negotiation Process	• To call bluffs
	• To control the direction of the discussion
	• To broach potentially controversial issues (rather than by statement)

Asking probing questions can be delicate. Questions should be framed so that the meaning is clear but the question itself does not appear aggressive. For example, "I hope you don't mind my asking how you can manage to meet that delivery time. My calculations predicted a greater delivery time and I would like to know where I might have made a mistake."

For example, when negotiating a purchase from a supplier in another culture, one will need to know about technical information, price, discounts, quantity, shipping dates, insurance, payment and shipping methods, repeat orders and quality control. Questions should be asked about all of these items, and each is potentially an issue to be negotiated. The questions refine knowledge about the importance to the other side of reaching an agreement, and create an understanding of what items the other side is willing to yield and what items the they are inflexible about.

Persuasion

The objective of the questioning phase is to determine the areas in which there is a need to focus to reach an agreement; the areas of agreement should be known, as well as those of potential discord. The commentary switches from one of questions and information gathering to one of persuasion. The goal is to persuade the counterparts to accept an agreement that provides both sides what they want.

The art of persuasion differs between cultures, and the persuasion process should take into account the different cultural aspects represented in a particular negotiating environment. As a general rule in all cultures, use inclusive statements such as "together we can increase our share in this market." The focus should be on what is being gained rather than what is being given up.

Persuasion should be handled according to a counterpart's cultural backgrounds (that is, high- or low-context cultures). A low-context culture might be represented by Canada or Germany, and be generally comfortable with facts, figures, direct comments and explicit statements. Communication and words are generally taken at face value.

Table 7.10—Negotiation tactics used in low-context cultures: Likely to succeed with high-context cultures?
• Arguing
• Offering exaggerated counter-proposals
• Ceasing communication (silence)
• Disagreeing
• Threatening the other side
• Attacking the characters of the other side
• Avoiding and dodging certain issues
• Expressing emotion
• Insisting on a final position
• Making a "take it or leave it" offer

The same persuasion tactics mentioned above would often be disastrous in dealing with a high-context culture, such as Singapore or Japan. In these cultures, the need to focus on relationship building, harmony, status, preserving face, avoiding emotion and embarrassment and the group as a whole would make these tactics ineffective. Silence would not be viewed as threatening but rather just as a break to contemplate the issues. Threatening and attacking individual characters and openly disagreeing would cause a loss of face, and the negotiations would come to a rapid halt.

Another disparity between the two cultures is reflected by the example for Americans, the signing of a contract represents the closing of a deal, while in Japan, the signing of a contract represents the opening of a relationship.

High-context cultures value long-term relationships and will work hard not to embarrass any member of the team. When negotiating with businesses in high-context cultures, relationships hold a high priority and the hard-bargaining style employed in low-context cultures will likely be unsuccessful. Normally, negotiations with high-context cultures will take longer, may require more consensus building and can be more costly. Changing suppliers, partners, or distributors can be costly, so the initial expense in developing a long-term relationship is warranted.

Concession and agreement

With the persuasion aspect of negotiations completed, negotiators can move on to the final phase, concession and agreement, when both sides make the concessions they feel they can "live with" to obtain the required agreement.

It is common to attach a concession to a counter-concession using "if" language. For example, "I will assume responsibility for insuring the cargo if you agree to assume the costs of customs duties."

Table 7.11—Cultural consideration checklist
☑ The understanding and appreciation of the foreign culture is the basis upon which all other competencies are built.
☑ To be successful in a foreign environment, one must respect local practices and customs and learn acceptable methods of conduct.
☑ Gaining knowledge about a target market's culture and business practices will only enhance the prospects for success.
☑ It is important to adapt to different cultural views and attitudes when trying to enter a target market or negotiate a business agreement.
☑ Successful communication is enhanced through an understanding and knowledge of the foreign country and culture.
☑ The importance of personal relationships varies throughout the world, but relationship-building skills are always an asset.
☑ When conducting business in a foreign culture, dedication and commitment to the business venture are critical to a successful outcome.

Some cultures are more contract-oriented than others. Some assert that contracts define the terms of the agreement and are legally binding, while others see contracts in a different light. At times they may be regarded as an insult— why would you need a contract to enforce an agreement between two friends: "Do you not respect our relationship?" At other times they may be viewed as merely a road map to where the relationship is headed but easily changeable should future conditions warrant. Other cultures, especially the litigious United States, view contracts as final, binding and enforceable in a court of law.

High-context cultures such as Japan and China may insist on escape clauses in contracts. They view the relationship as all-important and essential and believe each side has an obligation to nurture the relationship and keep it healthy. They do not see signed contracts as the answer. The issue of contracts highlights the differences between high- and low-context cultures. Low-context cultures regard unwritten and informal agreements as unenforceable, and they are uncomfortable with the uncertainty. High-context cultures view the relationship as long term, and the documents are far less important than is maintaining good relationships.

Chapter Summary

It is clear that culture plays an enormous role in developing successful relationships and that relationships are critical to positive outcomes in negotiations and business success. Differences between cultures make it extremely important to ensure that great care is taken to understand people who think differently and are driven by different values and beliefs, when entering into international business relationships.

Exercises

Exercise 1 (class discussion)
As a human resources professional within a North American organization that is increasing its international trade activities, you have been assigned to lead a workshop for key company personnel that will have direct contact with overseas business partners. Describe some of the typical cultural differences that they will need to be aware of, and how to deal with them.

(Estimated time 5–10 minutes)

Exercise 2 (class discussion or research assignment)
You are a top executive of a North American equipment manufacturer that is looking at the possibility of entering into a joint venture with a Japanese company. You are scheduled to travel to Tokyo to visit with the potential partner in one month and enter into final negotiations of an agreement. How should you prepare for the negotiations?

(Estimated time for class discussion 10 minutes. As a research assignment 45 minutes)

Exercise 3 (research assignment)
You are a top executive of a North American manufacturer, and you are scheduled to travel to Tokyo to meet a number of potential business partners for preliminary discussions. Do some online research and find out as much as you can about giving gifts in Japan. Then, select a gift that you will plan to buy and take to each meeting. In a single-page summary of your findings, describe your choice of gift and explain why the gift is appropriate. Also indicate any special care that must be taken when giving the gift to your hosts.

(Estimated time for research 45 minutes)

Exercise 4 (class discussion)

Read the "Saving Face" case below and discuss the case and the concept of saving face in class. If you are aware of this cultural way of viewing the world, how might it affect the tone of your written correspondence? What sort of issues need to be carefully dealt with and what sort of responses need to be carefully interpreted?

(Estimated time 15 minutes)

Table 7.12—Saving face...by Lothar Katz
Jim Lazar was becoming increasingly agitated. "Your product quality is simply unacceptable! None of my other suppliers have shipped me anything like this. For crying out loud, I can buy better products in Africa than what you're making here!"
He knew he was exaggerating. Nevertheless, Lazar wanted to make sure his supplier got the message loud and clear. He had not come all the way to Malaysia to exchange niceties and pretend that everything was fine. Product quality had been a problem of late, and he was not going to take that. The room fell silent. The Malaysians were all looking down, seemingly too embarrassed to talk. Their leader was blushing.
"OK," Lazar said, "We need a break. Let's meet again in the morning to discuss how you will fix this."
The next morning, Jim Lazar learned that his supplier had cancelled the meeting, quoting "urgent other matters." He called their office but was unable to reach any of his usual contacts. Back at his own desk a few days later, he was in for an even bigger surprise: the Malaysian supplier had cancelled the contract and returned the latest orders. While volumes were moderate, his company urgently needed these products to meet its own customer commitments. This was a major problem.
We have all heard of the concept of face. Unfortunately, Western business-people frequently underestimate how important it can be when working across cultures. Causing counterparts to lose face, as Jim Lazar did, does not necessarily end business relationships. However, stepping over this line, even if done inadvertently, inevitably leads to hurt feelings, loss of trust, weakened relationships and greater risks for your business success.
Harmony and Face Many cultures, especially in Southeastern Asia or in the Middle East, share a strong preference for preserving group harmony, a desire to continually maintain positive relations across all members of a group or organization. In such cultures, individual embarrassment represents a disturbance of the harmony of the group or groups to which the individual belongs. Whether an unpleasant situation centers on a single individual or the whole group makes little difference; in both cases, the group is likely to perceive a collective loss of face and react with a feeling of shame.

Table 7.12—Saving face...by Lothar Katz *(continued)*

Face is the external representation of a positive and harmonious self as viewed by others. The term is not limited to individuals. Families, groups, organizations, or even whole nations may have face in this sense. If a group views actions or behaviors causing loss of face as inappropriate, as in Jim Lazar's case, it is likely to turn against the person causing it. This may affect that person's organization as well. For instance, an Asian company perceiving face issues caused by a representative of a Western partner company may hold that against the company as a whole, not just the individual. Many actions carry the risk of causing loss of face. Examples are openly turning down someone's request, singling out an individual for public critique or praise, failing to show respect, or losing one's temper. The indirect communication approach often employed by members of such cultures reflects this: rather than saying "no," they use phrases such as "maybe, "we will see," or "this will need further analysis" to express disagreement in more face-saving ways. Similarly, they rarely confront problems openly, and sometimes do not even acknowledge them, which again serves as a way to preserve harmony.

What Can You Do If You Stepped Over the Line?

People often ask "How can I recover if I inadvertently caused loss of face?" The answer is that since relationships are affected, it is vital to make active efforts to regain your counterparts' trust by apologizing, expressing respect for the individual and/or group, and trying hard to build new bridges. In Lazar's case, an apology in the form of "I regret what might have been an unfortunate choice of words and would like to assure you that I have great trust in your ability to solve the quality problems. Let us please continue to work together towards our mutual business success" might help get the communication going again. However, he would have to continually demonstrate his respect for the Malaysian vendors through words as well as actions to win back their trust.

In some cases, your only hope may be to find a third party willing to act as a mediator. Assuming this person has the trust of the group you offended, he or she may be able to get the communication between the parties going again.

The Bottom Line

Seemingly small infractions of cultural rules can jeopardize and even disrupt your business. Avoiding face issues by adjusting behaviors is much more effective than trying to repair the damage later. Especially when doing business in Asia, it is vital to control your emotions and treat others with respect at all times, even when confronting problems. When it comes to conducting international business, keep in mind that the best guideline is not "Treat others as you want to be treated," it is "Treat others as they want to be treated"!

Lothar Katz is an International Business Advisor and the author of "Negotiating International Business—The Negotiator's Reference Guide to 50 Countries Around the World," released in 2006. He has a wealth of experience in achieving productive co-operation across cultures and driving business success on a

Table 7.12—Saving face...by Lothar Katz *(continued)*

global scale. A seasoned former executive of Texas Instruments, a Fortune 500 company, Lothar regularly interacted with employees, customers, outsourcing partners and third parties in more than 25 countries around the world. He teaches International Project Management at the University of Texas at Dallas' School of Management and is a Business Leadership Center instructor at the Southern Methodist University's Cox School of Business.

Source: © Lothar Katz, 2007 (www.leadershipcrossroads.com) Reprinted with permission

References/Resources

Geert Hofstede, Cultural Dimensions (www.geert-hofstede.com)

Going Global: An Introduction to the Cultural Aspects of International Trade (www.fitt.ca)

Centre for Intercultural Learning (www.intercultures.gc.ca)

8

International Business Practices

Ethics and social responsibility

Chapter Objectives

- Understand the importance of ethics and social responsibility in today's international business context

- Define the basic ethical challenges faced by international traders and how to deal with them

- Describe the value of integrating ethical individual conduct with responsible corporate business practices for the benefit of all stakeholders in global business

Overview

For the global trader, knowledge of business ethics, including bribery and corruption, child-labour constraints and human-rights issues is no longer a marginal consideration but essential for international success. An understanding of these issues, together with a firm commitment to conducting business in an ethical manner, will help address underlying injustices and re-generate eroded value in the business relationship. Fundamentally, ethical business conduct makes good business sense, in addition to being "the right thing to do."

The global trader needs to understand the widening importance of social responsibility in global business and how to handle the ethical challenges of international trade and investment and balance them with the demands of the business. Integrity and competency are two of the core values for all international trade professionals who have a responsibility to their profession, their organization and to society as a whole.

Cultural conflicts can undermine the benefits of increased contact among nations unless moral and ethical questions are raised and resolved. For example, the global trader needs to consider the following questions:

- Should countries apply their own values when dealing with other countries that may have radically different value systems?

- Should businesspeople trade with, or locate operations in, countries with oppressive political regimes?

- Should companies import products they suspect are made by child or prison labour?

- Should subsidiaries located in a foreign country continue to follow the ethical guidelines and practices of the parent multinational's home country?

- Should they follow "best" environmental practices in all their operations?

- Should businesspeople resist requests for bribes when they are abroad, even though bribes may be part of traditional business practice in a particular country?

- Should we export products deemed unacceptable by our own national standards?

- Should aid be "bundled" with trade when dealing with developing countries?

- Such ethical dilemmas will only become more difficult and complex as international economic interaction increases. There are no simple answers. Businesspeople involved in international trade must remain alert and sensitive to these issues.

International business ethics: changing times, changing perceptions

Just a decade or so ago, most business people had a primary—and laudable—focus: the success of their operation, in terms of orders, sales, profits and return to the shareholders. While these should still be primary goals, a new consideration has recently been added to the mix. Sometimes referred to as the "fourth dimension" or part of the "triple bottom line," this is the acceptance that carrying out business in an ethical manner, and being seen to do so, is as important as the other goals. It is true that some commentators disagree on the importance of ethics, but it will be seen that many potential problems—including ones that ultimately affect the "traditional bottom line" in adverse ways—exist for international businesses that ignore the principles of ethical conduct.

Table 8.1—What would you do?

If you are unsure about this, think of how you might react if one of your foreign agents requested a special commission to close an order with a client, and asked for it to be paid to a numbered Swiss bank account. Would you consider this a normal cost of doing business—after all, "everybody does it these days"—or would you be prepared to deny the request and risk losing the business? Take another example: If your order book was low and you learned that by leaving an "envelope" you could be sure of getting that lucrative contract, would you do it? Or would you refuse on ethical grounds to indulge in a bribe? Dealing incorrectly with issues of this kind could, at the very least, risk negative exposure in the media and, at worst, expose you to legal action and consequences.

Civil society

The anti-globalization movement so visible a few years back in Seattle, Genoa and Quebec City, was evidence that people were beginning to take a stronger stand for what they believed was right, led often by non-government organizations (NGOs) or individuals who felt strongly about the issues. In effect, these activists have publicly articulated the concerns of civil society as they have increasingly taken a firm stand on corporate social responsibility (CSR) issues. The global trader should have the understanding and insight to develop an informed view on CSR issues, and ought to put policies in place to deal with these changes and with the new demands on corporate behaviour. These changing perceptions are not only focused on the fairly straightforward issue of bribery and related corruption—they extend to child labour, human rights, environmental and sustainability issues and community involvement.

NGOs are increasingly influential and effective in their efforts to promote CSR, and are actively encouraging board-level representation and accountability in the area of CSR. Additionally, certain countries are including CSR considerations in their assessments of whether or not to provide financing for specific transactions or projects.

The public's concern with child labour and basic human rights has grown with the increasing supply of goods—textiles in particular—from the developing world. Many companies in the West have transferred production to factories in India, China and elsewhere in Asia to save costs and remain competitive. There is no doubt that in many of these countries costs are still saved by the employment of children, sometimes in appalling "sweat shop" conditions. The dichotomy is that the customers want the cheap shirt, but do not want it to be made in such circumstances and—as we have seen in the cases of well-known companies like Nike and The Gap—they are willing to go to great lengths to expose such abuse. Here is another issue to confront the manager of a global supply chain working with partners in the developing world.

Bribery and Corruption: Corrosive, Costly and Cancerous

Despite efforts to reduce bribery and corruption, never mind eliminate them, they are still endemic in many parts of the world. Apart from distorting normal trading arrangements, they can add greatly to the cost of doing business and generally only serve to enrich a few greedy people in positions of authority and tilt the playing field in favour of those with deep pockets. Business decisions based on personal reward rather than responsibility often turn out to be poor choices, bringing negative impacts to the corporation and to society.

While some argue that bribery is, in some regions, an accepted business practice, the current global environment is supported by a rules-based system that seeks to remove such distortions, and it is incumbent upon trade professionals to support and advance the fight against corruption and bribery.

Leading the fight for change is Transparency International. This organization, based in Berlin, was founded in 1993 and now has more than eighty branches around the world. Although it is active in many related areas, Transparency International's main visibility is through the regular publication of its "bribery perceptions index." This is compiled from interviews with people who regularly do business in about 140 countries, and lists those countries where bribery is most prevalent. Given that bribery cannot occur without a complicit action by the party providing the bribe, they also list those countries whose business people are perceived as most likely to bribe for competitive advantage.

Figure 8.2—Transparency International Corruption Perceptions Index 2006		
Country Rank	Country/Territory	2006 CPI Score
1	Finland	9.6
	Iceland	9.6
	New Zealand	9.6
4	Denmark	9.5
5	Singapore	9.4
6	Sweden	9.2
7	Switzerland	9.1
8	Norway	8.8
9	Australia	8.7
	Netherlands	8.7

Figure 8.2—Transparency International Corruption Perceptions Index 2006 *(continued)*		
Country Rank	**Country/Territory**	**2006 CPI Score**
11	Austria	8.6
	Luxembourg	8.6
	United Kingdom	8.6
14	Canada	8.5
15	Hong Kong	8.3
16	Germany	8.0
17	Japan	7.6
18	France	7.4
	Ireland	7.4
20	Belgium	7.3
	Chile	7.3
	U.S.	7.3
142	Angola	2.2
	Congo, Republic of	2.2
	Kenya	2.2
	Kyrgyzstan	2.2
	Nigeria	2.2
	Pakistan	2.2
	Sierra Leone	2.2
	Tajikistan	2.2
	Turkmenistan	2.2
151	Belarus	2.1
	Cambodia	2.1
	Côte-d'Ivoire	2.1
	Equatorial Guinea	2.1
	Uzbekistan	2.1

Figure 8.2—Transparency International Corruption Perceptions Index 2006 *(continued)*

Country Rank	Country/Territory	2006 CPI Score
156	Bangladesh	2.0
	Chad	2.0
	Congo, Democratic Republic	2.0
	Sudan	2.0
160	Guinea	1.9
	Iraq	1.9
	Myanmar	1.9
163	Haiti	1.8

Source: Transparency International (www.transparency.org)

In Canada, anti-corruption legislation was ratified in 1998 and is known as Bill S 21. Penalties in the Canadian case are potentially severe: summary convictions can carry up to $50,000 in fines and a maximum six months in jail. For an indictable offence, jail time can go as high as ten years.

The sectors most susceptible to bribery are major infrastructure projects, defence and aerospace, but it can occur whenever large sums are involved and where inadequate checks and balances are in place to prevent those in authority taking advantage of the situation. With extreme pressures on sales and project managers to achieve their financial targets and an increasingly competitive environment in most industries, this is understandable, and many follow the "when in Rome do as the Romans do" principle in deciding what action to take.

Specific steps to try and counteract this tendency started in the U.S. with the *Foreign Corrupt Practices Act (FCPA)* in 1977. Under this legislation, which was introduced after the well-known Lockheed bribery scandal in Japan, it is, among other things, forbidden by law to bribe any foreign public official. In 1996, the Organisation for Economic Co-operation and Development (OECD) developed an outline "Anti-bribery convention," primarily for its member countries, also outlawing the bribing of foreign public officials. This convention was subsequently ratified by 39 countries and became law. The convention specifies that it is a criminal offence to offer a loan, reward or benefit directly or indirectly to a foreign public official. No "benefit" means that it is illegal, for example, to offer to fund a scholarship for the official's daughter, and "indirect" means that making the bribe through a third party, such as an agent or distributor, is also illegal.

While this is a useful step, the legislation brings its own challenges. It is focused on public officials, leaving private business out of the equation, there is no specific protection for whistle-blowers and convictions have proven elusive. In one high-profile case, a Canadian engineering company was taken to court for bribing a foreign public official in Lesotho to the tune of C$260,000 in connection with a water-supply project. It was a complex case as the deal was done through an agent who subsequently died, and the company denied the allegations. However, the damage done to its reputation due to wide coverage in the press, and its subsequent difficulty in obtaining funding through international financial institutions serve as an example to others thinking of bribing their way to success.

Privacy and confidentiality vs. transparency

In a time of ever-increasing surveillance, triggered by attempts to crack down on real and potential threats including crime, corruption and terrorism and facilitated by advances in technology, a challenge that must be faced is maintaining the protection of confidentiality. As one can see from recent efforts to protect privacy with new legislation in some jurisdictions, a delicate compromise must be struck to preserve a balance between the legitimate need for corporate and personal security and exposing legal and ethical misconduct.

The ethical considerations around privacy are widely discussed in connection with, for example, medical records and confidential research, and there are restrictions on the use corporations can make of personal information supplied to them in the course of making a purchase (especially on the Internet). Companies are forced to ask whether they can use a private address to pass on to others, or send offers and product information to the e-mail address supplied, and most corporate websites will have a privacy policy. Some firms even quote it at the bottom of their e-mails. If a surveillance camera is in place, we expect there will likely be a warning, and the police have to justify and obtain permission if they wish to tap phones. Most of this is part of day-to-day life. The global trader, however, can come across different issues. He may be asked to pay a bribe when abroad and be instructed by his manager to ignore company policy and go ahead. What should he do? Some companies have clear policies for whistle-blowers, but it's a tricky call.

Facilitation payments

Regular international travellers, especially those who have lived abroad, know that the payment of a small (and occasionally not so small) fee is usually required if a telephone is to be installed with reasonable dispatch, an import or similar licence granted or goods cleared quickly through customs. The law recognizes that this is indeed a standard practice in countries where officials do not in all conscience earn a living wage, and allows so-called "facilitation payments" to officials for a routine action that is part of their regular responsibility. What is forbidden is to bribe to gain competitive advantage.

The question of facilitation payments remains, however, a contentious issue, because there is no clear definition of when they, in effect, become bribes. At one end of the scale one can argue convincingly that slipping a few dollars to a customs official to put a stamp on a routine document to clear legitimate goods through customs within a reasonable time frame (or to avoid holding them back on manifestly false pretences) is a facilitation payment. But what about approving a permit to add an extension to a factory, where a payment of around U.S.$500 or U.S.$1000 might be "expected"? The OECD convention prohibits payments when they are made to "obtain or retain business or other improper advantage in the conduct of international business." Facilitation payments are excluded from this but should be reasonable. What is the definition of reasonable? The only successful prosecution under the FCPA was on account of a claimed facilitation payment of U.S.$5000, so there is at least one precedent for "unreasonable"! As with so many ethical issues, it remains a question of judgment.

As we shall see later, international corporations like General Electric, which have taken the lead in stamping out this cancer, have clear policies in place, spend money and time on training staff and agents and ensure that there is total buy-in throughout their companies. Whatever the size of their operation, global traders need to be aware of the issues, the legislation and the ramifications of ignoring it and the most effective way to instil a total "no-bribe" culture within the organization. Only then can they be reasonably sure of avoiding exposure or prosecution.

Exploitative Child Labour: Critical, Complex and Compelling

The complex issue of child labour has received much attention in recent years as a result of action taken against well-known retailers that were thought to be employing children in unacceptable working conditions, either directly in their own subsidiary companies abroad or indirectly through suppliers. However, the problem has been around for a long time. Child labour was widely used in the Western world in the 19th century, and in many countries children played an important role in bringing in the harvest.

It has been many years since children were widely employed in developed countries (except to help out in the family business or on the farm), where education is obligatory and free, but this is far from the case in many parts of the developing world, including, for example, India. With the absence of a social safety net and much of the population engaged in agriculture, large families are still considered *de rigueur* and children are put to work to contribute to family income. Increasing urbanization has led to jobs for children migrating from the farm to the factory, highlighting the problem of working conditions, where unscrupulous employers pay miserable wages for long hours of virtual slave labour in indescribable conditions of heat and lack of ventilation, safety equipment and basic hygiene. The following case is based on recent events in the chocolate industry and illustrates some of the challenges associated with this issue.

Figure 8.3—Globalization and child labour: The cause can also be a cure

In providing jobs for millions of Africans, the globalized chocolate industry must also avoid engaging child labor.

Many chocolate lovers still have a bitter taste in their mouths from revelations that the candies they adore might have been produced by child labor in West Africa. In an ensuing uproar, cocoa producers, traders, suppliers, governments, unions and civil-society groups agreed to a solution brokered by two members of Congress. In 2001, they created a multi-sectoral partnership, the Cocoa Protocol, to address the conditions that perpetuate forced child labor on these cacao plantations.

Yet five years later, children still toil, picking cacao in unsafe and unfair conditions. Clearly, a sector-specific strategy cannot address the broad cultural, social and economic factors in West Africa that perpetuate child labor.

The number of children forced to labour in the cacao plantations is small. In 2000, the U.S. State Department, Knight Ridder and the BBC reported that some 15,000 children worked in conditions of forced labour picking beans in Ghana and the Ivory Coast. Trafficked from extremely poor countries, like Mali

---

Figure 8.3—Globalization and child labour: The cause can also be a cure

and Burkina Faso, the children worked on some of the 1.5 million small cocoa farms in West Africa. These farms produce more than half the world's cacao that's processed into candy, cookies or cocoa butter used for cosmetics.

Consumers and regulators don't know how to protect these child workers without jeopardizing the livelihoods of millions of their compatriots.

The news that forced labour was used to produce chocolate, a clear violation of existing legislation, raised a red flag for U.S. policymakers as well as processors and manufacturers of cocoa products. Under the *Smoot-Hawley Tariff Act* of 1930, the U.S. Customs Service is supposed to refuse entry to any goods identified as made by forced labour. But it rarely investigates or interdicts such products. Congressman Elliott Engel and Senator Tom Harkin pursued a new tactic. The House passed legislation requiring the U.S. Food and Drug Administration to develop a social label to reassure consumers that their cocoa products were free of child labour.

However, before the Senate could act, a panicked chocolate industry appealed for a non-legislative solution. The industry feared the U.S. chocolate market, with some $13 billion in sales, would collapse if the bill became law.

Harkin and Engel wanted to address child labour without undermining the fragile economies in question. They recognized that in the Ivory Coast alone, some 7 million individuals were engaged in cacao-related economic activity; but less than 1 percent of these workers were children. They also understood that a collapse of this trade could exacerbate rather than address the root factors—illiteracy, poverty and lack of economic alternatives—that perpetuate exploitation in the cocoa sector.

In September 2001, after intense negotiations, plantation owners, cacao traders and processors and chocolate manufacturers agreed to implement the Cocoa Protocol. All of the major chocolate company firms signed on and agreed to work with unions, civil society and government officials in a multi-sectoral partnership designed to ensure that all cocoa bean products are grown and processed without violating internationally accepted labour standards. Moreover, the signatories to the protocol agreed to develop and put in place a certification to assure consumers that processed cacao was not produced in these conditions by July 1, 2005.

But the companies did not meet that deadline. They were hampered by civil war in the Ivory Coast and the non-participation of companies that use cacao for cocoa butter products such as cosmetics firms.

After an in-depth investigation of conditions of cacao plantations in the Ivory Coast in 2006, BBC reporter Humphrey Hawksley found little evidence that industry efforts were changing farm conditions and concluded: "No one is in charge of the efforts put in place under the Cocoa Protocol. There's no place the buck stops. In the cocoa belt, it's only a short drive to find children working with machetes amid some of the worst poverty anywhere in the world."

Some NGOs and activists are frustrated and want to abandon the protocol. The International Labor Rights Fund filed suit against Nestlé, ADM and Cargill.

Figure 8.3—Globalization and child labour: The cause can also be a cure

Meanwhile, other NGOs such as Global Exchange want governments to adopt a social label and ban imports of cacao that can't be shown to be fairly traded. But a government-approved or -sanctioned social label is not a panacea. Although some countries, namely Belgium and South Africa, have put in place social labels for manufactured goods, they have not done so for bulk commodities such as cacao where it is difficult to separate out those commodities legitimately produced and those not. Moreover, policymakers don't yet know if such social labels could be challenged as a trade distortion at the WTO. In the face of these concerns, the two legislators as well as some NGOs, such as Free the Slaves and the National Child Labor Coalition, are willing to wait another year for the chocolate industry to develop its certification.

Forty-two countries in the chocolate supply chain endorsed the protocol and abide by its strictures. Industrialized country governments, international organizations, chocolate companies and foundations provide money and expertise to resolve complex problems in the sector. Under the watchful eye of Protocol participants, Ghana and the Ivory Coast have stepped up efforts to monitor labour conditions, reduce or eliminate school fees, and invest in the education of local children. Meanwhile, in countries such as Mali that have exported child labour, government officials teach families how they can raise family incomes if they let their kids go to school. These efforts are beginning to address the supply-side factors that can perpetuate forced child labour in the cocoa sector, while pushing cocoa processors and manufacturers on the demand side to stop procuring cacao from farms where forced child labour exists. And the changes do not undermine the cacao trade that sustains so many West Africans.

But a sector-specific strategy cannot address the economic and cultural factors that perpetuate forced child labour in West Africa: First, because of an oversupply of cacao, the real price of cacao remains low by historic standards. West African farmers have little leverage to bargain effectively for higher prices and thus they try to reap cost efficiencies from their workers. Secondly, the protocol cannot address the cultural mores that perpetuate child labour in the countries of West Africa. Lacking educational opportunities, parents view their children as an extra hand, not as individuals who deserve time for education or play. Childhood is both a construct and a luxury good, available only to children of adults who earn sufficient livelihoods for their families as a whole.

Consequently, while the Cocoa Protocol may reduce child labour in one sector, it cannot guarantee that children won't continue to work in other sectors. Their exploitation will only stop when policymakers in the industrialized and developing world meet their human-rights obligations and enforce the law; when companies take responsibility for their supply chains and develop strategies to ensure that their suppliers don't rely on forced labour; and finally, when policymakers address the lack of opportunities, power, and education as well as cultural mores that allow individuals to be abused. The Cocoa Protocol offers a model as to how policymakers working in collaboration with industry, unions and civil society might address these problems in one sector without distorting trade. But it's just a sector-specific start.

> ### Figure 8.3—Globalization and child labour: The cause can also be a cure
>
> Susan Ariel Aaronson teaches at the George Washington University School of Business and is the author, with Jamie Zimmerman, of "Trade Imbalance: The Struggle to Weigh Human Rights Concerns in Trade Policymaking," Cambridge University Press, 2007.

Source: © 2007 Susan Ariel Aaronson; YaleGlobal, Yale Center for the Study of Globalization, Washington, 13 March 2007 (www.yaleglobal.yale.edu/display

Child labour conventions

The worldwide movement to reduce and eventually eliminate child labour has been going on for many years, and some NGOs, like Save the Children, specialize in publicizing the issue and raising funds to combat it. One of the challenges is the confusing number of different standards. The International Labour Organisation (ILO) published a convention in 1973 that made some specific recommendations, and the United Nations—having initiated a treaty preventing bonded labour in 1956—went on to publish the Convention on the Rights of the Child in 1989. This noted that the child's interest must be paramount, that no hazardous work should be undertaken, that there should be a minimum age for employment (usually 18), that hours and conditions should be regulated and that work should not interfere with a child's education. The challenge with these initiatives was the failure by many of the countries, where child labour was widely used, to ratify the agreements or to observe the key recommendations. In 1997, the UNICEF State of the World's Children report focused on child labour. It called for an end to hazardous and exploitative child labour and recommended the adoption of codes by international companies specifying that neither they nor their sub-contractors would employ children in conditions that violated their rights. Recently, many large companies in the private sector, anxious to maintain their reputation with customers and the public at large, have taken the UNICEF recommendations to heart and included child labour in their company codes of conduct or integrity programes.

This issue has significant profile in the public's mind, and as with bribery, it is important to understand its complexity. Simply preventing child labour of any kind can be counterproductive, especially if the child happens to be the main or only breadwinner. The alternative to regular labour and wages may well be a life on the streets, or worse. So once again, a clear company policy and a code that adopts some or all of the above criteria will be beneficial.

Table 8.4—15-point code

Companies should adopt a 15-point code, which should:

1. Apply not just to the company, but also to its suppliers

2. Specify standards that are precise and measurable

3. Not prohibit child labour per se, but aim to prevent economic exploitation

Table 8.4—15-point code *(continued)*
4. Prevent abusive or exploitative forms of child labour
5. Prohibit employment of children under 12, guarantee minimum conditions for children under 18, and ensure no under-18's are employed in hazardous work
6. Provide that a company that stops a child from working because he/she is under age helps with their rehabilitation or return to full-time schooling
7. Stipulate maximum hours and ensure periodic holidays
8. Ensure that the child is paid regularly—at least every month—and preferably directly rather than through an agent
9. Ban corporal punishment
10. Prohibit debt bondage (bonded labour in exchange for debt incurred by parent)
11. Adapt the age of child employment to local laws where applicable, or prohibit it under the age of compulsory schooling
12. Allow working children to attend school
13. Be clearly communicated, allowing for translation where relevant
14. Be monitored for implementation by independent adjudicators, among others
15. Encourage building of relationships with sub-contractors to improve their child-employment practices

Source: Mendes, Professor Errol, University of Ottawa

Human Rights: Trade, Invest or Sanction

One could argue that human rights go back to the 1215 Magna Carta in Great Britain, or indeed even further back to the Persian and Mauryan empires, and they were, of course, included in the American Declaration of Independence. However, their importance in the 20th century was first highlighted by the adoption of the Universal Declaration of Human Rights by the United Nations in 1948, following the barbarism of the Second World War. Subsequently, there have been many additional international agreements, including the International Covenant on Economic, Social and Cultural Rights in 1976 and separate covenants on genocide (1951), racial discrimination (1969), torture (1984), discrimination against women (1981) and the rights of the child (as already mentioned). These were given additional focus by the creation in 2002 of the International Criminal Court with jurisdiction over genocide, crimes against humanity and war crimes (but with only 55 countries signing on, the U.S. being among several others declining).

We read about broader human-rights abuses in the press with discouraging frequency, and these circumstances all pose additional corporate challenges. Imprisonment without trial in China, gross abuse of the democratic process in Myanmar, imprisonment without trial in Guantanamo Bay, muzzling of the press for political ends in Iran and more recently in Venezuela, or the complete destruction of a wealthy and successful country in Zimbabwe are sad commentaries on the state of human rights in the 21st century. Likewise, in spite of many reports from human-rights organizations and the press, the conventions did not prevent genocide in Rwanda, ethnic cleansing in Bosnia, gross abuses in Darfur and torture all over the world.

Situations like this can pose a dilemma for the global trader who sees potential marketing or investment opportunities around the world and wonders whether to move ahead or not. Indeed, they are exacerbated by conflicts currently raging in many countries, particularly the Middle East and Afghanistan. In this context, work by the University of Heidelberg is an interesting reference point. Set up in 1991, its Institute for International Conflict Research tracks conflict zones and publishes an annual conflict barometer. It makes depressing reading. Tracking five grades of conflict from latent to all-out war compared with 2005 (already a highly conflict-ridden year), it shows that in 2006 the numbers of cases in 3 categories had increased markedly, there were 118 cases of crisis or severe crisis and 6 cases of all-out war. This has to be taken into account in assessing business opportunities and the risks involved, particularly if direct investment is contemplated in the country concerned.

Turning back to human-rights abuses, in some cases the decision regarding trade or investment is already made by the imposition of multilateral sanctions by an international body, such as the UN, or by a major group of countries, such as the EU. In other cases, a country may impose unilateral sanctions, as Canada did in Myanmar. Products may be subject to export controls, or investment may be proscribed in the targeted country, as is frequently the case with defence, financial and telecommunications sectors.

Economic sanctions or not?

Two views predominate in considering action when no restrictions apply. One view is that human-rights abuses are abhorrent, and the best way to demonstrate the corporation's position is to refuse to do business with or invest in the country concerned, and make this position publicly known to all stakeholders. While this may be a good political move at home, it is questionable whether it has much influence on the country concerned. When Indonesia invaded East Timor, the Canadian International Development Agency (CIDA) withdrew its aid funding for that country. This proved to be an ineffective gesture, as Indonesia simply went elsewhere for its support, and meanwhile the *persona non grata* Canadian private sector took several years to work its way back into that market.

In Iraq, multilateral sanctions succeeded in further impoverishing the local population, but did little or nothing to curb the activities or lifestyle of Saddam Hussein. As mentioned in the introduction, perhaps the only real sanctions success story is in South Africa, where the apartheid-ridden country became an international pariah, and—with the exception of a few countries that circumvented the sanctions—was shunned in business, sporting and other areas. This no doubt helped bring about the welcome change of regime.

The other view is that human rights tend to improve as the economy grows and strengthens, and because sanctions are usually ineffective and tend to harm the poorest people in the country concerned, it is better to trade and invest with a local partner, provided there is at least some assurance that the new operation will not be directly or indirectly complicit in abuses. Trade and/or investment will bring jobs and growth to the local economy, as the theory goes, and there will be a trickle-down effect from the introduction of better standards of behaviour from outside, which over time will improve local conditions in terms of human rights. The open question remains: how long does that take, and how much change does it bring about?

Corporate alignment with the Universal Declaration of Human Rights

While the media frequently focus on blatant human-rights abuses in a handful of rogue nations (as discussed above), the conduct of corporations in general is equally important. The importance of corporate alignment with basic human rights is growing because the forces of globalization are widening the gap between the rich and the poor. In this system, the most impoverished citizens on earth appear to be increasingly subject to forces that are beyond their control and, in some cases, this means that basic human rights are being impinged upon. Therefore, at a minimum, ethical conduct involves a solid understanding of the Universal Declaration of Human Rights (www.un.org/Overview/rights.html). These rights are of fundamental importance to anyone involved in international business and they should be studied carefully.

A careful review of these rights will reveal that all international business projects need to be scrutinized with these rights in mind. The declaration contains many important provisions that are relevant to corporate conduct and working conditions for employees. Whether it is foreign direct investment or a joint venture in a new factory, mining installation or some other major infrastructure project, these developments almost always require close collaboration with the local community to ensure that these rights are respected.

In many countries, particularly where government oversight is weak, it is argued by many that corporate conduct is often in violation of many of these rights. Therefore, the ethical challenge lies in the fact that the human rights noted below are often not enforced by law. However, ethical business professionals working for a company considering the establishment of operations in a country where regulatory oversight is limited need to know these provisions intimately to ensure that corporate conduct is judicious (i.e., even if enforcement of these rights by local legal authorities is unlikely).

For those who ignore these rights, they do so at their own peril. Apart from international agreements, there is a plethora of organizations watching over human-rights abuses, the best-known among them being Amnesty International, Human Rights Watch, The International Human Rights Association, The World Organisation against Torture, Freedom House, Anti-slavery International and Democracy Watch. Therefore, violations of these rights typically bring a swift response from these organizations, concerned citizens, the press, disenchanted shareholders and employees. It therefore pays dividends to understand these rights intimately and to have clear policies in place that require corporate conduct that respects them. Handling these issues correctly is not only the right thing to do as a good global citizen, it also makes good business sense.

Figure 8.5—The Universal Declaration of Human Rights
Adopted and proclaimed by United Nations *General Assembly resolution 217 A (III) of 10 December 1948*
PREAMBLE Whereas recognition of the inherent dignity and of the equal and inalienable rights of all members of the human family is the foundation of freedom, justice and peace in the world, Whereas disregard and contempt for human rights have resulted in barbarous acts which have outraged the conscience of mankind, and the advent of a world in which human beings shall enjoy freedom of speech and belief and freedom from fear and want has been proclaimed as the highest aspiration of the common people, Whereas it is essential, if man is not to be compelled to have recourse, as a last resort, to rebellion against tyranny and oppression, that human rights should be protected by the rule of law, Whereas it is essential to promote the development of friendly relations between nations, Whereas the peoples of the United Nations have in the Charter reaffirmed their faith in fundamental human rights, in the dignity and worth of the human person and in the equal rights of men and women and have determined to promote social progress and better standards of life in larger freedom, Whereas Member States have pledged themselves to achieve, in co-operation with the United Nations, the promotion of universal respect for and observance of human rights and fundamental freedoms, Whereas a common understanding of these rights and freedoms is of the greatest importance for the full realization of this pledge, Now, Therefore THE GENERAL ASSEMBLY proclaims THIS UNIVERSAL DECLARATION OF HUMAN RIGHTS as a common standard of achievement for all peoples and all nations, to the end that every individual and every organ of society, keeping this declaration constantly in mind, shall strive by teaching and education to promote respect for these rights and freedoms and by progressive measures, national and international, to secure their universal and effective recognition and observance, both among the peoples of Member States themselves and among the peoples of territories under their jurisdiction.
Article 1. All human beings are born free and equal in dignity and rights. They are endowed with reason and conscience and should act towards one another in a spirit of brotherhood.

Figure 8.5—The Universal Declaration of Human Rights *(continued)*

Article 2. Everyone is entitled to all the rights and freedoms set forth in this declaration, without distinction of any kind, such as race, colour, sex, language, religion, political or other opinion, national or social origin, property, birth or other status. Furthermore, no distinction shall be made on the basis of the political, jurisdictional or international status of the country or territory to which a person belongs, whether it be independent, trust, non-self-governing or under any other limitation of sovereignty.

Article 3. Everyone has the right to life, liberty and security of person

Article 4. No one shall be held in slavery or servitude; slavery and the slave trade shall be prohibited in all their forms

Article 5. No one shall be subjected to torture or to cruel, inhuman or degrading treatment or punishment.

Article 6. Everyone has the right to recognition everywhere as a person before the law.

Article 7. All are equal before the law and are entitled without any discrimination to equal protection of the law. All are entitled to equal protection against any discrimination in violation of this declaration and against any incitement to such discrimination.

Article 8. Everyone has the right to an effective remedy by the competent national tribunals for acts violating the fundamental rights granted him by the constitution or by law.

Article 9. No one shall be subjected to arbitrary arrest, detention or exile.

Article 10. Everyone is entitled in full equality to a fair and public hearing by an independent and impartial tribunal, in the determination of his rights and obligations and of any criminal charge against him.

Article 11.

(1) Everyone charged with a penal offence has the right to be presumed innocent until proved guilty according to law in a public trial at which he has had all the guarantees necessary for his defence.

(2) No one shall be held guilty of any penal offence on account of any act or omission which did not constitute a penal offence, under national or international law, at the time when it was committed. Nor shall a heavier penalty be imposed than the one that was applicable at the time the penal offence was committed.

Article 12. No one shall be subjected to arbitrary interference with his privacy, family, home or correspondence, or to attacks upon his honour and reputation. Everyone has the right to the protection of the law against such interference or attacks.

Figure 8.5—The Universal Declaration of Human Rights *(continued)*

Article 13.

(1) Everyone has the right to freedom of movement and residence within the borders of each state.

(2) Everyone has the right to leave any country, including his own, and to return to his country.

Article 14.

(1) Everyone has the right to seek and to enjoy in other countries asylum from persecution.

(2) This right may not be invoked in the case of prosecutions genuinely arising from non-political crimes or from acts contrary to the purposes and principles of the United Nations

Article 15.

(1) Everyone has the right to a nationality.

(2) No one shall be arbitrarily deprived of his nationality nor denied the right to change his nationality.

Article 16.

(1) Men and women of full age, without any limitation due to race, nationality or religion, have the right to marry and to found a family. They are entitled to equal rights as to marriage, during marriage and at its dissolution.

(2) Marriage shall be entered into only with the free and full consent of the intending spouses.

(3) The family is the natural and fundamental group unit of society and is entitled to protection by society and the state.

Article 17.

(1) Everyone has the right to own property alone as well as in association with others.

(2) No one shall be arbitrarily deprived of his property.

Article 18. Everyone has the right to freedom of thought, conscience and religion; this right includes freedom to change his religion or belief, and freedom, either alone or in community with others and in public or private, to manifest his religion or belief in teaching, practice, worship and observance.

Article 19. Everyone has the right to freedom of opinion and expression; this right includes freedom to hold opinions without interference and to seek, receive and impart information and ideas through any media and regardless of frontiers.

Figure 8.5—The Universal Declaration of Human Rights *(continued)*

Article 20.

(1) Everyone has the right to freedom of peaceful assembly and association.

(2) No one may be compelled to belong to an association.

Article 21.

(1) Everyone has the right to take part in the government of his country, directly or through freely chosen representatives.

(2) Everyone has the right of equal access to public service in his country.

(3) The will of the people shall be the basis of the authority of government; this will shall be expressed in periodic and genuine elections which shall be by universal and equal suffrage and shall be held by secret vote or by equivalent free voting procedures.

Article 22. Everyone, as a member of society, has the right to social security and is entitled to realization, through national effort and international co-operation and in accordance with the organization and resources of each state, of the economic, social and cultural rights indispensable for his dignity and the free development of his personality.

Article 23.

(1) Everyone has the right to work, to free choice of employment, to just and favourable conditions of work and to protection against unemployment.

(2) Everyone, without any discrimination, has the right to equal pay for equal work.

(3) Everyone who works has the right to just and favourable remuneration ensuring for himself and his family an existence worthy of human dignity, and supplemented, if necessary, by other means of social protection.

(4) Everyone has the right to form and to join trade unions for the protection of his interests.

Article 24. Everyone has the right to rest and leisure, including reasonable limitation of working hours and periodic holidays with pay.

Article 25.

(1) Everyone has the right to a standard of living adequate for the health and well-being of himself and of his family, including food, clothing, housing and medical care and necessary social services, and the right to security in the event of unemployment, sickness, disability, widowhood, old age or other lack of livelihood in circumstances beyond his control.

(2) Motherhood and childhood are entitled to special care and assistance. All children, whether born in or out of wedlock, shall enjoy the same social protection.

Figure 8.5—The Universal Declaration of Human Rights *(continued)*

Article 26.

(1) Everyone has the right to education. Education shall be free, at least in the elementary and fundamental stages. Elementary education shall be compulsory. Technical and professional education shall be made generally available and higher education shall be equally accessible to all on the basis of merit.

(2) Education shall be directed to the full development of the human personality and to the strengthening of respect for human rights and fundamental freedoms. It shall promote understanding, tolerance and friendship among all nations, racial or religious groups, and shall further the activities of the United Nations for the maintenance of peace.

(3) Parents have a prior right to choose the kind of education that shall be given to their children.

Article 27.

(1) Everyone has the right freely to participate in the cultural life of the community, to enjoy the arts and to share in scientific advancement and its benefits.

(2) Everyone has the right to the protection of the moral and material interests resulting from any scientific, literary or artistic production of which he is the author.

Article 28. Everyone is entitled to a social and international order in which the rights and freedoms set forth in this Declaration can be fully realized.

Article 29.

(1) Everyone has duties to the community in which alone the free and full development of his personality is possible.
(2) In the exercise of his rights and freedoms, everyone shall be subject only to such limitations as are determined by law solely for the purpose of securing due recognition and respect for the rights and freedoms of others and of meeting the just requirements of morality, public order and the general welfare in a democratic society.
(3) These rights and freedoms may in no case be exercised contrary to the purposes and principles of the United Nations.

Article 30. Nothing in this declaration may be interpreted as implying for any state, group or person any right to engage in any activity or to perform any act aimed at the destruction of any of the rights and freedoms set forth herein.

Working with local communities
When considering human rights, incoming investors need to be highly sensitive to local communities and the serious trouble they can get into if they ignore them. Shell Petroleum Development Corp. in Nigeria is a case in point. The challenges with its investment in the Ogoni tribal area led to a long period of disastrous public relations around the world and damaged its profile as a caring corporation. On the other hand, an international mining company investing in

Peru had extensive consultations with the local community and ended up routing one of its main access roads to the mine site many kilometres out of the way to avoid damage to a national park. Needless to say, it had a smoother ride to project completion. The introduction of the Internet and the cell phone has enabled disgruntled local activists to mobilize concerned citizens and block major developments with increasing regularity—and effectiveness—so investors need to involve local communities at an early stage to ensure their support.

Figure 8.6—Shell

Shell began to invest in earnest in the Ogoni region of Nigeria when oil was discovered there in 1958—before Nigeria achieved independence from British colonial rule. Shell's activities in the region have been widely accused of not only supporting the Ogoni people's exclusion from power within the national government structure, but also of eradicating the once lush agricultural region upon which the Ogoni have long depended for their survival.

A key figure in Ogoni people's struggle against oil exploitation and the Nigerian government was Ken Saro-Wiwa. Saro-Wiwa was eventually imprisoned and hastily executed by the Nigerian government in November 1995, following a sham trial. Despite a noted lack of protest from other governments, Nigeria was quickly suspended from the Commonwealth as a result. Shell's overall response to the Ogoni situation at the time was that it was up to government leaders, and not business to find a solution.

Although the TI Index (see above) grades Canada well on perceptions of bribing, it does not appear to have such a clean slate when it comes to working with local communities, particularly in the mining sector. Round tables on mining and developing countries were set up by the federal government in 2006 that identified 23 projects around the world where Canadian companies, in spite of their general assurances that their responsibilities were being taken care of,

---

Figure 8.7—Example

Sometimes a company will not have much control over perceived abuses. A Canadian oil company was an investment partner with a company in southern Sudan and was perceived by activists to be contributing to the funding by the central government of the civil war in that area. In fact, they had been model investors, working diligently with the local community, building schools and clinics and supporting the local infrastructure. Undeserved negative publicity resulted in a severe drop in their domestic share price and pushed the company into selling its 30 percent stake, but to a shareholder from a developing country whose reputation for safeguarding human rights and supporting local communities was far from stellar. It could be argued that it would have been better for this Canadian company to remain in Sudan, contributing to the local economy and setting a good example. The trouble was that this company did not, at that time, have an effective policy in place to deal with negative publicity of this kind, and there was no clear public evidence of its reputation as a good corporate citizen or of its investment philosophy.

had caused "significant adverse social and environmental problems." These examples are tracked in a "Canadian Mining Map" and cover projects as far afield as Bolivia and The Philippines. For example, Inco in Indonesia was alleged (and this word is important as some cases are clearly not proven) to have taken indigenous land for "paltry" compensation, and to have degraded land and water resources. In another example from the Democratic Republic of the Congo, Anvil Mining was alleged to have supplied logistics to the armed forces to suppress a rebel uprising, and the latter carried out a number of human-rights abuses. Most large companies, and some smaller ones, have a strong focus on the importance of working with local communities in their codes of conduct, and the best of these include arrangements for independent monitoring and evaluation. This helps to ensure that organizations practise what they preach. See also reference to the fifth generation of codes, referred to in Figure 8.8.

Fair trade

The development of the fair-trade movement in the 1980s provides another illustration of the growing strength of the consumer in shaping ethical business practices. The movement's thrust is that buying products direct from growers and producers in the developing world, under guarantees of fair wages, prices and working conditions, helps build local economies and reduce poverty. To bear the Fair Trade label, products must meet standards set by Fair Trade Labelling Organization International. These standards will vary according to the product—they could ensure a proper price for a farmer's coffee beans or reasonable wages for a tea estate's pickers. If factory conditions are involved (e.g., for textiles), the Fair Trade label could ensure that the supplier has decent wages and minimum health, safety and environmental standards in its operation.

All these developments underscore the public's awareness of ethical issues and the importance for international businesses that have to face bribery, child-labour or human-rights challenges. They must have clear policies in place, supported by detailed codes of conduct, employee- and partner-training programs and full buy-in throughout the organization.

Intellectual Property Rights

Intellectual-property rights have become a challenging issue in international trade. For some, the theft of these rights amounts to significant commercial losses that must be minimized. For others, the aggressive assertion of these rights in domains that impact basic human rights is creating vulnerabilities in the poorest nations that are unacceptable.

Protecting intellectual property

Failure to consider intellectual property (IP) issues can result in large or fatal losses when pursuing international markets. The consequences of being unprepared should not be underestimated—setting up joint ventures, distribution networks and other strategic alliances represents a significant undertaking when protecting one's IP. Yet protection from potential partners and in-country representatives provides no safeguard from the entire realm of pirates, counterfeiters and other dubious characters that have made it their business to profit at someone else's expense.

It is a phenomenon that goes far beyond losses for right-owners or individual companies but extends to the well-being and survival of entire sectors and national economies. Much is said about pirated CDs or DVSs, but the problem of counterfeiting and piracy extends to, for instance, aircraft parts, food, pesticides and medicines, just to mention a few.

The U.S. government estimates that piracy within China costs American companies $20–$24 billion a year in damages. If one includes European and Japanese firms, the losses on account of Chinese piracy are in excess of $50 billion annually.

Jayanthi Iyenga, a senior business journalist from India who writes on a range of subjects for several publications in Asia, Britain and the United States, reports on some of the latest findings in her article "Intellectual property piracy rocks China boat." In her article, she quotes the Secretary General of Interpol: "This is a multi-billion dollar problem that affects the safety of people, the security of governments, that is connected to organised crime, drug trafficking and terrorism."

The People's Republic of China has been trying to improve its legal system, which is less than 20 years old. They are committed to transforming China into a modern economy, and have undertaken the monumental task of creating a legal system to support that economy; however, it may take some time before one can be confident about their intent to check copyright, patent and trademark infringements.

A recent study on piracy by the Beijing Business Software Alliance (BSA), the international association of the world's leading software manufacturers, charged that Asian countries engage in extensive software piracy. The study found that 53 percent of the software installed on computers in the Asia-Pacific region was pirated in 2003, representing a loss of over U.S.$7.5 billion. It added that while U.S.$80 billion in software was installed on computers worldwide last year, only U.S.$51 billion was legally purchased.

The study also claimed that the Asia-Pacific region is the area with the fourth-highest software-piracy rate and the second-highest revenue losses. The piracy rates in the region range from 92 percent in Vietnam and China to 23 percent in New Zealand. Three of the four countries with the world's highest piracy rates are in the region.

Global traders need to invest time and resources into protecting this highly valuable asset. One option is to seek protection in individual countries separately by applying directly to national industrial/intellectual property offices. Each application may have to be translated into a prescribed language, which is usually the national language. National applications fees need to be paid, and it may be necessary to engage an IP agent or lawyer to ensure the application meets national requirements. Some countries have established regional agreements for obtaining IP protection for an entire region with a single application. Examples of regional IP offices include the European Patent Office, the Office for Harmonization in the International Market and the Eurasian Patent Office.

For more information on protection of intellectual property, refer to the World Intellectual Property Organization (WIPO) at www.wipo.int.

When intellectual property protection extends too far
Although the theft of intellectual property represents a real problem in some sectors (e.g., music, motion pictures, software, etc.), the extension of intellectual property rights into other important sectors, such as food and medicine, has become a highly controversial issue. The WTO's Agreement on Trade-Related

Aspects of Intellectual Property Rights (TRIPS) negotiated in the 1986–94 Uruguay Round, introduced intellectual property rules into the multilateral trading system for the first time that require member nations to respect intellectual property rules. While it may sound straightforward, this rule set is quickly creating ethical challenges that are threatening to many less developed nations.

For example, it is argued that some countries, such as the United States, issue patents too quickly without much research on whether or not the invention is truly novel (i.e., if it is really the first instance of this idea). In effect, if a patent that has been issued is challenged, it is left to the courts to decide whether or not the patent should have been issued in the first place. This led to a bizarre situation a few years ago where the United States Patent and Trademark Office (USPTO) granted a Texas-based company a series of patents on Basmati rice (i.e., strains of rice that have been grown in India and Pakistan for centuries). Eventually, after a lengthy series of challenges, most of these patents were revoked, but the implications of a system that creates intellectual property rights on food are considered too ominous for many. Indeed, as higher-yielding cereal crops are being created through genetic modifications, intellectual-property claims are being made on the very foundations of sustenance in many countries. Lower-yielding strains of plant are effectively rendered uncompetitive, and small farmers are being pushed out of business or are forced to adopt crop strains that are regulated by the monopolistic structures inherent to patented products. Farmers are then unable to save seed from one year to the next (an age-old practice), leading to extreme vulnerability from a food-security standpoint (i.e., in hard times, farmers may not be able to afford seed).

Similarly, in the area of medicine, multinational companies have been aggressively identifying the active ingredients in indigenous species of plants worldwide (in particular, those known for their healing potential) and filing patent claims on the chemical structures (or analogues of their chemical structures) in these plants to secure monopolistic rights for the resulting medicines. It has been argued that this is a form of unwarranted bio-piracy that capitalizes on public knowledge and the lack of technical sophistication in many countries. For example, a patent claim was granted a few years ago to the University of Mississippi Medical Center for the use of turmeric, an Indian spice, for wound healing (U.S. Patent Number 5,401,504). This was extraordinary because turmeric has been commonly used for this purpose in India for centuries. However, under U.S. law, it is necessary to find adequate evidence (i.e., printed or published information) that can establish precedence before a patent can be revoked. Fortunately, in this case, an adequate number of references were found, and when challenged, the USPTO revoked the patent. However, in many countries where literacy rates are low, such evidence could be difficult to locate. And again, the rights are first asserted, and then those who are potentially harmed by those rights must fight to nullify the claim. Given the costs and complexity of litigation and the time involved in undertaking such a challenge, the uniform application of these rights across national boundaries creates a situation that leaves the most impoverished nations at an extreme disadvantage.

Accordingly, those engaged in international trade need to understand the nuances of these situations to ensure that corporate claims on intellectual property are not impinging on well-established rights.

Codes and Integrity Programs: Theory to Practice

Codes of conduct have been around for decades but have changed significantly in recent years, paralleling changing perceptions of business ethics and the role of the corporation. These changes have been described by Professor Mendes as "the five generations," and their evolution can be summarized as follows:

Figure 8.8—The evolution of five generations of codes of conduct
• First generation: conflict of interest
• Second generation: commercial conduct, observing the rule of law
• Third generation: safe working practices, other third-party concerns
• Fourth generation: community and environmental issues
• Fifth generation: human rights, accountability and social justice

Source: Professor Errol Mendes, University of Ottawa, Canada

Company codes, very often simply called "guidelines" at the first-generation stage, were written mainly to protect the company from employees who might find themselves in a conflict of interest or exposed to confidential company information. It required that they work exclusively in the interests of the company, and this was consistent with the then-current view that profits and return on investment to shareholders were their primary, if not unique, responsibility. Without doubt, some still subscribe to this view.

Ethics as a positive impact

In the second generation of codes, ethical business conduct came into focus for the first time. The rationale here was to maintain the company reputation by making sure that employees complied with the law and did not engage in unethical practices. This would include bribery and related conduct, such as providing expensive trips or gifts. Here we see the beginnings of corporate social responsibility, and, bearing in mind recent business scandals, it is still highly relevant. The rule of law, and an effective judiciary to enforce it, is critical to successful international business. Many major corporations consider that high standards of ethical conduct are not only important to the success of their business, but give them a competitive edge.

Health, safety and employee rights

The third generation widens the focus to include health and safety concerns and employee rights, as well as relationships with other stakeholders, such as suppliers. The business rationale here is a more motivated workforce, satisfied customers and better public relations. It also reflects the growing interest of consumers in buying their products from "ethical" companies and investing their money in ethical funds. Codes that initially might have covered employees at home now begin to cover employees in premises abroad, to ensure that their conditions of work and employment are in line with stakeholder expectations.

With the expansion of the global supply chains, these issues have become much more important. International trade agreements (like NAFTA) increasingly include reference to labour standards, and whether a company is simply buying from a foreign supplier, is subcontracting manufacturing, working in a joint-venture partnership or outsourcing services that might otherwise be performed at home, labour standards cannot be ignored. This does not mean that wages have to be the same as in Canada (or wherever home base is), but they should be competitive with the local market, and preferably better. Working conditions should be of an acceptable standard and similar to those one would expect in a developed country, and workers should not be prohibited from collective bargaining to ensure that their working conditions are satisfactory and basic rights are respected. In practice, many multinationals provide an excellent working environment in their overseas operations (which is why so many local employees like to work for them), but unfortunately, there are still cases of abuse, appalling sweat-shop environments and exploitative child labour. Ethical global traders should not only avoid complicity in such abuses, but should do their best to stop them.

One case will serve to illustrate the challenge. Ivory Coast produces 43 percent of the world's coffee, and recent reports concluded there were around 15,000 children employed in the coffee, cocoa and cotton farms, many of them picked up from the streets of neighbouring countries and sold as slaves. The chocolate industry in the U.S. (the major importer of beans) adopted the Harkin-Engel protocol in 2002, the aim being to eliminate the worst forms of abuse, However, the International Labour Rights Fund reports that the ten major chocolate manufacturers (who control most of the supply from Ivory Coast) have yet to make significant changes in their supply-chain arrangements to resolve the issue, and depressed prices in cocoa beans exacerbate the problem.

Environmental protection and respect for local communities
The fourth generation introduces the concepts of environmental protection and respect for local communities. This was prompted in part by a few very public disasters, including Union Carbide's toxic gas escape in Bhopal, India, and the Exxon Valdez oil spill in Alaska. The Bhopal disaster occurred in December 1984, with the accidental release of 27 tonnes of methyl isocyanate into the atmosphere from a fertilizer plant. The initial death toll was reckoned to be around 3,000 with 15,000 related illnesses later. Amnesty International suggests 22,000 deaths as a conservative estimate. It was clearly one of the world's worst environmental disasters.

The Exxon Valdez disaster in March 1989 occurred when the tanker left port in Alaska with 53 million gallons of crude oil, struck a reef and discharged 11 million gallons into Prince William Sound. This resulted in the most extensive and expensive clean-up operation ever mounted and caused major damage to the sensitive ecosystem. Wildlife is still recovering, close to 20 years later.

Finally, one of the most damning indictments illustrating the chemical industry's apparent lack of respect for communities is their longstanding practice of exporting pesticides that have been banned (for heath reasons) in North America and Europe to less developed countries. The case below explains this problem in detail and shows how this is particularly hazardous for foreign workers and domestic consumers.

Table 8.9—The environment: examples

Pesticides return home on U.S.-bound produce

Thursday, August 16, 2007 by the Council on Hemispheric Affairs

For the period of May 2007, the USDA reported the total value of monthly agricultural imports to the U.S. amounted to U.S.$6.1 billion. Of that total value, 15 percent arrived here from Mexico, 15 percent from Canada, three percent from Chile and three percent from Brazil (USDA April 2007). Latin American produce historically has found a warm welcome in the U.S.; however, these products often carry on them dangerous pesticide residues. Most recently, on July 18, President Bush set an urgent timetable of 60 days for the newly formed Cabinet-level committee to announce safety limits on produce, especially on food products being imported into the U.S.

According to a Trade and Environment Database (TED) case study regarding pesticide use in Mexico, which is published online by American University, "Toxicity threatens U.S. consumers in the 'circle of poison' effect in which unregistered or banned pesticides are exported to Mexico and sprayed on crops whose produce is then exported back to the U.S." More specifically, dibromochloropropane (DBCP) was banned in the U.S. in 1979, yet it continues to be used on crops in developing hemispheric countries such as Nicaragua and Costa Rica, years after its cut-off date. Since then, there have been numerous reports of the chemical's baleful effects. But in the months to come, tropical plantation workers will finally have their day in a U.S. court, as they try to seek compensation for the residual harm arising out of pesticide use, which, for many of them, has ruined their lives. The trial began on July 19 in a Los Angeles courtroom and is expected to last two to three months.

Not acknowledged to be dangerous until symptoms are exhibited

The Pesticide Action Network of North America describes DBCP as a carcinogen, a ground water contaminant, a developmental or reproductive toxin and a suspected endocrine disruptor. The Environmental Protection Agency (EPA) has found that DBCP can potentially cause kidney and liver damage as well as cancer, especially if one is exposed to levels greater than the maximum contaminant level of .0002 mg/L for an extended period of time. The pesticide in question was manufactured by chemical companies like Dow Chemical and Shell Oil to be used as a fumigant for nematode worms in the U.S. until it was pulled off the shelves in 1979. It had been used as a spray on agricultural produce such as cucumbers, grapes, tomatoes, squash, carrots, okra, camellia and roses. The EPA (2006) established that by 1974, farmers in the U.S. were treating crops with 9.8 million pounds of DBCP, and by 1977, 831,000 pounds of it were in use in California alone. There is a considerable likelihood that DBCP often seeped into the groundwater supply during this period.

Table 8.9—The environment: examples *(continued)*

Banana plantations are a dangerous place

According to a press statement by the Dole Fresh Fruit Company on November 10, 2002, there were nine DBCP cases pending in the U.S. against the fruit company, in which plantation workers have alleged injury to them due to DBCP exposure. The latest set of lawsuits, filed in 2004 against Dole Fresh Fruit Company and Standard Fruit Company, have recently reached the point where the first case is about to be heard by a U.S. court. All told, five lawsuits involving at least 5,000 agricultural workers from Costa Rica, Guatemala, Honduras, Nicaragua and Panama are waiting to be heard.

Dole has been aware of the extent of the Nicaraguan injury claims for some time. In a 2002 press release, the company acknowledged that they "are aware of 295 DBCP lawsuits now pending against U.S. DBCP manufacturers, Dole and other banana growers, in which a total of 6,544 plaintiffs are now seeking (a total of) approximately U.S.$9.6 million in purported damages." Although a Dole press release on April 2, 2007 stated that the company was one of the first fresh produce companies in the 1970s to create programs to decrease pesticide use, DBCP was, in fact, used throughout the decade.

The lawsuit accuses Dole and Standard Fruit Companies of negligence and concealment during the time the pesticide was in use. Duane Miller, the lawyer representing around 50 Nicaraguan plantation workers, informed a hearing on July 19 that the workers "weren't told until the '90s—and they weren't told by Dow or Dole."

Fighting back

Duane Miller claims that the inherent toxicity of DBCP was recognized as early as the 1950s when scientists working for Dow Chemical observed the deleterious effect on the testes of laboratory animals exposed to the chemical. Examinations indicated a noxious condition in the reproductive organs. A study (Potashnik, 1979) released by the EPA, which was based on the examinations of 23 workers at a DBCP production plant, found that 18 out of the 23 men had azoospermia (no sperm was present in the semen) or oligospermia (a low sperm count). The severity of their condition was directly proportional to the time that they spent working in the plant that was producing the DBCP. For example, a group of 12 men with azoospermia logged in between 100 and 6,726 hours while a group of 6 men with oligospermia had exposure rates of 34-95 hours. Rabbits and other laboratory animals have been used to further prove the destructive manifestations of DBCP on reproductive and adrenal functions. One group of rabbits was subjected to 10 parts per million (ppm) of DBCP for 14 weeks which were compared against a control group of rabbits. Those injected with 10 ppm showed a significant decrease in the amount of sperm present compared to the control group.

Table 8.9—The environment: examples *(continued)*

Nicaraguans protest against approaching lawsuit

Monetary compensation for damages incurred seems to have taken precedence over social awareness for Nicaraguan workers. A court case would likely gain international attention and would inspire strong human rights and environmental legislation likely to positively affect all agricultural workers associated with the manufacture of the lethal chemicals. Many Nicaraguan banana workers signed a petition circulated on July 11 to fire their legal team in the upcoming lawsuit. There have been accusations, mainly by the union leader Victorino Espinales, that the lawyers have deceptively changed medical reports to make their future case more formidable; therefore, giving up any prospect that the case for the workers could be won. Since past lawsuits against companies like Dole and Dow have been settled out of court for monetary compensation ranging from U.S.$20 million in 1992 to U.S.$41.5 million in 1997, it would be safe to say that some Nicaraguan workers would rather directly negotiate with the drug companies for monetary amounts than establish important legal precedents. This seems to represent a sharp shift in feelings for the thousands of banana workers, including Espinales, who in the recent months had petitioned the Nicaraguan Congress for governmental relief from their plight.

The orientation of Nicaraguan President Daniel Ortega also has come under close scrutiny during this investigation into the use of poisonous pesticides, having reportedly met multiple times with top Dole officials. An offer of more jobs to the country was presented, but only if Nicaragua altered their legal system to make it more difficult to sue the giant drug corporations.

With or without Nicaraguans, Costa Ricans are victims

Although Dole claims to have halted any use of DBCP on its plantations in Latin America after 1979, the pesticide's continual usage in the region seemed to defy the U.S.'s ban: "In July 1991, 186 banana workers alleged that they were exposed to DBCP from the early 1960s to 1984, causing them serious and permanent sterilization" (American University, 1995). One TED case study was conducted in 1995 and investigated the sterilization of 1,500 plantation workers due to exposure to DBCP's harmful effects from its usage on Costa Rican banana crops. It is estimated that around 2,000 men were sterilized due to their exposure to DBCP throughout the 1970s. Workers were not even able to sue Dow Chemical and Shell Oil until March 1990, when the Texas Supreme Court narrowly voted in favor of the Costa Ricans' right to do so. Other grievances have been settled outside of court in order to salvage the good name of the corporations. The 1995 case study states that in 1992, a suit by Costa Rican plantation workers was settled out of court for a sum of U.S.$20 million.

Guatemalan pesticide use and its eventual arrival in the U.S.

The same issue was addressed in a 1997 TED case study on Guatemalan snow peas, one of the country's main agricultural exports to the U.S. The case study referenced an investigation conducted in 1995, in which it was estimated that Latin American campesinos were 13 times more likely than U.S. farmers to suffer from pesticide poisoning (Tansey, et al., *Eradicating the Pesticide Problem in Latin America*). Furthermore, the Environmental Working

Table 8.9—The environment: examples *(continued)*

Group (EWG), a non-profit organization, stated that the greatest number of Guatemalan pesticide violations came about as a result of U.S. imports of Guatemalan snow peas. The EWG concluded that 41 percent of the tested snow pea shipments exported to the U.S. from Guatemala during 1992–1993 were found to contain illegal pesticide residues (American University, 1997).

Pesticides used today hardly represent an improvement

As recently as December 2006, banned residential chemicals, endosulfan and diazonin, were found during air monitoring near an elementary school in Hastings, Florida. According to the Pesticide Action Network North America (PANNA, 2007), endosulfan is used in the U.S. as an insecticide mainly on cotton, potatoes and apples. Residential use of endosulfan was banned in 2000 after findings concluded that it is a neurotoxin with poisoning symptoms including tremors, convulsions, vomiting and hyperactivity. Diazonin is also a neurotoxin, but is still used as an insecticide on nuts, vegetables and fruits. The EPA banned its residential use in 2004. If repeatedly exposed to diazonin, asthma, cancer and gestational diabetes are some of the possible noxious outcomes. Endosulfan was used to combat insects on coffee plantations in Colombia. According to PANNA, more than 100 poisonings and three deaths were reported in 1994. A study by the German Federal Environmental Agency (February 2007) reported, "Excessive and improper application and handling of endosulfan have been linked to congenital physical disorders, mental retardations and deaths in farm workers and villagers in developing countries in Africa, southern Asian and Latin America."

What a U.S. trial could do

In light of the ongoing trial, U.S. investigations will hopefully direct their attention to the human rights abuses and manifestation of negligence committed by large fruit and chemical companies as well as demand stringent analysis of the methods and pesticides, like endosulfan, used in agricultural production. This could result in many U.S. citizens to question every organization [sic], from Dole Fresh Fruit Company, Shell Oil and Dow Chemical to the EPA, USDA and FDA, associated with the drug. Critics insist that pesticide use domestically as well as throughout Latin American has not always ceased, but instead, very likely has been masked or transformed, without benefit of reconsideration.

This analysis was prepared by Research Associate Jacquelyn Godin for the Council on Hemispheric Affairs, a non-governmental, non-partisan research organization based in Washington DC.

Obviously, most businesses are not involved in anything quite so damaging or controversial, but the ethical principles illustrated by this case are clear. Companies exporting to other countries may face choices where they have opportunities for ill-gotten profits in regimes where regulations are lax. Ethical practitioners must take a principled stand against being involved in such gains at all costs.

Government regulators and progressive businesses are certainly becoming more aware of these issues. Indeed, numerous business-led and government initiatives have emerged to address these issues as they arise. A handful of representative examples are included in the following list of organizations.

Environmental protection is an extremely important public issue, so company rationale for expanded codes of conduct is once again the maintenance of reputation and the protection of the company against lawsuits and other disruptive action by those affected by the company's activities. This is of particular importance to companies whose environmental footprint can be large; for example, in oil and gas exploration and mining. It can have greater importance and visibility if indigenous or other potentially disadvantaged communities are involved, such as in the aforementioned example of Shell in Nigeria.

Human rights
The fifth generation moves into the area of human rights and commits the company to comply with international human-right standards and behave in a manner consistent with the values of its home jurisdiction and the expectations of civil society.

State-owned enterprises, such as export credit agencies, also have ethics policies (often still under the corporate-social-responsibility heading). Export Development Canada is a good example.

An analysis by *Corporate Knights* (the Canadian Magazine for Responsible Business) investigated 21 Canadian companies operating in the extractive industries around the world and found that only five had a formal human-rights (HR) policy in place, six had made an explicit commitment not to be involved in HR violations, five had a mechanism to monitor HR policies and only four had signed on to the UN Global Compact. Clearly, much work remains.

Shell in Nigeria and investors in the Chinese Three Gorges project might have had fewer fall-outs with improved codes in place. Companies should also undertake to behave responsibly in countries where local requirements are less than would normally be acceptable in the home country. The fifth-generation criteria are less widely included in current codes, although progress is being made as the public becomes concerned about corporations that invest in countries where abuse is rampant.

Almost all major international corporations now have detailed codes of conduct that incorporate most, if not all, of the generations. Some, like General Electric and Alcan, set a fine example, by going further that just including all the issues listed above. They are absolutely clear where they stand on critical issues (like bribery) and ensure that the code is introduced throughout the whole organization and that employees at all levels accept it and sign off every year to confirm they have read it and will abide by it. In addition, senior managers undertake to "walk the talk" and set an appropriate example not just to employees, but to other stakeholders as well. These codes can often be viewed on the company websites.

Holding corporations to account
Civil society is keeping a close watch on corporations these days. An example of this is California based "Corpwatch," whose tag line is "holding corporations accountable." Set up in 1996, the organization "investigates and exposes corporate violations of human rights, environmental crimes, fraud and corruption around the world." Currently, its website includes the names of many well- known multinationals such as Starbucks, Barrick, Merck, Tata Steel and Wal-Mart,

Table 8.10—Websites
Arab Forum for Environment and Development: www.afedonline.org
Affiliated Network for Social Accountability Africa: www.ansa-africa.org.za
Canadian Business for Social Responsibility (CBSR): www.cbsr.bc.ca
CIES—Food Business Forum's Global Social Compliance Programme: www. ciesnet.com
Extractive Industries Transparency Initiative: www.eitransparency.org
Global Reporting Initiative: www.globalreporting.org
International Institute for Sustainable Development's international guide on CSR: www.iisd.org
International Finance Corporations Guidelines: www.ifc.org/policyreview
OECD Guidelines for Multinational Companies: www.oecd.org
The Business Social Compliance Initiative: www.bsci-eu.org
Project Finance and Equator Principles: www.equator-principles.com/principles.shtml
UN Global Compact launches principles for responsible business education: www.unglobalcompact.org
UN Global Initiative to Fight Human Trafficking and Modern Slavery: www. unodc.org/unodc/trafficking_human_beings.html
U.S. Climate Action Partnership, launched January 22, 2007: www.US-cap. org

which (from the allegations) would appear to be straying from the ethical principles to which they have subscribed either in their codes of conduct, OECD guidelines or industry norms. Apart from the actual damage caused by such actions, reputations are put at significant risk by such exposure.

Many industry groups, conscious of the importance of ethical issues, have established their own standards to which they hold members accountable. One example is the Extractive Industries Transparency Initiative (EITI), which was launched in 2002. It aims to "support improved governance in resource-rich countries through the verification and full publication of company payments and government revenues from oil, gas, and mining." Another initiative of this kind was the chemical industry's Responsible Care (RC) program; it originated in Canada in 1985 and is the chemical industry's global voluntary initiative under which companies, through their national associations, work together to continuously improve their health, safety and environmental performance. The OECD Guidelines for Multinationals adopted by member countries in 1976 as voluntary standards for private industry provide another yardstick by which to judge company ethical performance. They contain chapters on information disclosure, competition, financing, taxation, employment and industrial relations, environment, science and technology. Most major projects undertaken by corporations require extensive financing, and the Equator Principles provide benchmarks for financial institutions to determine, evaluate and manage social and environmental risk and to promote responsible environmental stewardship and socially responsible development. There is also the Global Reporting Initiative (GRI), first set up in 2000, whereby organizations publicly report their economic, environmental and social performance in so-called sustainability reports, using GRI guidelines. Over 1,000 organizations of all types in more than 60 countries now report in this way.

Global warming
Another ethical issue that represents a significant challenge for many companies is related to global warming. This has become a highly political issue ever since the 1997 Kyoto Protocol. Many governments, in response to highly alarming reports and public reaction to this crisis, are proposing incremental measures to reduce greenhouse gas emissions that will potentially impact many businesses worldwide. However, many countries have either not ratified the protocol (e.g., U.S./Australia) or continue to increase pollution in spite of ratification (e.g., Canada). Also, bringing the major countries of the developing world (e.g., China, India) on side to reduce emissions, while they are building up their economies, is proving to be a considerable challenge.

There are also conflicting sub-issues, such as the promotion of bio-diesel (i.e., plant-derived diesel fuel) and ethanol as alternative fuels. Fuel produced from corn or other crops requires extensive use of arable land, which is currently used for producing food for the world's six billion inhabitants, and is therefore a precious renewable resource. Massive depletion of this resource to meet the energy needs of the wealthy could cause demand spikes, food-price hikes and food shortages, which will exacerbate hunger and starvation in many parts of the world. Quite apart from that, considerable energy is also used in producing these fuels, so its benefit as an alternative fuel is not yet proven.

The global trader needs to be up to speed on these issues so that the environmental footprint of his organization's activities is recognized and managed effectively.

Diversity
In this era of globalization and its associated social, cultural and demographic trends, diversity in the workplace—at home and abroad—has become an increasingly important issue. Ideas, attitudes and customs from around the world need to be managed carefully to result in the acceptance of a common ethical policy that promotes fairness and social responsibility for the benefit of all stakeholders in international trade.

In March 2007, *The Globe and Mail* reported that 80 percent of the Canadian workforce is composed of women, visible minorities, First Nations people and people with disabilities. Working and managing relationships with such a diverse group certainly demands skills, but for the global trader it is ethnic diversity that is the most relevant to her future challenges.

In Canada we see ethnic diversity everywhere as new Canadians from around the world come to our welcoming shores, and we can already see cultural challenges as "hyphenated Canadians" form a larger percentage of the population in our multiculturally focused society. There is a massive Indian population in Toronto, for example, and they contribute in a major way to life in that city. The same is true of the Chinese community in Vancouver and the Haitian community in Montreal.

In the U.K., London has changed enormously in the past 20 years and is now one of the most multicultural cities in the world. These changes can cause friction at the local level, a situation exacerbated by the post–9/11 war on terror and the conflicts in Afghanistan and Iraq. This applies particularly in countries that do not make special efforts to encourage integration. The U.S. is a good example of an integration policy where, in spite of racial conflicts in the sixties and the increasing influx of Hispanics in recent years, the population generally considers itself to be American first and anything else afterwards.

A knowledge and understanding of the issues surrounding ethnic diversity at home will help the global trader handle the challenges of working and operating in different cultures, as outlined in the chapter on cultural considerations.

Ethical policy development

In summary, it is extremely dangerous for any business working internationally to ignore ethical issues, whatever the size of its operations. It risks legal penalties, loss of reputation and indeed, loss of business. The first step to mitigate this risk is to develop a clear and unambiguous policy contained in a code of conduct, integrity program or CSR commitment—the name is less important than the content. It can certainly be modelled on other examples, but it should be developed in conjunction with key staff, obtaining commitment during the process. It should be introduced throughout the organization at home and abroad and to agents, distributors, suppliers and other partners with whom the business is closely associated. Everyone must understand, accept and "sign off" on the policy, and senior managers should be clearly seen to "walk the talk."

Finally, independent monitoring should be set up to ensure compliance, and the policy and company position should be made clear to everyone, including customers and the public. A simple test can sometimes help with a decision on a difficult ethical issue: if the proposed action was to be reported on the front page of the local paper, would that damage the reputation of the organization, or would it be beneficial? If the answer is beneficial, or even neutral, there is a good chance the company is on safe ground—and doing what is right.

Professional associations

Almost all professional associations have a code of ethical conduct that members undertake to abide by as a condition for remaining a member in good standing. For example, as the professional accreditation organization for the FITT–CITP designation (Certified International Trade Professional), FITT is no exception, and a copy of the standards of ethical conduct expected—in fact, required—from its members is given on the next page.

Apart from competency, the key requirement here is integrity, whether to client, employer, other stakeholders or the public at large. As we have already seen from examples in this chapter, there may be times when integrity is put to the test. The standards are spelled out clearly, and when in a conflict situation or one demanding the exercise of judgement, the professional should use these as a reference point in coming to a resolution.

We have seen in the previous section how important it is for organizations operating internationally to have a formal code of conduct in place. While most larger corporations have these, this is by no means the case with smaller companies. If a professional joins such a company, there is an important role to play in ensuring that management understand the need for clear and explicit policies and for the professional to provide expertise in setting them up. These policies should cover all the main issues already discussed, and can be modelled in outline on the International Code of Ethics for Canadian Business, which was spearheaded by the Human Rights Research and Education Centre at the University of Ottawa. Reference can also be made to the United Nations Global Compact, which asks companies to "embrace, support and enact within their sphere of influence a set of core values in the areas of human rights, labour standards, the environment and anti-corruption." It then outlines ten principles in the areas of human rights, labour standards, environment and anti-corruption. Both these documents are guidelines or templates that companies can sign on to, but a complete code of conduct requires more detail and a higher level of commitment. Sample codes can usually be downloaded from company websites, and are also available from the Industry Canada website, Strategis. Their paper on voluntary code has been around since 1998, but is a useful basic guide.

Director's liability

High-profile fraud cases like the Enron and WorldCom debacles resulted in a much closer focus on responsibilities of directors to their shareholders. Accounting and reporting rules have been tightened significantly in the U.S. since the *Sarbanes-Oxley Act* of 2002 (now also adapted in Canada, Japan, Australia and France). Of course, directors have always had fiduciary responsibilities, but one of the areas where change is taking place is responsibility for social and environmental performance. For example, Stanford Law School's Directors' College program for senior executives now specifically includes "ethical concerns" in the shape of a workshop entitled "ethics and the corporation," thereby highlighting once again the importance of these issues and of having clear policies in place to deal with them as they arise. For the global trader to make decisions without considering ethical impacts is likely to be increasingly detrimental to the organization concerned.

FITT—CITP Standards of Ethical Conduct

Figure 8.11—FITT—CITP Standards of Ethical Conduct

Holders of the CITP designation have made a commitment to adhere to the following standards of ethical conduct. Most importantly, they are bringing a new level of accountability and increased recognition to the profession of international business and trade.

Ethical professionals should be governed by two basic concepts:

Competency. They must be able to successfully apply the competencies for their area of practice.

Figure 8.11—FITT—CITP Standards of Ethical Conduct *(continued)*

Integrity. They must have a keen sense of responsibility to their client or employer, to their profession and the public, and the sense of independence to allow exercise of their professional judgment without restriction or bias.

The Standards of Ethical Conduct reflect and are designed to ensure compliance by a CITP with these basic concepts; they also serve to enhance confidence in the integrity and service of the CITP. They are not in any order of priority, but should be applied as required to the specifics of a given situation.

Responsibilities to the individual

- Ensure the communication of rights, responsibilities and information to foster informed decision-making.

- Respect the customs and beliefs of others, consistent with the mission of the organization.

- Respect the confidentiality of information, unless it is in the public interest, or required by law, to divulge information.

- Promote competence and integrity with individuals associated with the organization.

Responsibilities to the organization

- Strive to provide quality services.

- Communicate truthfully and avoid misleading, or raising unreasonable expectations in others.

- Use sound management practices and use resources ethically.

Responsibilities to the community and society

- Serve the public interest in an ethical fashion and consider the effects of decisions on the community and society.

- Obey the law and foster an environment where fairness applies and discrimination, harassment or abuse of any sort is opposed.

- Contribute to improving the climate for international trade opportunities.

Responsibilities to the profession

- Develop and maintain competence in international trade management and practice within one's abilities.

- Support FITT in its efforts to enhance the profession of international trade.

- Practice with honesty, integrity, respect and good faith.

Figure 8.11—FITT—CITP Standards of Ethical Conduct *(continued)*

• Assist others to develop competence in international trade management and practice ethically.
 	
• Understand these standards and report to FITT when there are reasonable grounds to believe a CITP has breached them.
 	
Conflict of interest
 	
Conflict of interest exists when a CITP uses position, authority or privileged information to:
 	
    a)   obtain an improper benefit, directly or indirectly;
 	
    b)   obtain an improper benefit for a friend, relative or associate; or
 	
    c)   make decisions that will negatively affect the organization.
 	
A CITP shall therefore:
 	
    a)   conduct all relationships in a way that assures those affected that decisions are not compromised by a conflict of interest;
 	
    b)   disclose to the appropriate authority any direct or indirect personal or financial interest or appointment or election that might create a conflict of interest;
 	
    c)   neither accept nor offer personal gifts or benefits with the expectation or appearance of influencing a decision; and
 	
    d)   refrain from using FITT membership and credentials to promote or endorse commercial products or services where others would perceive this as a promotion or endorsement by FITT.

Source: FITT—CITP Standards of Ethical Conduct

Business Ethics Checklist

The following checklist can be helpful in researching and preparing to enter a new market:

Figure 8.12—Business ethics checklist
☑ See where the target country stands in the latest Transparency International table. ☑ Talk to others who know the country well about ethical practices there. ☑ Review your own company policy on these issues.

Figure 8.12—Business ethics checklist *(continued)*

☑ If there is no policy, put one in place as soon as you can.

☑ Do an ethics "due diligence" check on your potential partner in the target market, whether this is an agent, distributor or joint investor.

☑ If the partner is a supplier or joint-venture manufacturer, check their policy on child labour.

☑ Ask about their policy on fair trade.

☑ Review with your management team and outline a plan to ensure your organization will be in the best position to handle ethical challenges that may arise.

Chapter Summary

Thanks in part to some recent very public scandals involving major companies like Enron and World-Com, corporations have never been under closer scrutiny, especially if they operate internationally. There is an array of public activists, hungry media and zealous government prosecutors waiting to pounce on the unwary business executive.

To avoid problems, executives need to be guided by firm principles, defined for them and their teams in clear and unambiguous terms. These need to cover much more than basic tenets of civilized behaviour, and handle the challenges outlined in the first part of this chapter. This means dealing with bribery and other forms of corruption, not being directly or indirectly complicit in the exploitation of children and understanding the ramifications of human rights in different jurisdictions. Above all, it means working with an organization that has well-demonstrated attitudes and well-defined policies, and one in which these are followed to the letter and in the spirit at all levels, especially by the top management. To do this makes good business sense. To fail to do so is often unconscionable and, in addition, exposes the company to a wide range of potential problems, from expensive lawsuits to international public-relations disasters. The choice could not be clearer.

The issue of ethics and ethical conduct in international business is not a matter of imposing a view or standard on trading partners, national or corporate. It is not a form of dominance, but rather, a recognition that certain fundamental approaches to the conduct of business ought to be broadly acknowledged and actively supported for the ultimate enhancement of trading relationships at all levels. This is about the betterment of the international community, of which we all are part, and for which we all collectively share a responsibility—corporate, social and otherwise.

Exercises

Exercise 1 (class discussion)
You have recently joined a company as international sales manager and are preparing to enter some new markets in the developing world. You discover the complete absence of any policy regarding ethical issues and decide to present some proposals to your CEO. What would you include in your outline of the proposal?

(Estimated time 5–10 minutes)

Exercise 2 (class discussion)
You are CEO of a manufacturing company specializing in the supply of parts for the nuclear industry. Orders have been difficult lately as this is a highly competitive industry sector, and you are very much in need of some additional business. You are approached by an anonymous buyer with financing in place for a $5 million parts order. You suspect that this buyer could be a front man for a rogue and potentially threatening government that is under UN-sponsored sanctions. What do you do?

(Estimated time 5–10 minutes)

Exercise 3 (class discussion)
Your company is one of two final bidders in a major infrastructure project in Asia. December is approaching and your bonus will be based on results for the year. In addition, you have already invested considerable time and more than $2 million in preparing estimates and the bid for the project. You know you are up against a large foreign engineering firm with a reputation for not always playing by the rules, and you are concerned about the business ethics of the buyer. What will be your approach as you move forward?

(Estimated time 5–10 minutes)

Exercise 4 (short assignment)
Visit the Canadian Business for Social Responsibility website (www.cbsr.ca) and get a feel for the direction and activities of that organization. Then, visit the *Corporate Knights* magazine website (www.corporateknights.ca), download a few back issues of the magazine and identify at least one company that appears to be acting very ethically. What is it that the company is doing that makes it stand out? Is this exemplary example/activity a burden on the company, or does it help the firm in some way? Does this example of the company's behaviour exemplify its behaviour in all other areas of business, or does the firm use it in some way to put a friendly public-relations face on bad behaviour found in other areas of its operations? Would you want to work for this company (why or why not)? Summarize your findings on a single page and be prepared to hand it in or discuss your findings with the class at the discretion of your instructor.

(Estimated research time 60 minutes)

References/Resources

International Code of Ethics for Canadian Business, Human Rights Research and Education Centre, University of Ottawa (www.cdp-hrc.uottawa.ca/globalization/busethics/codeint.html)

Iyengar, Jayanthi, Business Journalist India (www.atimes.com/atimes/China/FI16Ad07.html)

Mendes, Errol P., and Clark, Jeffrey A. University of Ottawa: HRREC/CREDP, 1996: (www.uottawa.ca/hrrec/publicat/five.html)

Canadian Business for Social Responsibility (www.cbsr.ca)

Chemical Industries Responsible Care (www.responsiblecare.org)

Conflict Zone Barometer (www.hiik.de/start/index.hmtl.en)

Corporate Knights (www.corporateknights.ca)

Corpwatch (www.corpwatch.org)

Directors College (www.directorscollege.com)

Employee Rights in the Chocolate Industry (www.laborrights.org/projects/childlab/cocoa)

Export Development Corporation (www.edc.ca)

Extractive Industries Transparency Initiative (www.eitransparency.org)

Fairtrade Foundation, London, U.K. (www.fairtrade.org)

Financial Projects (www.equator-prinicples.com)

FITT—CITP Standards of Ethical Conduct (www.fitt.ca)

Industry Canada (www.strategis.gc.ca)

Mining Round Tables/mining map (www,halifaxinitiative.org/index)

OECD Guidelines (www.oecd.org/document/21)

Transparency International (www.transparency.org)

United Nations Global Compact (www.unglobalcompact.org)

World Intellectual Property Organization (WIPO) (www.wipo.int)

Market Research and Marketing

Strategic pursuit of trade

Chapter Objectives

- Define the basic elements of market research and marketing

- Recognize how marketing should fit within the organization of a global business

- Understand the "marketing mindset" required to remain competitive in the current and future global business environment

Overview

Successful marketing is the ability to create the perception that a product or service meets a set of predefined demand variables that are ultimately important to the consumer. Any firm, regardless of its size, must take into account a myriad of factors present within the foreign target market—and anywhere along the supply chain, for that matter—that will affect everything from the design of the product to the manner in which it is delivered and sold to the end-user.

The past decade has seen a tectonic shift in the way domestic and global business is done. Growing confidence in the quality of product and service supply from emerging markets, an explosion in the global availability of skilled knowledge workers and, not least of all, the ubiquity of the Internet, are all contributors to a global business environment that is more fluid than ever before.

The lifeblood of global competitiveness

Some marketing professionals, while referencing factors such as these, might claim that traditional marketing is dead, that the definition of customer has changed and that a new paradigm must be adopted to address the seemingly infinite market-segment diversity, especially in the context of Internet-based business. However, one fundamental fact remains true today: knowledge and communication are compulsory for achieving any business's ultimate goals of profits and return to investors and other stakeholders.

Today's ultra-competitive global business environment demands that the significance of marketing within the organization be heightened. In an increasingly global and networked business world, well-implemented market research and marketing activities are the lifeblood of successful global business ventures. High-quality and -value products and services may now come from anywhere. The marketing approach is one of the most important means of transcending these sales challenges and of taking maximum advantage of the opportunities presented by the current global economy.

Market Research: Trade Without Research = Tightrope Without a Net!

Informing the marketing approach is the collection and analysis of market research. It is used to gain knowledge of appropriate markets and potential customers: who they are, what they need, what they believe and what they are prepared to buy. Not only is this information vital to creating the messages that convince potential customers to buy, but it is often crucial to packaging and delivery of the product or service and even to the initial design and development stages. As emerging markets gain a higher global economic profile, the sources of supply and demand are shifting. Market research is critical to maintaining balance in global market share and to managing new opportunities and heightened competition. Depending on the methods used, market research can represent a significant business-development cost. However, as the adage goes, "failure to plan equals planning to fail," which could have far more serious implications if research and planning are not viewed as an integral function of the organization.

Market Research: What and Where

What research is needed?

Research can confirm the existence of a market opportunity and provide knowledge of that market's attributes. It can also give insight into how a new market could be developed. The marketer can determine what is important to customers and what is likely to influence their buying decisions. The research should also allow an analysis of the dynamics of the target market, the trends that characterize it, the forces driving demand and the costs of doing business.

Table 9.1—Typical factors that characterize a market	
Consumer-level market factors:	Socio-political market factors:
• income levels	• economy and currency fluctuations
• occupation	• government policy and regulations
• age	• political stability
• education	• internal or regional conflict
• sex	• health
• languages	• environmental performance and policy
• religion	• security and crime rate
• geographic location	• access to communications and technology
	• transportation and utility infrastructure
	• global and regional cultural differences

Where does the information come from?

While market research and analysis is an activity that is necessary for the marketing plan, one that allows for strategy building and decision making and one that is intended to reduce the risks involved in international transactions, there are associated resource implications that the company must determine. The financial, human-resource and opportunity costs need to be weighed against the organization's needs and financial situation.

Typical activities and sources of secondary and primary market research, some of which represent cost factors to be assessed by the company, include the following:

- Internet sources (search engines, competitor websites, discussion boards, etc.)

- online and offline commercial databases and subscription services

- periodical and trade publications

Secondary research
Research that has been collected and analyzed by others for a purpose other than, but related to, the current informational need, such as trade papers, market briefs and magazines.

Primary research
Research that is gained through direct observation, such as during a market visit or is obtained directly or indirectly by the researcher through interviews, surveys and statistical analysis.

- market guides and briefs
- market-research firms
- government representatives at home and abroad
- market visits
- commercial banks
- business associations and chambers of commerce
- bilateral business councils and industry associations
- other companies within the domestic market
- connecting with diasporas of the target market

Internet search engines: "product" + "country" + "buyer" = 1 million results

By now, companies preparing to become global traders instinctively look to the Internet and search engines as a potential means of collecting information about target market opportunities. The reality today is that there are well over 1 billion websites populating the virtual world, and much of the information that this represents either remains to be catalogued by the major search services or is simply inaccessible to them. Additionally, much of this information can be considered factually questionable.

This is commonly referred to as "the invisible Internet"—much of the critical information that a company might need that either resides in a database that cannot be indexed by search engines or that is available only through specialized online research firms and information brokers. That said, there is a wealth of information that can be obtained free or at a low cost by a market researcher that has taken the time to understand how each of the major search engines operate and how to best formulate search queries in order to obtain relevant results, the keyword being "relevant." Some of the more advanced search engines, such as Google, attempt to "guess" the relevance of search results based on the search keywords entered by the user. But most search engines operate best when Boolean search queries are used.

Figure 9.2—Basic structure of a Boolean search query

Query:

gears + steel - plastic + "United Kingdom" + importer buyers market

What it means:

Find all web pages that MUST INCLUDE some form of the words *gears*, *steel* and *importer* (note the plus symbols that indicate this). The results must also include the EXACT PHRASE *United Kingdom* (note the quotes around the exact phrase). The results must NOT INCLUDE the word *plastic* (note the minus symbol). The results MAY OR MAY NOT ALSO CONTAIN some form of the words *buyers* and *market* (no special notations used for these words).

Still, raw research conducted using general search engines can be very time-consuming, both in terms of locating relevant results and also in the process of verifying the accuracy of the information sources that are found. This makes the use of free and low-cost online services a valuable part of the research process. There are many of these kinds of services (some of which are listed in the final section of this manual), either for general business information or for information focused on a particular industry or geographic region, for example:

- **Manta** (www.manta.com): As an alternative to reviewing individual company websites to gain information on potential buyers and suppliers, Manta uses data from high-quality sources such as Dun and Bradstreet, Datamonitor and the ICON Group to provide searchable data on companies around the world. Much of this information is available through free registration, and somewhat more detailed information can be accessed at a nominal fee.

- **Alacra Wiki Spotlights** (www.alacrawiki.com): This site is composed of user-generated content containing information and resources on a long list of specific industries. The spotlight section of the website contains perhaps difficult-to-find resources for data on industry trends, financials and issues.

- **Technorati** (www.technorati.com): A *blog* or *weblog* is an online diary or e-magazine of sorts, usually written by an individual on a specific subject. Technorati is one of the Internet's largest databases of such websites, and a vast number of blog websites deal with specific business topics and industries. Quite often, blogs can be found that are written by known professionals and industry insiders and can contain valuable commentary and observations on a given market or business sector.

- **MarketResearch.com** (www.marketresearch.com): This site contains thousands of market-research reports from a wide variety of sources. While the reports are typically priced at under U.S.$1,000, some can be as expensive at U.S.$3,000 or more. However, locating report titles of interest and searching for those titles elsewhere on the Internet can sometimes locate more affordable sources. Additionally, some sites will provide fairly detailed abstracts of these reports, which can sometimes yield all the core information or statistics that a market researcher is looking for.

Skills and qualities of a market researcher

The market-research activity within a company may be conducted by a single individual with an in-depth appreciation for the product or service, for the overall business objectives of the company and for the market-development goals. It could be an internal function of the business or an outsourced activity. However the process is designed, effective market researchers embody the ability to collect and analyze quantitative and qualitative data that supports the company's strategic market-development objectives. The qualities of a skilled researcher also include

- a high degree of analytical skill and planning ability;

- strong creativity and imagination;

- good communication and people skills;

What makes a good researcher?
"Good imagination distinguishes great researchers...to wrestle with the unexpected and arrive at new understanding that challenges old ways of thinking is the crux of good research."
Indira Samarasekera, VP of Research, University of British Columbia

- strong self-motivation and initiative;

- an ability to efficiently absorb and interpret information;

- a degree of persuasiveness and sales skills; and

- the ability to use office and Internet technology effectively.

Ultimately, once the decision to proceed with market research has been made, the results analyzed and conclusions drawn, the company must decide whether to proceed with developing a full market strategy and plan. The company may conclude that the potential market is too small, that the cost of market entry outweighs the projected profits or that product modification would be too costly. If the market analysis supports a decision to proceed, the market strategy and plan provide the direction for how this is to be accomplished.

Recognizing Market Types

By understanding the different market types, global traders understand that they need to be ready to respond quickly to inquiries if they are coming from the U.S. or Europe.

In the case of Asia or Latin America, presenting a proposal or price list too quickly can be viewed as being overly aggressive. The best outcomes are usually a result of time spent developing the relationship.

Global markets may generally be categorized as one of three market types. Understanding the types of markets being targeted is an important step towards determining the suitability of the product and the company's ability to do business there. Market types can be loosely defined at the country level; however, a country may have many diverse market types within it, segmented along cultural or religious lines or by economic status. There are three basic types of markets:

Fast-paced markets
- Typical examples are the U.S., Canada and western Europe

- Requirements:

    - efficient delivery

    - fast, efficient communications

    - excellent quality assurance

    - good media profile (particularly consumer products)

    - good local partners if language is a challenge

Relationship-based markets
- Typical examples are many Latin American or Asian countries

- Requirements:

    - good communication skills

    - cultural sensitivity

    - fluency in local language for close contacts

    - building trust at senior levels

Developing markets

- Funded extensively by international financial institutions, or IFIs

- Typical examples are most African countries

- Requirements:

  - understanding of developing economies

  - patience—market penetration takes time

  - flexibility to deal with different situations

  - awareness of political situation

  - experience working with aid- or IFI-funded projects

Table 9.3—Ten Research steps for market selection

Screen potential markets

1. Obtain statistics that indicate product or service exports to various countries.

2. Identify five to ten large and fast-growing markets for the company's product. Look at them over the past three to five years. Has market growth been consistent year to year?

3. Identify some smaller but emerging markets that may provide ground-floor opportunities and that may have fewer competitors.

4. Target three to five of the most statistically promising markets for further assessment.

Assess targeted markets

1. Examine trends for company products as well as related products within the supply chain that could influence demand.

2. Ascertain the sources of competition, including the extent of domestic industry production and the major foreign countries the firm is competing against in each targeted market.

3. Analyze factors affecting marketing and use of the product in each target market, such as end-user sectors, channels of distribution, cultural idiosyncrasies and business practices.

4. Identify any foreign barriers (tariff or non-tariff) for the product being imported into the country. Identify any domestic barriers (such as export controls) that affect exports to the targeted country.

5. Identify any domestic- or foreign-government incentives that promote exporting of the particular product or service.

Table 9.3—Ten Research steps for market selection *(continued)*
Draw conclusions
1. After analyzing the data, the company may conclude that its marketing resources would be applied more effectively to a few markets or just one market. In general, if the company is new to exporting, then efforts should be highly focused. Exporting to one or two countries will allow the company to target its resources without jeopardizing its domestic sales efforts. The company's internal resources should determine its level of effort.

Understanding the Marketing Plan

What is marketing?

When the determinants of one aspect of the plan change, the determinants of the others may also change. Therefore, the marketing plan is fluid, not static.

Today's fluid global business environment requires a fluid marketing approach.

There is no single definition of what marketing is; it would appear to some that defining the process is as subjective as the activity itself. However, an oft-quoted overall definition is "the process of planning and executing the conception, pricing, promotion, and distribution of ideas, goods, services, organizations and events to create and maintain relationships that will satisfy individual and organizational objectives."[33] Whatever the specifics of the definition, most approaches to marketing start with recognizing that marketing is the activity that seeks to build understanding and communication between the company and the customer. Communication, however, requires the active involvement of both parties. An effective marketing approach must include ongoing collection and analysis of customer and market metrics through which a company can monitor and adapt to changes in market reaction and acceptance of its products, services and promotions.

Plan for change

The marketing plan is a living document. In an environment where the power of traditional trading giants has been weakened by emerging super economies, and in which supply chains have become increasingly global in nature, this has never been truer. Marketing requires continual tracking and monitoring of the environments in which the company and its competitors are doing business. Whether the gathering of information is a result of a formal procedure, the casual collection of market observations or the outcome of well-nurtured relationships and networks, the need for capturing information should be woven into the fabric of the company. In a very real sense, maintaining the market—not to mention growing it—is impossible without continuously revisiting the plan in order to compare marketing targets to actual performance. If a company lacks this commitment, awareness of emerging trends may arrive far too late.

Elements of the marketing plan

The plan itself is a written summary of the firm's export goals within a specific foreign market, the strategy to be followed, the organization of the resources needed to meet that strategy, and a feedback and reporting mechanism to measure progress. However they are arranged in practice, export marketing plans should contain at least the following conceptual elements:

---

[33] Boone and Kurtz. *Contemporary Marketing Wired*, Dryden Press.

- **Description of the business that the company is in:** The plan should describe company objectives and the characteristics that set it apart from its competitors. It should also highlight the company's competitive advantages and a winning value proposition.

- **Reasons for exporting to the intended market:** The plan should be clear about the reasons for exporting to the target market, the process that resulted in the selection of this market and on what basis the market was chosen over available alternatives. It should also define the role that sales to the target market will play in the business.

- **Sources of market research:** The plan should identify the sources of information that are appropriate for the product and the target market. These sources may include the Internet, specialized market-research firms, government representatives and direct contact with the market through visits and interviews.

- **Details of the target market:** In addition to describing the market, the characteristics of the target market should be compared to the company's strengths and weaknesses.

  - Market profile. Describe the segment being targeted and whether it is based on a regional area or a definable portion of the population.

  - Competitor analysis. Describe domestic and foreign competitors within the target market that offer a similar product and determine their strengths and weaknesses.

  - Customer profile. Is the end-user within the consumer or the industrial marketplace? Is the customer a government entity, such as in the case of capital projects, or is it a purchasing group that represents a particular industry, as is common in the retail-foods industry? How big is this market and what drives its buying decisions?

  - Cultural factors. How do cultural characteristics and beliefs affect the product and the ways in which it is presented to the market?

  - Market objectives. Ideally, this is described in easily quantifiable terms, such as "$X in sales in Y market by the year Z." What position does the company expect to hold within the market by that time? How will it achieve these objectives?

  - Pricing strategy. This is a major element in achieving market objectives. The pricing strategy will be based on the cost of entering and maintaining the market, expected profit margins, terms of payment and the price sensitivity of the market among other factors.

- **Details of the product:** Once the details of the target market have been given, this section should provide an analysis of the product or service within the context of the market characteristics. Are there similar products? What is the appeal? Are modifications required to ensure the expected product life cycle?

Typical market-research questions:

Will the product designed for the U.S. market need to be modified significantly for Asian markets?

How does one find reliable distributors in eastern Europe, and do the representation agreements need to be modified?

Will the profit margins be eroded due to currency fluctuations?

- **Market entry:** Will market entry be direct, or indirect through an intermediary? Can the company go it alone, or are partnerships required to fulfill the objectives? How will sales be conducted? Will the company need to establish a local presence?

  - Political characteristics. This should describe the market's political stability, its disposition towards foreign entities, its monetary policies and any barriers to the way in which the company intends to conduct its business.

  - Business and legal environment. Describes the tariffs, customs procedures, taxes, currency rules, import controls, health and safety standards, quality standards and an array of other factors that might affect the market objectives and financial viability.

- **Promotion:** From trade shows to the Internet, this describes the promotional program and the channel to be used, whether it is print advertising, radio or television broadcasting, trade fairs, online marketing or some combination of these. Determining the right promotional program relies on a thorough understanding of what is important to the customer, and how they will best perceive the product.

- **Logistics:** What is the optimal method of getting the product to the market on time, in good condition and with the required paper work? What appropriate warehousing and distribution methods are available?

- **Implementation:** What services, strategic relationships and/or advice are required to initiate all of the details of the plan? Who is responsible for executing the plan? What are the timelines and milestones? How will production capacities need to change, and what other skills are required within the company to ensure proper execution?

- **Monitoring progress and measuring results:** Reiterating the dynamic nature of the marketing plan, what process will be used to measure its success? How will this be quantified? If necessary, what alternative scenarios might be instituted to improve performance of the plan?

Market Planning and the International Business Plan

A company should have as many marketing plans as it has markets, so that the unique characteristics of the market may be served by unique solutions.

The marketing plan is not the only functional element of the international business plan, but the research and planning process does affect most other parts of the business. The overall international business plan provides the context and general goals of the company's global activities. The marketing plan specifies a particular foreign market, identifies a specific opportunity and describes the role that the market could play in achieving the company's strategic objectives. As an inherently dynamic activity, market planning is a role that should not be viewed as an independent department or division on a lateral plane with other business units. It should be considered as a function that permeates and informs the development, production, delivery and culture of all aspects of the business.

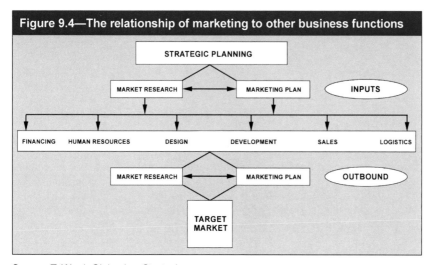

Figure 9.4—The relationship of marketing to other business functions

Source: T. Ward, Globeview Strategies

Knowledge of the target market, when translated into a realistic plan, is the business "proof" that is tested and re-tested when exposed to any of the company's stakeholders and, ultimately, to the market itself.

Finding the Right Mix: Elements of the Marketing Strategy

The marketing mix—sometimes referred to as the 4 Ps of marketing—is intended to describe the strategic elements that must come together in some combination to produce a successful marketing strategy. These are the initial P factors:

- Product: Selling the right product to the right market at the right time.

- Price: The act of selecting the pricing strategy that both fits the market conditions and the costs of doing business in the market.

- Place: A determination of the best way of getting the product to the customer.

- Promotion: Selection of the most effective means of making the customer aware of the value of the product.

In global business, there are other P factors that should be considered. The following examples round out the list to 10 P factors, although the number of strategic elements to be defined by the marketing plan could be much higher depending on the business the company is in and the unique aspects of the target market.

- Planning (business, market, account, sales and calls, etc.)

- Personnel (identifying the skills required to design, develop and deliver)

- **P**ractices (business practices within the culture of the target market)

- **P**artnerships (potential partners that may strengthen the opportunity)

- **P**ositioning (how the company wants to be perceived by clients and customers)

- **P**rotection (an assessment of the potential risks in all aspects of the transaction)

The concept of the marketing mix is a generally accepted rudimentary principle; however, there is debate on its current real-world applicability. In some cases, the marketing mix is interpreted as being too biased towards consumer markets, and could be an unsuitable approach towards industrial markets. In recent years, the marketing mix has been subject to new interpretations in order to address the unique attributes of service export modalities.

Adopting a "marketing mindset"

"The most successful business [person] is the [one] who holds onto the old just as long as it is good, and grabs the new just as soon as it is better."
Lee Iacocca, former Chairman of Chrysler Corp.

In an environment of increased global competition, it may not always be possible to effectively maintain and grow profits simply by juggling the marketing mix and altering the market plan in a reactive manner. While determining the role of marketing within the organization, companies must employ a proactive approach to market development, focusing more on the longer-term goal of market creation. The future profitability of the company relies on a vision of business modification and transformation based on predictions resulting from continual market research and analysis, and this has never been truer than in today's global business environment. Peter Drucker, a worldwide expert on management and marketing issues once said, "The business has two basic functions: marketing and innovation. Marketing and innovation produce results; all the rest are costs." To remain competitive, today's global businesses need to focus some of that innovation on maintaining a dynamic and vital attitude towards marketing.

Revitalizing the organization's view of marketing

To spread the marketing vision throughout the organization, the company must consider the marketing plan as a flow-through process rather than a document containing statements of intent. One alternative means of viewing the role of marketing is to consider the process-based "three horizons" approach to market strategy. This model is designed to not only strengthen competitiveness, but also to engender a proactive view of marketing that can give global businesses more control over their international growth objectives.[34]

The following illustrates this concept of short term through to long term, or moving from a market-penetration strategy through to a market-creation strategy:

- **Horizon 1**—*Demand-generation marketing* outlines the activities designed to drive short-term revenues and market share. The performance measurement of this horizon is based on behavioural outcomes that determine whether the customer is beginning or continuing to buy the product. This might characterize a traditional export-market-entry initiative with an existing product into a new market.

---

[34] Adapted from *Five Steps That Take Marketing to the Next Level*, Prof. Mohan Sawhney, Kellogg School of Management, Northwestern University.

- **Horizon 2**—This medium-term horizon focuses on *perception-changing marketing* and is measured in terms of the company's ability to build brands and relationships that drive or change the perception of the desirability of the product and the company itself. An example of this would be introducing a new and better product into a new export market.

- **Horizon 3**—The long-term horizon is *market-creating marketing*. "Thought leadership" is a concept gaining mass popularity and should be the ultimate goal of the marketing organization. This horizon focuses the marketing activity on the creation of new markets and new demand by driving a vision of future needs and uses. The way Microsoft designs and develops concepts and then transforms these concepts into products for the consumer is a prime example. This could also be described as creating a completely innovative product for an export market, and then going out and creating demand from customers that were previously unaware of the concept.

Table 9.5—The "three horizons" of marketing			
	Horizon 1: Generating demand	**Horizon 2: Changing perceptions**	**Horizon 3: Creating markets**
Marketing goal	*Revenue leadership*: Drive revenues and market share for in-market products	*Asset leadership*: Build brand equity and consumer equity	*Thought leadership*: Lead the creation of new markets and ecosystems
Marketing deliverables	Effective marketing campaigns and messaging	Compelling offerings and value propositions	"Visions of the future"—new experiences and ecosystems
Business impact	Revenue impact	Perceptual impact	Thought leadership impact
Time horizon	Short term (< 12 months)	Medium term (1–3 years)	Long term (5–10 years)
Functional interfaces	Outbound marketing: sales and partners as key interfaces	Inbound and outbound marketing, engineering and sales	Entire ecosystem— partners customers, suppliers and influencers

Table 9.5—The "three horizons" of marketing *(continued)*			
	Horizon 1: Generating demand	Horizon 2: Changing perceptions	Horizon 3: Creating markets
Key communication tools	Consumer and trade promotions, direct and online marketing, paid search and trade shows	Broad-reach advertising, public relations and contextual advertising	Experience prototyping, vision marketing, AR, evangelism and white papers
Success metrics	Pipeline velocity and volume, market share and revenues	Awareness, image, perceptions and consideration	Perceived thought leadership and strength of partner coalition

From market research to the creation of the marketing plan, managers that want to sustain and grow their business in a globally competitive and networked world need to view marketing as a core process of both the company's inputs and its target-market outputs or objectives. In this respect, the international marketing activity is one of the most important and all-encompassing aspects of participation in the global business environment.

Resources and Costs of the Marketing Activity

In practice, every company must recognize the limits on what it can accomplish during the market-planning process and what it is capable of within the market following the initial implementation of the plan. The costs of exporting and, indeed, the market planning process itself can be high, depending on what market research, planning and implementation measures the company deems necessary. These costs need to be factored into the pricing-strategy component of the marketing plan, and are an important determinant in the viability of pursuing the export opportunity. The following list outlines many of the costs associated with exporting due to the resources required or to the process itself that the company must consider:

- **Operational resources**

  - Foreign-market information needed to make sound decisions (information may not be readily available, adding to money and time spent in collecting the required information)

  - Increased paperwork (administration, shipping, customs and financial documentation)

- Staff and/or staff retraining and/or outsourcing (for expertise in the targeted market, marketing and promotion, financing, insurance, transportation and logistics and customs documentation, etc.)

- Expense of foreign travel in time and money (may be required for the market-planning process, and will almost certainly be required for sales and post-entry service)

- Language training or purchase of language services (required for relationship building, sales and promotional materials, etc.)

- Re-education to client market (for understanding of new cultures, political systems and environments)

- Development of new markets (may require a long-term commitment to maintaining a presence in the market for building relationships and negotiating contracts)

- Selection and hiring of qualified personnel in the target market (agents, distributors and transportation companies)

- Currency fluctuations

- Modification of the product, packaging and labelling due to target market requirements or preferences

- **Infrastructure resources**

  - Up-to-date computer systems

  - Full-time Internet access

  - Word-processing software with foreign-language capability

  - A reliable, high-quality fax machine

  - An answering service to answer business calls after hours

  - An accountant who understands international taxes and accounting

  - A bank that has an understanding of the export business

  - An insurance agent

  - Legal advice that includes familiarity with trade law

  - A good network of business associates

  - A good travel agent if a lot of travel is required

- **Human resources**

  - Country-specific knowledge

  - Local language

- Local representation

- Marketing infrastructure skills

- Export logistics/transportation knowledge

- Knowledge of local rules and regulations

- Trade-related documentation

- Awareness of financial options and arrangements

- Accounting practices of the target market

- Logistics of travel to and within the target market

Market Research and Marketing Checklist

The following checklist can be helpful when embarking on the market research process and the development of the marketing plan.

Table 9.6—Market research and marketing checklist
☑ Promote a company-wide appreciation for the role of market research and marketing.
☑ Define international marketing objectives within the parameters of the corporate strategic plan (e.g., market share vs. profit).
☑ Determine the nature and extent of research required (e.g., market dynamics, regulatory and legal issues, logistics capabilities and cultural considerations).
☑ Outline the resources to be used for market research and the creation of the marketing plan and understand the associated costs.
☑ Commit to continuous marketing research that captures the dynamic nature of trade in the current global environment.
☑ Ensure that market research includes learning about the competition. Such knowledge can be illusory, since non-traditional products, as well as firms, may be competing against your own product.
☑ Ensure that the market research helps to develop cultural sensitivity.
☑ Whenever possible, visit the marketplace and have face-to-face meetings with your potential customers. This is essential to success.
☑ Consider the need to attend trade shows for market research and product development or modification.
☑ Establish realistic time frames for implementing the marketing plan.

Table 9.6—Market research and marketing checklist *(continued)*
☑ Hire or otherwise access knowledgeable and experienced people to support your marketing plan.
☑ Consider whether establishing foreign partnerships or relationships with intermediaries within the market will help the implementation of the marketing plan.
☑ Have patience, but recognize the company's limits on costs and risk.

Chapter Summary

Market research and marketing are often under-valued and even less understood within many companies, particularly those where the core business functions revolve around product engineering or sales. Elevating the role of marketing to a position that envelopes every aspect of the business is what companies must do to not only maintain global market position, but also to plan for future growth.

The market research and marketing process does not stop once the export sale has been accomplished. The components of the international business plan that detail these marketing activities are as fluid as the dynamics of the market itself, and successful companies demonstrate the commitment to observing and measuring change. When analyzed, these observations allow the company to effectively alter their strategy to prepare for new competition and changing consumer demand, and also help to inform the direction of internal business units.

There is no one-size-fits-all approach to developing a marketing strategy. In going forward with the process of creating a marketing organization, a company must diagnose its available human resources, cost thresholds and potential exposure to risk to design a marketing activity that matches the potential gains of the opportunity at hand.

Exercises

Exercise 1 *(class discussion)*
Define the two main types of market research and identify some of the sources or processes involved in collecting them.

(Estimated time 5 minutes)

Exercise 2 *(class discussion)*
Your management team is currently reviewing your global business strategy and has decided to pursue a strategy of "market creation" vs. "market penetration." Discuss how your approach to promotion and company messaging might be different for each of these strategies.

(Estimated time 5 minutes)

Exercise 3 (small-group discussion)

In marketing, when we want to understand consumer or customer wants/ needs, we use a series of research tools that help U.S. narrow down options and ultimately validate our assumptions. Done properly, this process usually begins with informal interviews and loosely structured focus groups and then shifts to more formal activities, such as structured interviews and carefully structured questionnaires. As this process proceeds, we develop a more refined understanding of needs and our assumptions are typically tested or validated by asking the right questions to large samples of prospective customers or even mocking up a marketing mix and running a pilot test with typical prospective customers. This process can be time-consuming, but it ensures that the customer/consumer needs of a target segment are well understood and that the marketing mix is precisely tailored to those needs. This reduces project risk considerably, given that once a green light for a product/service launch has been given, promotional costs can easily reach into the millions for larger firms.

Work in groups in two or three to develop a list of typical market-research activities that could be self-managed by an exporting company looking at a new initiative in another country. Then, identify a list of activities that would typically be very difficult for them to undertake themselves (i.e., given the cultural, geographic and language barriers that are often present in distant markets). For the activities that the firm cannot undertake themselves, what strategy should they employ to ensure that the proper marketing research has been done before any substantial money has been spent on the development of a marketing mix for that market? What challenges would this present for the firm? Consolidate your thoughts on this issue and be prepared to discuss them with the class if your instructor asks you to do so.

(Estimated time 10–15 minutes)

References/Resources

Sawhney, Mohanbir. The Three Horizons of Marketing. Northwestern University, Kellogg School of Management Publications, 2007

Cook, Michelle. Create a Great International Marketing Plan. Global Trade Solutions, 2006

Canadian Marketing Association (www.the-cma.org)

Greenbook: Worldwide directory of market research companies and services (www.greenbook.org)

Marketing Magazine (www.marketingmag.ca)

Reaching the Customer: Developing Your Export Marketing Strategy (www. exportsource.ca)

The Virtual Trade Commissioner and Foreign Market Reports (www.infoexport. gc.ca)

Thought Leadership (www.prinfluences.com.au/index.php?artId=520)

Entering and Maintaining the Market

10

Strategic considerations

Chapter Objectives

- Identify strategic options for entering a market

- Outline distribution-channel options and how to manage them effectively

- Describe how to maintain distribution-channel communications

- Understand how to develop a strategy for establishing and maintaining a long-term presence

Overview

When a company has completed the process of market research and has confirmed that, given its resources, it is capable of successfully entering a specific international market, it is time to develop a strategy for market entry. A wide range of options exists for companies to approach the market, and to develop and maintain a long-term and successful presence there. These will be highlighted in this chapter.

Because so many options exist, it is critical to select the right market-entry strategy. Probably the first question to answer is whether to work directly with customers or to use some form of distribution, whereby a company's products or services are managed or impacted in one way or another by a third party. There are pros and cons to both options. Direct sales allow a product or service provider to minimize prices to end-users and to control the relationship directly; conversely, leveraging a company as a partner along the supply chain prior to its arrival at the ultimate customer may facilitate more reach into a market but can also increase end-user prices and complicate communications with customers.

When developing a market-entry and maintenance strategy, a variety of other factors must be considered. What method best suits a company's product or service? What is the layout of existing distribution networks, and what forces drive them? What is the competition doing, and what can be improved? What does the market research indicate are the drivers of customer buying behaviour? What investment needs to be allocated, in both the short and long term? How will the strategy need to be modified as the exporter progresses through the market-development cycle? Most importantly, what are the critical success factors that could determine the difference between success and failure in a target export market? All of these and more must be carefully considered as one develops an international market-entry strategy.

Market Entry: Time to Sell

As we have discovered, marketing is the "process of building understanding and communication between the supplier and the customer." Sales takes this process one step further, and can be characterized as the process of fulfilling the needs of customers with a satisfactory product or service, consummated by the exchange of money. One has not truly entered a market until a customer has paid money for the product or service being offered.

Commercial transactions are the ultimate goal of international trade and, indeed, trade of any kind. The pattern of international-market development often follows a series of stages, as indicated by the following table:

Table 10.1—Stages of exporting	
Stage	Description
1	Domestic-market establishment
2	Export research and planning
3	Initial export sales

| 4 | Expansion of international sales |
| 5 | Investment abroad |

Stage One: Domestic-market establishment

The domestic market is often an appropriate place to test products and fine-tune performance before tackling the complexities of international trade. It can also give a good indication of performance. However, in some instances, this stage of the export process does not serve any purpose at all. This may be the case for a Canadian software company, for example, that has developed a product specifically for a foreign market.

Because international-market development requires resources of time and money on the part of the exporter, it's important to ensure that a strong foundation has been built in the domestic market upon which to base future export-market-expansion activities, so that international activities do not compromise the company's core business.

Stage Two: Export research and planning

When companies begin trading abroad, they often target a country similar to their own in language, financial structures, legal and economic systems or culture. For example, Canadians entering the international marketplace usually address the U.S. market first.

Before venturing into an unfamiliar market, companies should prepare themselves properly. By analyzing how successful the proposed product or service may be in a potential market, the exporter can narrow the target markets down to three or four. A well-researched marketing plan can give the potential exporter the confidence to commit to exporting. Such concentrated effort is preferable to the common, and costly, mistake of "chasing orders around the world."

Another advantage to undertaking appropriate international-market-research and planning activities is that by creating a written document, potential problems and weaknesses can be identified more easily. This allows exporters to foresee potential challenges prior to making the investment of time and money that will be required for successful export-market development.

Stage Three: Initial export sales

When implementing an export plan, it is advisable to begin modestly by testing the market. A graduated strategy allows the novice exporter to acquire practical experience in a market without incurring unnecessary or unmanageable risk. Developing markets in phases allows the exporter to monitor their progress and make any necessary changes as they progress along the path to export success.

During this stage, the exporter should use initial shipments to become familiar with the mechanics of exporting (documentation, distribution channels, transportation and collections), to get to know the customer target group, to determine what product modifications may be necessary and to learn about regulations that might affect the business. This is also the stage at which to revise the initial plan.

Stage Four: Expansion of international sales

If initial sales have been good, planning for larger orders and expanded activity should follow. This stage is usually accompanied by intensified market research, more aggressive participation in international trade shows and other marketing activities and greater emphasis on strengthening networks and contacts in the target market. The firm may enter negotiations with potential local partners to strengthen its position in the market in win-win business relationships.

By the time exporters have reached this stage, they will have already learned a great deal about the export market through prior experience, which will assist them in making appropriate adjustments to their strategy as they proceed with strengthening their position in the market.

Stage Five: Investment abroad

If sales are brisk, profits encouraging and opportunities promising, the company may choose to expand its presence in the target market. It can, for example, open a local office, tighten relations with local partners, buy an existing local company, form a joint venture or invest in R&D or production facilities. The target market may serve as a stepping stone to adjacent markets and become a focal point for a larger trade strategy.

This final stage carries additional ramifications and responsibilities, beyond those of a company that is based elsewhere simply operating remotely in a foreign market. New issues come into play because the scope of a company's presence broadens when it takes on a permanent physical presence in the market. For instance, the investing company must take into account the impact on and interaction with the community and all other stakeholders—employees, local government, the environment, legal and tax compliance, transparency, public image and sustainability. All of these impacts must be managed seriously and carefully as a corporate citizen, with strong corporate social responsibility a policy that should be demonstrated at every opportunity.

Elements of trade

International trade once consisted almost exclusively of goods shipped from one country to another. In today's world and in the future, however, trade can take many forms, some of which are mixed together into one commercial item. Below is a table describing the basic elements of trade.

Table 10.2—Basic elements of trade	
Merchandise trade	Merchandise trade refers to trade in tangible goods—commodities and manufactured items. This can include raw materials (iron ore and logs), agricultural commodities (grains and sugar), semi-processed goods (steel tubing and plywood), components (automobile engines and assemblies) and finished goods (cars, clothing, food and television sets).

Table 10.2—Basic elements of trade *(continued)*	
Trade in services	Services represent in excess of 20 percent of world trade and one of the fastest-growing sectors worldwide. Trade in services is significantly different from trade in goods since services are invisible. Skills, knowledge and expertise are being traded across borders by architects, engineers, accountants, management consultants, trainers, translators and transportation and logistics firms, to name a few.
	The selling of services relies extensively on understanding client needs and building long-term relationships. Services are also embedded in the manufacturing process, and increasingly, companies are looking for ways to increase value through the position of value-added services.
Investment	Investment is becoming more important as an engine of growth in the international economy. Often, it is the price of admission into a market. Countries seeking to create employment for their citizens are more inclined to negotiate favourable terms for foreign investment than they are to surrender open and unrestricted access to their markets. Despite the WTO process of tariff reductions, there are still many ways that countries can restrict imports while favouring investment in their own economies. Moreover, multinational corporations are willing to invest internationally as a way of staying close to markets, tapping into additional human resources and acquainting themselves with new technologies or different business practices.
Technology transfer	This is another important way to gain market access with a partner. Technology, in the form of designs, formulas, production methods, specialized software or other technical know-how, including intellectual property such as patents and trade marks, is transferred to a partner under a licence agreement. The partner uses this technology to penetrate the market and pays an up-front fee or royalty on sales (or a combination of both). This can be applied in the service as well as the goods sector.

Market-Entry Options: Direct, Indirect, Investment and Strategic Alliances

When deciding upon the most appropriate method of entering an export market, two key points should be considered in the calculation: the value of a product or service and the population of potential customers. A useful analogy to demonstrate this point might be comparing manufacturers of nuclear power plants with manufacturers of vacuum cleaners.

Table 10.3—Example: Evaluating the choice between direct sales and distribution		
Variable	Nuclear power plants	Vacuum cleaners
Population of customers	Low	High
Value of product	High	Low
Requirement for stock	Low	High
Requirement for service	Extremely specialized	Relatively simple

Market-entry options depend on:
1. Value of product/ service
2. Population of customers

In the former example, the value of the product is very high, and the population of potential customers is very low—the federal government of a country could be the only entity in a position to purchase nuclear power plants. In this case, using distribution would not be the appropriate method; the manufacturer would be best advised to deal directly with the correct authorities and provide the high and unique level of technical support and clear communications required, without an intermediary. It should be remembered, however, that distributors or other channel partners can often provide the minor to intermediate levels of in-market service that are critical for reliable customer and product support. Manufacturers of vacuums would be ill-advised to try to sell to potential customers directly (that is, to every household in a market); strategic in-market partners would be far better positioned to reach, service and hold local stock for customers in a wide variety of channels much more effectively.

Trading strategies and methods

The recent profound changes in what is being traded internationally have also affected how trade is carried out. Apart from the traditional means of market entry—that is, exporting directly to end-users, or selling and buying through agents, distributors and trading houses—exporters now use a number of other mechanisms, such as various forms of investments, strategic alliances and licensing agreements.

Which channel(s) an exporter chooses will depend on a range of factors, including the following:

- the value of the product or service

- the population of potential customers

- the way business is conducted in the specific market and industry sector

- the exporter's experience in international trade

- the strengths and weaknesses of the exporting company

- the exporting company's financial capacity

- the product being sold

- the level of service customers demand

- trade barriers (tariffs, regulations and rules in the foreign market)

Direct exporting

As the name implies, a direct exporting strategy involves a company selling goods directly to a customer in an international market. There is a wide range of customers that a company can sell to, some of which act as intermediaries in the target market. (Even though an intermediary is involved, the export is still direct because the intermediary is a customer based in the target market.)

The most important types of customer for a company involved in direct exporting include the following:

- **Importers:** These companies operate by importing goods into their country. They are useful customers for exporters because they have researched the local market and are confident they can sell goods they import. They will also pay customs duties and taxes and arrange for import paperwork to be completed.

- **Wholesalers:** These are companies that purchase goods in bulk and distribute them to retailers or other customers in the local market. They are useful customers because they have established customers and take responsibility for selling, distribution and marketing from the exporter.

- **Distributors:** These are wholesalers that only carry non-competing lines of goods.

- **Retailers:** These are companies that sell to end consumers.

- **Government procurement departments:** These are local government departments that seek out providers of goods and services that are required for serving the public.

- **Consumers:** These customers can be reached directly using a variety of promotional techniques.

Finding customers

If a company wants to export directly to a selected market, it should contact its country's embassy in the foreign market and talk to the trade commissioners based there. They will be able to provide valuable information about important business contacts and will help organize business visits.

When a company has found a distributor, wholesaler or retailer that might be a good customer, it should make the following checks:

- Does the business have solid financial backing?
- Does the business have a reputation for paying invoices on time?
- Does the business have a wide coverage in the target market?
- How much stock will the business hold?

A company can usually obtain this information by requesting exhibits as part of a sales contract. These exhibits include actual sales contracts, rental contracts, inventory lists, customer lists, customer references and financial statements. These checks are essential to make sure that the company will not be working with a business that trades in unethical or illegal ways and that the company will receive payment for its goods in a timely manner. A business that does not have a wide coverage in the target market or one that cannot hold a reasonable amount of the company's stock is unlikely to be able to sell large quantities of the company's product. Because most distributorship agreements are exclusive for a certain territory, a company should look elsewhere if a distributor or wholesaler cannot provide its products with maximum market exposure.

Government procurement

Government departments in the target market can be an excellent customer for exporters. Government procurement can account for up to 20 percent of a country's GDP. For example, in Canada, the government tenders for goods and services worth over $100 CD billion every year.

Besides the wealth of opportunities associated with selling to foreign governments, a company obtains a certain level of prestige by being able to declare itself a government supplier. It will also find it easier to sell to other international marketplaces.

All governments put out tenders or requests for proposals (RFPs) to provide goods and services. A selection of tenders can easily be found by searching on the Internet. For example, DGmarket (www.dgmarket.com), a service of the Development Gateway Foundation, publishes lists of government tenders from nearly 200 countries organized by industry sector. Initial information is free to access and members can receive e-mail notifications when new tenders are published. B2Bpointer.com is a service provided by API Online. On this site, companies can perform a free search for public and private tenders.

Every government will have different standards and procedures for awarding tenders to companies, many of which place restrictions on foreign companies. However, countries that are signatories to the Agreement on Government Procurement (GPA) signed in 1994 do not make tender decisions based on the location of the supplier. Currently, 26 countries have signed the GPA, including Canada, members of the EU, and the U.S.

Companies must be very careful not to attempt to procure government contracts until they are ready to do so. In particular, companies should answer the following questions before attempting to enter a foreign market using government procurement as an export strategy:

- Do we have an offering that is ready to be sold and, ideally, has already been sold commercially?

- What is the largest order that we are capable of meeting?

- How rapidly could we meet a large order?

- What action would we take if a government requested a larger order?

- Do we understand all aspects of exporting, including which documentation we will require?

- Will our product require export permits?

- Is our product restricted to certain countries?

- Have we researched government funding cycles in our target market?

- Have we identified the competition in the market so that we can challenge them effectively?

- How can we adapt our marketing approach to be suitable for government procurement agents?

Business models

Companies can use a range of business models to organize their direct exporting efforts. Some businesses have an export department within the company that is responsible for exporting activities. Others establish sales offices in the target market. This business model enables companies to organize distribution and marketing more effectively. If a company wants to benefit from having personnel in the target market but does not wish to invest in sales offices, it can employ overseas sales personnel. However, companies new to direct exporting should start by selling to an intermediary or by contracting an agent. Agents represent the company on a commission basis and can engage in promotional work or help establish deals. Like distributors, they take on the selling responsibility for the exporter, but they do not act as a company customer. The advantages and disadvantages of using agents or distributors are summarized in Table 10.4.

Table 10.4—Considerations for working with agents or distributors		
	Advantages	**Disadvantages**
Agent	An expert who has established customer contacts represents the company. This greatly increases sales potential and can result in better deals being made.	The company must not work with other agents in that region or, sometimes, for the same product in other regions. The agent will negotiate pricing. Profit rates are reduced because of commission payments.
Distributor	The company must only deal with one customer, who becomes responsible for promotion, delivery and marketing of the goods. This reduces risk and effort.	The company loses control over pricing and promotion.

Advantages and disadvantages of direct exporting

Direct exporting as a market entry strategy has several advantages for a company:

- The company controls all its manufacturing processes, and the processes are based in the company's facilities. It therefore avoids risks associated with production overseas, such as the loss of reputation from poor production standards or the use of child labour. It is also less susceptible to the effects of political instability in the foreign market.

- A company can withdraw from the market relatively cheaply and easily if it needs to.

- Companies can obtain in-depth information about trade in the target market. This will enable them to make future decisions about whether to invest in facilities in the market.

However, direct exporting can be difficult, especially for companies new to international trade. Companies should consider the following disadvantages:

- Companies need to invest significantly in researching market information and preparing marketing strategies.

- Companies without exporting skills and experience can make expensive errors.

- Target markets in trade blocs are very difficult to break into.

- Intermediaries will be representing other companies and cannot be relied on to operate in the best interests of the exporting company.

- Exporting will be more difficult when the domestic currency is very strong in comparison to the target market's currency.

When is direct exporting a suitable strategy?

Direct exporting is a simple entry strategy that might be suitable for companies that want to expand their market share or maximize profits. A company of any size can start direct exporting activities, but not all will have the necessary resources in terms of skills, knowledge and finances. Direct exporters must make the export sale, arrange for shipping and insurance, organize permits and licenses, prepare all the paper work and process the letter of credit that provides for payment. These tasks are time-consuming and require skill to be performed correctly, and mistakes can result in serious business losses. Considerable time must also be spent researching the market so that goods or services can be promoted and priced appropriately.

Direct exporting is a strategy that might be very successful if the market selected is readily accessible and has similar regulations and customs to the company's country. If the target market has different regulations, legal systems, cultures, or ways of conducting business, and the company is inexperienced in international trade, direct exporting might be very difficult and risky. In these situations, companies should consider another strategy.

Depending on the market selected, the distance goods must be transported and the means of transportation, direct exporting can make goods too expensive for customers to purchase. It might also seriously impact profits made in the market.

With direct exporting, companies must be comfortable with a substantial element of risk. A direct exporter must assume responsibility for all losses during shipping and storage overseas. Substantial amounts must be invested in marketing and selling to the market and there is a risk that these expenses will not be recouped if the exporting activity is not successful. Political and economic instability in the market will also present the risk of business losses.

"The management staff is on call every minute of the year and they fully comprehend that the key to success is efficient service. CCL's headquarters in India is directly linked to its London and New York representatives through an international communications network, ensuring that the customers' requirements are processed and delivered with maximum efficiency and speed."
CCL website.

The main advantages of direct exporting are that it provides the exporter with a lot of control over the process of how the product is positioned and sold. It also presents an opportunity for high profits when markets are chosen carefully. If a company is interested in long-term growth in an international market, direct exporting can be a suitable entry strategy because it enables the company to gain knowledge of the market and develop distribution channels.

Table 10.5 summarizes the conditions for considering direct exporting as a market entry strategy.

Case study—Weathering financial storms through direct exporting

Continental Coffee Limited (CCL) Enterprises is an Indian company that Wealth Insight magazine declared one of the seven wonders of the Indian stock market in 2008. This small company started operations in 1995 dealing in instant coffee, and has always been 100 percent export oriented. It exports coffee to the U.S. and the U.K., major markets for quality coffee, and has seen sales rise by 34 percent year on year. Part of the reason for CCL's success is in offering personalized products to customers. The company also has a comprehensive and certified control system and tasting procedures to ensure high quality, which is essential in its targeted markets.

To start its international trade through direct exports, CCL took several actions. It engaged agents in London and New York and established a fast distribution network by locating its factory close to the Indian port of Chennai. It purchased a licence to use proprietary coffee production technology to ensure high quality. To establish a reputation for exceptional customer service, CCL has all managers on call 24 hours a day, every day of the year.

Source: www.cclproducts.com

Table 10.5—Conditions for direct exporting

Element to consider	Suitable conditions
Company goals	Strategic objectives are to maximize profits or expand market share.
Size of company	Any size company is suitable, although smaller companies might find allocation of resources difficult.

Table 10.5—Conditions for direct exporting	
Resources	The company must have skills and experience in dealing with exporting and marketing overseas, or must find partners who can help with it.
Product or service	Any product or service can be exported, but it must be suitable for the chosen market.
Remittance	This strategy will only be suitable if the costs added to the purchase price by shipping and insurance costs, storage fees, and duties and taxes will not make the product too expensive.
Competition	Main competitors must not be operating in a monopoly situation or receiving subsidies, because this can severely impact the possibility of success.
Intermediaries	No intermediaries are required, but importers and distributors will be beneficial customers to find.
Control	The company requires substantial control over production, marketing and selling activities.
Investment	The company must be able to invest substantial time and money into market research, marketing, selling and distribution issues.
Time	The company can enter the market slowly or rapidly.
Risk	The company must be able to handle risks associated with loss of goods in transit, non-payment for goods sent and unsuccessful market entry.
Flexibility	The company wants the ability to exit the market more quickly than would be possible if they had made a direct investment in the foreign market.

Source: www.cclproducts.com

Indirect exporting

Direct exporting requires considerable investment in time, money and skills. An easier option, especially for smaller companies, is to use indirect exporting to enter a market.

In indirect exporting, a company sells to an intermediary in their own country. This intermediary then sells the goods to the international market and takes on the responsibility of organizing paperwork and permits, organizing shipping and arranging marketing.

An indirect exporter can sell to the following intermediary customers:

- **Export houses (trading houses or export merchants)**. These are wholesalers that purchase goods and sell them to international markets. They use salespeople, stock lists and sometimes their own retail outlets to sell their purchased goods in foreign markets. Companies that sell to export houses will find the experience the same as selling to other domestic companies. They will be paid in domestic currency and domestic laws will govern the terms of sale. Export houses are useful customers for companies entering international trade because they have an expert knowledge of international markets and have established distribution and selling channels. One example of an export house is S & K Enterprises, located in Ontario, Canada. This export house specializes in exporting unusual mechanical and electrical products to the Caribbean region.

  Reputable members of trading houses are members of export merchants associations or trading house associations. These can be found by searching online. For example, the Quebec Export Trading House Association represents trading houses in Quebec and acts to encourage exports from the province and to train traders.

- **Confirming houses**. These companies represent foreign businesses that do not have a well-established reputation and cannot obtain credit to purchase goods from other countries. The confirming house takes on the responsibility of paying the company for the exported goods and ships them to the foreign business. Confirming houses will often be asked by foreign businesses to seek out certain goods for export. They are useful customers for companies entering international trade because they assume the risk of non-payment for the goods and they arrange transportation and shipping.

- **Foreign companies based in the company's country (buying offices)**. Many large companies and organizations establish offices overseas and purchase locally produced goods. They are useful customers for companies entering international trade because they arrange for shipping overseas and all export documentation.

Piggybacking

Companies who want to engage in indirect exporting sometimes use a system called piggybacking. In piggybacking, companies (often termed "riders") use the skills, experience or resources of a company that is more experienced in exporting (often termed the "carrier" company).

As an example, consider a small cosmetics manufacturer called Comelline based in Canada. It has developed a new anti-aging moisturizer called Comrenew and wants to sell it to the U.S., but does not have the expertise or the distribution channels to do so. Comelline approaches a larger Canadian cosmetics manufacturer, Bute, which is successful in the U.S. and the EU.

Comelline asks Bute to sell its new moisturizer, Comrenew, along with Bute's current product line. Bute agrees, because it obtains a new product line and obtains payment from the sale. Comelline benefits by selling its product overseas without having to establish distribution networks or invest in intensive marketing.

For a company to use piggybacking as a means of exporting, the following factors must be present:

- The product or service that the rider company wants to sell is complementary to the product line or function provided by the carrier.
- The product or service is suitable for the carrier's distribution and marketing chain.
- The product or service has a markup substantial enough to justify efforts by the carrier.
- The product or service has sufficient demand in the target market to predict substantial sales.

Carrier companies are paid either by commission or by purchasing the product and acting as a distributor.

Countertrade

Countertrade is the method most often used for indirect exporting, and is estimated by the UN to comprise up to 30 percent of international trade. In countertrade, payments for goods and services are made by deliveries of other goods and services as well as, or in place of, financial payments. Basically, it is an up-to-date form of bartering, in which one type of good is exchanged for another.

One form of countertrade is counter purchase, also known as buyback. This involves a buyer agreeing to purchase a set quantity of goods on condition that the seller purchases the buyer's products in return. If the selling company does not require the buyer's products, it can sell them to a third party.

Finding customers for indirect exporting

In some cases, the intermediary will contact companies. If a company wants to move into indirect exporting, it can find customers using the following strategies:

- Most countries have an exporter's association that can be found with a simple Internet search. By contacting the association for their country, companies can obtain lists of reputable export merchants.

- Chambers of commerce and trade associations will provide information about buying offices for specified products.

Advantages and disadvantages of indirect exporting

Indirect exporting is the cheapest entry strategy available to a company. It is flexible, and exporting activities can cease immediately if required. Its greatest advantage is that the intermediary companies handle all the exporting activities. No exporting experience or skills are required, and the intermediary company takes on all the risks associated with shipping and organizing payment from the international market.

The main disadvantage is that control of activities overseas is lost to the intermediary companies. A company interested in expanding into a target market will not gain valuable knowledge about how that market functions. It is also impossible for a company to establish after-sales service or additional value-added activities, and this can have an adverse effect on a company's reputation in a foreign country.

When is indirect exporting a suitable strategy?

This market entry strategy is one that should be considered by a company that wants to enhance its cash flow or increase its profits. However, it will not be useful for a company that wants to develop long-term market share. It is also not suitable for a company with a service to sell rather than a product.

A company of any size can engage in indirect exporting, but it is a strategy often chosen by smaller and newer companies. This is because once the intermediary business to sell to has been identified, the company does not have to worry about additional planning, marketing or expenses. It is also a very useful strategy for companies that cannot deal with considerable risk. With indirect exporting, the intermediary company assumes all the risks associated with exporting and selling the product.

Companies that choose an indirect exporting strategy must be able to make product adjustments as dictated by the businesses purchasing them. Buyers will also specify delivery times, levels of quality and packaging requirements. If the company cannot meet these requirements, it can lose the deal with the buyer.

Because the buyer takes responsibility for exporting and selling the goods, the company has no control over the market its products are sold to, how they are sold, how they are marketed or the price obtained for them. This makes it an unsuitable market entry strategy for companies that must control the export or marketing of their product to maintain its reputation. Companies that are interested in modifying their products to meet demand in other markets will also find indirect exporting unsuitable, because they will be unable to develop direct contact with the end user.

Table 10.6 summarizes the conditions in which indirect exporting might be a suitable market entry strategy.

Table 10.6—Conditions for indirect exporting	
Element to consider	**Suitable conditions**
Company goals	Strategic objectives are to maximize profits or enhance cash flow.
Size of company	Any size of company is suitable, but especially smaller companies that cannot devote human resources to international trade.
Resources	The company wants a market entry strategy that does not require special resources.
Product or service	The product must be in demand in an international market and the company must not want to trade in services.
Remittance	The company must be happy with the remittance offered by the intermediary company.
Competition	The level of competition in the market will not be a concern for the company.

Table 10.6—Conditions for indirect exporting	
Element to consider	**Suitable conditions**
Intermediaries	The company must be willing to deal with reputable trading houses or export merchants. A good working relationship will be required.
Control	The company does not need to have control over production, marketing and selling activities. It must also not have an interest in how its product is perceived overseas.
Investment	The company can invest in additional production or slight product modification if requested by the trading house or export merchant.
Time	The company is ready to trade immediately.
Risk	The company does not want to handle substantial risks.
Flexibility	The company wants to be able to withdraw from the trading relationship relatively quickly.

Table 10.7 compares trading houses, agents and distributors. Note that definitions vary from market to market, and a business arrangement may meet more than one criterion.

Table 10.7—Three common international distribution channels		
Trading house	**Agent**	**Distributor**
Purchases on own account and sells to foreign customers, sometimes both source and customer are offshore	Enters into a contractual agreement on behalf of the exporter	Purchases goods from the exporter or trading house and resells in the local market

Table 10.7—Three common international distribution channels *(cont'd)*		
Trading house	**Agent**	**Distributor**
May carry inventory, or just arrange a transaction without seeing the products	Does not normally take possession of goods	Carries inventory
Takes title to the goods, whether or not they take possession	Does not take title to the goods, payments flow directly to the exporter	Takes title and possession of the goods
Sets its own selling price	Does not set the selling price	Sets its own selling price
Assumes risk during brief ownership period	Does not take ownership risk	Assumes risk when goods are received until they are sold
Collects payment for goods sold	Receives commission when exporter is paid	Pays the exporter when goods are received
Trade names may or may not be used, depending on agreement with manufacturer	Trade names remain the property of the manufacturer	Trademarks may or may not be restricted, re-branding may occur
May specialize in one product or act as a broker for many products on an opportunistic basis	May represent several non-competing lines at same time, usually on an exclusive territory basis	Usually handles a wide selection of product lines
Conducts own marketing and sales activities	Executes export-marketing and sales-management activities in conjunction with manufacturer	Plans and carries out its own local marketing activities
Self-financed	Financed by manufacturer	Self-financed
Takes full responsibility for customer satisfaction, can provide after-sale service, may go back to manufacturer for warranty problems	Manages normal customer support activities, technical support and warranties are the direct responsibility of the manufacturer	Provides service and warranties, may go back to manufacturer for warranty problems
Is responsible for freight, customs and documentary and tax issues	Has no liability for freight, customs, logistics and documentary or tax issues	Assumes responsibility for local documents and taxes, sometimes freight and customs issues

Investment abroad
Pros:
- Control
- Safeguard of intellectual property
- Better market knowledge

Cons:
- Cost
- Time
- Management complexity

Investment

Investing in a wholly owned subsidiary is one way of acquiring presence in a foreign market. The high degree of control the parent company retains is particularly useful for complex products or services. Also, the risk of losing secrets to competitors is minimized. The drawbacks include the expense and time involved in establishing the subsidiary, the costs of staffing and overhead and the complexity of managing the enterprise from a distance. For example, excessive control by a head office may limit the ability of subsidiaries to respond quickly and flexibly to changes in local markets, while insufficient control may compromise the entire entry strategy.

Another form of investment—acquisition—involves the purchase of a company in the foreign market. If financial resources allow, this is a quick way to become established in a market. Sometimes it is not possible to buy all the shares in the foreign company; however, if an investor can buy a significant enough interest, he or she can influence the direction of the company through a position on the board.

These two forms of investment are referred to as mergers and acquisitions, or simply M & As. In both instances, it is important that the investment be accompanied by real expertise.

Table 10.8—Mergers and acquisitions (M & As)

The American Business Conference studied 34 high-growth, medium-sized U.S. companies that consistently outperformed similar U.S. companies in growth of exports, operating profits, foreign assets and sales (typically by a factor of five in growth of foreign sales). What they all had in common was early entry into the foreign market characterized by a flexible approach. There was especially rapid evolution in market development, from pure export to investment in local production, with 80 percent of international revenues coming from overseas production and only 20 percent from exports.

The factors that supported this investment-oriented approach to market development included the following:

- An ability to obtain intelligence on potential competitors, and to construct forward defence strategies by developing a strong presence in a potential competitor's home market

- More effective access to new technologies and processes developed abroad

- An ability to cross-source or cross-export to take advantage of particular skills or efficiencies in the company's foreign operations

- Broader access to ideas, resulting in new product applications

- An ability to realize the benefits of productivity improvements from foreign manufacturing processes

On this basis, the report concluded that "despite the conventional focus on exports… international competitiveness is increasingly becoming an exercise in investment with the creation, acquisition and development of overseas marketing, sales and distribution networks and the deployment of foreign-based production, service and research facilities."

Strategic alliances

Strategic alliances provide a variety of ways for firms to gain access to the resources they need to enter foreign markets. These alliances vary from participating in an overseas joint venture to exchanging products by means of a cross-licensing agreement.

Examples of strategic alliances include

- joint ventures;

- co-marketing;

- co-promotion;

- co-production;

- cross-licensing;

- licensing agreements;

- research consortia; and

- partnerships.

What these strategies have in common is that they can provide the technology, capital or market access a company needs to enter foreign markets but might not be able to afford or achieve on its own. Strategic alliances can enhance competitiveness, enabling firms to respond more quickly to competition, increase market share, solve technological problems, protect sources of competitive advantage and supplement internal resources and capabilities.

> Strategic alliances can provide the following:
> - technology
> - capital
> - market access
> - competitiveness
> - human resources

A strategic alliance can work well when

- its strategic objectives are clear;

- its partners are committed to these objectives, and they co-operate;

- it is efficiently organized and managed;

- the capabilities of the partners complement each other;

- the partners are well-informed and have reasonable expectations; and

- there is regular communication and face-to-face meetings to help build relationships.

Many different structures of strategic alliances can be used to accomplish different objectives and satisfy different time frames. The more common structures are either horizontal or vertical arrangements. Horizontal alliances include firms in the same industry. They are less common in the service sector where they are usually formed to achieve scale, to adjust for seasonal changes or to handle niche areas of expertise. Vertical alliances are relationships among organizations in different industries. This type of alliance is common in the service sector because it allows participants to offer complete solutions to clients. With little chance of competition between alliance members, firms can combine their skills to compete with much larger and more diversified organizations.

The most successful
agreements are mutually
beneficial for both
parties, i.e. win-win.

Properly focused, and with a well-defined set of objectives, strategic alliances offer great responsiveness and flexibility. Even small firms can use alliances to compete in global markets. The links formed are restricted by a company's ability to manage them, rather than by the company's capital and other resources.

Identifying and Implementing the Right Distribution Mix: Maximizing Coverage, Minimizing Conflict

The underlying objective of any export-development initiative is to reach into every possible corner of a market through every available channel. If it were feasible to sell farm equipment at gasoline stations, there would be tractors for sale at every service centre. This is clearly not the case, however, so understanding distribution-channel options that exist in a target market is critical in developing a strategy to maximize market coverage. The procedure in developing the right distribution mix generally involves identifying, selecting, setting up and supporting members of a global supply chain.

Steps in setting up
distribution:
• identify
• select
• set up
• support
• monitor

Distribution networks vary from country to country. For example, North American dealers of many kinds of equipment are usually independent from the manufacturers, from an ownership perspective. Therefore, it is sometimes possible to buy spare parts from a dealer of well-known brands of cars that were not manufactured by the original equipment manufacturer (OEM) but by an independent auto parts maker that copied the design and is selling "equivalent" parts at lower prices. This is not likely in Japan, where car dealers are usually partly or completely owned by the OEM and sell only parts made by the approved manufacturing facility. Therefore, the automotive-dealer channel in the Japanese market is effectively closed to companies who manufacture after-market parts; instead, they must rely strictly on independent auto-parts dealers.

The challenge is to identify customers and the channels through which products flow to reach them. Then, one must figure out if it is possible to access one or more of those channels—or identify an untapped one—and fill them with the products. Coca-Cola is an example of a product that has many distribution channels. Where can one buy a Coke? At a convenience store or grocery store, of course, but where else? Restaurants, vending machines, fast food outlets, airports, coffee shops, movie theatres, gas stations, hotel room minibars—almost anywhere. Manufacturers of products that have strong brand recognition and market dominance have relatively more power over their channel partners than do lesser-known brands because demand already exists and little promotion or effort is required to generate sales to customers.

Defining distribution channels

Distribution channels can be defined in several ways, including by geography, customer type and distributor type. Geography may be the easiest to define; a manufacturer can assign territories by drawing lines on a map, and distributors are permitted to work within their boundaries without fear of competition from other distributors of the same product within that area.

Territories may also be differentiated by distributor type; for example, construction tools may be sold exclusively through one retail chain of do-it-yourself stores as well as through contractors' specialty stores that do not generally cater to the general public.

Finally, channels can be separated by distributor type. For example, sandpaper can be sold in small and aesthetically designed packages for consumers through hardware stores, in larger quantity and different-sized sheets through suppliers to auto-body shops, and in bulk to factories through industrial-supply distributors. The product may be exactly the same and made in the same factory, but distributed by the manufacturer through three distinct channels.

Managing channel conflict

Inter-channel conflict, whereby distributors of the same product compete for the same customer, is a real issue—not only for the competing channel partners, but also for the manufacturer. When the product is identical, price is the only basis on which they can compete, particularly if there is not a significant service component. Although there may be real or imagined differences in service, customers will quickly use price to play the distributors off against one another, which tends to precipitate price cutting. When that occurs, distributors will see their profit margins decline or even disappear. At best, they will complain to the manufacturer about the situation, but at worst, they will discontinue the product line and possibly take on a competitive line.

Two ways that inter-channel conflict can be managed are through branding and pricing. Branding means creating a new name and image for a product, sometimes with minor modifications. One might be able to purchase a specific make and model of an electric drill from a hardware chain, and a slightly different "Professional Series" model with one or two minor changes from an industrial distributor, which is intended to have the effect of alleviating channel conflict. Pricing is another way to control distribution channels, whereby different discounts are granted for specific business types (wholesalers, dealers, distributors, etc.) to encourage their conformance within a defined channel structure. Simple volume discounts, with larger purchases earning lower prices, are also used to separate players in a global supply chain.

Exclusivity is a benefit that is often requested by international business partners that will be promoting a new product line, but that manufacturers are often reluctant to grant—both with good reason. In-market representatives may be concerned that they would do all the work to develop and promote the product, and then the manufacturer might take customers direct, or decide to work with another representative. Conversely, manufacturers are reluctant to make an exclusive commitment to a representative until time has demonstrated that they are the right company to partner with—if their initial judgment is wrong and the representative fails to move the product successfully, they may be stuck with them. Some countries even have laws that would require the manufacturer to "buy back" the rights to their own product to allow them to set up another representative. A common way of negotiating agreement on this point is to assign a limited period of exclusivity with mutually agreed sales targets.

The distribution mix is a critical concern for decision makers as they plan their international market-entry strategy; mistakes can be costly and result in insufficient sales, so careful attention must be paid to gathering accurate market information and doing due diligence on potential business partners in export markets.

Selling to Customers: Helping Them Make Informed Decisions

Selling is not about "convincing" customers to do something a seller wants them to do; it is helping customers make informed buying decisions. If managed properly, the sales process should result in a rewarding experience and a win-win situation for both parties. Costly mistakes can be made if the many variables in the context of export-market development are not managed correctly.

International sales factors

What factors exist in the international sales process that extend beyond domestic sales? Consider the following:

International sales factors
- distance
- cost
- market
- competition
- language and culture
- relationships

Distance

In international sales, customers are not across town or across the country; they are around the world. The real and perceived barriers associated with distance bring new variables, including time zones and the time it takes to travel to visit business partners. An important issue to consider is the perceived distance that customers will be aware of when they deal with a foreign supplier—it is advisable for suppliers to minimize perceived distance by responding to communications in one day or less, and to take every other available measure to be as easy to do business with as possible.

Cost

It costs money to do business internationally. The cost of visiting a target market may be several thousand dollars for travel and accommodation, plus other requirements for translators, brochure translations, trade shows and other necessary investments to generate sales in an export market.

Market

Finding information about a distant market is more challenging than doing so locally, because exporters do not have as much in-market familiarity as they do at home and must resort to primary and secondary information sources. To gain a real understanding of the nuances of a new market, it is essential to travel there to see it first hand.

Competition

To understand the competition, it is necessary to see it with one's own eyes, and to have personal discussions with potential customers and partners to discover what needs to be done to differentiate the product or service to gain a share of the market.

Language and culture

Unless English is the primary language in a target market, an exporter is well-advised to communicate in the local language whenever possible. This offers a competitive edge if the competition is not doing so, but is a must if the competition has adapted. The culture of the target market should also be taken into account, as described in Chapter 7.

Relationships

Many cultures around the world are highly relationship-oriented, whereby people "do business with their friends." To be successful in those regions, developing relationships and becoming a trusted ally is a necessity prior to earning sales.

Helping customers make informed buying decisions remains the goal, but the strategic sales approach must be customized to suit the target market to effectively turn international market opportunities into commercial transactions.

Distribution Channel Management: Maintaining the Market

Even once distribution channels have been established and products have been sold into the entrance of the supply chain, the job is not complete. In fact, it has just begun. Channel partners are an extension of suppliers and must be managed that way because they can improve the positioning, image and reputation of the supplier—or they can damage it severely.

They must be supported, motivated and supplied with all the tools they will need to be successful in their local market, including marketing support, technical training, performance monitoring and measurement and strategic objectives, among others. Successful international suppliers make it their business to be involved, albeit sometimes indirectly, by supporting every link in the chain up to and including the customer.

Finally, when managing distribution channels, it must be kept in mind that competition comes from two places. Clearly, manufacturers of similar products— traditional competitors—are competing to sell their products to final customers. However, competition also comes from within distribution channels, whereby channel partners who handle multiple lines of non-competing products are being pushed by suppliers to focus on their products instead of others. This makes distribution-channel support a critical success factor in ensuring that a supplier's products receive the attention they require to successfully sell through to end-users.

There is a trade-off between using direct and channel sales: in theory, the cost of using intermediaries to achieve wider distribution is supposedly lower. Indeed, most consumer-goods manufacturers could never justify the cost of selling direct to their consumers, except by mail order. In practice, however, if the producer is large enough, the use of intermediaries can sometimes cost more than going direct.

Therefore, many of the theoretical arguments about channels revolve around cost. On the other hand, most of the practical decisions are concerned with control of the consumer. The small company has no alternative but to use intermediaries, often several layers of them, but large companies do have the choice.

Distribution-channel management involves a number of decisions on the part of the supplier, as noted below.

Table 10.9—Channel decisions
1. Channel membership
2. Channel motivation
3. Monitoring and managing channels

Channel membership alternatives

1. Intensive distribution—Where the majority of resellers stock the "product" and where price competition may be evident (with convenience products, for example, and particularly the brand leaders in consumer-goods markets).

2. Selective distribution—Where suitable resellers stock the product—the normal pattern (in both consumer and industrial markets).

3. Exclusive distribution—Where only specially selected resellers (typically only one per geographical area) are allowed to sell the product.

Channel motivation

Motivating the owners and employees of independent organizations in a distribution chain requires significant effort, but there are many devices for achieving such motivation. Perhaps the most usual is "bribery." The supplier offers a better margin to tempt the owners in the channel to push their product rather than its competitor's, or a competition is organized among the distributors' sales personnel so that they are tempted to push the product. The ultimate goal is for the channel partner's personnel to be trained and motivated to almost the same standard as the supplier's own staff.

Monitoring and managing channels

In much the same way that the organization's own sales and distribution activities need to be monitored and managed, so will those of the distribution chain. In practice, many organizations use a mix of different channels; in some cases, they may complement a direct-sales force, calling on the larger accounts, with agents covering the smaller customers and prospects.

Distribution networks can be complex, so care must be taken in managing them carefully. This can be achieved with effective and regular strategic planning (in conjunction with partners, not dictated to them) and the writing of regular reports on channel and partner performance. These will provide data to help identify those partners that may be creating problems, identify specific problem areas and help correct these problems. This will also help the manufacturer "prune" the channels, creating stronger and more powerful alliances.

Because the funds that manufacturers have available to support distribution channels are always limited, effectively collecting information from the channels helps identify those partners in which further investments should be made, what investments will create the greatest return, and where no investment should be made at all.

Out of Sight, Out of Mind: The Importance of Communication

Probably every language and culture has an expression similar to "out of sight, out of mind"; one Latin American country's version is "an unseen saint performs no miracles." The point of this is that communications are extremely important in the support of international distribution channels, regardless of the quality of the product.

When maintaining a distribution network, ongoing communications are critical to long-term success. One of the key priorities of suppliers is to keep channel partners as focused as possible on their products rather than on others they manage concurrently. Personal visits are the best way to maximize the focus of—and relationships with—business partners.

There is no substitute for being there. While on a business visit, managers are able to see and confirm facts with their own eyes and experience, including partner facilities and processes and competitive products in action. They can meet the personnel of customers and partners and gain feedback, opinions and crucial insights that might not be forthcoming through more distant e-mail and phone conversations. They can get a feel for the business environment in which their products and services operate, and most importantly, they are able to develop relationships, rapport and trust with the people upon whom they depend for success.

Depending on the number of active international markets, constraints dictated by personnel availability and budgets and the level of in-market support that the product or service requires, it is not always possible to be there in person. In this case, regular communications with channel partners maintains an important virtual presence that helps fill the void between visits.

Communication priorities
Some common strategic priorities in maintaining communications with business partners include informing, motivating and relationship building.

Communication priorities:
1. informing
2. motivating
3. relationship building

Informing implies a flow of information in both directions: from a supplier to its channel partners and/or customers (outbound), and feedback from both to the supplier (inbound). Common outbound information includes product improvements, service updates, price change and others. Examples of inbound information include changes in competitive and market conditions, complaints and suggestions for product modifications.

Suppliers must use motivation to encourage their channel partners to take appropriate action to promote and sell their products and to persuade their customers to buy their products. Channel partners are nearly always motivated by money—generated by selling the product—and customers are usually motivated by the ability to save money, improve quality and productivity or to make their lives or jobs easier. Both groups are generally driven both by desire (to get something) and fear (of not having something or of failing in their assigned responsibilities).

It is difficult to build a strong relationship without meeting face-to-face, which is why occasional visits are highly recommended. Regular communications will help to maintain and strengthen established relationships. Even in cultures where business relationships are not as highly valued as others, they are always helpful in maintaining and growing business.

Examples of some different means of communication include

- newsletters;

- videos;

- e-mails;

- online bulletin boards;

- voice mail; and

- individual or group telephone calls.

Examples of key content in communications include

- product knowledge;

- service updates;

- corporate changes;

- feedback;

- best practices;

- success stories and "good tries"; and

- contests and incentives.

Some points to remember about communications:

1. Stick to core messages and keep them simple.

2. Keep messages relevant to the needs of the reader.

3. Use graphics and photos to make messages more attractive.

4. Visibility to all team members.

The core messages need to be communicated clearly throughout the organization. Every available communication channel should be used to review, remind and reinforce them. Multiple communication channels can and should be widely used to reinforce and support the core messages.

The best way to communicate is in person. The most effective communication approaches are like political campaigns. Leaders are out actively "pressing the flesh" and standing up to present their change and improvement themes and core messages. One should develop highly visible means of communication to publicize progress toward team and organization goals and priorities. A free flow of information and active communications is the lifeblood of a learning and growing organization.

Market-Entry Checklist

The following checklist can help identify the steps required for successful market entry.

Table 10.10—Market-entry checklist

☑ Successful market entry begins with domestic-market establishment and ultimately ends with investment in the new market.

☑ Selecting the correct market-entry strategy is a critical decision, and can mean the difference between success and failure.

☑ Selling directly to customers or through distribution is governed by the population of potential customers and by the value of the product or service being offered.

☑ When selling through distribution, understanding all available channel options, and how to manage them, is critical to the success of the market-expansion initiative.

☑ Competition comes not only from other providers of similar products and services but also from "non-competing" product lines that can occupy the attention of channel partners.

☑ Clear communications between suppliers and channel partners make it possible to adjust to changing market conditions.

☑ Selling is not convincing customers to do what you want; it is helping customers make astute purchasing decisions.

☑ Strong relationships are important to doing business between all cultures, and contact must be maintained through both personal visits and ongoing remote and electronic communications.

☑ Successful market entrants must possess management commitment, financial resources, staff and capacity to handle increased demand, language capability and availability to travel.

Chapter Summary

As we have seen, preparation and understanding are crucial to successfully entering a new international market. Developing and implementing the correct market-entry strategy at the outset can often make the difference between success and failure. Key components of a successful market entry include identifying and selecting the appropriate distribution channel options and ensuring clear communication with the business partners that are vital for success.

Exercises

Exercise 1 (class discussion)

You are a manufacturer of casual shoes for women, and you believe that a good market exists for your product line in Germany. What information do you need in order to be prepared to make the right decision on the most appropriate distribution channels through which to sell your products?

(Estimated time—5 minutes)

Exercise 2 (class discussion)

You are a domestic manufacturer of plastic injection moulds, and are interested in growing your business to the fullest extent possible over a ten-year period by taking advantage of export opportunities. Describe the stages of exporting, and how they apply to your company.

(Estimated time 5 minutes)

Exercise 3 (class discussion)

Assume that, as in the example above, you are a manufacturer of plastic injection moulds and you have successfully progressed to Stage 4 (market expansion) and are now ready to invest in the export market. What options may be available? Describe them, and discuss how viable they are in this scenario.

(Estimated time 5 minutes)

Exercise 4 (small-group activity)

Agents are individuals located in foreign markets who work for your company on commission to help bridge substantial language, cultural and customer-access barriers. They typically have no infrastructure for distribution and may even work out of their home office. They are best deployed when you need to reach a handful of high-dollar-value accounts and are most frequently used in businesses that have long selling cycles (e.g., defence procurement, large government acquisitions and large corporate accounts). Although agents often work for long periods of time with no pay (in anticipation of earning a significant percentage commission when a sale ultimately concludes), it is not uncommon for agents to secure millions of dollars of sales in a year and then get paid anywhere between 5 and 20 percent commission (depending on the industry).

Given this very basic explanation of how agents work, join together in a small group of three or four and develop a list of hiring criteria for an agent to be used to make sales of computers to the government of another country. What combination of skills, personal attributes and experience would constitute an ideal agent?

Also note that Canada has laws that state that Canadian business cannot be involved in bribery of foreign officials (for more information, Google the *Corruption of Foreign Public Officials Act*). Nevertheless, when an agent stands to earn a considerable amount of money, there is always a risk of corrupt dealings between your agent and that government and your firm can be implicated if this occurs. Discuss this issue and ensure that you understand how bribery works and offer suggestions of strategies that your firm might employ to ensure that you are not intentionally or inadvertently involved in such a scheme.

Be prepared to share your findings and suggestions with the class (if your instructor calls on your group to do so).

(Estimated time 15 minutes)

References/Resources

Fournier, Robert B. Department of External Affairs and International Trade. Cross Border Investment: New Directions and Challenges [speech] (Ottawa: June 1996).

Lancaster, G., and Massingham, L. Essentials of Marketing. McGraw-Hill, 1988.

ExportSource: Export Diagnostic (www.exportdiagnostic.ca)

Rob Wicking (www.wikipedia.com)

David Archer, Crash Course on Exporting, 2007 (www.atmexport.com)

CNET Networks Business: BNET (www.jobfunctions.bnet.com)

11 Trade Finance

Securing the deal

Chapter Objectives

- Differentiate between the four pillars of international trade finance

- Learn about traditional trade financing sources and instruments, emerging trade-finance models and alternative sources of financing

- Understand the importance of risk mitigation in trade finance

Overview

The pursuit of international trade opportunities and global commerce, no matter how successfully conducted through the planning, marketing and every subsequent step thereafter, becomes an expensive exercise in futility if buyer and seller fail, in the end, to exchange payment successfully.

Trade finance is a specialized subset of finance that deals specifically with import and export transactions. Traditionally, it has been the domain of banks, major financial institutions and government agencies, though like every other aspect of the global business environment, it has been subject to major changes. The evolution of trade finance is driven partly by technology and partly by changing business practices between the various parties involved in a trade transaction.

Trade finance is primarily about facilitating payment between trading parties, providing some element of security or risk mitigation and finally, offering financing solutions to the various parties in a given transaction, when that is needed. Increasingly, a fourth element is valued by international traders: the provision of timely information about the status of the transaction.

International Trade Finance

Financing in the global business environment

Short-term trade finance typically refers to transactions with a lifespan of up to two years, as distinguished from medium-term trade finance (up to seven years), and project finance (longer terms, often large capital projects or infrastructure projects.)

The challenges of managing international transactions, particularly the flow of merchandise across oceans and the flow of money across borders have resulted in the evolution of a highly structured and specialized form of financial service, called trade finance.

As with every other aspect of international trade and global business, the cross-border element and the unique challenges of operating in the global business environment add challenges and complexities to the settlement process, which can only be addressed by products with specialized features. Put simply, there are risks to contend with international business that extend far beyond the commercial risks generally encountered in the conduct of business in a domestic context. The importer and exporter may be fully committed to conducting business in good faith; however, if a military coup ensues, or civil unrest erupts, and goods cannot be shipped, or funding cannot be secured to pay for imports, the intentions of two commercial entities generally matter little.

As we have seen numerous times in the last three decades, economic conditions can deteriorate at alarming rates, as they did in Mexico, Argentina and Brazil as well as in parts of Asia during the Asian flu crisis.

Exporters to those markets during those periods would have been concerned with maximizing the likelihood of payment through appropriate mechanisms. Even if the importer was able and willing to pay, there have been instances where a country simply ran out of foreign exchange (historically, that meant U.S. dollars, but deals are increasingly denominated in Euros) and restricted the outward flow through exchange controls, effectively preventing payment to exporters.

Fortunately, the evolution of international trade and its various payment and financing mechanisms, together with its risk-mitigation capabilities, is such that these types of scenarios are well addressed by trade-finance solutions.

Trade finance in evolution

Trade-finance instruments have been used for hundreds of years, some in very similar form and based on the same principles and practices. Letters of credit, which are basically payment undertakings issued by banks in support of a trade transaction, are the perfect example of the enduring nature of trade-finance practices. These instruments have operated in the same way probably since they were first created.

Equally true, however, is the fact that trade finance is under significant pressure to evolve. Technology has now advanced to a level that enables fundamental changes to be introduced, such as the shift from paper- and labour-intensive transactions to Internet-based virtual payment systems that now facilitate hundreds of millions of dollars worth of global trade every year.

Managing Currencies, Managing Cash

Dealing in multiple currencies

The vast majority of trade transactions are concluded in U.S. dollars or, increasingly, in Euros, which adds a transactional complexity and an element of risk (or opportunity) for most importers or exporters, who must convert from a domestic currency to the currency of the transaction.

The U.S. dollar has historically been used as the primary currency of international trade due to its wide acceptance and stability, as well as its availability on a global basis. Those same characteristics make the Euro an attractive alternative— increasingly so as the U.S. imposes certain compliance restrictions based on the use and cross-border flow of its currency. There are expectations in some quarters that the RMB, China's currency, will play an increasingly important role over the coming years as well.

An importer must purchase U.S. dollars (or Euros) to pay for its merchandise, and an exporter, upon receiving payment, may have to sell U.S. dollars to acquire domestic currency (some companies will operate accounts in the currencies they use most frequently, but that is certainly not so in the majority of cases). It is in the purchase and sale of the U.S. dollar (or Euro) that risk and opportunity arise for global traders or for any company operating internationally. Sample scenarios are presented in the following table:

Figure 11.1—Currency risk and opportunity (U.S. dollar transaction between a European importer and a Mexican exporter)		
	Importer (Euro)	**Exporter (peso)**
U.S. dollar increases relative to Euro	The importer incurs higher costs to purchase the U.S. dollars required to pay for the items obtained in Mexico	The exporter is paid in U.S. dollars and converts to pesos, no impact

Figure 11.1—Currency risk and opportunity (U.S. dollar transaction between a European importer and a Mexican exporter) *(continued)*		
	Importer (Euro)	**Exporter (peso)**
Peso increases relative to U.S. dollar	The importer is purchasing U.S. dollars using Euros and is not impacted	The U.S. dollar is worth relatively less, so when the exporter is paid in U.S. dollars, the amount of pesos that can be acquired in selling U.S. dollars is lower, generating an exchange loss
Euro increases relative to U.S. dollar	The importer benefits, since the purchase of U.S. dollars required to pay for the transaction is now less expensive in Euros	No impact, as the exporter converts the same amount of U.S. dollars into pesos on payment

The financial markets have developed instruments, such as forward contracts, that allow for the purchase (or sale) of a given amount of currency at a pre-arranged price, effectively removing the uncertainty and the risk of transacting in a foreign currency. The market for such instruments exists because different parties have different expectations about the direction of a given currency over the period covered by such contracts, and are willing to speculate on those expectations.

Cash flow: cash and flow

The lifeblood of a business is cash flow. The existence of large receivables, the consummation of large deals or contracts and even the successful closure of a first international transaction are not as vital as healthy cash flow—especially for small- and medium-sized enterprises. Not only must the organization be doing business (cash) but the revenue must be coming in (flow) within reasonable and predictable timeframes.

SWIFT is the Society for World Interbank Financial Telecommunications. SWIFT is an integral part of the flow of payments and funds on a global basis. It also provides the standard message formats used to transmit trade finance instruments throughout the world.

Small businesses survive and thrive on good cash flow; larger commercial ventures will look for financing solutions, and large corporations and multinationals will typically be more concerned with risk mitigation.

Finance offers numerous solutions and instruments to ensure adequate cash flow; similarly, trade financiers have developed product and service offerings—in conjunction with other specialists—to help clients ensure adequate cash flow at critical stages in a trade transaction. Increasingly, the optimization of working capital is a value proposition offered by various providers to importers and exporters

Elements of Trade Finance

Trade finance instruments and techniques enable and ensure secure and timely payment of monies due, provided certain agreed commercial terms have been demonstrably met by the exporter or seller.

Given the need to conduct business across numerous jurisdictions with exposure to the fluctuations of at least two currencies, as well as delays/risks in effecting payment by other means, such as a cheque, both buyer and seller value the existence of a common settlement mechanism and infrastructure, as provided by trade finance.

While a cheque can take 30 to 45 days or more to "clear" when it is deposited internationally, electronic remittance can be sent and received within minutes, in part because of some of the shared communication and payment systems leveraged by trade finance bankers and providers across much of the globe.

Financing

The availability of numerous mechanisms to provide financing to one or more parties in a trade transaction—from the seller and buyer to one or more banks— is a second key contribution of trade finance instruments and specialists in the conduct of global commerce.

From pre-export production costs to settlement after delivery, a financing requirement can arise at any stage of a trade transaction. Increasingly, the ability of sellers to provide attractive financial terms to potential buyers is a competitive differentiator, and can often help "seal the deal."

Financing can involve accelerating the timing of payment to an exporter, or it can mean delaying a demand for payment from an importer, with one or more trade banks involved in the transaction providing the financing to a party in need. In addition to trade banks, financing can be provided by export credit agencies, factoring houses or the capital arms of large companies such as GE Capital or UPS Capital, both quite active in financing international trade.

Risk mitigation

Risk is a reality in even the most secure-seeming market or trade transaction, and trade financiers have developed a variety of mitigation processes and mechanisms that are fundamental to the secure conduct of international commerce.

Not only is this critical in terms of assuring successful conclusion of business, but it is also very important in reducing the overall risk profile of a transaction, and therefore, the cost of that transaction. Documentary letters of credit, for example, effectively shift a payment obligation from an importer—a commercial entity that may be a small business—to an established international bank, which greatly reduces the risk in that transaction. The replacement of a payment undertaking from an importer by a payment undertaking issued by a credible, stable commercial bank is referred to as "credit enhancement," in recognition of its positive impact on the transaction. The same can be said of payment undertakings that are shifted, for example, from a small local bank in a highly volatile market to a large global financial institution based in a secure market.

The risks that can be mitigated include everything from civil unrest and revolution in either country to financial crises, as well as commercial risks of insolvency or non-performance by either the buyer or the seller.

Risk-mitigation solutions can also be provided by financial institutions working in partnership with government entities called export credit agencies, or ECAs.

These agencies offer a range of guarantee, insurance and financing products and services that are often indispensable in the consummation of international transactions, especially in higher-risk markets.

The risks to be managed in international trade include the following:

- *Commercial risk* is the risk associated directly with the trading partner, including insolvency.

- *Bank risk* is the risk related to the financial health of the bank acting on behalf of the trading partner; this is typically the risk associated to the bank issuing a financial instrument or payment undertaking. Bank risk can be seen as "commercial," but we distinguish it here as a specific and key risk in trade finance.

    - *Sovereign* or *country risk* is the risk related to the country of the foreign bank and/or the trading partner. Such risks include risks of economic crisis, political risk and others.

    - *Currency* or *foreign-exchange risk* is the risk associated with changes in relative values of currencies, which can make a transaction more profitable, or more expensive, for either the importer or the exporter.

Information

The latest value proposition offered through trade finance is the provision of timely, accurate and detailed information about every aspect of a trade transaction, from the status of the shipment to the precise reporting of financial flows at any given moment in that transaction.

As the speed of conduct of international business increases, the need for near-real-time information is increasingly an expectation among traders, bankers and other business partners. Full visibility at every stage of a transaction is increasingly demanded by savvy business executives, and that same visibility is allowing trade-finance providers to offer new financing options and solutions to their importing and exporting clients.

Information is a form of currency, and the currency of knowledge about international trade transactions is increasingly provided through trade finance and its technology and mechanisms.

Trade Finance: Getting Paid

Trade-finance options

There are a variety of options in terms of payment mechanisms and other trade-finance solutions.

The basic and most common forms of settlement of international trade transactions are open account, documentary collections and documentary letters of credit. There are numerous features, variations and options related to these payment options that make them very flexible and enduring as business solutions.

Open account

Payments on an open-account basis are transfers of funds to the account of the exporter and may be effected prior to shipment or on delivery. Historically, open account has been used in trade between very stable and secure markets, such as between the United States and Canada or intra-EU, and in cases where the trading relationship is established and trusted.

Payment in advance presents the highest risk to the importer or buyer: even if the exporter acts in good faith, produces the promised goods and effects shipment, the cargo could be damaged or lost in transit and, depending on the terms of trade, the importer could sustain a total loss. Conversely, payment on delivery presents the highest risk to the exporter, in that the importer could become insolvent or the country of import could experience political turmoil, preventing payment.

Cases of outright fraud by either party are equally possible: the exporter could collect payment and ship an inferior product or nothing at all, or the importer could take ownership of the cargo, but refuse to remit payment or simply disappear.

Documentary collections

Documentary collections are a transaction type where banks act as intermediaries between the importer and exporter, agreeing to facilitate payment to the exporter only once a set of shipping documents have been prepared and presented to an intermediary bank. These documents typically include documents of title to the cargo, representing ownership of the goods and demonstrating that the goods have been shipped.

Documentary collections may also include a bank draft, which evidences the existence of a financial obligation.

Documentary collections afford some degree of incremental protection to both parties in comparison to open-account transactions. The importer is assured that no money will be transferred to the exporter without the presentation of a set of shipping documents to a neutral third party, and the exporter has assurances that once the goods are en route and shipping documents are available to prove this, payment will be forthcoming.

One should be aware that documentary collections do not erase all risk—the banks only act as intermediaries and will exchange documents for payment or a promise to pay at a later date. The banks do not verify documents, nor do they have any obligations or responsibilities beyond the most cursory expectation that they will ensure that the set of documents required has been presented.

Documentary collections are widely used, subject to a set of common rules or practices published by the International Chamber of Commerce in Paris.

Documentary letters of credit

Documentary letters of credit are probably the most secure trade-finance instrument available in terms of protecting the interests of both buyer and seller. As with documentary collections, banks act as intermediaries in facilitating payment to the exporter in exchange for the set of shipping documents agreed between buyer and seller.

International banks involved in trade finance represent the interests of their clients up to a point, but have legally binding responsibilities to act in objective and neutral fashion in facilitating trade. The reputation of a bank in respecting practices and regulations in this area is critical to its business, and banks take such obligations very seriously.

Between 60 and 70 percent of documents presented by exporters under documentary credits are in some way non-compliant with the terms of the letter of credit (L/C). In those instances, the protection to the exporter is minimal, as the importer can refuse the shipment or take advantage of the discrepancies to demand a substantial discount on the shipment. Some banks exercise judgment and will not identify "trivial" discrepancies, while others take a very literal approach to the examination of documents.

The fundamental difference is that banks are required to carefully verify that the terms and conditions of payment specified in a documentary credit have been fully complied with by the exporter. This requirement involves detailed verification of the documents presented by the exporter and requires a review of elements such as the shipment date, the description of goods and the presentation of various inspection certificates, if required. Documents of transport should also be verified, including negotiable bills of lading, which are documents of title to the goods and will, when presented in order, allow for timely clearing of the goods through customs.

While it is a long-established principle that the banks deal only in documents and have no obligation to verify the accuracy of said documents as they relate to the underlying shipment, the documentary letter of credit provides a high degree of comfort to buyer and seller. These instruments guarantee that payment will be effected against receipt of fully compliant documents presented by the exporter.

The exporter can expect payment, or a firm payment undertaking at a future date (depending on the terms of the letter of credit) from a bank, regardless of the ability or willingness of the importer to pay. The importer is assured that a payment will only be authorized by the banks involved if documents received from the exporter are fully compliant with the terms of the credit.

Documents travel from exporter to advising bank to issuing bank and finally, to importer. Payment flows in the opposite direction concurrently, from advising bank to exporter, issuing bank to advising bank and finally, from importer to issuing bank, all the while—in the most basic transaction type—mirroring the flow of the shipping documents. The basic transaction flow looks like this:

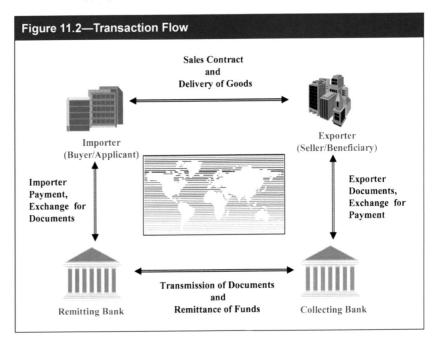

Figure 11.2—Transaction Flow

Documentary letters of credit are typically issued subject to a set of rules published and updated periodically by the International Chamber of Commerce in Paris. The broad global acceptance of these rules, their interpretation and their evolving authority through case law is a major reason for the effectiveness of letters of credit in international trade.

Confirmed documentary letters of credit

Documentary letters of credit offer numerous features that can be included in a given transaction, depending on the needs of the buyers and/or sellers. One major option available is to have a documentary letter of credit "confirmed."

In the event that an exporter is uncomfortable with the payment undertaking of the importer's bank, as represented by the letter of credit, an exporter may request that the letter of credit be issued with a clause allowing that it be confirmed—that is, another bank, typically one that is trusted by the exporter and located in the exporter's country, adds its own separate and independent payment promise to that same documentary letter of credit.

Rather than relying on the ability or willingness of an unknown bank to pay, or on the ability of a bank to send funds from an unstable market, the exporter simply presents documents to the confirming bank in exchange for payment.

Sight or term payments

Payment undertakings under collections or documentary letters of credit may be at sight or could be term payments. Payment at sight refers to payment immediately upon receipt of documents that are presented as per the collection or the letter of credit. Term payments, on the other hand, are future-dated, as agreed upon between buyer and seller. The payment due date can be based on the date of receipt of documents from the exporter (payable at 60 days sight), or based on the shipment date reflected on the transport documentation (payable 90 days after the "on board" date shown on the marine bill of lading).

Because of the combination of market needs and the features available through trade-finance products and services, an element of trade finance can provide value at almost every stage in a trade transaction.

Whether an exporter requires capital to secure parts and produce an item for export, or an importer must extend payment time frames to allow for the sale of the newly acquired goods to pay for them from the proceeds of sale, trade finance can offer solutions and financing options at every stage of a trade transaction.

Increasingly, as traditional trade-finance offerings evolve beyond traditional solutions and extend into supply chains and other business partnerships, the opportunity to secure financing extends across the full transaction life cycle. Some providers of trade finance, including trade-finance technology, claim to have identified many potential "triggers" for financing over the course of a trade deal, anywhere from between five and six triggers up to over 40 where financing may be provided.

The provision of financing extends beyond buyers and sellers; large trade transactions can sometimes challenge the financial resources of banks and even national governments, especially in emerging markets. Trade finance allows financial institutions to offer financing to other banks over extended periods where such needs exist. This financing can be provided based upon instruments such as documentary lettters of credit.

Payment risks

The payment options and their risk relative to buyer and seller can be represented as follows:

Figure 11.3—Payment options			
Payment options	**Payment timing**	**Risk**	**Usage**
Payment in advance	Buyer pays seller prior to production or delivery	High risk for buyer, fully secure for seller	Uncommon, unless the seller has leverage
Documentary credit	Payment authorized and effected only on presentation of fully compliant shipping/ commercial documents as agreed	Balanced risk, as documents generally represent title to the goods. Banks verify and authorize release of documents and payment	Secure option, often used in new trading partnerships or where a higher-risk market is involved
Documentary collection	Payment authorized and effected in exchange for shipping/ commercial documents	Favours exporter/ seller as the documents are not verified by the banks	Generally reserved for established and trusted trading relationships involving secure markets
Payment on delivery	Buyer pays seller on receipt of goods	High risk for seller, as payment can be withheld	Uncommon, unless buyer has leverage to secure such terms

Credit Insurance and Risk Mitigation

Trade-finance banks are in the business of assessing and mitigating the financial risks associated with international commerce; however, they are also limited in their ability and willingness to take on risk. Trade banks will often seek to reduce their own exposures through various means and mechanisms.

Confirmed letters of credit

Confirmation of a letter of credit involves taking on the full risk of the transaction. Banks will frequently seek to mitigate the risk of confirming risky letters of credit by seeking insurance cover, either from private-sector risk insurers or from export credit agencies (ECAs). ECAs are generally government agencies—though there is some movement towards privatizing these organizations—that can provide trade finance, risk insurance or various guarantee solutions in support of international trade.

Export credit and receivables insurance

It is possible, through ECAs or through private-sector providers (Atradius of the Netherlands, Euler of Germany, COFACE of France and AIG of the United States are among the largest), to obtain a wide range of insurance products and risk-mitigation solutions specifically created to meet the needs of international trade and global commerce. Canada's export credit agency, Export Development Canada (EDC) offers a comprehensive suite of trade-finance and risk-management products and services, and is recognized internationally as a top-tier ECA.

The range of risk-mitigation solutions available through ECAs, insurers and through other banks and financial institutions is comprehensive and can benefit importers and exporters as well as banks and other partners in the conduct of international commerce.

Bonds, guarantees and standby credits

There is a group of products and services that are frequently used in international business, including large capital projects. In general terms, these instruments are intended to provide for a guarantee of performance, failing which a financial penalty is triggered.

Bid bonds are often required when large tenders are published. They commit parties to submit a bid to a project or tender or forfeit a pre-defined penalty. Performance bonds are requested to ensure that parties contracted to execute a project will see it through to completion and will carry out their obligations as envisioned in the contract. Failure to perform as expected can trigger a demand for payment under a performance bond.

Bank guarantees (or guarantees issued by surety companies) and standby letters of credit are very similar instruments. These instruments provide for payment of an agreed amount in the event that an agreed activity is not completed, or an agreed obligation is not met.

Guarantees and standby letters of credit are not meant to be payment mechanisms, but rather a form of security, triggered only in the event of a failure to perform or a failure to pay.

Trade Finance Across the Supply Chain

Expanding the value proposition

The inexorable shift to open-account trade and the increasing emphasis on global supply chains and new sourcing models has resulted in a degree of "disintermediation" of banks in trade finance. Open-account transactions—direct payment at an agreed time against an invoice produced by the exporter—require little in the way of bank support, particularly when compared to documentary letters of credit. With open-account terms now common in trade transactions involving countries previously seen as (at least somewhat) risky, the role and value of banks in trade finance become a matter for serious review.

While there is some agreement in the market that letters of credit will continue to remain important to international trade, the increasing focus on open account and on global supply chains has forced trade bankers to identify new product and service solutions to be offered to the market.

One leading American Bank—JP Morgan Chase—has taken this shift so seriously that it acquired a leading logistics firm, Vastera, to expand its service offering beyond the traditional scope of trade finance.

Enabled by technology, leading trade banks are attaining high levels of visibility in clients' global supply chains and offering solutions across the full range of supply chain activities, including event-based trade finance, services related to merchandise classification, customs-clearance support and a range of evolving solutions related to international trade and global commerce.

Optimizing cash flow and working capital across the supply chain, assisting clients in managing days sales outstanding, offering discounting and finance solutions based on the status of a shipment and helping clients optimize inventory turnover—there is no shortage of opportunities for banks to add value.

In addition to effectively leveraging technology, to virtualize the most labour- and resource-intensive aspects of trade finance, the future of trade finance depends on the ability of trade bankers to meet client needs in the evolving business models driving trade.

Trade Finance: Helping to Close the Deal

Trade finance as a competitive advantage

The ability for exporters to offer "terms," or a financing package, to importers to close the sale is increasingly common in international trade and global commerce. Evolutions in the area of the supply chain and global sourcing, driven, some say, by the largest global retailers, include the expectation that exporters will carry a significant proportion of the financing burden of a transaction, despite the superior financial strength of these importing retailers.

The more traditional or historical view assumed the ability of exporters in certain parts of the world to secure financing at relatively lower, more attractive, rates. In doing so, exporters were able to offer financing options to importers based on a lower cost of funds, again increasing the probability of securing a sale.

Access to competitively priced financing—or lack of it—is frequently cited as a key element of global competitiveness in various industry sectors, from capital projects to service-sector exports.

Risk and ownership (related to a shipment) can transfer between seller and buyer at various points in the life of a transaction, as determined by the terms of trade or Incoterms selected by the buyer and seller in the sales agreement. Similarly, financing can be triggered at various points in a transaction, from pre-shipment financing to favour the exporter, to import financing (an exporter paid immediately by the bank, while an importer is permitted to reimburse 90 days later, for example) at the "end" of a trade transaction, which assists the importer.

Favourable terms can make a significant difference even in pursuing opportunities with governments, particularly in emerging or developing markets. Likewise, the ability of banks to offer financing to other banks in less solvent markets (or in markets where foreign currencies may be in limited supply) can be very helpful in securing business.

A lack of ability or willingness to offer financing terms to potential trading partners can be sufficient reason to terminate negotiations before other aspects of the transaction, such as the superior quality of the merchandise being sold, can even be fully presented or evaluated.

Trade finance is not merely about payment or about the end result of a deal: it can be a vital element of business development in international trade and global commerce.

Banks, ECAs and IFIs: Trade Finance the Traditional Way

A three-way partnership

Banks, from small local ones to world-class global financial institutions, have always been the primary providers of trade finance. Their global reach, extensive network of partner banks (correspondents), large financial capacity and technical expertise ensure that they remain a formidable force in the business of trade finance.

In recent years, the number of banks that can afford to profitably maintain the full suite of trade-finance capabilities—including the transaction-processing capability—has steadily decreased. Nonetheless, the banks that remain committed to the business of trade finance have driven costs down, invested in technology and sought to expand partnerships as well as extend their products and solutions beyond traditional offerings.

Banks work very closely with private risk insurers and/or government ECAs to provide trade-finance solutions for the full range of transaction types, all over the globe. ECAs arguably expand banks' ability to provide trade finance, both in terms of geographic breadth, and in terms of depth within an industry, with a particular foreign bank or in a given market.

Even as ECAs in various parts of the world consider new operating models, with some of them shifting more towards providing guarantee products as opposed to financing solutions, the partnership between banks and ECA's remains a critical element of the global environment related to international trade finance.

International financial institutions (IFIs), or multilaterals, such as the International Finance Corporation of the World Bank, as well as the various regional development banks—the Inter-American Development Bank (IADB), the Asian Development Bank, the Islamic Development Bank and others—play major roles in facilitating trade and supporting global commerce.

The business models and mandates for export credit agencies vary widely across the globe. Some operate with strong commercial orientations, while others lean more towards a public-policy orientation. There is no single optimal ECA model, and as trade professionals, it is advisable to be aware of the options available.

EDC, Canada's export credit agency, is widely recognized as a world-class ECA.

Several IFIs have some form of trade-finance support program, generally a guarantee framework that covers international banks who support trade by providing confirmations on letters of credit issued by local banks in higher-risk markets. The IFIs seek to encourage strong (international) banks to provide steady and reliable trade finance in their respective regions.

IFI trade finance programs include

- The IFC Global Trade Finance Program (International Finance Corporation/World Bank);

- The European Bank for Reconstruction and Development Trade Facilitation Program;

- The Asian Development Bank Trade Facilitation Program; and

- The Inter-American Development Bank Trade Finance Facilitation Program.

Other Sources of Trade Finance

Non-bank providers of trade finance
GE Capital has been an active provider of trade-finance services for many years. Likewise, UPS Capital has been active in trade finance for over a decade, providing niche financing solutions, often in partnership with the United States Export-Import Bank (the American ECA) under their small-business programs.

Investment bankers and hedge-fund managers are also becoming increasingly active in the trade-finance arena, competing directly with traditional providers of financing to companies pursuing international commerce.

Several hedge funds based in London and New York perceive opportunities to generate attractive returns by providing funding to support trade involving emerging markets. These funds engage former trade bankers to originate, assess and structure the deals and are proving to be a serious new force in the market.

Technology: Trade Finance Evolves

Trade finance and technology
Historically, technology has been applied to trade finance to enhance the efficiency of current business processes and service-delivery models. Processes that were paper- and labour-intensive remained fundamentally unchanged, but could be completed more securely and cost-effectively through the introduction of trade-banking technology.

More recently, technology, particularly the Internet, has evolved to allow for a shift to transformational evolution in the business of international trade and trade finance.

Sophisticated trading platforms, including trade-financing solutions, were developed and deployed globally and covered the most sophisticated global markets, just as they now cover a number of key emerging markets with the necessary information and communications infrastructure to support the implementation of such technologies.

GTM, or "global trade management' providers aim to cover the full transaction cycle, including the payment and financing elements of international commerce, and have done so with increasingly convincing success.

Technology has begun a critical shift from an enabler of existing processes to a transformational force in international commerce, including trade finance.

Project Finance, Countertrade and Other Flavours

Medium- and long-term financing

Medium-term financing arrangements are structured for repayment periods of up to five years, while the repayment periods of long-term financing arrangements can range between 5 and 15 years. Banks or other financial institutions offer such financing programs, often in support of large projects. In offering them, the financial institution assumes the risk of non-payment arising from the failure of the buyer or the buyer's bank, or from political instability in the buyer's country. In certain circumstances, the financial institution and the exporter can share the risk in different proportions.

The following are the most common medium-term and long-term financing mechanisms.

Buyer credits

A buyer credit is used to finance an export over a medium or long term. With this method, funds are lent directly to the foreign buyer. These credits are best suited to large transactions involving capital goods or to turnkey projects. Buyer credits are generally extended on a non-recourse basis to the exporter, as the importer enters into a direct financial relationship with the lending bank. The creditworthiness of a buyer credit is based on the buyer's integrity and ability to repay. It may be supported by the guarantee of a government, a government agency or a bank in the buyer's country.

Supplier credits

In the case of a supplier credit, a financial institution purchases from the exporter a foreign buyer's debt (to the exporter) for products or services purchased. Arranging this type of financing may be easier and more economical than arranging a buyer credit because the bank or lender does not have to negotiate directly with the foreign buyer. Supplier credits are generally suited to transactions with a value between U.S.$100,000 and U.S.$5,000,000, with terms of payment ranging from six months to five years.

Forfaiting

Forfaiting, or forfait financing, is a medium-term form of seller credit provided by trade banks. A bank purchases medium-term (up to five-year or, in special cases, seven-year) promissory notes due to the exporter from a foreign buyer.

The value of the promissory notes is discounted at a fixed rate so that the exporter receives cash, after deduction of the interest charge or discount. Generally provided along with a guarantee from the buyer's bank, the promissory notes are discounted by the exporter's bank on a non-recourse basis to the exporter.

The exporter benefits by passing on the credit risk and currency exposure to the bank, turning a term-credit sale into a cash transaction and receiving fixed-rate financing. If this method of financing is decided on in advance, the discount fees and all other finance costs can be incorporated into the contract price. It also eliminates the need for extensive documentation.

Countertrade

Countertrade is an arrangement in which a sale to an importer is conditional on a reciprocal purchase by the exporter. It therefore includes any international trade contract in which the reciprocal obligations of the parties are substituted for payment in kind. Instead of being paid in cash for a shipment, the exporter receives products—or even certain kinds of services—from the target market. Types of countertrade common in international trade include barter, counterpurchase, advance purchase, buybacks, bilateral and offset arrangements.

Countertrade was very popular in the centrally planned economies of the former Soviet bloc because the governments of the region were chronically short of hard currency and were therefore committed to a policy of promoting exports. For similar reasons, countertrade is used extensively in the developing world.

Export leasing

It is mostly private companies that specialize in this type of financing, with programs designed for specific industries, such as the motor-vehicle, aircraft and industrial equipment sectors, although some banks can provide export-leasing services through subsidiaries. Exporters, working in conjunction with leasing companies, may undertake this form of trade financing to gain a competitive edge and to offer their buyers an alternative means of financing. The buyer alone concludes the leasing arrangement. Exporters can use such arrangements when dealing with countries where import restrictions prevent the buyer from purchasing foreign equipment outright. Export leasing can also be used when a country's tax regime favours leasing over outright purchase, so that the importer can acquire capital goods more cheaply. Export leasing is a medium- to long-term method of financing. Depending on the mechanism used, the exporting firm receives cash for its transfer of title to the leasing company and the delivery of the capital equipment to the buyer. The leasing company then collects regular payments from the leaseholder.

Project financing

Project financing differs from all other types of financing previously outlined in that it is based entirely on the feasibility and profitability of a project. Project financing secures repayment for a sale out of the cash flow that the project is expected to generate when it comes into production. The assets of the project serve as collateral, and the lenders also have recourse to the cash flow created by the project. The loan is granted mainly on the basis of the project's capacity to generate sufficient revenue to service the debt. In the case of default by the project operator, the lenders may take control over the collection of revenue, or may seize the assets specifically pledged or others pledged as additional collateral. Project loans are long-term and may be structured and secured in many ways. They require extended gestation periods before completion, as well as innovative financing.

Trade Finance Checklist

Figure 11.4—Global supply-chain checklist
☑ Understand the four core elements of trade finance
☑ Appreciate the importance of managing and optimizing risk
☑ Understand the risk-mitigation options available through features of trade-finance products as well as through insurance and guarantee programs
☑ Understand the range of financing options available across the lifespan of a trade transaction and their importance to cash flow
☑ Appreciate that there are numerous sources of trade finance across the globe, including numerous non-bank providers
☑ Appreciate the competitive value of trade finance

Chapter Summary

Trade finance is a critical element of the pursuit of opportunities in international trade. Ensuring the delivery of expected goods or services and assuring timely payment are fundamentally important to both buyer and seller. The techniques of trade finance have evolved over hundreds of years to successfully and securely facilitate global trade under every imaginable condition.

Trade finance effectively combines risk-mitigation capabilities with global-payment facilitation, a wide range of financing techniques and the ability to provide very detailed information about the status of payment and the status of a given shipment.

The World Trade Organization noted, in a paper: "Short-term credit/trade finance has been associated with the expansion of international trade in the past century, and has in general been considered a routine operation, providing fluidity and security to the movement of goods and services. Short-term finance is the true life-line of international trade."[35]

Exercises

Exercise 1 (class discussion)
It is often said, incorrectly, that a letter of credit is "just like cash." Consider the features of a documentary letter of credit and the process involved in obtaining payment under a letter of credit and identify the ways in which payment facilitation under a documentary credit differs from a cash settlement.

(Estimated time 10-15 minutes)

---

[35] Improving the Availability of Trade Finance During Financial Crises, WTO Publications, 2003.

Exercise 2 (class discussion)
As a senior finance executive in a company exploring its first export transaction with a promising new buyer in a dynamic emerging market, prepare a briefing to your CEO that addresses an approach to risk, identifies the major exposures involved and proposes three risk-mitigation options.

(Estimated time 10–15 minutes)

References/Sources

Asian Development Bank Website (www.adb.org)

Export Development Canada (EDC) (www.edc.ca)

Warfield, Gerald, Harry Venedikian and Gerhard Schneider. Export-Import Financing. Wiley and Sons Inc., 1986

European Bank for Reconstruction and Development Website (www.ebrd. com)

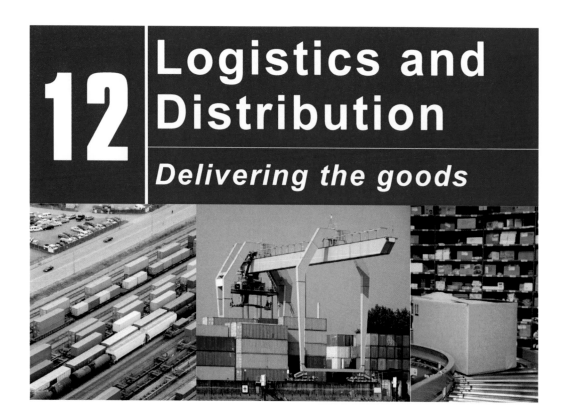

12 Logistics and Distribution

Delivering the goods

Chapter Objectives

- Understand how products move in the global economy and how to make informed decisions on freight and logistics

- Understand freight and logistics terminology

- Recognize the current developments and issues, including global security measures, in the logistics environment

- Describe issues related to local regulatory compliance

Overview

This chapter reviews the vital area of logistics and distribution. It identifies some of the key issues involved in materials management and physical distribution and explains the competitive advantages that firms can gain by effectively managing the logistical function and applying advanced logistics to optimize their international trading activities.

The movement of goods, services and information is both a process within global commerce and an end result of it, balanced by the exchange of money in return. A key component of logistics—physical proximity (or lack thereof)—can alone negate an otherwise viable business opportunity. A strong understanding of the elements of global logistics and the forces that affect the logistical environment is important when making international business decisions.

Logistics: Your Competitive Advantage

The Canadian Professional Logistics Institute (CPLI) defines "logistics" as follows:

> "Logistics is a group of services that is concerned with the effective movement of materials and information from their source to the point of consumption."

Logistics includes a spectrum of activities designed to move goods—and increasingly, services—from the producers to the customers as quickly and cost-effectively as possible. At first glance, this may seem to be a fairly simple process involving cargo assembly, packaging, handling, inspection and transportation. More and more, however, logistics is being viewed as a key strategic capability that binds virtually all functions together within and between companies. It has an impact on, and a direct relationship to, product development, manufacturing, marketing, sales and even financial management.

Logistics is significant in domestic transactions, but it is critical in international trade, due to greater distances and the borders between producers and customers. Recent trends in international commerce, driven by evolving trade agreements and ongoing advances in communications, electronic tracking technologies and other factors, have led to the emergence of global supply-chain networks that will continue to shape the future of world trade.

Logistics consists of two key functions:

- Materials management, which involves the movement of raw materials or components from domestic or foreign suppliers to the company's production line and through the manufacturing process

- Physical distribution, which involves the movement of goods or services from the manufacturing process to the customer

On the following page is a diagram illustrating the logistical environment.

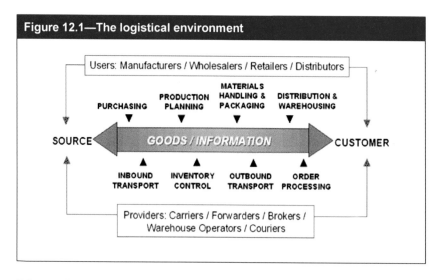

Figure 12.1—The logistical environment

Materials Management: Reliability and Cost-Effectiveness

Before companies embark on ambitious ventures abroad, they should ensure that their supplier systems can sustain the added demands of international trade. Materials management is a service function, representing the consolidation of the purchasing, traffic and warehousing functions into one management responsibility.

The integrated chain of materials-handling activities in a company's production process may flow in the following sequence:

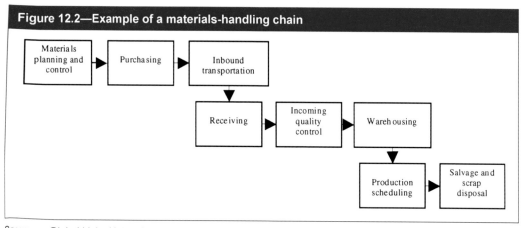

Figure 12.2—Example of a materials-handling chain

Source: Global Links Network

Materials-management planning begins as the needs for materials and services are determined and normally ends at the point of manufacture or distribution of a marketable product. It can be defined as "the first half of the logistical chain."

The goals of purchasing, traffic and warehousing are similar: to create and maintain a regulated flow of quality materials and services at acceptable costs to satisfy the objectives of a manufacturing or commercial enterprise. These functions are related, and unifying them into a team effort is a natural progression.

Inbound transportation refers to transportation of materials into the production process. Outbound transportation is the distribution of the components or goods created in the production process. Similar terminology is used to describe the storage of materials before and after they have entered the production process: inbound warehousing and outbound warehousing.

Physical Distribution: Options and Strategies

The physical path of products does not always follow the distribution (sales) channel. In the case of "drop shipping" or even commissioned sales arrangements, products may bypass one or more steps in the established channel between manufacturer and customer, because there is no need for them to physically handle the shipment.

The distribution of products occupies the other end of the logistical chain. A company engaged in international sales should know the alternatives available for moving goods from the plant to the customers. A company will generally choose the most cost-effective strategy to distribute goods in international markets. The cost-effectiveness of the strategies depends on each company's circumstances.

Logistical considerations should be taken into account during the selection of export-distribution channels. Key factors include the business practices of the country or region where the goods are going, the modes of transportation available and their accessibility and costs, and any need for the company to maintain local representation.

The role of freight forwarders

For a small-volume shipper with limited time and resources, or for a large-volume shipper exporting into a new or unfamiliar market, using a freight forwarder makes eminent sense. A freight forwarder

- has detailed knowledge of distribution modes and methods used around the world;

- can consolidate small shipments;

- may offer volume-rate opportunities;

- provides documentation and makes freight arrangements; and

- offers specific logistical services such as crating, marking and warehousing.

The freight forwarder can perform virtually all distribution services for the client. Freight forwarders control more than 80 percent of export shipments of finished goods from Europe to North America. Because of the complexity of documentation and regulations and the variety of options available, freight forwarders' expertise can bring significant benefits to customers who can then focus on their core businesses.

Shippers planning to use the services of a forwarder should ensure that the forwarder they choose is reputable. The Canadian International Freight Forwarders Association (CIFFA) represents the leading forwarders in Canada. It has a self-regulation strategy and has introduced an insurance program to give shippers financial protection.

One of the important services forwarders offer, apart from handling documentation and organizing transportation, is the tracking of shipments. For this reason, another important factor in choosing a freight forwarder is that they have a reliable presence near both the point of origin and the destination; some forwarders have their own offices in both, while others have relationships with agents in other locations.

Transportation: Issues and Challenges

The market price of the product must include the cost of delivering it into the hands of the customer. Distribution costs can represent the largest component of a product's market sales price after the manufacturing cost and can strongly affect the exporter's ability to compete in a given market over time. Effectively managing and controlling these costs is a challenge, especially in times of rising fuel prices and increasing security measures.

Until quite recently, exporters tended to resist contracts that assigned them responsibility for transportation and distribution. However, integrated logistical systems give companies more control over distribution and transportation and reduce risks and costs. These systems give firms better leverage to seek volume discounts and better rates from carriers. Better control also allows the exporter to ensure that the firm does not pay for services it does not want. The exporter can develop direct and ongoing relationships with carriers who offer real benefits in terms of reliability, dedicated service and communication. It becomes easier for them to do business with their customers as a potential obstacle in the trade transaction is removed.

To handle transportation and distribution, the exporter will need qualified personnel to arrange, monitor and control the freight function. Any traffic function is a cost centre, and its utility (usually expressed in terms of transportation freight savings) must be balanced against the cost of the resources deployed.

In the past, most medium- and large-sized companies employed extensive traffic departments that dealt exclusively with the transfer of the firm's goods. More recently, many companies have moved away from employing such costly resources in such a narrow field. If the traffic department does still exist, it is smaller, more focused on research and service, and part of a larger, integrated logistical system. Transportation and distribution services are contracted to logistics specialists such as freight forwarders, consolidators, carriers, customs brokers and foreign distributors.

A firm's decision to keep managing transportation and distribution may depend on the location of the export market. North American communications and transportation networks are so well established and well served that it is simple for even a small-volume exporter to handle its own transportation and distribution services.

In the case of overseas exports, currencies, languages, complex documentation and the difficulties of arranging distribution services prompt many companies to use the services of a third party, such as a freight forwarder. Third-party assistance would also be advisable for younger firms just entering international markets. Such firms face enough challenges already, without also having to deal with the complexities of overseas transportation and distribution.

Modes of Transportation: Making the Right Choice

The physical path of products does not always follow the distribution (sales) channel. In the case of "drop shipping" or even commissioned sales arrangements, products may bypass one or more steps in the established channel between manufacturer and customer, because there is no need for them to physically handle the shipment.

In international trade, greater distances between the buyer and seller increase costs, which can impair competitiveness because the potential buyer will compare imported products with similar domestic products partly on the basis of their delivered cost. Transportation costs must be controlled while efforts are made to ensure the merchandise is delivered promptly and in good condition. The modes of transportation selected depend on the cost of shipping, the transportation time required, the importer's preferences and competitors' prices. Logistical analysis shows what mode or modes of transportation the exporter will need to optimize costs and maximize customer satisfaction in an international transaction.

There are four major modes of transportation choices (the fifth—pipelines—is not usually a choice):

Table 12.3—Four major modes of transportation	
Ocean freight	There are three types of ocean carriers: conference carriers, independent shippers and tramp vessels. Conference carriers primarily carry manufactured products and charge standardized rates, providing the exporter with stability in both price and routes. Independent shippers have lower rates, serve the major routes regularly and accept reservations on a first-come, first-served basis. "Tramp" lines offer the lowest rates but do not offer regular service because they go wherever they are hired to carry freight on a "spot" basis.
	Ocean freight is generally shipped in standard steel containers measuring between 20 and 40 feet, although bulk commodities are also carried by specially designed ships. Exporters can ship full container loads (FCL) or less-than-container loads (LCL). One of the main functions of freight forwarders is to sell LCL freight by the cubic metre and then consolidate various customers' products into full containers. Ocean freight is generally the least expensive but slowest mode of transportation.

Table 12.3—Four major modes of transportation *(continued)*	
Air freight	Air freight offers the benefits of fast delivery, greater security and lower insurance costs because it is in transit for a shorter period of time. However, it is the most expensive way to ship products. Some kinds of products lend themselves to air freight due to time sensitivity or perishable nature, for example, fresh fish, flowers, or desperately needed spare parts. Freight forwarders consolidate small air shipments into special containers made specifically for different models of aircraft. Air freight is charged by weight or dimensions, whichever is greater. Certain goods are not permitted to be shipped by air, such as dangerous chemicals or materials that are sensitive to air-pressure changes because accidental spills, fires, or other incidents could threaten the safety of an aircraft, its crew and passengers, or people and installations on the ground.
Railroad	Rail freight offers relatively fast shipment over land at lower costs than trucks, provided there is a high volume of product to be moved and that the points of origin and destination are both conveniently located on a railway line. A common rail route in Canada is between the highly populated central part of the country to the ports on both coasts, where container and bulk freight is transferred to and from ocean freighters.
Trucking services	Trucks are involved, in one way or another, in nearly every movement of goods between suppliers and customers. Long-haul trucks generally move full trailers (FTLs) between customers or distribution hubs that are several hours' to several days' driving apart; freight forwarders and trucking companies accommodate small less-than-truckload (LTL) shipments through consolidation. Short-haul trucks are generally smaller, and usually transfer freight from one local transportation hub to another or provide delivery services from a warehouse to a customer.

Customs brokers

Customs brokers are companies dedicated to ensuring that documents are completed and duties and taxes paid to the government when goods cross borders. To do this job, they have specialized knowledge about Harmonized System (HS) tariff classification codes, documentation requirements and regulations. Due to the complexity (and legal ramifications) of these issues—and their direct involvement in the logistics process—using a customs broker is usually recommended. In fact, because customs brokers are closely linked with freight forwarders, in many cases they are different divisions of the same company. Some logistics companies are so vertically integrated that they can offer freight, customs, warehousing, distribution, insurance and even corporate travel services—all under one roof.

In some countries one is not required to use customs brokers to clear a shipment through customs (one can do it for him/herself), and in others it is. Two main reasons it is required are to avoid errors due to complex regulations and to ensure ease of collections by the government of taxes and duties payable.

Advanced Logistics: New Delivery Considerations

Transportation, as a major component of logistics, generally involves the straight-line movement of goods through four major modes: air, sea, rail, and road—or some combination thereof, usually referred to as multi-modal transportation. Advanced logistics refers to the new technologies that have dramatically affected how goods are handled as they are transferred from one leg of their journey to another in distribution centres and other transportation nodes.

Transportation nodes—or hubs—receive shipments from various points of origin and channel them through warehouses and other distribution centres onto the next part of the journey to their ultimate destinations. Some hubs handle two or more different modes of transportation; for example, all ports transfer their cargo to trucks and sometimes also to trains.

Some of the key components of advanced logistics include sophisticated software, computerized conveyor systems, automated warehousing operations and electronic scanning of bar-coded packages. A large courier company, for example, handles more than 15 million packages per day, made possible by complex systems that integrate the latest materials-handling software and machinery. Bar codes are tracked throughout the process to provide real-time tracking of shipments, and innovative materials-handling equipment with high-speed cameras and scanners has the flexibility to push shipments off one conveyor onto another with a lightning-fast mechanical apparatus. Driving the process is CTM (complete-transportation-management) software, which is able to make optimized decisions about route programming, cargo load planning, mixed pallet building, lowest-cost carriers and other automated decisions.

While logistics companies are often the heaviest users of advanced logistics systems, their customers—manufacturers and purchasers—have the opportunity to integrate their systems of internal business management with their external distribution networks through computerized systems integration. This facilitates an optimized supply chain that allows all partners to work together to shorten lead times, minimize inventory, cut costs and maximize efficiency and productivity.

Incoterms™: Must-Know Trade Terminology

International trade usually involves the shipment of goods, often over long distances. By definition, the shipments travel across borders, which implies they can travel from one language, culture and set of business regulations to another, creating potential for confusion and misunderstanding between business partners.

To respond to this problem, the International Chamber of Commerce established, published and trademarked a set of rules called Incoterms™ (International Commercial Terms) in 1923 to clearly define the rights and obligations of each party involved in an international shipment. Most recently updated in 2000, Incoterms have been recognized as a practical and efficient way to simplify the international trading process and capture the essence of the logistical aspects of the transaction under discussion by using a series of abbreviations to describe the basic terms of purchase or sale, such as FOB (free on board) or CIF (cost, insurance, freight). Experienced traders understand that using these terms is an important part of assigning responsibilities, costs and risks between the exporter and the importer.

The most important issues defined by Incoterms are the nature and extent of the seller's delivery obligations and the point at which the title (ownership) of the goods passes from the seller to the buyer. Once the title passes, the buyer is obliged to pay for the goods and assumes responsibility for any subsequent damage to them. The additional vital issue linked to Incoterms is that payment is usually triggered when sellers show, with documented proof, that they have fully met their obligations.

Incoterms are highly detailed and specific—so much so that detailed training courses for logistics professionals are available in many countries to ensure that they are clearly understood, together with the rights and obligations they imply for buyers and sellers involved in international commerce.

The following table shows the 13 Incoterms, along with their three-letter abbreviations:

Table 12.4—Incoterms	
EXW	Ex Works
FCA	Free Carrier
FAS	Free Alongside Ship
FOB	Free On Board
CFR	Cost and Freight
CIF	Cost, Insurance and Freight
CPT	Carriage Paid To
CIP	Carriage and Insurance Paid To
DAF	Delivered At Frontier
DES	Delivered Ex Ship
DEQ	Delivered Ex Quay
DDU	Delivered Duty Unpaid
DDP	Delivered Duty Paid

Below is a useful example that contrasts two commonly used Incoterms and demonstrates that not only do they indicate the points where ownership (risk) and responsibility for payment of freight costs are transferred from seller to buyer, but also that cost and risk may change at different points along the journey. The choice the exporter makes will depend on a number of factors, including his competitive position and how much risk/cost he believes he can pass on to the customer.

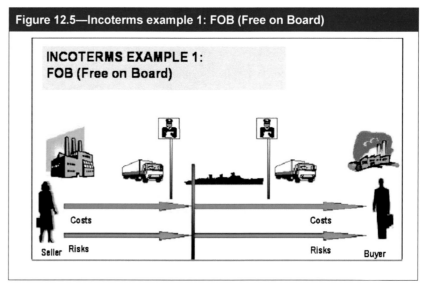

Figure 12.5—Incoterms example 1: FOB (Free on Board)

Source: International Trade Centre Geneva/Trade Facilitation Office Canada.

Cost of transportation and ownership (risk) is transferred from seller to buyer at the same point.

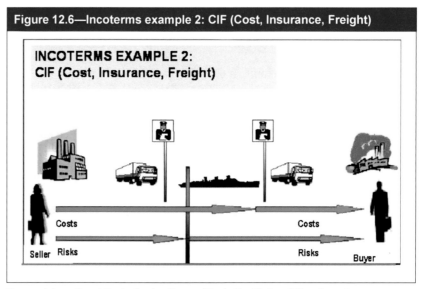

Figure 12.6—Incoterms example 2: CIF (Cost, Insurance, Freight)

Source: International Trade Centre Geneva/Trade Facilitation Office Canada.

Cost of freight and risk of damage are transferred from seller to buyer at different points along the transportation route.

Documentation: Requirements and Examples

International shipments cannot move without accompanying documentation. Documents serve a number of purposes, including communicating information about the buyer, seller and the products being shipped to the many parties involved in and regulating the movement. Aside from those directly involved in transporting the goods, other parties have an interest in the transaction, including government agencies who monitor traffic of merchandise for tax, security and statistical reasons.

Every country has its own set of documentation requirements. Some documents are universally required (for example, commercial invoices), while others are unique to a country based on its own internal requirements. Moreover, some documents are required for certain points of origin and not for others. Finally, others apply only to some types of goods.

There are literally hundreds of international trade documents in use around the world. Which ones to use depends on many factors as set out by each different government, and care should be taken to research the requirements specific to every movement of goods across borders. Below is a table showing some examples of different kinds of commonly required documents in use today.

> Documents used in international trade can be like computers: one spelling mistake or other "minor" error can have disastrous consequences, including having shipments delayed, rejected or even, in some cases, payment denied.

Table 12.7—Examples of export documentation	
Commercial document	**Purpose**
Commercial: Invoice	Identify supplier and customer, value of transaction, and duty and tax information
Financial: Letter of credit (L/C)	Provide banking information, release funds to supplier at appropriate time
Shipping: Bill of lading (B/L)	Identify supplier, contents, destination and transportation particulars
Regulatory: Certificate of origin	Ensure shipment is in compliance with appropriate trade rules
Health and safety: Dangerous-goods certificate	Ensure dangerous shipment is authorized

Health and Safety: Dangerous Goods Certificate

Product compliance means that products must conform to regulations designed to ensure that when used, they do not harm consumers, property or the environment. Product-safety regulations may be enacted by different levels of government within the same country and may vary between jurisdictions. It is therefore very important for exporters and importers to research the regulations thoroughly.

Packaging

Standards and regulations in effect in other countries also cover product packaging. Companies contemplating export sales should obtain a copy of the relevant legislation to ensure that their products are in compliance. The information sources on foreign packaging are similar to the sources for foreign safety standards.

Labelling

Labelling of goods refers to information provided on the product itself or on the package in which it is sold. This information is of two types: that required by law, and that provided by the manufacturer. What has to be on the product, as well as what cannot appear on it, is regulated in most countries. The labelling of food items is one of the most regulated areas, as these labels often must contain a list of ingredients and their components, a "best before" or "sell by" date and storage instructions. Choice of language(s) is also often a regulated issue, and sometimes two or more are required.

Many groups are concerned with the packaging of goods to be exported, including

- the exporter and the importer;

- transport companies;

- government inspectors in the exporting and importing countries;

- port and warehouse authorities;

- insurance companies;

- freight forwarders and customs brokers;

- health ministries;

- consumer-protection agencies;

- occupational-safety organizations;

- shareholders of public corporations handling or distributing the products; and

- final customers.

Experienced exporters and export-packaging companies can determine the kind of packaging needed so that products can be

- exported without damage to the integrity and quality of the goods;

- transported without damaging or harming people, other goods or the environment; and

- transported at minimal cost.

Security: Mitigating Risks

Security of shipments has always been an issue, but in recent years new threats have emerged to make it an even more important consideration. Not only must shipments be kept safe from physical damage and theft in transit, but the potential threat of terrorism—where the shipment itself could pose a hazard to its surroundings—has precipitated new initiatives to ensure public safety.

Threats to the cargo

Keeping contents free of physical damage caused by mishandling in transit has always been an issue, but with the advent of containerization and advances in handling equipment, products are safer as they move from origin to destination. Steel containers protect the contents inside them, and provided the containers are "stuffed" correctly using proper packing materials and methods, the goods inside should arrive intact. Further, new technologies such as RFID (radio-frequency identification) have become available to monitor temperatures and other variables throughout the journey.

An entire industry has developed to ensure that valuable shipments arrive intact at their intended destinations. The risks of minor losses through pilfering, or major losses through outright container theft, can be mitigated through tamper-resistant seals and packaging, satellite tracking technologies, and in some cases armed security escorts. A container of computer equipment can be valued at hundreds of thousands of dollars and could easily be illegally resold, as many criminals are aware. For this reason, there exist numerous security precautions and procedures to ensure that vulnerability to crime is minimized throughout the many transportation routes and hubs within which products travel en route to their destinations.

Threats from the cargo

Since the 2001 terrorist attacks in New York, the potential use of transportation networks as a conduit for terrorism has received increasing attention around the world. In particular, the government of the United States has initiated a number of initiatives to reduce the risk of indiscriminate damage caused by threats that could conceivably be contained in freight shipments. Some of these include inspections, electronic scanning and many initiatives, such as the C-TPAT (Customs-Trade Partnership Against Terrorism) program, whereby foreign suppliers voluntarily follow prescribed security procedures in an attempt to ensure that shipments are not compromised by threats of this nature along the global supply chain. Smuggling is another issue of great concern to authorities, and is addressed in similar ways.

Although some security programs are "voluntary", there are often clear advantages to participating, such as when saving several hours or days in transportation time across a border can mean the difference between success or failure of a customer relationship.

Finally, shipments of hazardous materials must comply with special regulations to ensure that in the event of an accident or train derailment, their contents do not pose a serious threat to the public. Examples of dangerous goods include toxic, corrosive or flammable materials. Specific steps must be taken to provide extra protection against potential impacts that could release hazardous materials into the environment, as well as procedures on how to handle the situation if it does occur.

Logistics and Distribution Checklist

Table 12.8—Logistics and distribution key points
• Logistical factors are key considerations in evaluating the viability of business opportunities.
• Regardless of whether the manufacturer or importer pays them, transportation costs directly affect the price consumers must pay for products.
• Materials management addresses inbound traffic of inputs to production; physical distribution addresses the outbound traffic of finished products.
• Transportation decisions are made by considering factors such as shipment time, suitability of the mode of transportation and cost.
• Security issues involve protection of the cargo and protection from the cargo.
• Incoterms provide detail on the obligations of the buyer and seller with regard to ownership risk and payment of freight costs.
• Advanced logistics is the application of technology to the planning and execution of freight movements throughout the supply chain.

Chapter Summary

When compared with domestic business, international trade implies commerce with longer distances and more regulatory considerations precipitated by the crossing of borders. More documents must be created, more parties are involved, more and longer transportation routes must be travelled and more specialized expertise is required.

For all of these reasons, a thriving industry has sprung up not only moving goods from origin to destination, but also managing those movements in an optimized, efficient and cost-effective manner. Logistics professionals—freight forwarders, customs brokers and transportation companies in particular—play a critical role as they continually work to reduce costs and build the efficiencies that are driving the growth of the global supply chain.

Exercises

Exercise 1 (paired student activity)

Partner with another student and try to solve this problem. You are a plant manager of an automotive manufacturer in Mexico, and a large and critical machine has just broken down and stopped your production line, costing $1,000 per hour in lost profit. A replacement machine is available in Toronto and can ship immediately. A trucking company says they can have the machine there in 72 hours at a cost of $5,000, and an air freight company can fly have the machine at your plant in 12 hours at a cost of $70,000. Strictly from a financial perspective, which option makes the most sense? Are there other issues to consider when deciding between the two options that have been presented? What would you do? Be prepared to share your insights on this case with the rest of the class (if your instructor calls upon your group to do so).

(Estimated time 10 minutes)

Exercise 2 *(class discussion)*
You are the new export manager of a company, and have found that your employer has never included freight costs in its quotations to international customers. Furthermore, some customers—often with little experience in international freight—have complained that freight costs are too high. How can you improve the competitive position of your company?

(Estimated time 10 minutes)

References/Resources

Canadian Professional Logistics Institute (www.loginstitute.ca)

Canadian International Freight Forwarding Association (www.ciffa.com)

International Chamber of Commerce Official Incoterms (www.iccwbo.org/incoterms)

13 Law, Policy and Regulation

Toward common ground

Chapter Objectives

- Understand the challenges in developing and securing adherence to a common set of legal and regulatory standards

- Learn about the major components of the existing (and emerging) regulatory and legal framework in the conduct of international trade

- Review issues such as extraterritoriality and dispute-resolution options

Overview

The legal and regulatory environments, along with the public-policy considerations related to international trade, are fundamental aspects of the pursuit of international trade and global commerce. The sheer size and scope of the global machinery—regional, national and global—that exists to help shape and manage the legal and regulatory elements of international business reflects the importance of this area to the conduct of global commerce.

Individual legal traditions, broadly applied treaties and regulations overseen by multilateral entities such as the World Trade Organization and the veritable web of bilateral and multilateral trade agreements are all part of the legal and regulatory framework that underpins global commerce and enables a relatively orderly conduct of business.

There is no suggestion that the system works perfectly—in some respects, it might not even work all that well—yet there must be recognition of the mammoth challenge posed by attempts to develop an effective, fair and widely accepted legal, regulatory and policy framework.

The areas affected by legal, policy and regulatory considerations cover every aspect of trade and global commerce. An uninformed approach by business executives can be disastrous to any business venture, and perhaps to the whole enterprise; frequently, errors in this area are not discovered until a crisis or dispute arises.

This is very much the case of an ounce of informed prevention being worth a pound of painful and expensive cure.

The International Regulatory Framework

Common ground?
The policy, legal and regulatory elements of the global business environment serve multiple, often contradictory, purposes.

Laws and regulations that originate within the borders of a nation may exist to protect the rights of an individual or those of an organization, or to ensure the support and promotion of various categories of national interest; however, these elements must also operate effectively within the international arena, in the context of broader, international agreements, laws and institutions.

Given the large number of legal traditions and regulatory regimes and the endless variety of public-policy objectives, it may seem unrealistic to suggest that there ought to be committed, focused attempts to find common ground across the international community. Despite the seemingly insurmountable challenges of doing so, the international business environment and the system of global trade are supported by a far-reaching framework of "common ground." The trade rules overseen by the World Trade Organization; the multitude of bilateral and multilateral trade agreements, legal principles and practices governing international shipping; and the regulations related to the use of instruments of international trade finance are examples of the reality of "common ground" in an area as complex and full of self-interest as this one.

The recognition—indeed, the development and active support—of common ground in the international regulatory framework, in law and at some level, in public policy, is essential to the long-term survival and effectiveness of the global business environment. This includes, perhaps somewhat paradoxically, agreements about what constitutes a healthy competitive environment for international business and what measures ought to be used to ensure fair competition.

Public-trade law

Public-trade law governs the import and export of goods between countries. This area of law is characterized by agreements among countries rather than between private individuals or companies. These international agreements establish a structure for the domestic trade legislation applied by countries across the globe. Their effect is to limit and define the measures countries may take to protect their domestic markets against foreign imports.

> The distinction between strict and verbatim interpretation of law— "black letter law" and the "spirit" of the law— is important in domestic commerce, but highly critical in international business, given the varying ways in which laws are promulgated, interpreted and applied across the globe and across cultures.

Many countries have enacted legislation governing export controls, tariffs, customs, countervailing duties, anti-dumping duties and the subsidization of exports. These laws fall within the internationally accepted devices used by governments to protect their local industries. Their purpose is to protect local manufacturers from unfair international competition, develop new industries, promote secondary manufacturing, maintain an adequate supply of locally produced goods and protect national security. In addition, these laws protect the free market in international trade by attempting to moderate or eliminate discriminatory or unfair trade practices of other countries.

The customs tariff continues to be the principal means of taxing and controlling the flow of goods into many markets. While alternative measures, such as outright bans, quotas and surtaxes are available, most major trading nations employ these measures only in exceptional circumstances. Although some national tariffs have lost significance because of various trade agreements and the negotiation of lower tariffs through GATT, tariffs remain an important obstacle to imports in many sectors.

Trade agreements—NAFTA as a sample

The North American Free Trade Agreement (NAFTA) between Canada, Mexico and the United States came into effect on January 1, 1994, and has often been identified as an example of a generally successful trade agreement by proponents of such arrangements. NAFTA focuses and reinforces the FTA, which had several of its provisions improved by extending them to Mexico. All basic components of the FTA remain unchanged under NAFTA, including measures to protect cultural industries, social services and basic products under supply management, as well as the Auto Pact. However, its provisions have been extended to cover all three member countries.

While NAFTA is held by some to be a shining example of effectiveness and success in the negotiation and management of trade agreements, it, like most trade agreements, has detractors and opponents among the three signatories to the deal, interestingly. Allegations of lost employment, reduced net value of trade, net transfer of benefit to trading partners, unacceptable exposure in sensitive industry sectors, loss of sovereign independence and risks of increased integration are commonly levelled at the NAFTA.

Certificates of origin

Administration and enforcement of NAFTA is generally based on a customs document known as the certificate of origin. The document certifies that the goods described in it qualify as "originating goods" under the rules of origin of NAFTA. Essentially, when an importer seeks NAFTA tariff treatment for imported goods, the importer must declare that the product qualifies as an originating good on the basis of a valid certificate of origin. The valid certificate of origin would have to be provided by the manufacturer or the exporter. Falsifying a certificate of origin is subject to severe penalties. The customs services in the member countries have significant powers of verification and audit. Advance rulings are available to assist manufacturers, exporters and importers.

Trade Policy: National Interest, Global Citizenship

Striking a balance

Protection of national interest is clearly a key function of a government, and in the areas of international trade and global business, the range of areas where such protection is necessary is very broad and often quite sensitive. It is equally correct to observe, however, that pure self-interest often masquerades as legitimate national interest, and the definitions of these terms, together with the boundaries associated to each, often blur.

The trade policies of individual national governments are, in theory, supposed to be shaped or framed by the agreements, regulatory context and practices adopted by members of the international community. Recurring challenges include the reality that visions and opinions related to the evolution of the international trade system and the environment for global business cover a wide range of views, underpinned by differing political philosophies, economic belief systems and objectives. The international community is far from homogenous, and views related to the optimal legal and regulatory regime vary widely.

Secondly, national self-interest remains the primary driver for most members of the international community, even in areas where shared interests and opportunities for broader benefit are widely recognized, supported and promoted. Economic and financial interests cede priority to very little else except perhaps security concerns, and even then, not easily.

The most extreme opponents of globalization allege that the national interests of developed countries (some more than others) are so completely their priority that they intentionally and systematically subjugate most of the developing world under debt loads that purport to be development aid, but are in fact highly lucrative means of assuring some level of interest payment, as well as long-term market access, including access to certain highly prized resources.

These realities acknowledged, is there a balance to be struck between national interest (legitimate or not) and good global citizenship? This type of question, perhaps a bit theoretical on its surface, will become increasingly important to executives and leaders venturing internationally over the coming short term. Debates already exist about carbon emissions versus economic interests, sustainability versus competitiveness, and environmentally and socially sound practices in project finance versus the profit imperative. They will all grow in importance, and are likely to be managed effectively through a positive, creative and empowered framework for international law and regulations, given that the impacts of these issues cross borders.

The consequences or outcomes of these debates are fundamental and transnational—even global—in scope. Global citizenship may be an option, but it will become a matter of sound business and political judgment, if not an outright question of survival.

Law and International Trade

Legal systems and jurisdiction
The legal systems, traditions and precedents which evolve and guide the conduct of business on a domestic basis are fundamental to the conduct of international business and to the successful conclusion of international trade transactions.

Executives pursuing business internationally must be aware, at least in broad terms, of the existence of very different legal models and of their potential applicability in a given deal or transaction, as well as the consequences associated with having business dealings under the jurisdiction of an unfamiliar legal system.

U.S. anti-terrorist laws, anti-money laundering provisions and foreign-assets tracking can impact, restrict or entirely derail transactions that are deemed by American authorities to be illegal according to U.S. law. Letters of credit issued by international banks are verified against extensive compliance lists issued by the Office of Foreign Assets Control (OFAC) to ensure that the financial instruments do not involve countries subject to embargo or individuals, for example, whose assets have been seized by the United States.

Legal systems and the treatment that can be expected under each vary significantly; individuals and firms venturing internationally must prepare for the possibility of expensive, protracted and perhaps ultimately ineffective legal action, given the difference in some areas, between legal theory and practical enforcement and remedy. Concerns about excessively litigious business practices and expensively disproportionate awards are also the reality in certain markets, most notably in the United States.

Overview of major legal systems
United States
The United States is a federal state, although one with a significantly stronger central government than Canada. The U.S. Constitution establishes the division of powers, giving each state jurisdiction over most local matters that do not have national or international implications. Thus, much of commercial and corporate law is, as in Canada, governed by the individual states. All states except Louisiana have a common-law system. However, the United States has codified its common-law systems more than Canada has, particularly in commercial matters. Each state has adopted a form of the Uniform Commercial Code, which facilitates the legal aspects of conducting business throughout the country. It is important to realize that the Uniform Commercial Code as adopted by the various states in the U.S. is not always the same. Thus, from state to state, there

In global trade, instruments of settlement such as letters of credit are often denominated in U.S. dollars and settled through a U.S. financial centre or even as U.S.-based bank. Thus, it is common for transactions that have no other connection to the United States to fall under the legal and regulatory powers of the U.S. government, by virtue of the use of American currency and U.S.-based financial institutions in the transaction.

may be some differences in how a particular state applies its own version of the Uniform Commercial Code.

To a large extent, many of the various pieces of commercial legislation (for example, the *Sale of Goods Act* and the *Personal Property Security Act*) enacted by provinces in Canada have provisions that are similar to those found in the U.S. Uniform Commercial Code.

Another important feature is the extraterritoriality of U.S. law. Like Canada, most countries do not impose their legislation outside their borders. U.S. laws do not respect this limitation, thus requiring businesses to address U.S. legal issues even when they or their transactions have little connection with the United States.

Other notable features of U.S. law are as follows:

- It permits significant punitive damage awards in civil lawsuits (including treble damages in some cases). These awards act as a deterrent against non-compliance with government regulations and breach of constitutional, contractual or other rights. In contrast, there is no Canadian legislative or jurisprudential basis for treble damages.

- As a society, the United States is more prone to resolve disagreements by lawsuits. Litigation is frequently used as a tool in business competition. The widespread and common practice of lawyers' contingency fees promotes easy access to the courts. It is much more common to see jury trials for commercial matters in the United States.

- Since the United States is a litigious society, its jurisprudence is extremely well-developed in business matters. This reduces uncertainty in the law and facilitates the structuring of legal transactions.

European Union

European integration preserves the social and linguistic character of each country while fostering fiscal, economic and political interdependence. The Treaty of Rome established pan-European institutions such as the European Parliament, the EU Commission and the European Court of Justice. Under the guidance and rule of these institutions, the trade barriers among the member countries are being eliminated and various trade practices are being harmonized and standardized.

The central institutions enact laws that apply throughout the EU. These take the form of regulations, directives, decisions, recommendations and opinions.

A regulation has general application, is binding in its entirety and is directly applicable in all member states. It requires no implementing legislation. For example, there are regulations about the provisions in technology licences that might be considered anti-competitive.

A directive is binding on each member state to which it is addressed, but the choice of form and method is decided by each national authority. Directives are usually implemented through each member's national legislation in ways that are roughly consistent but not identical. For example, the directive on "rental and lending rights and on certain rights related to copyright" requires every member

A business entering the European market must consider not only the applicable regulations, directives and decisions governing the transaction, but also the national laws of the individual states involved. One way to take full advantage of the European Union is to incorporate a subsidiary in one of the member states. That subsidiary becomes entitled to the benefits of EU membership, including guaranteed access to the internal markets of other EU states.

to enact laws to protect authors, performers and record and film producers, but the manner and timing in which that is accomplished may differ.

In global trade, instruments of settlement such as letters of credit are often denominated in U.S. dollars and settled through a U.S. financial centre, or even as U.S.-based bank. Thus, it is common for transactions that have no other connection to the United States to fall under the legal and regulatory powers of the U.S. Government, by virtue of the use of American currency and U.S.–based financial institutions in the transaction.

A decision is binding in its entirety upon those to whom it is addressed, while recommendations and opinions have no binding force, but act as guidelines.

Most western European countries that are not EU members have individually negotiated free-trade agreements with the European Union. This means that their industrial goods enter the union tariff-free, and that EU goods enter those countries duty-free. Most of those countries intend to join the union in the near future.

It has been stated by several legal commentators that the EU is most likely the closest example that the world has of a "true free trade zone." The EU has the most harmonized systems of law to date and continues to attempt to implement a common currency, the Euro, across its membership. The EU likes to refer to its goal of the "four freedoms" when describing its vision. These four freedoms are

- unrestricted movement of goods;

- unrestricted movement of capital;

- unrestricted movement of services; and

- unrestricted movement of people.

Islamic Law

The Shari'a is the term given to the Islamic legal system, currently practised in Iran, Pakistan and a growing number of Middle Eastern and Asian states. It derives primarily from the Qur'an, the holy religious text for those of the Muslim faith. Islamic law is more restrictive of parties' freedom to contract than is western law.

The major difference between Islamic and western commercial law is the prohibition on "unearned or unjustified" profit. This concept forbids payment of interest on loans and prohibits any transaction in which the gain of each party is not defined at the time the contract is made. Thus, for example, Islamic banks claim not to charge interest on their loans. Borrowers will still repay more than they received from the bank, but the difference is specified in a repayment agreement and is not termed interest.

It is important to note that, like most systems of law, the Shari'a may be practised differently among various countries adopting Islamic law. Independent research into the particular practices of a country is crucial. The Shari'a will likely appear to be quite different from what westerners are accustomed to. It is also important to realize that the Shari'a is very closely tied to the religious beliefs of the people

Where a contract violates the prohibition against "unjustified profit," an Islamic court will not enforce it. In practice, courts in countries adopting Islamic law do not always apply that law. This uncertainty limits confidence that the courts in Islamic countries will uphold contracts the parties freely enter.

where it is practised. Thus, it is critical that a westerner be cautious when negotiating legal agreements in such countries. In particular, it is a good idea not to voice any criticisms of the Shari'a legal system to avoid offending the religious beliefs of the other side.

Asian Legal Systems

Most Asian legal systems are based on systems similar to civil codes. This means that, rather than strictly following a large body of previously decided case decisions, most Asian countries have a codified set of legal principles that they follow. Previous decisions may be persuasive to the court, but such decisions are not binding.

However, it would be a mistake to think that Asian civil code systems are the same as their western counterparts (for example, those of Quebec or Europe). Although many Asian countries have codified their legal principles, such legal principles often reflect a culture with different values. The introduction of western legal systems is a relatively new phenomenon, and most Asian countries are still developing theirs.

Hong Kong and Singapore are exceptions that have a common-law-based legal system. This is undoubtedly a result of the historical occupation of these countries by the British. As of 1997, Hong Kong reverted to the possession of the People's Republic of China but stated that it would preserve the current legal system (strongly common-law-based) for a period of 50 years. Singapore continues to have a common-law system. Even these "versions" of common-law systems are significantly different from western common-law systems.

It is also important to note that countries such the People's Republic of China and North Korea are communist, centrally planned state economies. As a result, the laws in these countries can be quite different and far more restrictive than western laws.

In general, law has not historically enjoyed the same status in Asian countries as it has in western countries. For example, historically, China referred to two concepts: "li" (meaning proper behaviour according to relationships) and "fa" (law). Chinese philosophy has always regarded "li" as being superior to "fa" in terms of governance of behaviour. Chinese legal historians have remarked that in China, it was thought that one who had to call state courts to put a fellow citizen in the wrong was considered uncultured and lacking in the virtues of modesty and readiness to compromise. Furthermore, because of the harsh punishments used by the Qin dynasty, law was thought of as the tool by which tyrants oppressed the people. The "legalist school of thought" (those who favoured governance by law) was largely replaced by the Confucian school of thought, which advocated governance by a set of Confucian principles. The Confucian principles were societal norms that prescribed conduct between individuals according to their relationships (for example, husband and wife or ruler and subject).

As a result, the Chinese have never based their dealings on a firm legal infrastructure, preferring to rely on societal norms. During the shift from a legalistic to a Confucian approach, China was the largest nation in Asia, and its way of thinking, it has been argued, had a profound impact on the Asian countries around it.

As a result, westerners doing business in China and many other Asian countries may find that their Asian counterparts do not seem to pay as much attention to legal agreements. To many Asians, legal agreements are often seen to be a form of general understanding that may be modified according to the parties' relationship rather than as firm binding commitments. It is not surprising that many Asian entrepreneurs spend more time "getting to know" the western entrepreneur. In part, this may be due to the fact that Asians often base their dealings on the development of a relationship rather than on legal principle.

In many cases, the views of western and Asian cultures can be seen to be on opposite ends of a spectrum. Western law strongly values certainty, while Asian thought values flexibility in an arrangement. With the development of Asian legal systems, the divergence between western and Asian approaches is narrowing. However, it is important to still be aware of the differences that exist.

Newest jurisdiction: The Internet
Advances in technology, including the advent and now widespread use of the Internet for domestic and international business purposes, raise many challenges in terms of legalities and regulatory issues.

The United Nations has recognized the growing importance of the Internet and e-commerce, and has devised a set of principles intended to assist in responding to this technological evolution:

The UNCITRAL Model Law operates on the following principles:

- Equivalence. Electronic communications shall be the functional equivalent of paper-based documents. Given proper standards, electronic documents can be treated and given the same value as paper documents.

- Autonomy of contracts. Contracts may be in the form of electronic documents. However, this should not result in a change in the substantive terms and conditions of a transaction.

- Voluntary use of the electronic communication. Parties may choose to enter into an electronic transaction or not at all. It is not mandatory.

- Solemnity of the contract and the primacy of statutory requirements respecting formalities of contracts. The requirements for a contract to be valid and enforceable, such as notarization, remain the same.

- Application to form rather than substance. The law should be applicable to the form rather than the substantive terms of the contract. Whatever statutory elements are required to be present must still be present, for example, consent freely given, an object, cause or consideration.

- Primacy of consumer-protection laws. Consumer-protection laws may take precedence over the provisions of the Model Law.

The Internet crosses national boundaries and poses challenges in terms of recognition of electronic communications and signatures in legal contexts; there are legitimate concerns about security and the ability to ensure authenticity of sources as well as security of messages "in transit" across the web. The legal and regulatory framework related to the use of the Internet in business and trade is in its early stages of evolution, but clearly represents a new "jurisdiction" in considering the legal and regulatory context of the global business environment.

Intellectual property and technology

The main types of intellectual property (IP) rights are

- patent;

- industrial design;

- trademark;

- copyright; and

- trade secrets.

The owner of IP rights may use, sell or license them to others. Brand-name recognition is becoming increasingly important in today's competitive world. In addition, technology (for example, computers and software) and media content (for example, the Internet) have emerged as very significant business issues. Intellectual-property laws can help businesses obtain certain legal rights to brand names, technology and media content, among other things, and are thus an important legal topic to study.

For IP connected to special items such as semi-conductor chips and plants, some countries have legislation that tracks international initiatives (the Washington Treaty on Intellectual Property in Respect of Integrated Circuits, and the International Union for the Protection of New Varieties of Plants).

Patent and industrial-design rights do not exist except by application to the patent office and the industrial-design office, resulting in the granting of a patent. An application should not be confused with a grant; an application is merely a request that will be examined for its merits, and no protection exists until granted. There may ultimately be no grant, and if there is a grant, it typically occurs years after filing the application. In contrast, a trade secret or copyright exists outside the process of application and grant. Trademarks exist outside the process of application and grant but can advantageously be the subject of that process.

The World Intellectual Property Office (WIPO), which is a specialized agency of the United Nations system of organizations, is responsible for promoting and harmonizing IP laws around the world. Its headquarters is in Switzerland.

The World Trade Organization's (WTO) Agreement on Trade-Related Aspects of Intellectual Property (TRIPS) built on existing conventions of WIPO (namely the Paris Convention for patents, trademarks and industrial designs and the Berne Convention for copyright) and added new or higher standards where existing conventions were silent or thought to be inadequate. TRIPS addressed the applicability of the basic principles of the General Agreement on Tariffs and Trade (GATT), the provision of adequate IP rights, enforcement measures, multilateral dispute-settlement mechanisms and transitional implementation arrangements (especially for developing countries).

Extraterritoriality

Extraterritorial application of laws

Extraterritoriality refers to the practice of some countries or regions, most notably the United States and the European Union, to apply their legal standards to subsidiaries or affiliates of domestic companies when they operate in foreign jurisdictions. Some instances of this practice involve the application of laws to companies (including foreign-owned and foreign-based ones) seeking to do business in the United States or the EU.

Countries do not tend to attempt to apply their laws beyond their borders; however, the United States and the European Union often consider the effects that activities outside their borders have on their internal economy. If, for example, the offenders were outside a country but committed an offence inside the country (for example, implemented a price cartel inside through subsidiaries, agents or branches), the offenders might be under the jurisdiction of that country's courts. Conversely, if trademark infringement outside the United States were hurting a U.S. business, the offender and the foreign activities might be under the jurisdiction of the U.S. courts. This is not restricted to commercial matters—for political matters, the United States has two anti-boycott laws (under the *Export Administration Act* and the Internal Revenue Code), both of which are extraterritorial and reach the foreign subsidiaries of U.S. corporations.

Extraterritorial application of laws may have significant impact on businesses pursuing international business. Exposure arises when a business executive is faced with a legal or compliance requirement that may not have been contemplated or anticipated, or when the company is in a dispute that proves difficult to resolve. Extraterritoriality may present the challenge of having to choose between compliance with one of two or more contradictory laws based on an assessment of the relative consequences, including the likelihood of legal action.

> Extraterritorial application of laws and regulations can generate significant ill will and can subject companies engaged in global commerce to severe financial penalty and legal consequences; contravention of such laws may even result in a company being prevented from doing business in the country applying its law on this basis.

GATT and the WTO Agreement

GATT is the starting point in any discussion of international public trade law because it preceded the WTO Agreement. GATT was a multilateral treaty signed by 23 countries in 1947. GATT served four basic functions:

- it was a framework for the negotiation and reduction of tariffs and other trade barriers;

- it was a code of rules governing international trade between contracting parties;

- it was a forum for negotiating and solving international trade disputes; and

- it was an international institution that assisted in making rules governing international trade among the member countries.

There were eight rounds of trade negotiations under GATT, the most recent being the Uruguay Round, which began in 1986 and ended on April 15, 1994. Each round lasted several years and bears the name of the country or city in which it commenced. These negotiations successfully lowered tariffs in many developed countries on manufactured and semi-manufactured goods from an average of 40 percent in 1947 to the present level of about 6 percent.

GATT covered international trade in goods worth over three trillion dollars (U.S.) annually. One of the objectives of the Uruguay Round was to extend GATT to cover a limited number of services, although the main concern of GATT was always trade in goods and, more particularly, the reduction and fixing of tariff barriers and the issue of agricultural subsidies.

The most important achievement of the Uruguay Round was the creation of the World Trade Organization (the WTO) via the WTO Agreement. The WTO Agreement (like GATT) is an agreement among countries rather than individuals or corporations. Thus, the rights it creates and the obligations it imposes are enforced by governments, not by the businesses affected. Whereas GATT concentrated on multilateral rounds of negotiations, the WTO provides a permanent negotiating forum. As of May 2007, 150 countries were members of the WTO. There are also 31 "observer countries" that must begin accession processes within five years of attaining observer status (see list at www.wto.org, under Membership). Any country wishing to be a member of the WTO must agree to a number of listed agreements (see www.wto.org, under Accessions), which also includes GATT (1994).

Membership in the WTO may require nations to effect amendments and additions to domestic law to ensure that the responsibilities, commitments and obligations associated with WTO membership have legal standing at home.

The WTO is a complex organization, as might be expected given its broad and ambitious mandate.

As under GATT, the Most Favoured Nation (MFN) clause directs that members are bound to grant no less favourable treatment to other members' products than they do to the products of any other country. The WTO also encompasses another provision from GATT—that of "national treatment," the requirement that once goods have entered a market, those goods must be treated no less favourably than the equivalent domestically produced goods. These two principles are the two fundamental and most important concepts under the GATT and WTO.

The WTO attracts a great deal of negative attention from anti-globalization activists, non-governmental organizations and other individuals and entities, based on the view that the organization favours certain members and seeks to impose the views of its most powerful members on the rest of the international community. The WTO is often portrayed as an ineffective, bureaucratic organization debating minutiae in exotic locales while fundamental issues remain unresolved, and major initiatives—such as agricultural trade issues, which, if resolved could bring some measure of economic gain to developing countries— languish in "negotiation limbo" for decades.

The WTO has been assigned five principal tasks:
- to facilitate the implementation of the results of the Uruguay Round of trade negotiations;
- to provide a forum for multilateral trade negotiations and a framework for the implementation of their results;
- to administer the dispute-settlement process;
- to administer the Trade Policy Review Mechanism; and
- to co-operate with the International Monetary Fund (IMF) and the World Bank in working toward the achievement of greater coherence in global economic policy making.

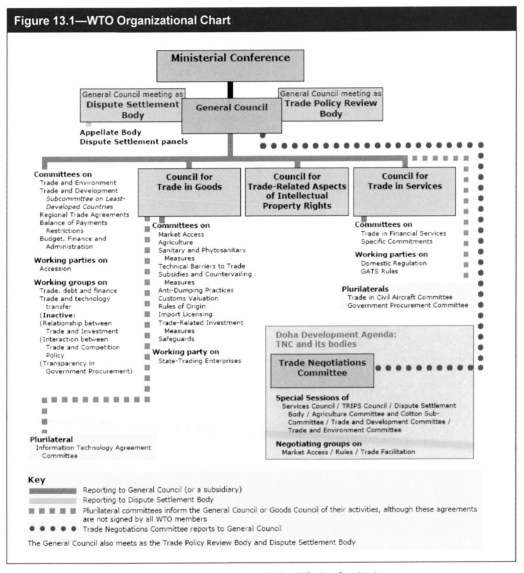

Figure 13.1—WTO Organizational Chart

Source: WTO Website (www.wto.org/english/thewto_e/whatis_e/tif_e/org2_e.htm)

International Security

Security concerns and international regulation

International security has been an element of the conduct of trade and global business in various forms for many decades, but arguably has never been in such a central position on the world stage as it has in the post–9/11 period.

Security concerns have increased global vigilance in financial matters, including tightening monitoring and enforcement related to money-laundering activities, both in relation to organized crime and now relative to the potential financing of terrorist organizations.

Cross-border communications are monitored, as are financial transactions, to a degree and at a level of detail not previously seen, at least publicly, in international business and global commerce. The monitoring of financial transactions and messages transmitted through SWIFT (the Brussels-based Society for World Inter-bank Financial Telecommunications) by the U.S. Treasury, Office of Foreign Assets Control (OFAC) clearly illustrated the degree to which security measures have been expanded.

Customs clearance and security issues are also subject to increased attention, and are becoming an important element of the international regulatory and legal framework. C-TPAT (the Customs Trade Partnership Against Terrorism) is another recent example of the role of international regulatory activities in international security. C-TPAT is a supply-chain security initiative under which companies exporting to the United States can be designated as "low-risk" based on previous history. While compliance is voluntary, the impact of non-compliance can result in loss of business in the U.S., costly delays at customs and a loss of competitive advantage.

International security concerns will continue to materially impact the conduct of global commerce, the ease of travel of business executives and others and the overall cost of business. The international legal and regulatory framework will certainly expand as it relates to security issues, and the potential collision of security concerns, commercial interests and questions of national sovereignty will be key to the global business environment for many years.

Rules Against Dumping and Unfair Trade Practices

Anti-dumping

The WTO authorizes countries to take protective measures against dumping. Dumping is a form of discriminatory pricing: it is the term used to describe a situation in which a seller sets different prices in different national markets. In short, dumping is the selling of goods abroad at prices below those at which the goods would sell in the exporter's home market. This would occur, for example, if a Canadian toothpick manufacturer was being put out of business because its U.S. competitor, who sells toothpicks in the United States at $1 per box, is selling them in Canada at $.25 per box. Dumping is considered an unfair trade practice that distorts prices or profits, disrupts markets and injures local producers of competitive products. As a result, dumping is regulated domestically in many countries through legislation that gives local force to the rights granted under the WTO Agreement.

Subsidies

Subsidies, like dumping, are sometimes considered unfair trade practices that distort markets, profits and prices and injure producers of competitive products.

Defined by the WTO Agreement on Subsidies and Countervailing Measures, subsidies mean:

- any financial or other commercial benefit conferred on persons engaged in the production, manufacture, growth, processing, purchase, distribution, transportation, sale, export or import of goods as a result of any scheme, practice or thing done, provided or implemented by the government of a country other than [the national government]; and

- any income or price support that confers a benefit.

WTO regulations recognize that "generally available subsidies" do not distort trade and thus should not attract countervailing duties. It is only specific "targeted subsidies" that distort trade and attract countervailing duties.

Subsidies are government programs or other government benefits that are either generally available to the entire economy (for example, government-built highways), available to similar persons across a wide range of industrial sectors (for example, small-business-development financing) or are specifically targeted. Targeted subsidies are those programs or benefits that are available only to certain enterprises. For a subsidy to be countervailable, it must provide a financial or commercial benefit and be specifically targeted. Generally, available subsidies are not countervailable. Similarly, any exemptions from internal taxes or duty drawbacks to which the goods may be entitled because of their export from the country of origin or country of export are not countervailable.

Unfair trade practices
The following partial list is illustrative of export subsidies that GATT has ruled are unfair trade practices and are thus subject to the imposition of countervailing duties:

- The provision by governments of direct subsidies to a firm or an industry contingent upon export performance

- The provision or requirement by governments of internal transport and freight charges on export shipments on terms more favourable than domestic shipments

- The allowance of special deductions in the calculation of taxes for expenses directly related to exports or export performance that are more generous than those granted for production for domestic consumption

- The full or partial exemption, remission or deferral of direct taxes specifically related to exports (i.e., taxes on wages, profits, interest, rents or royalties) or social-welfare charges paid or payable by industrial or commercial enterprises

Countervailing duty
Countervail, or a countervailing duty, is the special duty imposed upon imports that have benefited from a foreign government subsidy in their country of origin. The duty is usually an amount equivalent to the subsidy, and it is intended to eliminate any competitive advantages a foreign exporter gained through receiving the subsidy. As in the case of dumping, the countervailing duty may be imposed only on subsidized imports that have caused injury or retardation or are threatening to cause injury to a domestic industry.

Technical Standards

European CE markings

Technical, safety and quality standards are major elements of the international trade and global business environment. European standards, such as those represented by CE Markings (Conformité européenne), are an example of such standards.

> "A CE Marking on a product is a manufacturer's declaration that the product complies with the essential requirements of the relevant European health, safety and environmental protection legislation, in practice by many of the so-called 'Product directives.' Product directives contain the 'essential requirements' and/or 'performance levels' and 'harmonized standards' to which the products must conform. Harmonized standards are the technical specifications (European Standards or Harmonization Documents) that are established by several European standards agencies."

CE Marking on a product indicates to governmental officials that the product may be legally placed on the market in their country, facilitates the free and unencumbered movement of duly marked goods within the EFTA and EU countries and permits the removal or withdrawal of unmarked, non-conforming products by customs and enforcement authorities.[36]

Health and Environmental Regulations

Evolving priorities

Health and environmental considerations are becoming increasingly high priorities in international business and global trade. Environmental regulations, by way of illustration, impact many elements of the conduct of business, both domestically and internationally.

Questions of sustainability and sustainable development, together with increasingly common requirements to conduct environmental-impact assessments on international projects, are illustrative of the increasing importance of an area that was once considered very much on the "fringe" of business.

Export credit agencies—government agencies that play a significant role in financing trade as well as international projects—are now actively classifying projects in terms of risk and social/environmental impact, and are declining to support higher-risk projects. Such requirements arise from a combination of sources: the lobbying and political actions on non-governmental organizations, the broad agreement of ECAs whose countries are members of the OECD, and domestic regulations and public policy initiatives that place increasing emphasis on environmental issues. It remains true that ECAs are carefully monitored by various NGOs due to the practices of certain agencies that have directly or indirectly contributed to environmental damage, displacement of populations, funding of corrupt regimes and a host of similar unsavoury outcomes.

Health concerns and regulatory requirements apply across a range of products, most commonly agriculture and food products, and are regulated by a combi-

---

[36] Wellkang Tech Consulting. (www.ce-marking.org/what-is-ce-marking.html)

nation of international standards as well as extensive domestic legislation and government oversight. Health certificates are commonly required in trade transactions that involve the transport of food items across borders.

Dispute Resolution: Negotiation, Mediation, Arbitration, Legal Action

Processes and mechanisms

Commercial disputes in international trade typically involve controversies such as

- disputes with agents, distributors or licensees;

- collection of monies due on a contract;

- breach of contract or of warranty;

- patent, copyright, trademark and trade secrets;

- secured creditors' rights, i.e., seizure of assets; and

- enforcement of foreign judgments.

Because of the expense, inconvenience and complexity of litigating international business disputes, it is usually in the best interests of all parties to explore settlement before engaging in more formal means of dispute resolution. The investment in time and cost and the risk of an unfavourable result suggest that in most cases compromise is preferable. In particular, it is important to realize that court litigation with respect to international business disputes can lead to very uncertain results.

Moreover, litigation can be very costly. The initial legal cost is usually at least U.S.$25,000 and can take three to ten years to resolve in court. Costs and delays increase further when an international transaction is involved. In contrast, alternative forms of dispute resolution such as mediation and arbitration can be resolved in less than 90 days. The costs of mediation and arbitration vary depending on the complexity of the matter, but are usually less expensive than litigation. A downside to arbitration and mediation is that they take up considerable time in the short term. In other words, instead of having a long litigated court trial over years, the parties have to be prepared to devote a large amount of time over a short, intense period (for example, 90–120 days). However, this is frequently preferable to long, drawn-out litigation.

Mediation

When a dispute arises between two or more parties, usually the first step is to have the parties discuss, negotiate and attempt to settle the dispute between themselves. The parties will either meet in person or discuss the matter on the telephone without involving any outside persons. If these attempts at settlement are not successful, the parties may seek the assistance of an independent, external person.

One method of attempting to resolve the dispute is by means of mediation. In mediation, an external, neutral mediator is used to help the parties resolve their dispute. The purpose of the mediator is to facilitate discussion and settlement between the disputing parties. Usually, the mediator is an independent third party with no vested interest in the outcome of the mediation. Unlike arbitration or court litigation, mediation is non-binding: there is no winner or loser, and the parties are not bound by the mediator's decision (if there is one).

Some agreements, particularly long-term contracts and contracts with public bodies, contain mediation or conciliation clauses. These typically outline a formal mediation procedure the parties must undergo before taking adversarial actions such as arbitration or litigation.

Arbitration or litigation
When a dispute cannot be settled by negotiation or mediation, the claiming party must decide whether to arbitrate or litigate.

Arbitration is a method of dispute resolution in which the disputing parties have an outside person (the "arbitrator") hear their sides of the dispute and agree to be bound by the arbitrator's decision. It is in many ways similar to mediation, with the notable exception that the arbitrator's ruling is final and binds the parties.

Litigation refers to when the disputing parties decide to commence formal legal proceedings and have their dispute decided by a court of law.

To decide between arbitration and litigation, the contract must be reviewed; if it contains a valid arbitration clause that encompasses the dispute in question, a party will generally be prevented from suing in court. There are few exceptions to this principle, given the worldwide trend favouring commercial arbitration to resolve international disputes. However, arbitration or mediation are not useful from a practical standpoint if one suspects that the other side is not genuinely interested in resolution. In such cases (for example, fraud), litigation may be a better route.

Litigation in court
Even if the contract does not require arbitration, the parties may voluntarily resolve the dispute through arbitration or some other means. However, most disputes that are not settled in this way are resolved through litigation.

Where to sue
If the claiming party (the "plaintiff") decides to litigate, the first decision is where to sue. In international disputes, a plaintiff usually has at least two possible venues in which to commence litigation: its own place of business, or the jurisdiction of the opposing party (the "defendant"). Where there are numerous defendants and complex international transactions, there will be a number of possible jurisdictions.

Government agencies
In addition to courts, some government agencies that can provide remedies. For example, the U.S. International Trade Commission is an independent quasi-judicial federal agency. It may make determinations in investigations that involve unfair trade practices, mainly allegations of infringement of U.S. patents and trademarks by imported goods. In Canada, the Canadian International Trade Tribunal and Canadian Competition Bureau are often involved in the investigation of unfair trade practices. Actions from these agencies are usually started by a written complaint from a business regarding a breach of laws by a competitor.

International commercial arbitration

In recent years it has become common practice to resolve international business disputes through arbitration, for many reasons. The parties in international disputes are usually subject to the legal systems and judicial procedures of different countries. At least one of the parties will be on unfamiliar ground if the parties litigate in the courts. Litigation leads to conflict over which legal system should govern the procedures and which country's laws and rules should apply. Where the parties' respective cultures and business practices differ widely, a less formal means of resolving disputes is preferable. Arbitration is a neutral procedure that is not dominated by the legal system of either party.

Defining arbitration

Arbitration is a device that entrusts the resolution of a dispute to an independent person or persons (an arbitrator) whose authority derives not from a court system (like a judge's authority does), but from the consent of the parties as contained in their contract or other mutual agreement. Like a contract, the result of arbitration binds both parties and is enforceable by a court.

Arbitration services, or information on arbitration, may be secured from several sources, including:

- International Chamber of Commerce (ICC);

- American Arbitration Association (AAA);

- Centre for Public Resources;

- European Convention on International Commercial Arbitration;

- United Nations Conference for International Trade Law (UNCITRAL), which is the explicit base for the Canadian federal and provincial arbitrations acts and whose commentary can be used to interpret the acts;

- London Court of International Arbitration (LCIA);

- British Columbia International Commercial Arbitration Centre (BCICAC);

- Québec National and International Commercial Arbitration Centre;

- Japan Commercial Arbitration Association;

- China International Economic and Trade Arbitration Commission (CIETAC); and

- World Intellectual Property Organization Arbitration Centre.

Besides selecting a set of rules, the arbitration clause should address the governing law to be applied to the arbitration, the language and the place of the arbitration and the number of arbitrators. If these details are omitted, they will be determined by applying the rules of the chosen institution or by the arbitrator's decision during the preliminaries.

Law, Policy and Regulation Checklist

Table 13.2—Law, policy and regulation checklist
☑ Understand the impact and implications of multiple legal traditions and jurisdictions in international trade.
☑ Understand the political imperatives, the concept of extraterritoriality and the issues of policy and national interest that affect the global legal and regulatory framework.
☑ Appreciate the basic principles that guide legal interpretation and action in major legal systems and jurisdictions.
☑ Review the importance of balancing national interests and objectives with the broader "good" of the global business environment.
☑ Understand the various dispute-resolution mechanisms and options available to businesses engaged in international business.
☑ Appreciate the challenges related to enforcement of intellectual property and the critical importance of an effective framework related to the Internet and e-commerce.

Chapter Summary

Questions of policy, regulation and international law are critical to the successful and effective pursuit of international trade and global business. The framework of agreements, treaties, laws and regulations that enables a remarkably organized flow of business across the globe, despite numerous systems, philosophies and opposing interests, is broad in impact and impressive in resilience and evolution.

While interests and objectives often compete between nations and commercial entities, there is an important requirement to seek, support and expand a "common ground" in the international regulations governing the conduct of trade and business, as the international community faces an increasing list of challenges and issues that are international in scope and global in their impact and consequences.

Executives venturing internationally for any reason, even in the early stages when the "venture" consists primarily of marketing trips, do so at significant risk if they do not take account of the legal, regulatory and policy context within which they propose to operate. Expert advice in legal matters—especially when crossing borders—is highly advisable. Somewhat like insurance, it may feel like a questionable "sunk cost" to some if there is no dispute or legal challenge to overcome, but it may save the deal—and perhaps the enterprise as a whole—if indeed something does "go wrong."

Exercises

Exercise 1 (class discussion)
Discuss the relationship between domestic commercial law and local regulations versus international regulations, agreements and treaties. How does the WTO relate to domestic laws governing the conduct of international trade?

(Estimated time 10 minutes)

Exercise 2 (class discussion)
Consider the ways in which technology and the evolution of virtual business models has created a new legal jurisdiction: the Internet. To what extent is this simply the combination of traditional national jurisdictions? Does the Internet present legal and regulatory challenges that go beyond those that arise within the context of national legal systems?

(Estimated time 10 minutes)

References/Resources

Legal and Regulatory Issues in the Information Economy, e-ASEAN Task Force, UNDP, 2003

SWIFT (www.swift.com/index.cfm?item_id=61228)

World Trade Organization Website (www.wto.org)

Website of Michael Geist (www.michaelgeist.ca)

14 The International Business Plan

Putting it all together

Chapter objectives

- Understand why careful planning is crucial prior to implementation of international business ventures

- Recognize the components of an international business plan

- Understand the scope of international business initiatives

- Describe the inherent risks in international trade

Overview

As the adage goes, "if you fail to plan, you're planning to fail." This applies to any business, and even more so to international trade. Again and again, research has shown that companies who plan carefully are more successful than those who do not. Target markets become more distant from the home office as products become global; the success variables rise in number and complexity, and the costs and potential risks likewise increase. These costs and risks must be managed carefully, and planning takes on an even greater significance.

Gambling vs. risk taking

All businesses must take risks, but what is the difference between gambling and risk taking? Risks can be mitigated through planning, and some control over the outcome is retained after the decision to "go" is taken. With gambling, all control over the outcome is lost once the money is on the table.

Although everyone knows that planning is important, some managers—at their peril—still do not find the time to do so. Developing international markets carries significant risks, which can be mitigated through careful collection of information and analysis of data. In the possible event that, for whatever reasons, a would-be exporter "just cannot compete" in a new export market—regardless of the money invested, products adapted and marketing efforts expended—it is preferable to arrive at this conclusion sooner rather than later. There are innumerable cases of failed international business ventures that could have been avoided if looming risks had been detected sooner through careful planning.

Another adage is "nothing ventured, nothing gained," which speaks to the importance of taking risks. Risk taking is an unavoidable part of business; the key is to manage the risk through planning. One can never hope to have all the necessary information prior to making a "go" decision, because for the majority of business cases, the introduction of a product into a new market is done without the benefit of previous history or track record for the product in that particular market. However, planning bridges the gap between the imperative to take on new initiatives to grow the business and making poor decisions that could have been avoided had more information been collected and evaluated.

The Importance of the International Business Plan

International business plans might be thought of as road maps that set out a framework for success. They identify goals and objectives and establish metrics with which success can be measured.

Although highly dependent on the individual business case, on average it takes a three-year commitment to establish a successful presence in a foreign market. This process may require tremendous human, technical and financial resources during the developmental period. We know that maintaining commitment is crucial to the success of international business ventures, so carefully assessing the feasibility of the venture is an essential step before going global and making that commitment.

But why plan? After all, it takes significant time to identify information resources, gather data and construct a plan—wouldn't this time be better spent just going out there and doing it?

Planning is essential to any business, whether domestic or international. The plan outlines the specific reasons why the corporation is expected to succeed in its ventures. It defines a direction and a purpose. A plan will establish where a business is going and show how it proposes to get there. It is the internal benchmark against which success and failure can be measured.

A business plan is a valuable management tool that can be used for a wide variety of purposes, such as

- to set goals and objectives for the company's performance;

- to provide a basis for evaluating and controlling the company's performance;

- to communicate a company's message to managers and staff, outside directors, suppliers, lenders and potential investors;

- to help the planner identify the cash needs of the business; and

- to provide benchmarks against which to compare the progress and performance of the business over time.

A comprehensive and detailed plan forces the planner to look at a company's operations and re-evaluate the assumptions on which the business was founded. In doing so, the planner can identify weak spots as well as strengths in different parts of the company's operations. When thoughts are translated onto paper, this has the effect of highlighting potential problems that can easily be overlooked when one simply conceptualizes a plan.

The purpose of planning

Ultimately, planning gives a firm greater control by allowing it to anticipate events instead of simply reacting to them. With a plan, a firm can lead, not follow. The need for planning is all the more important in international trade, which is both more complex and riskier than purely domestic business. To manage and reduce risk, international traders must grasp that complexity and develop the necessary know-how. Planning is absolutely essential; below you will find a table outlining some of its purposes.

Table 14.1—The purpose of planning	
Purpose	**Rationale**
Definition of objectives	Articulates the direction in which a company is moving and specifies the criteria for measuring success.
	Specifies the measures that should be taken to improve business operations and performance.
Evaluation mechanisms	Helps management develop a better understanding of the business, how it functions, what its strengths are and where its weaknesses lie.
	Assesses external risks a company faces.
	Specifies the means to be used in monitoring progress.
	Helps managers test the export readiness of a company and identify which resources are available and which are still needed for international trade.

Table 14.1—The purpose of planning *(continued)*	
Purpose	**Rationale**
Management tools	Measurement tools (e.g., benchmarking, tracking mechanisms) can help to achieve the firm's objectives. Communications tools help the company reach its employees, shareholders, investors, creditors and partners. Testing tools assess the feasibility of any proposed business venture, especially one in the international arena, prior to implementation.
Identifier of options	The plan should provide management with different alternatives and options in order to choose the best one and to identify backup strategies in the event that unforeseen circumstances develop later.

The Planning Process: Gathering the Information

The international business plan is subject to repeated adjustment and revision to keep it current with the changing circumstances of the company. The very act of planning changes the nature and assumptions of a business. The plan is a feedback mechanism through which new information is continually incorporated into the company's operations. Planning always precedes action; therefore, planning must be thought of as a continuous cycle. The analytical tools presented in this chapter are not intended to be used just once. If they are to be useful, they should be used several times as part of a process of improvement and incremental adjustment.

Plan-preparation guidelines

Below are guidelines for preparing a comprehensive business plan:

1. The objectives for producing the plan should be clearly defined. Who is going to read the plan, and what will they need to do? These objectives can help decide how much emphasis to put on various sections.

2. Enough time and resources should be allocated to thoroughly research the plan. A plan is only as good as the research that went into producing it.

3. Drafts of the plan should be shown to others. It can be very useful to obtain feedback from others inside and outside the business.

4. The plan should be original and done specifically for each business case. A common mistake entrepreneurs make is to borrow heavily from a sample plan and simply change the names and some of the numbers. There are two big problems with this approach. First, the emphasis placed on various sections of the plan must reflect what is important in the particular business in question. Second, a good plan should flow like a story, with the sections working together to demonstrate why the business will succeed. Plans

that borrow too heavily from other plans tend to be disjointed, with some sections contradicting others and various key issues left unaddressed.

5. Key points should be outlined in each section before writing starts, and then reviewed to ensure that the sections are consistent with each other, that there is little duplication and that all key issues have been addressed.

6. Financial projections should be believable. For many readers, the financial section is the most important part of the plan because it identifies the financing needs and shows the profit potential of the business. In addition, a good financial plan will give the reader confidence that the author really understands the business.

7. The executive summary should be done last. In some ways it is the most important section of the plan because people will read it first—and it may be the only section they read. A good executive summary should be short (two pages at most), should highlight what is important in the plan and should excite the reader about the business opportunity.

Steps in the planning cycle

Attaching the word "cycle" to planning implies that it happens more than once. International business plans need to be reviewed periodically because new information is coming in all the time that has an impact on both planning and operations. There are at least five major steps in the planning cycle of an international trading venture:

Step 1: Defining the mission statement

The mission statement describes the firm's primary purpose, its direction and what management expects to accomplish; it explains what the company does and what needs the company fills. These objectives and goals should be expressed in a concise manner to ensure they are clearly and quickly understood.

Putting the mission statement into words is a crucial executive act. Uses of a mission statement are, among others,

- to communicate the company's values to customers as a marketing tool;

- to provide consensus on company goals;

- to orient staff to the prime business purpose; and

- to create performance expectations.

A mission statement is worthless unless

- there is visible executive commitment;

- everyone buys into it; and

- it is put into practice.

Step 2: Defining the current status of the business

This step involves preparing a comprehensive summary of everything that is significant about current operations. A skills audit is a component of this, and may include

- language capabilities;

- existing contacts and personal relationships;

- summary of ability to handle tasks associated with new international business opportunities;

- recent in-market travel experience; and

- experience with logistics and documentary requirements.

Step 3: Determining corporate strategy

The results achieved in the second step allow planners to identify ways of improving the company's performance and to build those into the plan. The planners can use their planning tools to test various scenarios and devise an optimal corporate strategy.

Step 4: Identifying international opportunities

Once an optimal domestic strategy has been articulated, planners can use the results to identify promising international business opportunities.

Step 5: Revising the business plan

Once one or more potentially attractive ventures are identified, they should be incorporated into the overall corporate plan. The plan itself should be adjusted to accommodate any impacts on the existing business arising from the proposed international transactions.

Companies who possess multi-ethnic workforces are often more capable of doing business internationally than those who do not, because their language and cultural skills may be leveraged to handle the new and diverse tasks associated with international operations.

This cycle should be repeated with every major new business venture— even those that do not involve a change in the direction of a business. Every initiative may influence the operations of a business and, therefore, should be incorporated into the planning process.

Once a company has developed and implemented a comprehensive plan, ongoing adjustments to it need not be time-consuming. The plan should be flexible enough to incorporate ongoing course corrections quickly, without absorbing the precious time of the planners.

Assembling the Components of the International Business Plan

Information base

When the planning process has been defined, it is time to begin assembling the components of the plan. Information must be gathered and processed into a comprehensive plan that communicates the business initiative, describes the business case and explains why it will be successful. The first part of this is an internal analysis, which helps create a base—where the company is at this moment—from which to expand. Below is a table containing a number of items that need to be evaluated and relevant details, along with spaces to detail the source of the information and the findings or results of the exercise.

Table 14.2—The information base			
Item	**Details**	**Source**	**Findings**
Corporate structure	• ownership • management • divisions • key assets		
Corporate history	• foundation • key milestones • awards • major changes		
Strategic objectives	• mission statement • short- and long-term objectives • timetable		
Description of top management and key staff	• names • positions • qualifications • contributions • job-output measures		
Description of business	• industry served • customer base • assets • operations		
Market analysis	• market location • size • characteristics • trends • opportunities		

Table 14.2—The information base *(continued)*			
Item	**Details**	**Source**	**Findings**
Product evaluation	• features • advantages • life cycle • replacement/ extension strategy		
Competitor analysis	• number • size • market share • advantages • disadvantages		
Human resources	• number of employees • skill levels • performance gaps • development programs		
Suppliers	• functional areas • supplier relationships • replaceability		
Current financial performance	• sales • gross and net income • financial goals achieved • trends		
Financial forecasts	• sales projections • income forecasts • cash flow forecasts • profit forecasts		
Financing strategy	• financing needed • sources of financing		

Market Evaluation

Without sales there is no business, and the market is where the sales come from. This makes accurate market evaluation absolutely critical to the success of an international business initiative.

Evaluating foreign markets is one of the most difficult tasks facing the prospective international trader. Doing a comprehensive and useful analysis of a domestic market is difficult enough, but doing a comparably detailed analysis of a foreign market is immeasurably more difficult. The key steps in this process are as follows:

1. Acquiring information in sufficient quantity and detail to allow the company to make an informed decision

2. Ensuring the information is comparable to the kinds of information the company is used to dealing with, that the information derived from different countries was collected in the same way and, therefore, that it measures the same things

3. Establishing the accuracy and reliability of the information

Chapter 9 is dedicated to the process of international market research and marketing, but the following can serve as a brief introduction and a template that can be used in preparing the business plan. The table below summarizes the types of information that planners should look for to develop a useful view of a foreign market and the opportunities it offers. Planners would need to develop such a matrix for each prospective market and compare the results to assess the most promising opportunity.

It may be difficult to find information about every category listed in the table, and indeed some of this information may not exist or be badly flawed. Business planners have to do the best they can with whatever data are available. Ultimately, the global entrepreneur will fill in as much of the picture as possible, assess what is available and rely on advice, extrapolation or intuition to bridge whatever is missing. Planning is a business necessity, but it is not an exact science.

Table 14.3—Planning information			
Item	**Details**	**Source**	**Findings**
Size of the target market	• in absolute dollars • as a percentage of the economy		
Recent and future trends	• growth or contraction • technological changes • likely future developments		

Table 14.3—Planning information *(continued)*			
Item	Details	Source	Findings
Market for a specific segment	• description of segment • size of the market for the product • current and future trends		
Impact of imports	• volume • value • as a percentage of the total market • origin by country		
Canadian imports in the sector	• volume • value • trends • sources		
Customers	• ideal customer profile and characteristics • income levels • spending on the sector or iproduct • priorities • preferences		
What do customers care about?	• price • features • quality • timeliness • service • other factors		

Table 14.3—Planning information *(continued)*			
Item	**Details**	**Source**	**Findings**
Purchasing	• purchasing decision makers • reasons for making purchases • channels through which purchasing is conducted		
Factors influencing buyers	• cultural characteristics • level of development • religion • attitude to foreign products • consumerism • fashion • political attitudes • social consciousness • technology • importance of the buyer/ seller relationship		
Competitors	• names • countries of origin • description (background, resources, strategies) • annual global revenues • employees worldwide • in-market employees • in-market sales • annual sales in this sector • market share • strengths and weaknesses		

Table 14.3—Planning information *(continued)*			
Item	Details	Source	Findings
Competing or alternative products or services	• product or service names and descriptions • features relative to our offerings • price comparisons with alternative offerings • share of the market		
Emerging opportunities	• by product and service • prospects and forecasts • emerging trends • special projects • government procurement • new market entrants		
Sales techniques	• distribution channels • available promotional techniques (fairs, advertising, special events) • after-sales service		
Sources of market intelligence	• own government resources • target-government resources • customers • sector specialists • intermediaries		
Sources of marketing assistance	• professional marketers • agents and distributors • media representatives • consultants		

Table 14.3—Planning information *(continued)*			
Item	**Details**	**Source**	**Findings**
Regulatory framework	• customs and tariffs • quotas and import restrictions • health and safety regulations • environmental regulations • hiring standards • technical standards • corporate law • incorporation • taxation • investment and partnering • repatriation of profits		

The above table provides a comprehensive list of the components of an international business plan. The next step is to use the information to formulate the plan.

Export Market Penetration: Step by Step or Full Speed Ahead?

When the process of data collection and evaluation has been completed, the company is ready to begin the final part of the planning process: developing a strategic plan, defining—from a high-level perspective—how the market opportunities that have been uncovered will be accessed. The strategic plan should be accompanied by an implementation plan that describes the specific tasks and actions that will be undertaken to achieve the strategic objectives as the company begins forward momentum toward international market penetration.

A key consideration in action planning is how quickly to enter the market, which is driven largely by the chosen market-entry strategy. This decision must be made when all of the market research and resource evaluations have been completed. If market entry is done too quickly, the potential for costly mistakes increases; conversely, if it is done too slowly, opportunities may be missed and competitors will have more time to react. Some points to consider include these:

Finding the right strategic partner can be a key to success. Ron Foxcroft, the inventor of the Fox 40 whistle, met the right partner on a plane, which gave him instant access to distribution in 137 countries.

1. What distribution strategy will be used? Will customers be approached directly or through distribution? Identifying, selecting, and setting up distribution channels can take longer than directly contacting customers, depending on the uptake of the channel; however, in some cases, finding an appropriate strategic partner can create instant access to customers the partner already has.

2. Does the business opportunity require immediate action? Examples might include a request for proposal (RFP) or an urgent requirement to solve an immediate customer problem.

3. How rapidly is the market changing? A fast-changing market might be consumer electronics, while a slower-changing market could be the grocery market. The former would require a more rapid entry strategy.

4. How quickly are competitors moving to adjust to the new opportunities? Some companies—particularly small- and medium-sized firms—can respond more quickly to new opportunities than larger enterprises.

5. Is the opportunity market driven or product/service driven? Market-driven opportunities feature unfilled demand that already exists, while product/service-driven opportunities are "push" efforts by companies to secure a niche in a market that has existing competition. Market-driven opportunities tend to demand a faster entry strategy.

6. Are internal resources already in place to begin the international business initiative, or do they need further development?

7. What is the confidence level for success? Failure can be costly, and although success can never be fully assured, the more confident one is in success (based on careful research and analysis), the more quickly the exporter can and should move.

Pricing strategy

When planning the entry methodology and speed at which it is implemented, another factor to consider is the pricing strategy to be used; some examples include premium, penetration, skimming, economy, predatory pricing and even dumping, although this is illegal according to World Trade Organization (WTO) and other rules. Some markets are more price-sensitive than others, but apart from rare cases, prices are always important. A common strategy to get a foothold in the market, particularly with customized products and services where one order is not exactly the same as the next, is to begin with particularly low prices (also known as "buying the business") to demonstrate quality and earn customer confidence and loyalty, then gradually increase prices to return to reasonable profitability. An example of this might be in the export of translation services, where the translation firm is seeking to establish credibility and demonstrate quality. This strategy is more difficult when producing standard products and services because it is harder to raise prices when customers can easily compare them.

Developing Contingency Plans and Exit Strategies

A comprehensive summary of the resources needed to pursue an international opportunity can be used to perform the final step in the planning process: the cost-benefit analysis of the proposed venture. The expected costs of the venture should be compared to the potential benefits to arrive at one of three possible decisions.

1. The costs are too high relative to the potential benefits. Therefore, the venture should be abandoned.

2. More planning is needed to explore ways of reducing costs or enhancing benefits before the company can proceed.

3. Potential benefits are attractive enough to justify the expected costs. Therefore, the company can implement the plan.

Contingency plans—including an exit strategy—should be part of any international business plan. Nobody implements a plan knowing that they will have to revert to an alternative strategy, or worse, that they will fail, but everyone should be prepared for these eventualities. Retreat is an option even for the world's mightiest armies.

A crucial factor is to know early in the process if the program is proceeding according to plan. If it is not, immediate steps should be taken to correct the problem. The most important enabling factor is a measurement system, whereby results are communicated to decision makers quickly and for evaluation and follow-up action.

Table 14.4—Diagnosing market issues	
Problem	**Possible cause**
Lack of sales	Product problem, poor market research
Distributors not performing	Poor choice of partners, poor support
Customer complaints	Product or service problem
Excessive costs, poor ROI	Failure to anticipate costs
Sense of problems, unclear why	Poor measurement system

Most of these problems can be avoided with proper planning. When problems occur once export market development is in progress, there exist two options: identify the problem and take corrective action, or exit the market.

The International Business Plan Key Points

Figure 14.5—International business plan key points to remember

☑ Planning is a way to increase the probability of success in pursuing international business opportunities.

☑ International business plans can be used to set goals and objectives, to determine cash requirements, to communicate messages to staff, to benchmark the company vs. the competition, and to provide a basis for measuring performance.

☑ When preparing a plan, goals should be clearly communicated, sufficient time and resources should be allocated, drafts should be shared with others, key points should be outlined before writing, the plan should be original and believable and the executive summary should be done last.

☑ Key steps in market evaluation include establishing reliability of information, ensuring the information is similar in format to the type of information already possessed and is available in sufficient quantity and detail to be useful for planning purposes.

☑ The final step of an international business plan is a cost-benefit analysis, which should show that the cost outweighs the potential benefit so the plan should not be implemented, that the conclusion is unclear, so more research and analysis is necessary, or that there is a good probability of success and the plan should be implemented.

Chapter Summary

Proper planning based on appropriate research and analysis is critical to international business success. International commerce, when contrasted with domestic operations, brings greater costs and business risks as a result of increased geographical distance, cultural differences, gaps in knowledge and lack of familiarity with the market.

As companies implement their international business plans and progress through the stages of exporting they will, knowingly or not, be having an increasing impact on the business, social and cultural environment of the export market. They should recognize this and take steps to ensure that they behave with corporate social responsibility, transparency and sustainability and are perceived to have a positive impact on the local community and all stakeholders.

A detailed inventory of company resources and capabilities must be weighed against information gathered from careful market research and analysis. With this information, a comprehensive international business plan can be generated that minimizes risk and maximizes the opportunity for success in export markets, allowing a company to grow and prosper in the global economy.

Exercises

Exercise 1 (small-group activity)

Work in small groups of two or three to formulate answers to the following three questions.

1. You have been promoted to Export Development Manager of a manufacturer of energy-efficient appliances, and have been assigned to open new export markets for your company. Define some of the most important factors you would consider as you began developing a new international business plan.

2. Define some of the benefits of creating an international business plan.

3. Assume that your company has no current policies stating a commitment to a sustainable business model. Build an argument in favour of committing to sustainable business to present to senior management along with your business plan. Be sure to address the four foundational pillars of sustainable business.

   a. Sustainable development—the need to balance the need for economic growth with environmental protection and social equity

   b. Corporate social responsibility—that ethical managers should consider the needs of society, not just the interests of the shareholders or their own self-interest

   c. Stakeholder theory—that there are many groups and individuals who can affect or who are affected by the achievement of the organization's objectives

   d. Corporate accountability theory—that the firm has both a legal and an ethical responsibility to provide an account for the actions of the firm

(Estimated time 30 minutes)

References/Resources

ExportSource (www.exportsource.gc.ca)

Ron Foxcroft (www.fox40world.com)

Index

accountability, 60, 76, 175, 196, 206, 234
acquisition, 8, 10, 15, 23, 111, 137, 250
Africa, 6, 7, 10, 12, 13, 32, 44, 51, 52, 153, 154, 170, 180, 181, 182, 185, 201, 203
African Development Bank, 44
after-sales service, 109, 110, 135, 139, 246, 330
agents, 64, 68, 90, 119, 139, 175, 179, 205, 227, 236, 239, 240, 242, 248, 256, 260, 285, 307, 313, 330
Agreement on Subsidies and Countervailing Measures, 311
Agreement on Trade-Related Aspects of Intellectual Property, 306
aid effectiveness, 52
air freight, 287, 294
alliance, 142, 251
American Arbitration Association, 315
Andean Community, 45
anti-corruption measures, 26
anti-dumping duties, 299
anti-globalization movement, 175
anti-money laundering provisions, 301
anti-terrorist laws, 301
APEC. *See Asia-Pacific Economic Cooperation*
arbitration, 313, 314, 315
ASEAN. *See Association of Southeast Asian Nations*
Asia, 7, 10, 12, 13, 15, 50, 52, 60, 70, 153, 154, 161, 163, 166, 170, 171, 175, 194, 210, 218, 264, 304
Asian Development Bank, 275, 276, 280
Asia-Pacific Economic Cooperation, 50
Association of Southeast Asian Nations, 48
Australia, 41, 162, 176, 204, 206
Austria, 177
Auto Pact, 43, 299

bar code, 102
barter, 278
Belgium, 177, 182
Berne Convention, 306
best practices, 122, 258
bilateral, 7, 9, 22, 43, 45, 46, 47, 48, 216, 278, 298
bill of lading, 98, 271
border congestion, 50
border control measures, 47
Border Infrastructure Fund, 50
BPO. *See Business Process Outsourcing*
brand
    loyalty, 59, 109, 152
    recognition, 17, 252
    value, 17, 114
branding, 123, 253
Brazil, 24, 41, 43, 47, 71, 118, 198, 264

breach of contract, 313
bribery, 175, 176, 178, 183, 193, 196, 202, 209, 256, 260
BRIC countries, 43
business
    development, 5, 38, 48, 52, 53, 87, 98, 147, 214, 274, 299, 311
    model, 15, 72, 73, 83, 103, 108, 137, 238, 262, 334
    plan, 72, 122, 123, 222, 229, 321, 322, 324, 327, 331, 333, 334, 335
    practices, 31, 54, 63, 68, 72, 79, 149, 164, 168, 173, 193, 219, 224, 235, 264, 284, 301, 315
    process, 1, 15, 71, 100, 107, 114, 143, 146, 147, 160
    relationship, 22, 86, 153, 164, 166, 174
    venture, 24, 152, 165, 168, 298, 322, 324
Business Process Outsourcing, 11, 102, 107, 143
buyback, 246
buyer credit, 277
buying offices, 244, 246

Canada, 10, 16, 21, 24, 32, 34, 35, 36, 38, 39, 40, 43, 44, 45, 46, 47, 48, 49, 50, 51, 52, 53, 54, 59, 61, 99, 116, 118, 126, 127, 131, 136, 137, 145, 155, 160, 162, 167, 192, 197, 198, 203, 204, 206, 218, 238, 244, 245, 260, 267, 273, 285, 287, 299, 301, 302, 310, 314
Canada-Chile Free Trade Agreement, 48
Canada-Costa Rica Free Trade Agreement, 49
Canada-Israel Free Trade Agreement, 48
Canada-U.S. Free Trade Agreement, 38, 43, 44
Canadian direct investment, 45
Canadian International Freight Forwarders Association, 285
Canadian International Trade Tribunal, 314
Canadian Manufacturers and Exporters, 25, 38
capital markets, 14, 15, 163
carbon emissions, 26, 300
cargo, 87, 88, 89, 168, 267, 269, 282, 288, 293, 294
Caribbean Community, 10, 45, 50
CARICOM. *See Caribbean Community,*
cash flow, 4, 80, 246, 247, 260, 274, 278, 279
CCFTA. *See Canada-Chile Free Trade Agreement*
CE Marking, 312
Central America Four, 45, 49
certificate of origin, 300
Certified International Trade Professional, 2, 205
channel partners, 236, 252, 253, 255, 257, 259
child labour, 182, 183, 184, 193, 197, 209, 240
Chile, 44, 45, 48, 49, 177, 198
China, 5, 7, 8, 10, 11, 12, 13, 22, 26, 28, 34, 42, 43, 83, 98, 99, 139, 162, 163, 169, 175, 185, 194, 204, 304, 305, 315
China International Economic and Trade Arbitration Commission, 316

CIF. *See cost, insurance and freight*
CIS. *See Confederation of Independent States*
CITP. See Certified International Trade Professional
civil
    codes, 304
    society, 25, 29, 175, 180, 181, 182, 202
    unrest, 5, 264
clearance, 79, 85, 87, 118, 274, 310
code of conduct, 112, 205, 206
collateral, 278
co-marketing, 251
commercial
    activity, 100
    enterprise, 284
    entity, 6, 267
    law, 303, 317
    partnership, 13
    perspective, 11, 16, 70
commodity prices, 10
common law, 301, 304
communication channel, 258
competition, 22, 24, 29, 34, 41, 49, 54, 59, 91, 92, 97, 101, 121,
    140, 142, 145, 146, 152, 203, 214, 219, 224, 228, 229, 232,
    238, 247, 251, 253, 254, 255, 256, 299, 302, 332, 334
Competition Bureau, 314
competition policy, 24, 49
competitive advantage, 6, 16, 85, 88, 90, 144, 150, 176, 179,
    251, 274, 310
competitive intelligence, 75, 101, 119, 141
competitiveness, 23, 26, 40, 46, 50, 58, 60, 68, 98, 109, 214,
    224, 250, 251, 274, 286, 300
competitor, 120, 126, 164, 215, 310, 314
concession, 164, 168
Confederation of Independent States. *See CIS*, 11, 12
conflict of interest, 196, 208
consumers, 22, 40, 45, 70, 78, 92, 126, 145, 181, 196, 197, 198
    237, 253, 255, 291, 294
container, 79, 286, 287, 293
containerization, 293
Convention on the Rights of the Child, 183
copyright, 125, 194, 302, 306, 313
corporate social responsibility, 27, 28, 60, 73, 139, 175, 196,
    234, 334
corruption, 26, 50, 174, 175, 176, 179, 202, 206, 209
cost, insurance and freight, 289, 290
Costa Rica, 44, 45, 49, 198, 199
cost-benefit analysis, 333, 334
counterfeiting, 194
counter-offer, 86
counterpurchase, 278
countertrade, 245, 246, 278
countervailing duty, 311
crating, 284
credit, 5, 15

credit report, 29
cross-border, 24, 49, 50, 82, 131, 144, 265
cross-cultural marketing, 151, 152
cross-cultural relationships, 150
cross-licensing, 251
cultural
    awareness, 139, 150, 151
    backgrounds, 167
    context, 150
    differences, 5, 64, 68, 148, 150, 151, 169, 215
    diversity, 45, 152
    filters, 154
    preferences, 73
    sensitivity, 63, 218, 228
currency fluctuation, 215, 221
customer needs, 63, 68, 135, 147
customer service, 78, 86, 103, 163, 242
customs broker, 79, 84, 91, 287
customs duties, 87, 168, 237

Denmark, 176
developed market, 14
developing country, 192
development bank, 19, 27, 115, 274
dictatorship, 22
digital network, 99
digital supply chain, 115
direct sales, 108, 109, 110, 236, 256
discriminatory pricing, 310
disintermediation, 14, 108, 273
dispute resolution, 297, 313, 314, 316
dispute settlement, 5, 29, 46, 49, 81, 306, 308
distribution, 38, 62, 69, 70, 78, 101, 131, 137, 138, 193, 219,
    222, 231, 232, 233, 236, 237, 239, 242, 243, 244, 245, 248,
    250, 252, 253, 255, 256, 257, 259, 260, 282, 283, 284, 285,
    286, 287, 288, 294, 311, 330, 331, 332
distribution channel, 231, 252, 255, 259
distribution network, 242, 257
distributor, 51, 138, 178, 209, 237, 238, 245, 252, 253
diversity, 4, 45, 67, 150, 152, 204, 205, 214
documentary letter of credit, 87, 270, 271, 279
Doha Development Agenda, 13, 46, 50
Doha Development Round, 51
domestic market, 30, 34, 58, 59, 62, 74, 75, 86, 216, 233,
    259, 327
due diligence, 5, 6, 87, 209, 253
duties, 85, 87, 89, 168, 191, 237, 243, 287, 299, 311

e-business, 113, 114, 116, 119, 121, 122, 123, 124, 125, 126
ECA. *See export credit agency*
e-commerce, 6, 59, 76, 78, 79, 81, 91, 100, 104, 108, 109, 110,
    123, 124, 305, 316
economic
    growth, 7, 11, 12, 19, 47, 60, 64, 73, 335

integration, 10, 43, 82
performance, 35
power, 7, 10
economy, 10, 11, 17, 21, 23, 28, 34, 35, 37, 38, 40, 42, 43, 45, 46, 53, 54, 64, 83, 85, 98, 105, 108, 130, 131, 136, 140, 146, 150, 186, 192, 194, 214, 215, 235, 307, 311, 327, 332, 334
Electronic Data Interchange, 75, 98, 102, 104
electronic scanning, 288, 293
e-marketplace, 112, 113, 114
emerging
economy, 11,
market, 280
powers, 28, 83
enabling technologies, 83, 106, 107
end user, 59, 108, 109, 142, 214, 219, 221, 232, 247
entrepreneurship, 21, 64, 65, 66
entry strategy, 87, 241, 242, 246, 250, 332
environmental footprint, 202, 204
environmental impact assessment, 312
environmental protection, 60, 73, 197, 312, 335
e-procurement, 71, 115, 117
Equator Principles, 27, 203, 204
ethical conduct, 27, 63, 175, 186, 196, 205, 206, 209
ethics, 2, 154, 174, 175, 196, 206, 208, 209
EU. See European Union
Europe, 7, 10, 12, 15, 16, 43, 60, 63, 83, 153, 162, 197, 218, 284, 304
European Convention on International Commercial Arbitration, 315
European Court of Justice, 302
European Union, 7, 9, 10, 11, 12, 16, 21, 24, 28, 48, 49, 115, 238, 245, 269, 302, 303, 306, 307, 312
exchange rate, 20, 35, 74
exit strategy, 333
explicit communication, 157
export
controls, 185, 219, 299
credit agency, 21, 273, 276
documentation, 73, 245, 291
financing, 29
house, 91, 244
management, 68
market, 43, 73, 90, 151, 224, 225, 232, 233, 234, 235, 254, 260, 285, 320, 333, 334
process, 62, 88, 90, 233
strategy, 239
exporting
direct, 237, 239, 240, 241, 242
indirect, 243, 244, 245, 246, 247, 248
Export Administration Act, 307
Export Development Canada, 53, 82, 273
extractive industries, 26, 202
extraterritoriality, 297, 302, 316

face-to-face communication, 155
facilitation payment, 179
Fair Trade, 193
Fair Trade Labelling Organization International, 193
FDI. See foreign direct investment
financial
expenses, 80
flow, 24
institution, 267, 277
loss, 142
management, 4, 88, 282
manager, 80
markets, 8, 9, 28, 266
plan, 323
resources, 27, 74, 250, 259, 271, 320
risk, 4
services, 7, 8, 49, 61, 111, 132
supply chain, 29, 80, 81
transaction, 310
financing solution, 29
Finland, 176
fixed-rate financing, 278
foreign
assets tracking, 301
culture, 67, 164, 168
direct investment, 11, 27, 28, 40, 41, 45, 47, 54, 94, 186
exchange, 20, 28, 264, 268
investment, 8, 10, 11, 54, 82, 83, 235
Foreign Corrupt Practices Act, 178
forward contract, 266
forwarder, 284
France, 35, 41, 97, 130, 144, 160, 177, 206, 272, 314
fraud, 202, 206, 269
Free and Secure Trade, 50
free on board, 289
Free Trade Agreement of the Americas, 47
freight forwarder, 79, 91, 284, 285, 286
full container load, 286

GATS. See General Agreement on Trade in Services
GATT. See General Agreement on Tariffs and Trade
General Agreement on Tariffs and Trade, 44, 306
General Agreement on Trade in Services, 17, 18, 145, 146. 147
Germany, 35, 41, 42, 59, 117, 118, 130, 139, 159, 161, 167, 177, 259, 273
global
business environment, 2, 6, 7, 8, 9, 10, 11, 12, 19, 20, 21, 23, 24, 25, 26, 27, 30, 31, 54, 58, 59, 71, 82, 83, 91, 92, 93, 126, 214, 224, 226, 264, 288, 299, 306, 310, 312, 316
competition, 34, 41, 59, 101, 224
economy, 21, 40, 43, 44, 83, 131, 136, 140, 150, 214, 234
leader, 67

markets, 23, 35, 58, 59, 62, 126, 252, 276
organization, 58, 70
power, 11, 13
globalization, 19, 31, 34, 58, 82, 130, 175, 186, 204, 300, 308
good faith, 207, 264, 269
goods surplus, 35
government procurement, 48, 49, 145, 239, 330
Gross National Income, 52
gross world product, 100
growth potential, 44

hard currency, 278
Harmonized System, 287
hazardous materials, 293
hedge fund, 276
high-context, 152, 153, 160, 161, 164, 165, 167, 168
Hong Kong, 10, 21, 51, 52, 83, 162, 177, 304
Hong Kong Ministerial Declaration, 52
human rights, 4, 10, 174, 175, 182, 184, 185, 186, 187, 191, 192, 193, 196, 200, 201, 202, 206, 209

Iceland, 49, 176
IDA. See International Development Association
IFC. See International Finance Corporation
IFI. See international financial institution
ILO. See International Labour Organization
image, 101, 152, 156, 160, 226, 234, 253, 255
IMF. See International Monetary Fund
implementation plan, 331
implicit communication, 157
import
    controls, 222
    restrictions, 46, 278, 331
    valuation, 87
inbound warehousing, 284
Incoterms, 274, 288, 289, 290, 294
independent shipper, 286
India, 5, 7, 11, 12, 13, 15, 17, 43, 83, 93, 94, 99, 145, 175, 180, 194, 195, 197, 204
Indonesia, 48, 162, 185, 193
industrial design, 306
industrialized countries, 20
industry sector, 53, 92, 93, 130, 210, 236, 238
information supply chain, 29, 80, 81, 82, 92
information technology, 30, 100, 116, 135, 140, 144
infrastructure projects, 26, 134, 178
innovation, 43, 53, 54, 58, 59, 60, 99, 140, 144, 145, 147, 224
insolvency, 267, 268
insourcing, 27
intangible, 105, 137, 139
integrated supply chain, 86
integrative trade, 27, 78, 82, 83, 84, 85, 91, 92, 93
integrity, 67, 119, 121, 122, 183, 205, 207, 277, 292
intellectual property, 10, 13, 25, 46, 48, 49, 51, 123, 125, 193,

194, 195, 235, 306, 316
intellectual property rights, 46, 49, 50, 194, 195
inter-channel conflict, 252
inter-company trade, 8, 24
intercultural effectiveness, 88
intercultural understanding, 164
interest rates, 61
intermediaries, 26, 79, 229, 237, 243, 255, 269, 330
Internal Revenue Code, 307
international
    carrier, 89
    development, 7, 18, 27
    exchange-rate system, 20
    financial institution, 18, 21, 115, 178, 219
    investment, 8, 9
    security, 22, 310
    trade, 4, 5, 6, 8, 15, 18, 20, 22, 23, 24, 25, 27, 28, 29, 30, 34, 40, 44, 53, 62, 64, 66, 68, 80, 81, 82, 83, 84, 85, 86, 88, 92, 98, 100, 132, 150, 169, 174, 193, 195, 204, 207, 208, 232, 233, 234, 236, 240, 241, 242, 244, 245, 247, 264, 265, 267, 268, 271, 273, 274, 275, 276, 278, 279, 282, 283, 286, 291, 294, 298, 299, 300, 301, 307, 308, 312, 313, 316, 317, 320, 321
    trade law, 98
International Bank for Reconstruction and Development, 18
International Chamber of Commerce, 269, 271, 288, 314
International Development Association, 18
International Finance Corporation, 18, 275, 276
International Labour Organization, 20
International Monetary Fund, 19, 308
inventory, 6, 62, 68, 80, 88, 90, 94, 109, 110, 238, 249, 274, 288, 334
inventory control, 88
investment, 2, 8, 9, 10, 11, 15, 19, 26, 27, 40, 41, 43, 44, 45, 46, 48, 49, 51, 52, 53, 54, 68, 78, 82, 83, 86, 89, 92, 94, 98, 100, 104, 117, 131, 133, 134, 136, 145, 164, 165, 174, 185, 186, 191, 192, 196, 232, 233, 235, 243, 250, 256, 259, 313, 331
investment capital, 15
investment flows, 47
IP. See intellectual property
Iran, 185, 303
Ireland, 41, 177
Islamic law, 303
Israel, 44, 45, 48, 49
Italy, 35, 99, 130, 139

Japan, 12, 21, 35, 41, 42, 43, 45, 48, 60, 61, 71, 99, 130, 139, 156, 159, 161, 162, 167, 168, 169, 177, 178, 206, 252, 315
Japan Commercial Arbitration Association, 315
joint venture, 91, 93, 94, 169, 186, 209, 234, 251
just-in-time, 108, 109

knowledge-based industries, 7

Korea, 44, 49, 99, 162, 304

labelling, 88, 102, 227, 292
labour market, 35
leader, 64, 67, 139, 141, 170, 200
leading economies, 9, 17
leads, 62, 66, 72, 101, 152, 170, 315
leasing, 278
legal remedy, 25
legal system, 194, 200, 301, 303, 304, 315
less than container load, 286
less-than-truckload, 287
letter of credit, 87, 241, 270, 271, 273, 279
level of competition, 246
litigation, 195, 313, 314
loading, 89
logistics
    management, 68
    supply chain, 28
    system, 85
London Court of International Arbitration, 315
low-context, 153, 160, 161, 164, 165, 167, 168, 169
low-cost market, 15
lower-cost country, 143
Luxembourg, 41, 177
luxury items, 84

mail order, 255
Malaysia, 48, 162, 170
manufacturing cost, 285
manufacturing supply chain, 108
market
    analysis, 218
    dominance, 252
    entry, 59, 68, 121, 144, 146, 218, 222, 224, 232, 236, 240,
        242, 243, 246, 247, 252, 258, 259, 331
    entry strategy, 68, 121, 232, 240, 242, 246, 247, 253, 259,
        331, 332
    orientation, 59
    planning, 87, 222, 226, 227
    research, 2, 61, 68, 72, 86, 88, 90, 101, 123, 126, 133, 140,
        141, 214, 215, 216, 217, 218, 221, 224, 226, 228, 229,
        230, 232, 233, 234, 243, 327, 331, 333, 334
    segment, 98, 214
    share, 59, 68, 75, 108, 110, 131, 136, 144, 214, 224, 225,
        226, 228, 241, 242, 246, 251, 326, 329
    strategy, 59, 62, 218, 224
marketing
    mix, 223, 224, 230
    plan, 72, 114, 123, 215, 220, 222, 223, 224, 226, 228,
        229, 233
    vision, 224
marking, 88, 89, 284
materials management, 78, 282

mediation, 313, 314
member states, 7, 9, 18, 115, 302
merchandise export, 42
merchandise trade, 42, 45, 47
mergers and acquisitions, 8, 11, 24, 250
Merx, 115
Mexico, 42, 43, 44, 45, 47, 49, 50, 198, 264, 265, 294, 299
MIGA. See Multilateral Investment Guarantee Agency
Model Law, 304
money laundering, 301, 309
most economically advanced countries, 20
Most Favoured Nation, 308
multilateral
    institution, 18, 27, 29
    negotiations, 46
    sanctions, 185
    treaty, 307
Multilateral Investment Guarantee Agency, 18
multi-modal transportation, 288
multinationals, 8, 17, 27, 70, 197, 202, 266

NAFTA. See North American Free Trade Agreement
national interest, 298, 300, 316
nationalization, 5
Netherlands, 41, 176, 273
networking, 101, 142
new technologies, 84, 235, 250, 288, 293
New Zealand, 176, 194
NGO. See non-governmental organization
niche, 17, 58, 59, 107, 126, 251, 276, 332
non-competing products, 255
non-discrimination, 40
non-governmental organization, 20, 25, 26, 27, 308, 312
non-recourse basis, 276, 278
non-resident, 134
non-tariff barriers, 10, 20, 46
non-tariff measures, 49
non-verbal communication, 153, 154, 155
North American Free Trade Agreement, 10, 43, 44, 47, 55, 197,
    299, 300
North-South trade, 7, 13
Norway, 49, 176

ocean freighter, 287
OECD. See Organisation for Economic Co-operation
    and Development
Office of Foreign Assets Control, 301, 310
offset arrangement, 278
offshoring, 15, 82, 93
oil prices, 17
on-demand manufacturing, 102
online payment system, 81, 118
online tools, 74, 98
open account, 268, 269, 273, 274

order processing, 88, 91
Organisation for Economic Co-operation and
    Development, 13, 14, 20, 21, 50, 51, 178, 179, 203, 312
outbound warehousing, 284
outflow of value, 85
outsourcing, 7, 15, 27, 71, 72, 82, 83, 92, 93, 107, 124, 131,
    143, 144, 145, 146, 147, 172, 197, 227
over-quota tariffs, 51

packaging, 62, 73, 88, 91, 102, 107, 137, 151, 214, 227, 247
    282, 292, 293
packing, 67, 89, 293
Pakistan, 11, 177, 195, 303
pallet, 288
Paris Convention, 306
partnership, 10, 13, 22, 23, 92, 180, 181, 197, 267, 275, 276
patent, 194, 195, 306, 313
payment mechanisms, 29, 268, 273
payment terms, 62, 63, 80, 118
pension funds, 9, 15
Personal Property Security Act, 302
physical assets, 113
physical supply chain, 29
piggybacking, 245
pilfering, 293
piracy, 194, 195
Poland, 11, 140
political borders, 70
political stability, 11, 215, 222
positioning, 6, 58, 152, 255
poverty reduction, 22, 51
predictability, 40, 145
pre-shipment financing, 275
price cartel, 307
pricing, 23, 24, 62, 143, 163, 220, 221, 223, 226, 240, 253,
    310, 332
pricing strategy, 221, 223, 226, 332
primary sales, 108
principle of scarcity, 23
Prior Information Notice, 116
privacy, 112, 125, 126, 160, 179, 188
procurement processes, 115
product life cycle, 221
production
    capacity, 73
    costs, 267
    facility, 38, 234
    line, 103, 108, 282, 294
    process, 283, 284
    schedule, 89
    supply chain, 78
    system, 41
productivity improvements, 250
profit margin, 109

profitability, 23, 60, 68, 86, 106, 140, 141, 142, 224, 278, 332
project finance, 26, 27, 301
promissory note, 277, 278
prosperity, 29, 34, 47, 54, 85, 86
protectionism, 17, 21
public policy, 9, 16, 298, 299, 312
public trade law, 307
punitive damage, 302
purchase order, 86, 87

quality of life, 22, 34, 46, 50, 85
Québec National and International Commercial Arbitration
    Centre, 315
quota, 51
quota-free access, 51
quotation, 86, 103, 111, 118

Radio Frequency Identification Technology, 6, 102
receivables, 80, 266, 273
reciprocal purchase, 278
relationship marketing, 138. 139, 140
reputation, 59, 114, 121, 178, 183, 188, 192, 196, 202, 205, 210,
    237, 240, 242, 244, 246, 247, 255
request for proposal, 332
request for quotation, 86
research, market. See market, research
retailers, 78, 80, 94, 109, 180, 237, 274
return on investment, 117, 196
revolution, 130, 267
RFID. See Radio Frequency Identification Technology
RFQ. See request for quotation
risk
    insurers, 28, 273, 275
    management, 87
    mitigation, 27, 264, 265, 266, 273, 279, 280
RosettaNet, 104, 105
rule of law, 187, 196
rules of origin, 51, 300
rules-based system, 40, 176

Sale of Goods Act, 302
sales
    contract, 87, 238
    forecasting, 78
    process, 85, 254
sanctions, 22, 185, 186, 210
secured creditor, 313
Security and Prosperity Partnership, 50
security risk, 119
selling proposition, 4, 17
SEPA. See Single European Payments Area
service export, 137, 224
service trade, 35, 135
shareholder, 192

shipping carrier, 98
shipping documents, 267, 269, 270
Singapore, 45, 48, 49, 162, 167, 176, 304
Single European Payments Area, 7
small- and medium-sized enterprises, 46, 266
Smart Border Declaration, 50
SME. *See small- and medium-sized enterprises*
social responsibility, 26, 27, 28, 60, 73, 76, 139, 174, 175, 196,
    204, 234, 334, 335
social structure, 22, 151
sourcing, 4, 5, 6, 8, 26, 27, 30, 78, 79, 83, 84, 85, 86, 90, 92,
    93, 102, 111, 273, 274
South Korea, 99, 162
South-South trade, 7, 13, 14, 21, 51
stakeholder, 60, 196
standards, 5, 17, 20, 26, 27, 34, 47, 67, 73, 84, 100, 102, 103,
    104, 105, 144, 174, 181, 182, 183, 186, 187, 193, 196, 197,
    202, 203, 205, 206, 208, 222, 238, 240, 292, 305, 306, 307,
    312, 313, 331
start-up, 4, 61, 84
stock exchange, 15, 26
strategic alliance, 251
Strategic Highway Infrastructure Program, 50
strategic objectives, 222, 251, 255, 331
strategic plan, 228, 331
subsidiary, 71, 135, 180, 250
subsidies, 21, 22, 46, 145, 243, 308, 311
Summit of the Americas, 47
supplier credit, 277
supply chain, 2, 6, 27, 29, 70, 71, 72, 78, 79, 80, 81, 82, 83, 85,
    86, 90, 92, 93, 94, 98, 102, 103, 104, 105, 108, 110, 111,
    115, 117, 119, 137, 145, 176, 182, 197, 214, 219, 232, 252,
    253, 255, 274, 279, 288, 293, 294, 310
supply chain
    management, 2, 71, 80, 85, 102, 111, 117
    model, 27, 83, 90
    strategy, 108
sustainability, 4, 8, 26, 28, 60, 61, 72, 175, 204, 234, 300,
    312, 334
Sweden, 176
Switzerland, 20, 41, 49, 176, 306

Taiwan, 162
tangible goods, 234
target market, 62, 63, 87, 90, 138, 143, 144, 152, 154, 163, 168,
    209, 214, 215, 216, 219, 221, 223, 224, 226, 227, 228, 234,
    237, 238, 239, 240, 241, 245, 246, 254, 255, 278, 327
tariffs, 10, 14, 46, 48, 49, 51, 222, 236, 299, 307, 331
tariff
    barriers, 10, 20, 46, 308
    classification codes, 287
    reductions, 49, 235
    treatment, 300
tax regime, 278

taxes, 85, 222, 227, 237, 243, 249, 287, 311
technical assistance, 19, 51
temporary entry, 49
tender, 115, 116, 124, 238, 273
terms of trade, 35, 269, 274
terrorism, 179, 194, 293
Thailand, 48, 162
time zone, 111, 254
title, 29, 248, 249, 270, 272, 278, 289
total quality, 63
trade
    agreement, 44, 49, 55, 299
    balance, 35
    barriers, 86, 236, 302, 306
    commissioners, 54, 55, 237
    deficit, 35, 85
    disputes, 18, 307
    fair, 88, 222
    finance, 9, 15, 27, 28, 68, 84, 264, 265, 267, 268, 269, 271,
        273, 274, 275, 276, 277, 279, 298
    liberalization, 46, 47, 50
    mission, 88, 116
    office, 52
    receivables, 80
    secrets, 306, 313
    show, 116, 139, 222, 226, 228, 234, 254
    surplus, 35, 37
Trade and Investment Enhancement Agreement, 48
Trade Commissioner Service, 53
Trade Data Online, 53
Trade Point Development Centres, 20
Trade Point Program, 20
trademark, 194, 306, 307, 313
trading house. *See also export house*, 244, 248
trading partner, 34, 81, 92, 268
tramp vessel, 286
transaction cycle, 277
transaction documentation, 89
transfer pricing, 24
transhipments, 34
transparency, 26, 40, 50, 78, 80, 81, 101, 109, 145, 179,
    234, 334
Treaty of Rome, 302
treble damages, 302
two-way trade, 45, 48, 50

U.S. Constitution, 301
U.S. International Trade Commission, 314
U.K. *See United Kingdom*
uncertainty, 67, 169, 262, 302
UNCTAD. *See United Nations Conference on Trade and
    Development*
UNDP. *See United Nations Development Programme*
unfair trade measures, 46

unfair trade practices, 298, 310, 314
Uniform Commercial Code, 301, 302
unilateral sanctions, 185
United Kingdom, 24, 35, 41, 42, 71, 99, 130, 177, 216
United Nations, 11, 19, 183, 184, 187, 189, 191, 206, 305, 306
United Nations Conference for International Trade Law, 315
United Nations Conference on Trade and Development, 11, 20,
    107
United Nations Development Programme, 19
United States, 7, 12, 15, 21, 24, 28, 34, 35, 36, 38, 39, 41, 43,
    44, 45, 47, 49, 50, 70, 71, 99, 162, 169, 194, 195, 267, 273,
    276, 293, 299, 301, 302, 303, 307, 310
unloading, 89
Uruguay Round, 44, 195, 307, 308
U.S. *See United States*

validation process, 87
value
    chain, 6, 11, 13, 17, 78, 82, 83, 91, 93
    proposition, 4, 17, 28, 59, 87, 140, 141, 144, 146, 221,
        266, 268, 273
value-added network, 104
value-added services, 108, 111, 235
value-based approach, 92
venture capital, 61
vertical relationship, 86
vertical supply network, 109
virtual business networks, 71
volume discount, 253, 285

warehousing, 36, 89, 90, 91, 108, 109, 134, 222, 283, 284,
    285, 288
wholesalers, 26, 78, 237, 244, 253
wholly owned subsidiary, 250
WIPO. *See World Intellectual Property Organization*
working capital, 266, 274
working conditions, 180, 186, 193, 197
world
    economy, 10, 17, 43, 98, 146
    trade, 13, 131, 235, 282
World Bank, 18, 19, 26, 44, 115, 275, 276
World Intellectual Property Organization, 194, 315
World Trade Organization, 11, 13, 18, 44, 46, 133, 139, 145,
    146, 279, 298, 308, 332
WTO. *See World Trade Organization*

FS-GBE-PG-EN-05-MAN

Printed in Canada